PLOTTO

The Classic Plot Suggestion Tool
for Writers of Creative Fiction

by William Wallace Cook

Norton Creek Press
http://www.nortoncreekpress.com

Plotto
The Classic Plot Suggestion Tool for Writers of
Creative Fiction

by William Wallace Cook
Foreword by Robert Plamondon

ISBN 978-0-9819284-7-0

Originally published by Ellis Publishing Co. 1928 as:" Plotto: A
New Method of Plot Suggestion for Writers of Creative Fiction"

Foreword

If you're like me, plotting your fiction can be a real struggle. Sure, characters and key situations can appear like magic, but extending these into a complete story can be frustrating. What if there were a tool for this very problem, so you can navigate these uncharted waters as quickly as possible? A tool that starts with what you have—a situation, perhaps, or a group of characters—and sets you on the road to new possibilities?

Plotto does all of this. Created by a master of "organized creativity," William Wallace Cook, one of the most prolific writers in history, *Plotto* has been highly prized by professional authors since its publication in 1928, and is still in demand today, with copies of the original edition selling for up to $400. This Norton Creek Edition is an exact reproduction of Cook's work.

To keep the book's length down to 300 pages, Cook uses a telegraphic format that you will soon appreciate, as it saves your time as well as space, so the time you spend studying the introduction is soon rewarded.

Because *Plotto* was written in the Twenties, its situations are old-fashioned and the terminology is sometimes politically incorrect. Since Cook himself wrote both westerns and early classics of science fiction, you can see how substituting "star ship" for "stagecoach" or "male stripper" for "dance hall girl" will be within the range of any writer using the system.

Robert Plamondon

The Soul, with its human faculties which put it in immediate touch with the Universe, is a Divine Instrument, an Aeolian Harp which is not played upon by the Winds of Chance but by all the Winds of Destiny that blow from the four quarters of Human Nature; and this Music of the Soul is a Divine Harmony which the Creative Imagination, alone of the human faculties, interprets in Creative Art. To this high interpretation, through fictional narrative,

𝔓𝔩𝔬𝔱𝔱𝔬 𝔦𝔰 𝔡𝔢𝔡𝔦𝔠𝔞𝔱𝔢𝔡.

INTRODUCTION

THE PLOTTO METHOD. Plotto achieves creative art in fiction by a new Method of plot **suggestion.** Suggestion is based on Themes (or Masterplots) and Conflicts.

THEME. Every story has a Theme, or an underlying proposition that indicates its type. The Theme may be clear-cut and distinct, or shadowy and vague; it is always in evidence, and differentiates one type of story from all the other types. Around each Theme any number of distinctly different stories may be written.

A story may be constructed with, or without, a certain Theme in mind. Rarely perhaps does a writer begin a story with a set Theme in front of him. He may develop his plot from a situation, or Conflict; nevertheless, as the plot develops the Theme develops with it. The writer will **feel** the Theme and, consciously or unconsciously, combine his Conflicts to a certain pattern. This pattern, plain in the finished work, will conform to a Theme. When a story is built around a Theme, the Theme becomes a Masterplot.

The Plotto Method enables the Plottoist to begin his story with a Masterplot and marshal his situations or Conflicts in conformity to it; or, it enables him to begin with a situation or Conflict and consciously to watch the particular Theme as the plot unfolds.

MASTERPLOTS WITH INTERCHANGEABLE CLAUSES. Each Plotto Masterplot classifies in general terms and in a single terse sentence a certain type of story. Each Masterplot consists of three Clauses: An initial Clause defining the protagonist in general terms, a middle Clause initiating and carrying on the action, and a final Clause carrying on and terminating the action. Suggestions for exemplifying the action with concrete situations are offered by the Conflicts.

THE CONFLICTS. Desire, in some one of its many forms, is responsible for the awakening of Purpose. Something from without, impinging upon something within, excites a feeling or an emotion, and the soul flows into Purpose, and Purpose into action. Then, somewhere on the path of rising action, Purpose encounters Obstacle. At this point, and at this point only, do we establish what writers of creative fiction call a **situation.** Purpose alone never made a situation; Obstacle alone never made one; but strike the flint of Obstacle with the steel of Purpose and sparks of situation begin to fly.

Plotto, as a Method of plot **suggestion** for writers of **creative** fiction, is founded upon this law: **Purpose, expressed or implied, opposing Obstacle, expressed or implied, yields Conflict.**

PURPOSES AND OBSTACLES. How many Purposes are there in the world? Not many, although their variations are infinite. Perhaps, in the last analysis one General Purpose would comprehend all the Purposes: TO ACHIEVE HAPPINESS. That is the end and aim of life on this planet. But happiness has a different meaning for most of us. There is the happiness of love and courtship, of married life, of achieving wealth or power by all the many methods, good or evil, that may be contrived by the thinking mind. Religion may be the road to happiness for some, and revenge the road to a doubtful happiness for others. The virtues or the faults of a human soul set the pattern of Purpose for that soul.

Plotto concerns itself with but one General Purpose in its application to three general goals of endeavor:
1. To Achieve Happiness in Love and Courtship.
2. To Achieve Happiness in Married Life.
3. To Achieve Happiness (Success) in Enterprise.

Yet, while this one General Purpose runs through all the Conflicts, a host of subordinate Purposes will appear in them, opposed by an infinite number of Obstacles.

There is one Supreme Purpose in every life: TO LIVE; and there is one Supreme Obstacle each life encounters: DEATH. Complicating the scheme and giving zest to the plot of life are innumerable subordinate Purposes and Obstacles, dealing with all the enterprises of which life is capable.

Overshadowed by the Supreme Purpose of LIFE, and the Supreme Obstacle of DEATH, we wage our mimic wars of conquest and gain; but, at any minute, the Supreme Purpose may fail, and Death come striding into our finite calculations and calling a truce. There is also a Paramount Purpose in all the lesser activities of our existence, opposed by a Paramount Obstacle; and they marshal their secondary Purposes and Obstacles to keep us "on our toes" and fighting valiantly for all we have, or hope to have. Blessed be Purpose! And thrice-blessed be Obstacle!

The Conflicts in Plotto are brief statements of Purpose in active opposition with Obstacle—situations which are to be combined with other situations. For instance: "A, in love with B, is not favored by F-B, father of B." Here is the implied Purpose, "To Achieve Happiness in Love," meeting an Obstacle bluntly expressed.

Purpose and Obstacle give concrete exemplification of the Theme in every form of fictional narrative, whether short story, novelette, or novel.

THE SHORT STORY. Purpose and Obstacle at grips in one dramatic situation will define the short story, since it is calculated to leave a single dominant impression upon the reader's mind. Ordinarily, this form of narrative fiction will be woven about a plot of the simplest construction. There will be the main situation as suggested by a chosen Conflict, the Conflict leading up to it and the Conflict carrying on and terminating the action. These three Conflicts may be reduced to two, if the main Conflict should in itself possess the qualities of a terminal Conflict. Conflicts too long, or too involved, for short story purposes will usually be found to be broken Conflicts. When such a Conflict is selected for the main situation, it is possible to use only that part of it which contains the most dramatic appeal.

THE NOVELETTE. This form of narrative fiction may be considered as a long short story, or as a short novel. If the former, the Conflict suggesting the situation will be elaborated with dramatic material concerned with the Purpose and Obstacle. If, on the other hand, the novelette partakes of the character of a short novel, the Paramount Purpose and Obstacle will involve subordinate Purposes and Obstacles all cumulative in power and bearing upon the story's climax or crisis. Here, as everywhere, the imagination must exercise constructive judgment.

THE NOVEL. The full-fledged novel may be considered as consisting of several short stories all leading up to, and intimately bound up with, the Paramount Purpose and Obstacle that give the complete story its unity. Construction here plays its most discriminating rolé, for the subordinate situations must grow toward a single, decisive crisis. The effect must be cumulative. If the main Conflict shall involve the crisis—and it should—all the subordinate situations dealing with the Theme will be so selected as to grow naturally in dramatic strength toward the climax. Here no rules of construction will take the place of taste and discrimination. The constructive imagination, properly exercised, will deal capably with the situations, and the creative imagination will work a miracle of dramaturgic power.

ORIGINALITY. The Conflicts all come from the vast storehouse of Human Nature. They are there, millions upon millions of them, waiting for the imagination to select them and group them in an original combination. For there is "nothing new under the sun." Originality in creative work comes from our own individual use of the tools so bountifully provided by the Divine Creator. All that is possible to a mortal craftsman is the combining of old material into something new and different.

Originality is the ideal of the Plotto Method; and it is realized by disregarding the references prefixed and affixed to the Conflicts and (or) interpreting the Specific as well as the General, Conflicts in terms of the Plottoist's own experience. Nothing in the Specific Conflicts will be used literally, but the concrete exemplification in such Conflicts will serve as a suggestion, lending wings to the creative imagination for its own high flight.

For orginal combinations of Conflicts the Classification by Symbols will be found a treasure-trove of suggestions. If the main Conflict selected is built around A, or B, alone, the A or B group should be scanned; if around A and B alone, the A and B group will yield suggestions, or the A or B group may be found to serve; or, if several characters are involved in the main Conflict, reference may be had to that particular group of symbols. If a certain group of symbols proves too limited, drop one of the lesser character symbols and consult the group represented by those remaining. This course may be followed, in the search for original combinations, until only the protagonist remains in the situation. Somewhere along the line of search the imagination is certain to find exactly what it is looking for.

CONFLICT GROUPS AND SUB-GROUPS. The Conflicts in Plotto are classified in three main groups:
   1. Conflicts in Love and Courtship.
   2. Conflicts in Married Life.
   3. Conflicts in Enterprise.

ᐯ The Conflicts in Love and Courtship are re-grouped as follows:
Conflicts in Love's Beginnings.
Conflicts in Love's Misadventures.
Conflicts of the Marriage Proposal.
Conflicts in Love's Rejection.
Conflicts of Marriage.

All the sub-groups are classified, for convenience of reference, under the middle, or "B," Clauses of the Masterplots; and these form the only subdivisions of the main group, "Married Life." Conflicts of the third group, "Enterprise," fall into the following general classifications:

Conflicts in Misfortune.
Conflicts in Mistaken Judgment.
Conflicts in Helpfulness.
Conflicts in Deliverance.
Conflicts in Idealism.
Conflicts in Obligation.
Conflicts in Necessity.
Conflicts in Chance.
Conflicts in Personal Limitations.
Conflicts in Simulation.
Conflicts in Craftiness.
Conflicts in Transgression.
Conflicts in Revenge.
Conflicts in Mystery.
Conflicts in Revelation.

Inasmuch as dramatic situations are a product of the emotions, and the emotions, by reason of their complexity, have defied a hard and fast classification, it follows naturally that the Conflicts themselves will defy a rigid classification. The groupings noted above are more or less arbitrary, yet they will be bound to serve. Some Conflicts in Misfortune might easily fall into the sub-groups, Mistaken Judgment, Simulation, etc., and Conflicts in other sub-groups might logically be re-classified. Nevertheless, the classification in each case will exemplify in the Conflict the particular sub-group in which it has been placed.

MECHANICAL STRUCTURE. There is, of course, a mechanical structure underlying every properly constructed story. There are some very intelligent people who believe in the "divine afflatus" as something apart from hard, consistent, carefully calculated effort. Overlooking the old adage that "Genius is an infinite capacity for taking pains," these wise ones will have their back-handed slap at anything mechanical in its application to Art.

It remains, however, that a good story must have a carefully developed plot for its framework; and the plot in itself, is purely mechanical. It is the logical devising of means to an end, a motivating of all the parts into a harmonious whole. A plot may be simple, or it may be complex, but an interesting story without some sort of plot is inconceivable. This machinery must not creak or complain as the story advances. A discriminating imagination must oil it so well with logic and plausibility that the god in the machine shall not be ruffled by the turning wheels. Plausibility is attained when fine discrimination, true judgment and a facility with words so cover the necessary mechanism that it does not intrude at any point upon the completed work. And therein lies the art of the story teller. Plotto, at least, holds this to be true; and, as a corollary of the position thus taken, exalts the **imagination** as the greatest force in the world.

IMAGINATION. If a story is a skeleton structure of plot, overlaid with a felicity of thought and phrase that may be called the flesh, then the pulsing heart of the creation, the one factor that gives it life and beauty, is the imagination. But this imagination must be rightly controlled.

The demands of fictional narrative would seem to predicate an imagination of three types: Mediocre, Constructive and Creative. A mind positively brilliant in its mastery of scientific research, or of the pursuit of trade, might be hopeless in meeting the demands of fictional narrative. Nevertheless, Plotto believes sincerely that a **desire** to write successful fiction is predicated upon the **ability** to write successful fiction; and that, given the technical requirements of experience and a fair education, not often will the mediocre imagination be found hopeless. Intensive training should develop constructive power; and it is but a step, in the interpretation of suggestion, from the constructive to the creative. Originality is the soul of creative art, and originality is nothing more than the interpretation of suggestion in terms of individual experience.

Each life is the sum of many experiences, and character indicates the reaction of those experiences upon the soul. In other words, life is a combination of situations, or Conflicts, with a spiritual signification drawn from the Conflicts themselves. So a story plot, which holds the mirror up to life, is a combination of Conflicts, selected to the pattern of a single Theme, or Masterplot. Life, with its multitude of experiences, is general; the imagination, dealing with a cross-section of life, makes the story plot particular. And imagination does this through the interpretation of suggestion.

SUGGESTION. The ideal of the Plotto Method, as stated elsewhere, is the interpretation of Conflict suggestions in terms of individual experience. Some of the Conflicts are General. Thus, Conflict No. 31 reads: "B, rescued from an accident by A, whom she does not know, falls in love with him." The nature of the accident, and the character of B and of A, are circumstances left to the constructive imagination. In dealing with these circumstances, references to other Conflicts, prefixed and affixed to this general suggestion, will offer further suggestions for inventing the circumstances.

Many of the Conflicts are Specific. Thus, to quote Conflict No. 647: "B, a respectable working girl seeking employment, follows the advice of a supposed friend, A-5, and finds herself in an immoral dance hall where she is compelled to dance with patrons and serve drinks." References to other Conflicts will suggest the cause of B's necessity for seeking employment, and other references will suggest a finalé for B's unhappy plight. The constructive imagination might use Conflict No. 647 literally, but Plotto would not approve of such literal use. The ideal method is for the imagination to use the dance hall merely as a suggestion for something equally pertinent to the situation; in other words, use the concrete example in interpreting an equivalent for this specific suggestion as to B's misfortune. Herein lies the opportunity for originality, and the way to creative work.

DEVELOPING THE PLOT FROM A MASTERPLOT. For purposes of illustration, we will select a Masterplot from the Masterplot Chart and build up a short story plot in tabloid form.

A 11   A Person Swayed by Pretense,
B 11   (49) Assuming a fictitious character when embarking upon a certain enterprise,
C 2   Emerges happily from a serious entanglement.

The B Clause "originates and carries on the action." Prefixed to this B Clause in parentheses is the number, (49). On the back of the Masterplot Chart, we find that No. (49) refers us to a sub-group of Conflicts beginning with Conflict No. 1173, this particular B Clause serving as a title for the sub-group:

1173

(2b, c, d, e, g, h)   (1187; 2f)
A, a pretender, encounters B, who is also a pretender * A and B are pretenders,

yet neither knows the other is not what he or she seems to be ** (773; 772 ch A to B & A-4 to A)   (806 ch B-4 to B)   (1462)

The reference numbers prefixed to this Conflict offer lead-up suggestions. Numbers 1187 and 2f form a complementary suggestion, or a combination of two Conflicts appropriate to the main situation.

1187.   A is a poor clerk who, with a limited capital, dons a dress suit and takes a "fling" in high society.

2f *-**.   B, poor and humble but pretending to be wealthy and aristocratic, meets rich and influential A, and they fall in love.

Thus we have our two pretenders, neither knowing that the other is not what he or she seems to be.   No. 2f has a carry-on suggestion:

1461a.   B fights a hard battle with her conscience; she finds it a losing battle and makes an important revelation in order that she may achieve peace of mind.

A and not B is the protagonist of 1461a, but we manipulate the Conflict by changing A to B.   This Conflict has a reference, No. 358 **-***:

358 **-***.   A, in order to win B, is compelled to confess his true rank and station.

We can now eliminate our main suggestion, Conflict 1173, so that our tabloid plot will read:

2f *-**.   B, poor and humble but pretending to be wealthy and aristocratic, meets rich and influential A, and they fall in love.

1187.   A is a poor clerk who, with a limited capital, dons a dress suit and takes a "fling" in high society.

1461a.   B fights a hard battle with her conscience; she finds it a losing battle, and makes an important revelation in order that she may achieve peace of mind.
358 **-***.   A, in order to win B, is compelled to confess his true rank and station.

We have manipulated the combination Conflict by allowing 2f *-** to precede 1187; and if we keep the reader in ignorance of the fact that A and B are pretenders and allow the revelation to come at the end of the story, we shall achieve a double surprise and find ourselves with the plot of O. Henry's story, "Transients in Arcadia."   Yet any number of stories, true to the Masterplot, may be built around these suggestions.

By changing the first two situations and selecting different Conflicts, the plot will develop along criminal lines:

2h.   B, a criminal, assumes an alias and makes use of stolen funds in evading the the law * B, a criminal in disguise, meets A, and they fall in love **

1c.   A, a crook, pretends to be an honest man in order to forward his love affair with B.

Or, we could make our plot more dramatic by having the second situation read:
3a.   A is a judge, and B is a fugitive from justice posing as a woman of wealth and fashion * A, a judge, falls in love with B, a criminal **

This might be followed with:
1292.   B seeks happiness as a reformed transgressor * B, seeking happiness as a reformed transgressor, has her old transgression discovered **

727.   A, a judge presiding at a murder trial, finds himself unexpectedly confronted with a circumstance that makes his work a torture to his soul.

These changes in the plot would make necessary a change in the C clause of the Masterplot:

C (1). Pays a grim penalty in an unfortunate undertaking.

CONFLICT MANIPULATIONS. Characters in the Plotto Conflicts are represented by symbols (see "The Plotto Character Symbols," page 17). These symbols may be readily changed or transposed, as an aid in manipulating the Conflict suggestions. Thus, "261 ch A-3 to A," indicates that A-3 in the Conflict is to be changed to A; and, "578b tr B & B-3," indicates a transposition in which B-3 takes the place of B and B of B-3.

The character symbols are changed, or transposed, in the auxiliary Conflicts to agree with the character symbols of the Conflict whose ramifications are being studied.

In many instances the Conflicts are "broken"—that is, divided into two or more parts. The end of the first part is marked with a star (*), of the second part, with a double star (**), of the third part with a triple star (***), etc. Thus, "-*" indicates that the Conflict is to be used up to the first star; "*-**" indicates that the first part of the Conflict is not to be used, but only that part between the first star and the double star; "-**" indicates that all of the Conflict is to be used up to the double star, etc.

DEVELOPING THE PLOT FROM A SELECTED SITUATION. The most practical way to illustrate the Plotto Method of developing a plot from a single situation, or Conflict, will be to select a Conflict and follow the Method through, step by step. For this purpose, the first Conflict, 1a, may be used:

1

(a) (112) (117) (148) (656)
A, poor, is in love with wealthy and aristocratic B * A, poor, in love with wealthy B, pretends to be a man of wealth ** (209) (187)

The simplest combination will consist of three Conflicts—the Conflict selected as the working basis for the plot, the one Conflict leading up to it, and the third Conflict terminating the action, both auxiliary Conflicts taken from the references prefixed and affixed to the main, or basic, situation. For example, as a lead-up Conflict No. 112 may be used, followed by 1a, and this in turn followed by No. 209.

It develops, however, that the second part of the broken Conflict, 1a, may be eliminated; and that, with this elimination, 1a -* may logically precede Conflict 112, giving the three-Conflict plot as follows:

1a -*. A, POOR, IS IN LOVE WITH WEALTHY AND ARISTOCRATIC B.
112. A loves B; and B's father, F-B, promises him B's hand in marriage if he will successfully carry out an enterprise of great difficulty and danger.
209. A carries out successfully a very difficult enterprise when promised the hand of B in marriage by F-B, father of B * A, discovering secretly that B loves a rival, A-3, refuses to hold B to a promise of marriage made by her father, F-B **

Nobility of character on the part of A is suggested by this heroic renunciation. The character of B, of F-B and of A-3, as well as the "enterprise of great difficulty and danger," may be left to the creative imagination.

Again using Conflict 1a for our main suggestion, we might begin with Conflict 656 for a lead-up:

656

(751)   (961)   (1000)   (1079)

A's ancestral acres have been heavily mortgaged and he is about to lose the property * A, by hook or crook, seeks to save his mortgaged paternal acres from foreclosure ** (500)   (860)   (874)   (1029)

Reaching backward into the causes of A's unfortunate condition, we will select lead-up suggestion No. 1079. Many other Conflicts in Personal Limitations, Misfortune, or some of the other groups would serve us equally well, or better; but we will content ourselves with

1079

(127a)   (656)

A's character weakness is betting; * and he seems unable to conquer the failing although he invariably suffers loss ** (367a)   (524a)   (902)

Here we have a suggestion as to the character weakness which caused A to squander his fortune and mortgage his ancestral acres. We shall assume now that none of the references prefixed or affixed to 1079 appeals to our imagination, so we shall proceed on our own initiative—a course which Plotto earnestly recommends to the Plottoist in the working out of every plot. A further study of Personal Limitations suggests

1075

(a)   (850b)   (902)

A, struggling hopelessly against a character weakness, forms a platonic friendship for B (838 ch A to B & A-2 to A)   (850a, b)   (364d)   (1075b)

Thus we have A, struggling hopelessly against a character weakness that has wrecked him financially, forming a platonic friendship for B. If we consider it expedient to bring about a dramatic first meeting of A with B, the Conflicts are brimming with such suggestions. But we will not go into that in this skeleton plot, our object being to simplify the references as much as possible. Conflict 1075b, a reference appended to 1075a, offers this suggestion as to B's influence over A: "A's admiration for his friend B, and his desire to please her, inspires him to bring out the best in his nature." Also appended to 1075a is a reference to Conflict 364d, which seems quite apropos at this point:

364

(d)   (850a, b)   (1075a, b)

A, with the help of B, overcomes an ignoble weakness * A's gratitude to B blossoms into love; and, when A is sure he has rehabilitated his character, he proposes marriage to B and is accepted ** (826)   (828)

This Conflict may be called a terminal Conflict, in the sense that it brings our love story plot to marriage, the finalé of most such plots. But we are not ready, as yet, to close the action, inasmuch as we are merely leading up to the main situation, 1a; so we shall use only the first part of this broken Conflict: "A, with the help of B, overcomes an ignoble weakness."

At last we have the female protagonist, B, firmly fixed in the plot, and we need not go back further into the lead-ups.

1079. A's character weakness is betting, and he seems unable to conquer the failing although he invariably suffers loss.

656. A's ancestral estates have been heavily mortgaged and he is about to lose the property * A, by hook or crook, seeks to save his paternal acres from foreclosure **

1075a. A, struggling hopelessly against a character weakness, forms a platonic friendship for B.

1075b. A's admiration for his friend B, and his desire to please her, inspires him to bring out the best in his nature.

364d -*. A, with the help of B, overcomes an ignoble weakness.

1a. A, POOR, IS IN LOVE WITH WEALTHY AND ARISTOCRATIC B * A, POOR, IN LOVE WITH WEALTHY B, PRETENDS TO BE A MAN OF WEALTH **

From this, it is manifest that A's platonic association with B has gone the way of most platonic associations (see Conflicts 9a, b, c), and his gratitude has blossomed into love. A, by inference, is so deeply in love with B that the best in his nature is, for the time, eclipsed by his desire to win B. He resorts to simulation in forwarding his suit—thinking less of saving his ancestral acres by a wealthy marriage than he is of his own future happiness. Conflict 1a has a reference to Conflict 187 for carrying on the action:

187

(145) (956 -*) (1105) (1119)

A, in love with B and wishing to propose marriage, finds it impossible because B is so busy he can never find her alone. He seeks to make an opportunity by stratagem. (163; 91) (352a)

We will discard this suggestion, for the reason that it will plunge A deeper into the questionable methods into which his ardor has already lured him. He is pretending to be a man of wealth when he is almost a bankrupt; but he has overcome his passion for gambling, thanks to B's influence, and he is ready to husband his remaining resources and save what he can from the wreck of his material fortunes. A carry-on suggestion appended to Conflict 187 is a two-Conflict combination, 163; 91:

163. B learns that her lover, A, has fallen into desperate misfortunes.

91. B, in love with A, seeks to save A from disaster.

We are now approaching the climax of the action. A's pretensions to wealth, B secretly discovers, are a hollow mockery. She learns that he is faced with disaster; and the Conflicts, if desired, will offer suggestions as to just how she discovers this secret. B is in love with A and ready to overlook his shortcomings, so she hastens to his rescue. We will depart, at this point, from the references and show B, on her own part, indulging in a bit of simulation. Turning to the sub-group, Simulation, we select Conflict,

1155

B, the friend of A, learns that A is desperately involved in debt * B, unknown to A, settles with A's creditors and frees him from debt **

This happy turn of affairs, naturally, cannot long remain unknown to A. If he has pride, let him pocket it; or let his pride be humbled by B's proof of her great love for him. If this course cannot be made to serve, the Conflicts will offer many suggestions for estrangement and reconciliation; but, in our plot, we will not have A a cad. Of the thousands of changes possible in such a series of actions as we are studying, we could eliminate the Conflicts from 163, inclusive, onward and place A in a better light by using this suggestion from Revelation:

1451a. A fights a hard battle with his conscience; he finds it a losing battle, and makes an important revelation in order that he may achieve peace of mind.

But we will not make the change. We will proceed to close the action with Conflict 364d *-**: "A's gratitude to B blossoms into love; and when A is sure he has rehabilitated his character, he proposes to B and is accepted."

The nature of the Conflicts, and their pliability, often calls for useless repetition. The statement in 364d that "A's gratitude to B has blossomed into love," is redundant. That fact has been known for some time, and has formed the basis for much of the action; and we simply ignore it here.

The latter part of this love story plot would stand as follows:

1a. A, POOR, IN LOVE WITH WEALTHY AND ARISTOCRATIC B, PRETENDS TO BE A MAN OF WEALTH.

163. B learns that her lover, A, has fallen into desperate misfortunes.

91. B, in love with A, seeks to save A from disaster.

1155. B, in love with A, learns that A is desperately involved in debt * B unknown to A, settles with A's creditors and frees him from debt **

364d *-**. A's gratitude to B blossoms into love; and when A is sure he has rehabilitated his character, he proposes to B and is accepted.

In the Classification by Character Symbols, all terminal Conflicts are marked by the parentheses number of the C Clauses. For instance, 364d exemplifies C Clause (9), "Achieves success and happiness in a hard undertaking." This Conflict, 364d, will be found, marked "9", under the A and B symbols of Conflicts in Marriage in the Classification by Symbols. An elusive terminal situation may be run down by consulting this Classification.

INDIVIDUALIZING PLOTTO. It is possible for the Plottoist to individualize his Plotto by adding material of his own. Every writer has newspaper clippings or other memoranda filed away for possible use. Let all this be catalogued in a loose-leaf book under the Conflict numbers to which each bit of material applies, and a notation to that effect penciled opposite the Conflicts thus amplified. This will broaden the usefulness of Plotto, often with concrete exemplifications of the Conflicts from real life.

Plotto Chart

Masterplots with Interchangeable Clauses

NOTE

A Plotto Masterplot consists of three clauses: An "A" Clause, a "B" Clause and a "C" Clause.

The A Clause is the Protagonist Clause.

The B Clause originates and carries on the action.

The C Clause carries on and terminates the action.

Any A Clause may be used in conjunction with any B Clause and with any C Clause. For the purpose of bringing all the B Clauses in juxtaposition with all the A and C Clauses, it is merely necessary to turn the narrow page.

Suggestions for evolving a plot to the pattern of the Masterplot selected will be found in the Plotto Conflicts. The Conflicts are listed in sub-groups; and each sub-group is listed under the full text of the B Clause which the sub-group exemplifies.

On the page immediately following the Masterplot pages will be found an index of the respective Conflict sub-groups under the parentheses number of the B Clause.

The C, or Terminal, Clauses are also numbered in parentheses; and Conflicts suggesting these terminations will be found opposite the C Clause numbers in the Classification by Symbols.

"A" Clauses   "B" Clauses

1. A Person in Love,

(1) Engaging in a difficult enterprise when promised a reward for high achievement,
(2) Falling in love at a time when certain obligations forbid love,
(3) Seeking to demonstrate the power of love by a test of courage,

2. A Married Person,

(10) Suffering an estrangement due to mistaken judgment,

3. A Lawless Person,

(13) Seeking by craftiness to escape misfortune,
(14) Falling into misfortune through the wiles of a crafty schemer,

4. An Erring Person,

(21) Falling into misfortune through mistaken judgment,

5. A Benevolent Person,

(25) Seeking to save a person who is accused of transgression,

6. A Protecting Person,

(28) Facing a situation in which the misfortunes of one greatly esteemed call for courage and sagacious enterprise,

7. A Person of Ideals,

(31) Living a lonely, cheerless life and seeking companionship
(32) Seeking to conceal identity because of a lofty idealism,

8. A Person Influenced by an Obligation,

(38) Committing a grievous mistake and seeking in secret to live down its evil results,
(39) Forsaking cherished ambitions to carry out an obligation,

9. A Person Subjected to Adverse Conditions,

(43) Seeking to overcome personal limitations in carrying out an enterprise,

10. A Resentful Person,

(46) Seeking retaliation for a grievous wrong that is either real or fancied,

11. A Person Swayed by Pretense,

(47) Finding (apparently) an object greatly coveted, and obtaining (apparently) the object,

12. A Subtle Person,

(50) Being impelled by an unusual motive to engage in crafty enterprise,

13. A Person Influenced by the Occult and the Mysterious,

(54) Becoming involved in a puzzling complication that has to do with an object possessing mysterious powers,
(55) Becoming involved in a mysterious complication and seeking to make the utmost of a bizarre experience,

14. A Normal Person,

(61) Becoming aware of an important secret that calls for decisive action,

15. Any Person,

(62) Becoming involved in any sort of complication,

"B" Clauses

(4) Being impelled by inordinate fancy to exercise mistaken judgment in a love affair

(5) Becoming involved in a hopeless love affair, and seeking to make the best of a disheartening situation,

(6) Challenging, in a quest of love, the relentless truth that "East is East, and West is West, and never the twain shall meet,"

(11) Confronting a situation in which courage and devotion alone can save the fortunes of one beloved,

(15) Finding a sustaining power in misfortune,

(16) Being delivered from misfortune by one who, in confidence, confesses a secret of transgression,

(22) Following a wrong course through mistaken judgment,

(26) Seeking secretly to preserve another from danger,

(29) Aiding another to hide from the world a fateful secret,

(33) Resisting secretly and from an honorable motive a mandate considered discreditable,

(34) Embarking upon an enterprise of insurrection in the hope of ameliorating certain evil conditions,

(40) Embarking upon an enterprise in which one obligation is opposed by another obligation,

(44) Seeking by unusual methods to conquer personal limitations,

(48) Assuming the character of a criminal in a perfectly honest enterprise,

(51) Devising a clever and plausible delusion in order to forward certain ambitious plans,

(56) Seeking to test the value of a mysterious communication and becoming involved in weird complexities,

(57) Seeking to unravel a puzzling complication,

"B" Clauses

(7) Becoming involved in a love affair that encounters unforeseen obstacles,

(8) Confronting a situation in which wealth is made conditional upon a certain course of action in a love affair,

(12) Falling into misfortune through disloyalty in love,

(17) Bearing patiently with misfortunes and seeking to attain cherished aims honorably,

(18) Rebelling against a power that controls personal abilities and holds them in subjection,

(23) Becoming involved in a complication that has to do with mistaken judgment and suspicion,

(27) Refusing to betray another's secret and calmly facing persecution because of the refusal,

(30) Enlisting whole-heartedly in the service of a needy unfortunate and conferring aid of the utmost value,

(35) Becoming involved in a complication that challenges the value of cherished ideals,

(41) Finding an obligation at variance with ambition, inclination or necessity,

(45) Seeking to forward an enterprise and encountering family sentiment as an obstacle,

(49) Assuming a fictitious character when embarking upon a certain enterprise,

(52) Encountering a would-be transgressor and seeking to prevent a transgression,

(58) Engaging in an enterprise and then mysteriously disappearing,

(59) Engaging in an enterprise and becoming involved with the occult and the fantastic,

"B" Clauses

(9) Being put to a test in which love will be lost if more material fortunes are advanced,

(19) Meeting with misfortune and being cast away in a primitive, isolated and savage environment,

(20) Becoming involved with conditions in which misfortune is indicated,

(24) Becoming the victim of mistaken judgment in carrying out an enterprise,

(36) Undergoing an experience that results in a remarkable character change,

(37) Seeking against difficulties to realize a cherished ideal,

(42) Falling into misfortune while seeking honorably to discharge an obligation,

(53) Opposing the plans of a crafty schemer,

(60) Becoming involved, through curiosity aroused by mystery, in a strange enterprise,

"C" Clauses

(1) Pays a grim penalty in an unfortunate undertaking.

(2) Emerges happily from a serious entanglement.

(3) Foils a guilty plotter and defeats a subtle plot.

(4) Undertakes a role that leads straight to catastrophe.

(5) Emerges from a trying ordeal with sorely garnered wisdom.

(6) Makes the supreme sacrifice in carrying out an undertaking.

(7) Reverses certain opinions when their fallacy is revealed.

(8) Achieves a spiritual victory

(9) Achieves success and happiness in a hard undertaking.

(10) Meets with an experience whereby an error is corrected

(11) Discovers the folly of trying to appear otherwise than as one is in reality.

(12) Rescues integrity from a serious entanglement.

(13) Comes finally to the blank wall of enigma.

(14) Achieves a complete and permanent character transformation

(15) Meets any fate, good or evil.

16

THE PLOTTO CHARACTER SYMBOLS

Characters in the Plotto Conflicts are represented by symbols. These symbols indicate the relationship of the auxiliary characters to the protagonist. This relationship is invariably explained in the text of the Conflicts, with the exception of the symbols A and B—these being the symbols of the male, and the female, protagonists. These symbols give a certain uniformity to the characters and facilitate character changes or transpositions. Protagonist A, or B, might be a criminal, an officer of the law, an employer, etc., but the numeral is never used in connection with the protagonist symbol—the explanation is given in the text.

A,	male protagonist		B,	female protagonist
A-2,	male friend of A	.	B-2,	female friend of B
A-3,	male rival or enemy of A		B-3,	female rival or enemy of B
A-4,	male stranger		B-4,	female stranger
A-5,	male criminal		B-5,	female criminal
A-6,	male officer of the law		B-6,	female officer of the law
A-7,	male inferior, employé		B-7,	female inferior, employé
A-8,	male utility symbol		B-8,	female utility symbol
A-9,	male superior, employer, one in authority		B-9,	female superior, employer, one in authority
F-A,	father of A		F-B,	father of B
M-A,	mother of A		M-B,	mother of B
BR-A,	brother of A		BR-B,	brother of B
SR-A,	sister of A		SR-B,	sister of B
SN-A	son of A		SN-B,	son of B
D-A,	daughter of A		D-B,	daughter of B
U-A,	uncle of A		U-B,	uncle of B
AU-A,	aunt of A		AU-B,	aunt of B
CN-A,	male cousin of A		CN-B,	female cousin of B
NW-A,	nephew of A		NW-B,	nephew of B
NC-A,	niece of A		NC-B,	niece of B
GF-A,	grandfather of A		GF-B,	grandfather of B
GM-A,	grandmother of A		GM-B,	grandmother of B
SF-A,	stepfather of A		SF-B,	stepfather of B
SM-A,	stepmother of A		SM-B,	stepmother of B
GCH-A,	grandchild of A		GCH-B,	grandchild of B
CH,	a child			
AX,	a mysterious male person, or one of unusual character		BX,	a mysterious female person, or one of unusual character
X,	an inanimate object, an object of mystery, an uncertain quantity			

Note: BR-A, BR-B, SR-A, SR-B, SN-A, SN-B, D-A, D-B, CN-A and CN-B may on occasion be merely BR, SR, SN, D, and CN.

Where necessary to indicate a male friend of B, or a female friend of A, the symbols aB-2, bA-2 may be used. Likewise, bCN-A, female cousin of A; aCN-B, male cousin of B, bGCH-A, female grandchild of A, aCH, male child, etc.

X added to any character gives to the character a suggestion of mystery.

(50) Being Impelled by an Unusual Motive to Engage in Crafty Enterprise

1

(a) (112) (117) (148) (656)
A, poor, is in love with wealthy and aristocratic B * A, poor, in love with wealthy B, pretends to be a man of wealth ** (187) (228) (233) (347a -*)

(b) (171) (734) (1106 -* ch B to A) (1146)
A, of humble birth, falls in love with aristocratic B * A, of humble birth, in love with aristocratic B, pretends to be a man of high social standing ** (139) (153) (209) (1200)

(c) (918a) (926) (928a)
A, in love with B, finds that B considers him too perfect for married happiness * B considers her lover, A, too perfect for married happiness; so A simulates a "hard-boiled" character in order to prove that he is not so perfect as he seems ** (1167) (1170) (1216) (1227 a, b, c)

(d) (148) (149) (160)
A, elderly, is in love with youthful B * A, elderly, in love with youthful B, seeks to forward his love affair by simulating youth ** (40 a, b) (75b) (78) (97) (156) (330a)

(e) (59) (1146) (1175a)
A, a crook, outlaw, gambler, pretends to be an honest man in order to forward his love affair with B (280a, b, tr A & A-3) (318; 236; 267) (252a)

(f) (230) (1060) (1101)
A is in love with B, who is devoted to scientific pursuits * A, who knows nothing of the sciences, pretends to be engaged in scientific research ** (179a, b, c) (181 a, b, c)

(g) (234a -*) (1061) (1150)
A falls in love with romantic B * A, in love with romantic B, pretends to be a hero ** (234a *-**) (1150; 851; 885a) (1227b, c)

(h) (43 -*) (101b) (898 -*)
A quarrels with his sweetheart, B, and fears he is losing her love * A, fearing he is losing the love of B, pretends to take poison with suicidal intent ** (249)(262a, b, c) (1461b)

2

(a) (949a) (954) (968)
A, a poor clerk, finances a "fling" in high society * A, a poor clerk financing a "fling" in high society, meets wealthy and aristocratic B (1146 ch A to B) (1187 ch A to B), and they fall in love ** (1461a ch A to B) (146a, c)

(b) (1146) (1175a) (1197)
A, a fugitive from the law and using a fictitious name, falls in love with B * A, craftily engaged in a secret enterprise, falls in love with B (1146 ch A to B) (1169 ch A to B) who has also embarked upon a crafty enterprise ** (91) (224) (233) (876a)

(c) (232) (420) (818b)
A, one of the "idle rich," gratifies his love of adventure by frequenting the slums in the character of a city "tough" * A, disguised as a city "tough," meets B, and they fall in love ** (114) (220) (358)

(d) (818a) (1197) (1198)
A is mistaken by B for A-8. B has corresponded with A-8 but has never seen him * A, falling in love with B, pretends that he is A-8 ** (82a) (97) (822)

(e) (1170) (1329)
B, wealthy, devotes much time to settlement work; and, in carrying out her phil-anthropic enterprises, she pretends to be a shop girl * B, while posing as a shop girl, meets A, and they fall in love ** (115) (336b) (1461a ch A to B; 358 **-***)

(f)   (916)   (974)

B, poor and humble but romantic, acquires unexpectedly a small sum of money; thus financed, she pretends for a time to be wealthy and aristocratic * B, poor and humble but pretending to be wealthy and aristocratic, meets rich and influential A (1163c) and they fall in love ** (117)   (152a)

(g)   (850a)   (1159 ch A-4 to A)

B, a maid, uses the wardrobe of her wealthy mistress and pretends to be a distinguished personage * B, poor but pretending to be wealthy and aristocratic, meets rich and influential A (1148a) and they fall in love ** (885a) (1060)

(h)   (876a)   (1244a)

B, a criminal, assumes an alias and makes use of stolen funds in evading the law * B, a criminal in disguise, meets A (1169)   (1175a)   (1181) and they fall in love ** (97)   (1208)

3

(a)   (2h)   (926)   (949b)

A is a judge, and B is a fugitive from justice posing as a woman of wealth and fashion * A, a judge, falls in love with B, a criminal ** (359)   (727)

(b)   (106 -*)   (925 -*)

A, a detective, falls in love with B, the criminal he has arrested and is returning to the scene of her crime for trial and punishment (106 *-**)   (53)   (359)   (986)

4

(a)   (298a ch BX to B; 58a ch AX to A; 1184)   (1172)

A, seeking to uncover duplicity by crafty enterprise, encounters the unexpected * A, seeking to uncover duplicity, falls in love with B, supposed to be guilty of the duplicity ** (62)   (64)   (1167; 826)

(b)   (739; 1401) (1170)

A recovers property belonging to an unknown woman, B * A, in a spirit of altruism, restores property to an unknown woman, B—and falls in love with her ** (21) (792a)

5

(168)   (603b, c, d)

A, carrying the news of the death of his friend, A-2, to B, the girl to whom A-2 was betrothed, (70 ch A to A-2), is mistaken by B and her parents for A-2. B and her parents have never seen A-2 or A (26a, b) * A, posing as his dead friend, A-2, falls in love with B, and withholds the news of A-2's death ** (1385)   (1461a; 73)

6

(a)   (14b -*)   (101b)

A, traveling the highroad, drops a purse of money unnoticed * B, who has long desired to know A, picks up a purse he has dropped and restores it. A and B fall in love ** (54a, b)   (1357)

(b)   (2h)   (3a -*)

A, a judge, loses his brief case * B finds a lost brief case belonging to A, a judge, and restores it to him; and the acquaintance, thus begun, ripens into love ** (801) (822)

7

(a)   (898)   (1073)

A is crude, unhandsome and repellant to the ladies, although he desires to be a gallant * A receives from A-7 a small object of mystery, X, which A-7 declares will make him redoubtable in love. A takes X and fares forth to try it ** (8a) (1330) (1347)

(b)   (1403)   (1418a)

A is in love with B and fears his affair is hopeless * A, in order to prosper his love affair with B, secures a love philtre from the Seventh Son of a Seventh Son—a philtre that is guaranteed to bring him the love of B ** (249)   (1433b; 1363)

8

(a)   (7a, b)   (1061)

A has a repellant personality and, knowing it, he is timid in love * A is timid in love but, armed with a love charm, X, he becomes bold, and wins success ** (161, (378)   (454)

(b)   (7a, b)   (1330)
A's love affair with B is not prospering.   A secures a love philtre and mixes it secretly in a cup of tea; but B's maiden aunt, AU-B, drinks the tea (1332) (1334a) (1375)

9

(a)   (13a)   (36)
A and B, both single, craftily covenant and agree to ban love in their associations * A and B, engaging in an enterprise, mutually covenant and agree to ban love; but love enters into their little scheme in spite of their platonic notions ** (207) (260a, b)

(b)   (244 ch B to B-3)   (325)
A and B, young and single, enter into a business co-partnership * A and B, entering into a business co-partnership, ban love with every legal device—but in vain ** (178)   (212a)   (213)

(c)   (83)   (84a)
B's cattle ranch was left to her by her father; and every man B hires as foreman makes love to her sooner or later, and is discharged * B hires A as foreman on her ranch, and he promises to keep his place and not make love to her; but B falls in love with him, and is presently glad to learn that A's sole purpose in taking the job of foreman was to win her love ** (181a)   (828)

10

(a)   (665)   (1309a ch A to A-8; 1309b)
B is a criminal, and A is the detective who has arrested her * B, a criminal arrested by A, a detective, brings her charms to bear upon A in the hope of effecting her escape ** (3b)   (230 tr A & B)

(b)   (873)   (876a)
B, poor and in great misfortune, is befriended by wealthy A * B, poor, seeks to win the love of wealthy A ** (186)   (230)   (431)

(c)   (239)   (745)
B makes love to A in an attempt to escape misfortune (182a)   (406)

11

(a)   (1279a ch B to M-B; 57 ch B to M-B)   (124 -* ch B to M-B)
B's mother, M-B, a middle-aged widow, introduces A, her youthful lover, to B* B's mother, M-B, plans that her youthful lover, A, shall transfer his affections to B.   M-B's plans are successful ** (83 ch B to M-B)   (324 ch B to M-B & B-3 to B)

(b)   (124 -*)   (168 -*)
B, middle-aged, and A, a youth, are in love with each other * B, elderly, in love with youthful A, seeks to have A transfer his affections to B-3, who is nearer his own age ** (11a ch B to B-3 and "daughter" to "friend")   (93a)

(c)   (3a, b)   (4a)
B, who is unworthy, finds that she has won the love of worthy A * B, unworthy, seeks to have her lover, A, transfer his affections to B-3, who is worthy ** (263) (324)

(15)   Finding a Sustaining Power in Misfortune

12

(a)   (2b)   (1173)   (750; 784-*)
A and B, each secretly, suppose themselves transgressors of the law * A and B, supposing themselves fugitives from the law, meet in a foreign country and fall in love ** (11c)   (624)   (784*-**)   (1050)

(b)   (688)   (918a)   (921)   (750; 784-*)
A, unmarried, and B, married, are shipwrecked and cast away on a desert island * A, unmarried, and B, married, fall in love when B supposes A to be her ideal.   And then B makes a discovery ** (307)   (1461c)

13

(a)   (32)   (340)
B is discouraged regarding her romantic affairs * B, discouraged regarding her love affairs, meets with a "sign" which prophesies her marriage within a year ** (56) (1342a ch A to B)

(b)   (15a, b)   (34)   (229)
B, as the world would have it, is an "inferior" person * B, an "inferior" person, falls in love with a "superior" person, A; and A's apparent love for her gives her the power to bear patiently the misfortunes of her humble estate ** (53)   (270)

14

(a)   (641)   (645)   (818a)   (873)
B, almost overwhelmed by misfortune, meets A, and they fall in love * B, winning the love of A, finds the courage to bear patiently with her hardships ** (827) (850a) (892 ch B-3 to A)

(b)   (60 ch A to A-3)   (647)
B finds herself in a great city, penniless and the victim of evil intrigue *'B, helpless and in misfortune, meets a stranger, A, and they fall in love ** (24a, d)   (82a) (144)

(c)   (564a ch A to A-8)   (577 ch B to B-8)
B, an attractive young widow, meets A, an equally attractive young widower * B, a widow, and A, a widower, meet in a cemetery where each comes with flowers for her and his lost spouse—and they fall in love ** (40a)   (67)

15

(a)   (23a)   (31)
B, plain and humble working girl, falls in love with A (68)   (243)

(b)   (29)   (32)
B, plain and humble "slavey," secretly adores A * A does not dream that humble B is in love with him ** (87)   (270)

(2) Falling in Love at a Time When Certain Obligations Forbid Love

16

a)   (453)   (10a)
A, a detective, has arrested B, a criminal, and is returning her to the scene of her crime for trial and punishment * A, a detective, falls in love with B, a criminal whom he has arrested ** (49)   (986)   (126)

(b)   (250)   (1186)
A has taken vows that proscribe the love of woman * A, although he has taken vows that proscribe the love of woman, nevertheless falls in love with B ** (224) (221a, b)   (248)

17

(690)   (688)
A, unmarried, and B, married, thrown together in a solitary and lonely environment, fall in love (53)   (438 ch A to A-8)

(b)   (561 ch A to A-8 & A-3 to A)   (503b ch A to A-8 & A-3 to A)
A, unmarried, out of sympathy for B, who is unhappily married to brutal and tyrannical A-8, falls in love with B (568a ch A to A-8)   (568b ch A to A-8 & A-3 to A)

18

(462 ch B to B-3)   (3a)   (4a)
A falls in love with B; but A already has a wife, B-3, whom he has never loved, a wife whom he considers it his duty to care for (417)   (557 ch B to B-3) (368a, tr B&B-3)

(41) Finding an Obligation at Variance With Ambition, Inclination or Necessity

19

(a) (117) (24a, b, c)
A falls in love with B, and renounces wealth which he was to inherit by marrying BX (223) (43)

(b) (118) (1041 ch A to GF-A)
A, under threat of being disinherited, is ordered to commit an act that will prove a grievous injury to a near relative of B's, the woman he loves. A refuses (130) (313)

20

(a) (1058) (1138)
A seeks to buy an object, X, from B, an object he greatly desires. B will not sell * A and B, while engaged in a commercial transaction, fall in love ** (41a, b, c)

(b) (1148a) (1153)
A meets B while engaged in an enterprise of indirection, and clever B finds a flaw in his explanations; B, also, is entangled in a snare of indirection, and A's suspicions are aroused * A and B are mutually involved in a snare of indirection; nevertheless, they are drawn to each other and fall in love ** (163) (50)

(c) (125b) (745)
A is a young lawyer, retained by B to help her settle the involved estate of her deceased father, F-B * A and B, during their meetings as lawyer and client, fall in love ** (107) (69)

(23) Becoming Involved in a Complication That Has to do With Mistaken Judgment and Suspicion

21

(4a) (1167) (1168) (1169) (1170)
A meets B and thinks she is a transgressor; and B, on her part, thinks A is a transgressor * A and B, each thinking the other is a transgressor, nevertheless fall in love ** (69) (97)

22

(a) (850a, b) (250) (885a tr A & B)
A is a woman-hater, but he is rendered a service by B which causes him to revise his opinions of the opposite sex * A, a woman-hater, falls in love with B ** (153) (826)

(b) (259-1) (262a)
A has an experience with B which causes him to become a woman-hater (22a) (1002 ch B to B-3)

23

(a) (3a) (15a, b)
B, an "inferior" person, falls in love with A, a "superior" person, and seeks to win him in marriage (212a) (254)

(b) (331) (346-*)
B, of an inferior race, falls in love with A, of a superior race (229) (226)

(c) (255) (282b)
A, of an inferior race, falls in love with B, of a superior race (225) (227)

(d) (293) (330a)
A, wealthy and of high social position, falls in love with humble B (228) (358)

(20) Becoming Involved With Conditions in Which Misfortune is Indicated

24

(a)   (806 ch B-4 to B)   (812a ch A-4 to A)
A loses his heart to B, a woman he does not know, and wishes to marry her (1d, e) (103)

(b)   (818b)   (788)
A, attracted by the loveliness of B, loses his heart to her (71b)   (128)

(c)   (1364 a *-** ch B to A)   (1410)
A sees a photograph of B, a woman he does not know * A, studying a photograph of unknown B, falls in love with her ** (27)   (31)

(d)   (22b ch B to B-3; 839 tr A & A-2)   (22b ch B to B-3; 1461b)
A, hearing of the character and charms of B, a woman he has never met, falls in love with her and resolves to win her in marriage (29)   (54a, b)

(e)   (74a, b)   (924b)
A, of an inordinately romantic temperament, sees the hand of B; and, because of the hand's shapeliness and beauty, falls in love with the owner, B (27)   (2c)

25

(101b)   (24b)
A, falling in love with B (32) (38), whom he does not know, seeks an introduction (139)   (36)

26

(a)   (169 tr A & A-2)   (6a, b; ch B to B-3)
A and B have never seen each other; but, through their fathers, F-A and F-B, who are old friends, it is arranged that A and B shall meet and marry (117 ch BX to B) (118)

(b)   (72)   (1183 ch SR to B)
A and B have never seen each other; but they correspond, and through their correspondence become betrothed (1461c)   (31)

27

(946)   (1203)   (1208)   (1258 ch A-6 to A)
B, unworthy, wins the love of worthy A, and tense complications result (11c) (359)

28

(a)   (452 ch A to A-8)   (1248)
B, very ill and under the doctor's care, fancies herself in love with the doctor, A (162a)   (1462)

(b)   (688)   (148 tr A & B)
B, suffering misfortune with A, fancies herself in love with him (307)   (147)

29

(38)   (916)   (925-*)   (926)
B knows nothing of A, having fallen in love with him at "first sight' (31)   (223) (226)

30

(32)   (1185)
B, a stenographer, is in love with A, junior partner of the firm employing her (274) (754)   (213)

31

(2f, h)   (8a)
B, rescued from an accident by A, whom she does not know, falls in love with him (45a, b)   (59)   (207)   (220)   (255)   (616)   (801)

32

(31)   (10a)   (641)   (765)
B, desiring love, has never had a lover, and feels the misfortune keenly (185)   (195)
(850a, b)

33

(668)   (670)
B, daughter of M-B, a widow, desperately opposes, and for very good reasons,
M-B's intention to marry again (59 ch B to M-B)   (65 ch B to M-B)

34

(327b)   (15a, b)
B, humble and self-effacing, worships A, her love alone seeming a sufficient reward
of happiness (87)   (91)   (186)   (270)

35

(32)   (10b*-**)
B, a plain girl who has no lover, is persuaded by her friend, B-2, to accept an escort
to a dance—A, a man she does not know (68)   (96)   (891 tr A & A-3)

36

(13a)   (32)
B is attractive, but no man pays her any attention * B, attractive, and humiliated
because of her lack of admirers, resorts to simulation to gain contentment ** (83)
(58a, b)

37

(1279a)   (1d tr A & B)
B, middle-aged, loves and is beloved by A, a youth (59)   (124)

38

(13a)   (35)   (36)
B considers love and marriage the great adventure, and eagerly proceeds with
them (64)   (88)   (143)   (146)

39

(38)   (15a, b)
B, unmarried, cherishes motherhood as her ideal (68)   (90a; 60)   (84)

(21) Falling Into Misfortune Through Mistaken Judgment

40

(a) **(41a, b)** **(129)**
A presents his sweetheart, B, with a novel; and the story, unknown to A, contains a character described as an adventuress in terms that exactly fit B.   Or, the novel which A, by mistake, wraps up and sends to B was a gift to A from a former sweetheart, her name and his on the fly leaf, and various love passages marked.   Or, there is something left by chance between the pages of the book at which B takes offense.   Or, some of the incidents of the story (which A has not read), approximate events in the affair of A and B with slighting references to B (80a)   (208)   (210)

(b) **(6a, b)** **(1461d)**
A encounters disappointment in love when B fails to answer a note he sent her (316)   (218b)   (306)

41

(a) **(1c)** **(9b)**
A, in love with B, refuses the wise counsel of B in business affairs, and an estrangement follows (300)   (315)

(b) **(1079)** **(1132)** **(808b tr A & B)**
A has promised B, the woman he loves, that he will give up a practice which B considers discreditable * A, yielding to temptation, proves false to a promise he made his sweetheart, B, and an estrangement follows (85a)   (97)   (163)

(c) **(118)** **(1315 ch A-3 to F-B)**
A persists in taking measures against one of the family of B, A's sweetheart, in spite of the protests of B.   An estrangement follows (43)   (259)

42

(a) **(292)** **(3a)**
A, in love with B, discovers that B is in love with B-2 (1413a ch A-5 to B2)   (315)

(b) **(1330)** **(1368)**
B, in love with A, discovers that A, Narcissus like, is in love with A (57)   (1347)   (1374)   (1375)

43

(70) **(73)** **(75b)**
A, in love with B, quarrels with F-B, father of B * B's father, F-B, is mysteriously slain, and innocent A is arrested for the crime ** (91)   (828 tr A & B & ch B-5 to A-5)

44

(a) **(598 ch A to A-4)** **(1029 ch A to A-4)**
A, a publisher in love with B, receives a manuscript novel from A-4, in which a woman character, approximating B physically and temperamentally, is made the rogue of the story * A, a publisher, rejects a novel because of personal pique (208)   (292)   (317)   (260a ch A-3 to A-4)

(b) **(44a)** **(131)**
A is so absorbed in his love affair with B that it has a disastrous effect upon his business enterprises (311)   (260a ch A-3 to A-4)

45

(a) **(28a, b)** **(29)** **(30)** **(31)**
A discovers that B, unhappily married, is —innocently on his own part—in love with him (55)   (61)   (274)

(b) **(806 ch B-4 to B)** **(818a)**
A, kind to humble B and considering her merely as a friend, is amazed to learn that she is in love with him (270; 251)   (254)

46

(205)   (22b)
A meets B, his love of other days, and is surp..sed to find that his success in distant
lands (967)   has no charm for her that is not discounted by the meager opportunities of the home country (207)   (211)   (21)

47

(a)   (1399)   (1436)
A asks that B allow herself to be hypnotized in order that he may learn where
buried treasure has been concealed (1394) * A hypnotizes B, and B dies of psychic
shock ** (53)   (633)   (1262)

(b)   (1220a)   (1159)
A persuades his sweetheart, B, to assume a fictitious character for the purpose of
acquiring gain by transgression—with unhappy consequences for both of them
(50 tr A & B)   (1192; 1200)

48

(606)   (619)   (631 ch A-1 to A-8)   (654)
A knew very well that he would suffer adversity all his life when, in order to cancel
an obligation he gave his daughter, D-A, in marriage to A-8, a man she did not
love (284 ch B to D & A-3 to A-8)   (313 ch F-B to A, B to D-A, A to A-3 & A-3
to A-8)

49

(70; 73; 690 add B)   (688-*)
A and B, lovers, meet with tragic misfortune but escape death * A and B, lovers,
escaping death in a tragic misfortune, each believes the other has perished ** (105)
(794 ch A-2 to B)

50

(126)   (1201)
A, in love with B, impersonates another person at B's instigation * A's pretentions
accepted, it develops that the person impersonated has a wife, who immediately
claims A as her husband ** (95)   (163)   (225)

51

(a)   (1290a)   (1316)
A loves B, and, when A confesses to B that he once committed a murder, B's health
declines and she worries herself into her grave (1433a)   (53)

(b)   (68 ch B to B-3)   (1304)
A confesses to B, his sweetheart, that he once committed a transgression, and the
result of the confession proves disastrous (1269 ch A to B & A-2 to A)   (249)

52

(a)   (1209a)   (1298)   (694)
A, a fugitive from justice, hiding in the bush, through error shoots and kills B, his
sweetheart, when he hears some one approaching his hiding place (746 ch B to A)
(787)   (802b ch A to A-6)

(b)   (808a)   (475)
A, seeking to benefit B, undertakes an enterprise which results disastrously (52b)
(761b; 385a)   (578a)

53

(11c)   (14a)   (17a,b)
A loves B; B dies; and A becomes demented through grief * A thinks B has merely
gone away for a time, and spends years in a vain search for her ** (1345)   (1365)
(1375)

54

(a)   (8a)   (117)
A is in love with B.   One evening, as usual, A calls to see B; but, where her beautiful
home had stood, no later than the evening before, there is now only an ancient, time-
stained tomb—the tomb of B, who had died a hundred years before A was born
(1433b)   (1446c)

(b)   (7a)   (1441a)
A, investigating a psychic mystery, falls in love with B * B, apparently in her early
twenties, is dazzlingly beautiful; but she is really very old, and in her case the
ravages of time were stayed in early youth by a psychic shock.   A's love dissolves
the spell; and, under A's eyes, B ages and her beauty fades ** (1433b)   (1461b)

55

(250) (288)
A really loves B, although he has taken vows that prohibit love for woman. A lives to regret his vows (106) (205) (207)

56

(38) (766)
B is convinced that several eligible men are in love with her * B is unaware of the fact that she is the victim of egotistical self-deception ** (65) (86) (184) (194a)

57

(226) (243) (264)
B, in a fit of discouragement over an unhappy love affair, meditates suicide and writes a note to her friends telling of her motives * B, contemplating suicide, writes a note explaining her motives; then she changes her mind—and loses the note ** (742) (758)

58

(a) (32) (36)
B invents a wholly imaginary lover, AX; and, most unexpectedly, a man of AX's name and general characteristics, presents himself to her (1184) (4a)

(b) (32) (36)
B pretends that she is engaged to be married to an imaginary lover, AX, buys herself an engagement ring, and has the betrothal announcement published in a newspaper (298a ch A to AX; 4a ch A to AX) (1187 ch A to AX)

(c) (62) (83)
B, single, pretends that she is a married woman and assumes the name of "Mrs. Blank" (1242a) (947) (946)

59

(31) (1146) (1175a)
B, aristocratic, wealthy, romantic, falls in love with A, a designing rogue masquerading as a person of "quality" (103; 93a) (90a) (228)

60

(90a, b) (676) (916) (55) (148) (217 tr A & A-3) (237) (247)
B is abandoned by A, the man with whom she eloped (665) (737a) (738)

61

(82a, b) (87)
B, in male attire, is suddenly revealed to A, the man she loves, in her true sex (220) (244) (264) (359)

62

(36) (145)
B is harrassed by gossip concerning men falsely rumored to be in love with her, and by relatives of the supposed lovers calling on her and making complaint (83) (102) (14a, b, c)

63

(2f, g, h) (10b)
B, in love with A, sends A a gift which, she mistakenly thinks, will forward their mutual happiness (40 ch A to B) (153 ch A to B) (333 ch A to B)

64

(15a) (23a, b) (34) (38) (916) (232) (272) (302) (421)
B is persuaded into a secret marriage by A, the man she loves (400) (415) (426)

65

(1105) (1121)
B is so fully aware of the fact that she is beautiful and attractive that she thinks every man is in love with her * A, whom B favors but who does not love her, seeks B out and bluntly tells her of her egotistical self-deception (1067) (679) (88)

(50) Being Impelled by an Unusual Motive to Engage in Crafty Enterprise

66

(a) (259-1-2-3) (226) (262a, b) (1105)
A, his love rejected by B, revenges himself by cutting off B's long hair (173) (1326 ch A to A-8)

(b) (335) (334a)
A, his love rejected by B, seeks revenge on the sex by becoming a heart-breaker, and a betrayer (96 ch B to B-3) (98 ch B to B-3)

(c) (284) (263 tr A & A-3)
A, his love rejected by B, seeks revenge by making love to eligible, wealthy women and getting money from them (387 ch B to B-3) (422b ch B to B-3)

67

(220) (330a)
A, elderly, wealthy, is in love with youthful B.* A seeks by a stratagem to discover the sincerity of B's professed love for him ** (93a ch B to A) (82a tr B & A)

68

(98) (658) (1306) (96)
A wronged B, the woman he loved, but secretly; and A craftily retains his own high place in society while leaving B to bear the heartache and shame alone (951) (1461a)

69

(27) (1146) (1173) (1175) (10c) (14b) (147) (61)
A, in love with B and thinking B has committed a crime (1172) (1206) (1292) (1293a, b, c), declares to the police that he committed the crime himself (828) (833) (787 ch A to B)

70

(100) (129) (132) (240)
A's family is at war with B's family; and A, in love with B, disguises his identity when calling on B (5) (73) (352a, b)

71

(a) (250) (1095) (101a)
A seeks to escape annoying manifestations of love * A, in order to escape annoying manifestations of love, pretends ι1ι that a wax figure, X, is his invalid wife; ι2ι pretends that he is married; ι3ι pretends that he is engaged to be married (2c) (24a, b, c, d)

(b) (143) (145)
B, in order to escape annoying manifestations of love, resorts to simulation (83) (84a) (58a, b, c)

72

(70) (299)
A, in love with B, pretends to be his deceased friend, A-2 (26a, b ch A to A-2) who was betrothed to B. B and her family, hearing of A-2's death at last, believe A to be the spectre of A-2 (73) (353) (362)

73

(70) (275) (276) (311) (312) (303)
A and B are in love, but B's parents, F-B and M-B, do not favor A; and A and B plan to elope, marry, and then seek forgiveness of B's people (154a, b) (314)

74

(a) (101b) (1389b)
A, young and romantic, sees a ruinous old house in a city street, a house said to be deserted. * A, his curiosity aroused, secretly watches the house; then, one day, he sees a beautifully rounded arm and a small, shapely hand (953 ch A to B) (403) emerge from behind a broken blind and place something on the window sill ** (24e) (1335)

(b)   (259-3)   (968)   (1104)   (1134)   (513)
A, hearing a woman's voice calling for help in a house he happens to be passing,
rushes up the steps, through the front door—and into a romantic complication
(664)   (407 ch A to A-8; 274)

75

(a)   (266)   (280a)   (290)
A and A-3 are in love with B.   A-3 seeks by craftiness to eliminate A (79)   (1228)
(1253)   (1267d)   (1265a tr A & A-3)

(b)   (75a)   (76)
A, through the wily manoeuvers of A-3, his rival in love, is innocently lured into
a compromising situation by B-5, woman confederate of A-3 (347b ch B to B-5)
(315)

76

(75a)   (157)
A and A-3 are rivals for the hand of B.   A-3 plans to forward his own aims at A's
expense (138)   (245)   (79)

77

(160)   (158)
A and A-3 are in love with B (85a).   F-B, father of B, seeks to discover by secret
enterprise which lover is the more worthy (111 add A-3)   (112 add A-3)

78

(137a)   (157)   (171)
A and A-3, in love with B, are persuaded by capricious B to undertake a dangerous
enterprise to prove their love (342)   (212b)

79

(111)   (112)   (115)
A's rival in love, A-3, pretends to be A's friend in order to lure him into an undertaking in which he will lose his reputation or his life (75b)   (612)   (1226 ch A-5
to A-3)   (1228)   (1229 ch B to B-8)   (1233)

80

(a)   (157)   (171)   (918a)   (926)
A, in order to insure the happiness of B (85a), whom he loves devotedly and who,
he thinks, loves his rival, A-3 (177 ch A to A-3)   (1175a ch A to A-3), flees secretly
so it may appear that he, and not A-3, committed a certain transgression (906 ch
A-2 to A-3)   (97)   (122)

(b)   (137a)   (139 ch A-2 to A-3)
A and A-3 are rivals for the love of B, and A learns that B prefers A-3.   A, in order
to insure the happiness of B and A-3 slays himself and leaves his estate to B and
A-3   (248 ch A to A-3)   (268 ch A to A-3)

81

(97)   (252a, b)   (260a)   (283)   (290)   (293)   (301a)
A kidnaps his sweetheart, B, (206)   (284)   (311)   from an automobile while she
is on her way to marry A-3, A's rival in love (367b)

82

(a)   (103)   (105)
B disguises herself and meets A, the man she loves, as an Unknown * B seeks to
discover whether A really loves her **(142)   (246a)   (249)   (250)   (357)

(b)   (103)   (141)   (162a)
B resorts to simulation in order to discover whether A, the man she loves, really
loves her (93a)   (82a)

83

(102)   (143)   (145)   (148)   (207)   (870a)
B pretends that she is engaged to be married in order to be free of certain annoying
experiences (21)   (207 tr A & B)

84

(a) (947) (976) (1212a)
B, in order to be free of unwelcome lovers, invents a mechanical figure, X, which she pretends is her husband (354b) (2c)

(b) (101a) (1095)
A, annoyed by unwelcome love affairs, pretends that he has an invalid wife, BX (71-1) (1f)

85

(a) (114) (178) (188a)
B, in love with A, treats A harshly in an attempt to arouse his anger and spur him into proving his abilities (125a) (225)

(b) (162a) (249)
B seeks to prove A's love for her by a stratagem * B deliberately manoeuvers herself and A into a compromising situation, and then places the responsibility squarely upon A ** (876b) (212b)

86

(32) (36) (38) (68) (124) (871) (1105)
B, unmarried and impelled by an unusual motive, pretends that she is engaged to be married to a fictitious person, AX, and has the announcement published in a newspaper (58a) (1242a)

87

(34) (91) (162a) (163)
B disguises herself as a boy, in order to be near A, whom she secretly adores (144) (146) (147)

88

(291) (330a) (659) (745) (916) (993)
B, in order to carry out an enterprise considered necessary, offers to sell herself in marriage to the highest bidder (182a) (269) (351a)

89

(223) (225) (228) (246)
B, thinking a symbol of lost love, X (1384), has a magic power of its own, seeks to regain love by wearing the symbol (1368 ch A to B) (746)

90

(a) (240) (290) (59) (66b, ch B to B-3) (1175a)
B elopes with A, who promises her a theatrical engagement (60) (142) (226) (415)

(b) (218a) (324) (678 ch SR-B to B-3)
B's ambition is to do B-3 an injury; so she elopes with A, who is engaged to marry B-3 (221 ch B to B-3) (224) (247)

91

(27) (29) (98) (1167) (1170) (1180)
B, in love with A, seeks to save A from disaster (595) (608) (610) by shrewd enterprise (92) (94a) (114) (125a)

92

(27) (126) (163) (1181) (1185) (1195) (1197)
B is in love with A, who has been arrested on a criminal charge by A-6 (753) (1084) (1101) * B, in order to help her lover, A, escape from A-6, the officer who has arrested him, makes love to A-6 ** (183 ch A to A-6) (230 ch A to A-6) (866)

93

(a) (59) (103) (164)
B, wealthy, pretends to lose all her money in an unfortunate investment, by way of discovering which of her lovers loves her for herself alone (210-3) (214) (361a.b) (366)

(b) (186) (199) (200)
B, seeking to prove whether or not A really loves her (141), has recourse to a stratagem (82a) (93a) (87)

94

(a) (3a, b) (14a, b, c) (925-*) (949)
B and A are in love. B-3, by craftiness (138) (215a) steals A away from B (216); *
then B, matching her own craftiness against B-3's, steals B-3's thunder and wins
A back again (359) (361a, b) **

(b) (337a) (340)
B's friend, B-2, an attractive married woman, seeks to save A, B's fiance, from the
wiles of a designing woman, B-3, and restore him to B. B-2 does this by winning
A away from B-3 (337b) (322b)

95

(27) (91) (291) (113) (311)
B will lose her lover, A, if she allows A to proceed with an enterprise (225) (125a)
(1201) (1267a) (1278a) instigated by herself. To avoid losing A, B defeats
the enterprise by making a confession (50)

(13) Seeking by Craftiness to Escape Misfortune

96

(703) (925-*) (937) (121) (239) (947)
A betrays B and does not marry her as he promised (60) (68) (98) (188b ch
A to A-8)

97

(260a) (280a) (284)
A, in love with B, seeks to save B, by secret enterprise and at any cost from threatening misfortune (236) (267) (351a)

98

(1185) (1247)
A is one of the "idle rich", who craftily retains his high place in society in spite
of the fact that he has secretly betrayed a young woman B (1325) (1326 ch A to
A-8) (1328) (1349) (1262)

99

(259 ch B to B-8) (321a ch B to B-8) (13a) (38) (325)
A and B, both unmarried, enter into a business association. They covenant and
agree that love between them shall be taboo (808a) (822)

100

(275) (276) (299) (1298)
A, in love with B, is determined to see B, although the determination will surely
involve him in misfortune unless he resorts to crafty enterprise (1209a) (70)

101

(a) (250) (918) (926)
A is so besieged by match-making mammas that their meddling seriously interferes
with the practice of his profession. He resolves to escape the annoyance by a
stratagem (84b) (1163b)

(b) (718b) (949a)
A is a sentimental person, fancy free but yearning for love * A is a poet, fancy free,
who keeps his lightning rods up in the hope of attracting a bolt of the divine passion
** (14b) (24a, b, c, d, e) (25)

102

(32) (325)
B is falsely suspected ot being in love with various men. She decides to free herself of the suspicion by a stratagem (86) (952 ch A to B) (1204)

103

(104) (143)
B is in doubt as to which of her many lovers are in love with her money, rather
than with her, and she resolves to settle the doubt by secret enterprise (82a) (93a)

32

104

(188a) (189) (290) (291)

B, if she wins a certain contest, also wins A-3, a lover of wealth and distinction whom she does not love, although she does love riches and social prominence; and if she loses the contest, she wins A, a poor lover whom she does love (356) (239) (933) (355)

(10) Suffering an Estrangement Due to Mistaken Judgment

105

(49) (585 ch "wife of A" to "sweartheart of A")

A believes that his sweetheart, B, is dead; and B, at a distance, learns of this mistaken belief on A's part (82a) (162a) (357)

(15) Finding a Sustaining Power in Misfortune

106

(259 ch B to B-8) (898) (681a)

A is a crabbed, disagreeable person whose misfortune it is to find no pleasure in life * A, a crabbed, disagreeable person, falls in love with B (4a) (9a, b) and, under the inspiration of love, his character undergoes a transformation ** (41a, b, c) (131; 115) (359)

107

(131) (85a) (156)

A's little world seems to crumble about his ears when he fancies that his sweetheart, B, is false to him * A, discovering that B is still true to him, undergoes a character transformation; pep, persistency and eloquence return, and lead him to success and happiness ** (360a) (369) (370)

108

(750) (43) (1167)

A, sweetheart of B, is condemned to die for a transgression he did not commit * A, unjustly imprisoned, is pardoned and restored to liberty when B appeals to high authority, A-9 ** (895) (350)

109

(249) (259-3) (283) (284) (291) (313)

A loses his sweetheart, loses his liberty on a false charge (43) (747) (731) (623) (608), escapes prison and survives shipwreck (650) (686) (688) (690), at last to reach the island where great treasure is buried (1394) (1369) (1403) (1436) (1406; 1408) (1393). And he recovers the treasure (360a) (963; 907)

(1) Engaging in a Difficult Enterprise When Promised a Reward for High Achievement

110

(1a, g) (4b) (22a)

A, in love with B, is promised her hand in marriage if he will: [1] successfully accomplish a work of great difficulty (209) (225) (111) (112) (113) (114) (115) [2] demonstrate his ability by securing a position at a salary which the parents of B think necessary for her comfort and happiness (1374) (1377b); or, [3] solve a puzzling mystery (1352) (1377b) (1384) (1392) (1399)

111

(22a) (20a) (1e)

A, in love with B, is required by F-B, father of B, to secure a certain amount of money before he will be seriously considered as a son-in-law (628) (1101) (1269) (1297)

112

(1f, g) (4b)

A loves B; and B's father, F-B, promises him B's hand in marriage if he will carry out successfully an enterprise of great difficulty and danger (209) (313)

113

(111)   (114)
A, in love with B, struggles to accumulate enough money to be able to marry (117)
(1001a)   (1028)

114

(125)   (291)   (595)   (748)
B informs A, the man she loves, that he will lose her love unless he overcomes his lack of enterprise and makes the determination to win his dominant trait (132)
(604)   (606)   (662)   (757)

115

(1061)   (1062)   (1063)   (1064)   (1090)
B is in love with A; but, before she will promise to marry him, she stipulates that he must do big work, wonderfully big work (1093; 1098)   (1073)

(9) Being Put to a Test in Which Love Will be Lost if More Material Fortunes are Advanced

116

(117)   (118)
A loses wealth by marrying B against the wishes of a rich relative, who disinherits him (363a)   (366)

(8) Confronting a Situation in Which Wealth is Made Conditional Upon a Certain Course of Action in a Love Affair

117

(26a, b ch B to BX)   (1432 ch A to F-A & NW to A)
A, a wanderer, is left a fortune by F-A, his father, in case he can be found and will marry BX, a woman he has never seen (116)   (132)   (230 ch B to BX)

118

(302)   (1432 ch A to GF-A & NW to A)
A will be disinherited by his wealthy grandfather, GF-A, if he does not perform an act which will prove a grievous injury to F-B (276 ch F-A to GF-A), father of B, the woman A loves (116)   (116; 1041 ch A to GF-A)

(2) Falling in Love at a Time When Certain Obligations Forbid Love

119

(128)   (476a)   (476b ch A to A-8 & A-3 to A)   (477 ch A to A-8 & A-2 to A)
A, unmarried, elopes with B, the wife of his dearest friend, A-2 (400 ch A to A-8 & A-3 to A)   (418 ch A to A-8 & A-3 to A)

120

(17a)   (140)   (409 ch A to A-8 & A-3 to A)
A, unmarried, falls in love with married B; B's husband, A-8, will not divorce B, nor will she divorce him (457)   (129)   (133)   (148; 210)

121

(27)   (32)   (34)
B, unmarried, seeks motherhood because of a lofty ideal that does not shrink from public censure (945)   (946)

(25) Seeking to Save a Person Who is Accused of Transgression

122

(260a)   (280a)   (1177 ch A to A-3)   (1181 ch A to A-3)
A and A-3 are both in love with B (84)   (235)   (286). A seeks to protect A-3 from arrest (80a, b)   (147)

(39) Forsaking Cherished Ambitions to Carry Out an Obligation

123

(70) (1315 ch A-3 to F-B)
A, to protect a parent, F-A, is compelled to take measures aginst F-B, father of B, the girl A loves (41c) (248) (282a)

124

(37) (1279a) (148)
B is older than A and feels that it will be unjust to permit A to marry her, although she dearly loves him * B suffers remorse after rejecting A's love ** (11a ch B to B-3 & M-B to B) (11b, c) (326-1) (251) (268) (325)

(28) Facing a Situation in Which the Misfortunes of One Greatly Esteemed Call for Courage and Sagacious Enterprise

125

(a) (114) (158)
B, in love with A, who is unfortunate and unenterprising, sees an opportunity for A to make great gain and influences him to take advantage of it (180) (284; 351a)

(b) (260b) (265b)
B, in love with A who is forgetful and absent-minded, is asked by A to marry him. B tells A to call on her for his answer on a certain day at a certain hour. If he can remember to come, B is resolved to accept him (367b) (284)

(c) (88) (745)
B is in love with A, who is engaged in settling the estate of B's deceased father, F-B * B's father, F-B, deceased, was heavily in debt, and A, wealthy, pays the debts unknown to B ** (367b) (808a)

126

(27) (291) (244) (695b)
B, sweetheart of A, persuades A to seek wealth by transgression (628) (628 ch B to B-3) (637) (296) (701)

(41) Finding an Obligation at Variance With Ambition, Inclination or Necessity

127

(a) (291) (311)
A believes that B will not marry him until he becomes wealthy (638) (621) (850b)

(b) (1061) (1062) (1079) (1092)
A believes that B will not marry him until he overcomes his personal limitations (252a) (853) (855) (857)

128

(24a, b, c, e) (25) (3a) (494 ch A to A-8 & A-3 to A)
A, in love with B, discovers that B is married to A-8 (134a, b) (558 ch A to A-8 & A-3 to A)

129

(128) (159) (170) (185) (196)
A and B are in love; but certain unhappy conditions prevent the cherished culmination of their romance (371 ch B to B-3) (397) (402 ch A to A-3 & A-3 to A)

130

(220) (148) (330a)
A is on his way to marry B and has only a few hours before the ceremony. He meets with misfortune (154a) (314) (634) (664) (711a, b)

131

(1a, b, c, d, f, g) (14a, b, c)
A is so much in love with B that his business languishes and he devotes all his time to courtship (41a) (85a) (115) (311)

132

(123) (118) (3b)
A, if he carries out a certain obligation, will be unfaithful to B, and will lose her love (116) (291; 700) (95) (986) (1007)

133

(17a, b) (120)
A loves B, and is compelled to stand helplessly by while B undertakes a dangerous enterprise (516 ch A to A-8) (893) (956) (1137a)

134

(a) (290) (299) (300)
A, and the woman he loves, B, are lost in the woods; and it is evident that they will have to remain in the woods all night (351b) (870a)

(b) (70) (73)
A, and B with whom A is in love, find themselves trapped in a ruinous old house from which escape seems impossible. Night is coming on, and B accuses A of seeking to compromise her so that he may win her in marriage (147) (360a, b) (876b)

135

(139 ch A-2 to F-A) (75a ch A-3 to F-A) (1d) (148 ch A to F-A)
A and his father, F-A, are both in love with B and wish to marry her (156 ch A to F-A) (282a) (983 ch A-8 to F-B; 269 ch A-3 to F-A) (351a ch A-3 to F-A)

136

(997a) (1022)
A and A-3 are in love with B*. Obliged to carry out the orders of A-3, A is commanded to [1] commit suicide, or [2] to leave the field clear for A-3 ** (209) (351a) (352b) (884 ch A-5 to A-3)

137

(a) (27 add A-3) (139 ch A-2 to A-3)
A and A-3, twin brothers, are both in love with B (80b) (821 ch "son SN" to "brother A-3")

(b) (678) (668 ch "mother M-B" to "sister SR-B")
B and SR-B, twin sisters, are both in love with A (215a ch B-3 to SR-B) (216 ch B-3 to SR-B) (238 ch B-3 to SR-B)

138

(04b) (238)
A, engaged to marry B, receives a request from B-3, his former sweetheart, that he come and see her (170) (172) (349)

139

(885a ch A to A-2) (997a) (885a ch B to A-2; 997)
A discovers that his best friend, A-2, is in love with B, the girl A is seeking to marry (157 ch A-3 to A-2) (174 ch A-3 to A-2) (122 ch A-3 to A-2) (75a, b, ch A-3 to A-2) (175 ch A-3 to A-2) (350 ch A-3 to A-2)

140

(259 ch B to B-8) (898) (32) (325)
A and B, associating in platonic friendship, find that love will not be denied (22a) (97) (366) (367a, b) (837)

141

(145) (992) (55) (111) (113)
B, in love with A, has worn A's engagement ring for years (129) (142) (162a) (234a) (249) (363a)

142

(162a) (82a, b) (87) (93a, b)
B, in love with A, discovers secretly that A no longer loves her, although he is willing to marry her as he has promised (324) (256) (287) (261) (325) (326-2)

143

(38) (908) (916)
B has so many lovers that she has no time to give to any one or anything else (96) (102) (931)

144

(646)   (654 ch A to B)
B, in the hands of enemies of A (616)   (719) is being forced to do their bidding
(666)   (1010) by threats of violence against A, the man she loves (1135a without the
clause in parentheses)   (1135a, with the clause in parentheses)

145

(921)   (976)   (1100)
B, an attractive girl, is so absorbed in serious pursuits that she subordinates everything else, even love, to her high ambition (1f)   (31)   (84a)

146

(142)   (158)   (170)   (266)
B loves A; but A's rival, A-3, makes a captive of B (81 tr A & A-3) and intends
compelling her to marry him (352b)   (851)   (884a ch A to B & A-5 to A-3)

(29)   Aiding Another to Hide from the World a Fateful Secret

147

(644)   (648)   (801)
B shares with her sweetheart, A, an important secret which, if revealed, would
bring misfortune to B (224 tr B & A)   (596)   (1408)   (1409)   (660b)

**(4)   Being Impelled by Inordinate Fancy to Exercise
Mistaken Judgment in a Love Affair**

148

(38 ch B to A)   (949a)   (954)
A, because of his romantic surroundings (197)   (210-1), imagines himself in love
with B (152; 211)   (69; 214)   (3a; 176a, b, c)

149

(1073)   (912a)
A, a widower, elderly, wealthy, temporarily bewitched by the vernal season, ima-
gines himself in love with B, a servant in his own household (616)   (658)   (33 ch
M-B to F-B)   (151)

150

(120 ch A-8 to A-2)   (476a ch A to A-2 & A-3 to A)   (900)
A, unmarried, elopes with B (405 ch A to A-2)   ('77 tr A & A-2; 403 ch A to A-2;
468 ch A to A-2; 784) the wife of his best friend, A-2; then B leaves A to elope with
A-3 (951)   (925)   (918b)   (705)

151

(149)   (210-2)   (232)   (27)   (38)   (220)   (239)
A, fancying himself in love with B, corrects the error when his fancy is discredited
(314)   (865)   (880a)

**(36)   Undergoing an Experience that Results in a
Remarkable Character Change**

152

(a)   (982a ch A to A-8 & NW to A)   (916 ch B to A)
A is a youth who is "wild" and hard to manage; he falls in love with B (812b; 230
tr A & B)   (224) and his character is transformed (234a)   (289)   (367a)

(b)   (1220b)   (1244b)
A's secretary, B, is a criminal, "planted" in A's home by A-5, a crook * B, a criminal,
confederate of A-5, a crook, falls in love with her employer, A ** (144)   (616)

(20)   Becoming Involved with Conditions in which Misfortune is Indicated

153

(218b)   (976)   (1042b)
A, in love with B, has a valuable gift sent to B by a jeweler. * Through error, or by
evil intent, packages are transposed; and the gift received by B, as from A, very
nearly proves disastrous to A's love affair ** (170)   (172; 1136)   (349)

154

(a)   (73)   (311)
A, planning to meet B at a country church where they are to be secretly married,
becomes lost in a storm and does not reach the church until B, and all the others,
have left (261)   (316)   (154b)

(b)   (160)   (75a)
A's rival in love, A-3, learning of the plans of A and B for a secret marriage, sends
an automobile to the church with a confederate, A-5, who lures B away by telling
her A has sent for her (146)   (885)

155

(916 ch B to AX)   (954)   (923 ch A to AX)   (954 ch A to AX)
AX, a gay young blade traveling through the country, takes refuge from a storm
in a rural church.   To his astonishment, he is hailed at once as a bridegroom, and
is hurried to the altar where a pretty girl, B (38)   (166) in an exhausted condition,
seems waiting for him. . In a spirit of recklessness (421 ch A to AX), he allows himself to be married to her; and when she, after the ceremony, seems to realize that
he is not the man she thought he was, he hurriedly makes his escape (389 ch A to
AX)   (432b ch A to AX)   (451 ch A to AX)

156

(1a, b, d, f, g)
A, a pretender, in love with B, secretly discovers B making fun of his pretentions;
he retires from the scene in disgust, hurt and indignant, and gives B up (320)
(344)   (922b)   (1171)

157

(704)   (1021b ch A-2 to A-3)   (913 ch A-2 to A-3)
A and A-3, once bosom friends, become enemies through their rivalry for the love
of B (122)   (174)   (352b)   (906 ch A-2 to A-3)

158

(159)   (171)
A's rival for the hand of B, A-3, is more energetic and enterprising than A and
seems to be more favored (85a)   (177)   (265a)   (364a)

159

(25)   (940-*)   (24a, b, c, d, e)   (37)
A is in love with B and does not know he has a more favored rival, A-3 (127a, b)
(139 ch A-2 to A-3)   (267)   (319 ch A-2 to A-3; 294a ch A-2 to A-3)

160

(171)   (75a)
A has a rival in love, A-3, whose assurance is the key to his extraordinary resourcefulness (158; 114; 1134; 81)   (80a)   (366; 1242b)

161

(7a)   (1377 tr A & A-2)
A discovers that a certain "charm," X, with which he has won success in love, is
no charm at all.   The person who gave him the charm tells him that faith in it is
all that counts.   Let a man be sure of himself, with or without a charm, and he is
bound to conquer love (182b)   (350)

38

162

(a)   (736)   (740)   (913 ch A-2 to B)   (928a)
B, in love with A, is uncertain of A's affections (47a, b)   (67)   (82a, b)

(b)   (39)   (96)   (98)
B has been betrayed, and her child is to be born out of wedlock * B, a poor unfortunate, meditates suicide as the only way out of her misfortunes ** (188b) (945)   (946)

163

(114)   (125a)   (126)   (608)   (623)   (777)
B learns that her lover, A, has fallen into desperate misfortune (91)   (92)

164

(564a ch A to A-8)   (2e)
B, a rich widow, has so many suitors she finds it difficult to make a choice (82a, b; 142)   (102)   (103)

165

(203)   (201)   (164)
B loses her watch (or a locket), and has her lovers search for it.   The picture of A, the lover B favors, is in the watch (301b)   (360b)

166

(64)   (73)   (154a)
B, running away from home to marry A, arrives in an exhausted condition at the church where she is to meet A.   Scarcely realizing what is going on, she is married to a man who, as her senses clear, she discovers is not A but AX (155).   She swoons on making the discovery, and AX disappears (402 ch A to AX)   (451 ch A to AX)

167

(280b)   (634)
B, her first lover having died, after some years falls in love a second time.   AX, the man she loves, greatly cast down, tells B he is already married, and to a woman he does not even know, BX.   He recites the circumstances (365b ch B to BX) (365c ch B to BX)   (365d); * and then strangely, even implausibly, it develops that BX is B.   (166 ch B to BX) **

(b)   (647)   (648)   (665 ch A-3 to A)   (659)   (18)   (162b)
B, failing miserably in her chosen line of work, takes "the easier way" and becomes the mistress of A (279)   (359)   (743a)

(5)   Becoming Involved in a Hopeless Love Affair, and Seeking to make the best of a Disheartening Situation

168

(603b, c, d)
A, and his friend, A-2, traveling together, meet with a tragic accident in which A-2 is killed.   Before he dies, A-2 requests A to carry the news of his death to his sweetheart, B (130 ch A to A-2)   (112 ch A to A-2)   (175 ch A-3 to A-2).   A proceeds with his mission (14a)   (139)   (5)

169

(26a, b)
A falls in with his friend, A-2, who is on his way to meet B, a girl he has never seen but to whom he is betrothed * A and A-2 meet with a tragic adventure and A-2 is killed **(603b, c, d)   (168)

170

(177)   (178)   (182)   (212a)
A and B, lovers, have a violent quarrel, and B returns a gift, X, she has received from A (57)   (208)   (349)

171

(941)   (944)   (964a)   (921)   (946)
A, a humble lover, has a rival for the love of B—A-3 (75b)   (899 ch A to A-3) (925-*) who is cultured, polished and a man of the world (75b)   (239 ch A to A-3)

172

(212a)   (213)   (222a)
B, estranged from her lover, A, whom she dearly loves, sends a telegram to another person and unconsciously puts A's name and address at the top of it (194b)   (1136)

173

(215a)   (216)   (221a)
B wore a certain ornament when her false lover, A, proposed to her. She has an odd conviction that the same misfortune will befall any other woman who wears the ornament (238)   (849; 1245)

(57)   Seeking to Unravel a Puzzling Complication

174

(160)   (157)
A and A-3, rivals in love, agree to meet at a certain hour, call on B, and ask her to choose between them (183)   (816a; 1265b)

(3)   Seeking to Demonstrate the Power of Love by a Test of Courage

175

(75a)   (76)   (93b add A-3)
B puts the love of two suitors, A and A-3, to the test (78)   (79)

176

(a)   (175)   (93b)
B, seeking to make a test of her lover's devotion, capriciously sends him into desperate danger (212b)   (342)

(b)   (175)   (59)
B, seeking to make a test of her lover's devotion, capriciously plunges into danger to see if he will follow her (851)   (85b)

(c)   (164)   (162a)
B promises A that she will marry him if he will successfully carry out a difficult enterprise (212a, b)   •

(23)   Becoming Involved in a Complication That Has to do With Mistaken Judgment and Suspicion

177

(77)   (112)
A mistakenly believes that F-B, the father of B, the girl he loves, is his enemy (300)   (311)   (322a)   (360a)

178

(29)   (31)   (24a, b,.e)
B promises to meet A, her lover, at her home and introduce him to her parents. A, arriving in advance of B, is mistaken for A-7, a man who is expected to call and apply for the position of butler (70; 352a)   (702 ch A to F-B; 1164 ch A to F-B & A-8 to A)

(11)   Confronting a Situation in Which Courage and Devotion Alone Can Save the Fortunes of One Beloved

179

(131)   (1042b)   (158)   (170
A, by mental telepathy, becomes aware of a terrible danger threatening B, the woman he loves (144)   (146)   (1137a)

(b)   (217)   (223)
A, at a long distance from B, and in a lonely country, hears an agonized call from his sweetheart over the phone (483 ch "wife" to "sweetheart")   (1154a)

(c) (1389b) (1f)
A has a clairvoyant vision apprising him of danger that threatens his sweetheart,
B (694) (873) (1172)

180

(70 ch A to A-3) (208)
A, a man of great strength and skill, is in love with B. F-B, father of B, sure of
A's prowess and proud of it, in order to lure the champion of a rival clan, A-3, into
a wrestling match with A (726b), offers the hand of B to the victor of the bout
(652b) (350) (142; 94a; 933 ch B to A)

181

(a) (41b) (114) (234a-*) (176b) (162a) (164)
A, riding his cow pony through the bleak hills, sees B, on a mettlesome horse, her
bridle-rein broken, plunging helplessly toward the brink of a cliff.   A, with a rattle
of spurs, overtakes B and snatches her clear of the saddle.* Thereupon, love is
declared and accepted (188a) (241) (360a) **

(b) (135 ch A to SN & F-A to A) (148 ch A to SN)
A's son, SN, is determined to marry B, whom A thinks is unworthy * A, seeking
to prevent his son, SN, from marrying B, makes love to B and plans to marry
her himself (241 ch A to SN & F-A to A) (159 ch A to SN & A-3 to A) (156)

(c) (885b) (1426b)
A and A-4 held prisoners in a strange lost city, escape with the help of B, a supposed goddess * A is in love with B; and B, rescuing A and A-4 from their captors,
flees with them when they effect their escape (157 ch A-3 to A-4) (1395)

(21) Falling Into Misfortune Through Mistaken Judgment

182

(a) (56) (143) (235) (1105)
B, thinking she has received a proposal of marriage from A (192a) (195), accepts. Later, she discovers it was A-3 (76) (160) who proposed (260a) (266) (318)

(b) (148) (137b ch SR to B & B-3 to SR-B)
A is in love with B. Intending to propose marriage to B, he discovers that he has proposed to B-3 * A, thinking he is proposing marriage to B, finds that he has proposed to B-3, who accepts him ** (137b ch SR-B to B-3) (261) (284) (3,0)

183

(142) (162a) (659) (665) (669 ch A-5 to A-3)
B, while in an irresponsible state of mind, promises to marry A-3 (1d) (239 ch A to A-3); and later, realizing what she has done, regrets the promise (404) (10, tr A & A-3)

184

(56) (62)
B takes the opposite meaning of an ambiguous sentence and accepts A's statement (196) (288) as a proposal of marriage (65) (307)

(50) Being Impelled by an Unusual Motive to Engage in Crafty Enterprise

185

(312) (299)
A is in love with B and is determined to ask her to marry him, but B is so closely guarded that A is in despair because of his lack of opportunity * A seeks by subtlity to make an opportunity to ask B to marry him ** (81) (82a tr A & B) (352a)

186

(816b) (743a)
A, in order to rescue B, who is ill and without funds, pretends to be in love with her and proposes marriage (142) (230) (373) (393)

187

(145) (956-*) (1105) (1119)
A, in love with B and wishing to propose marriage, finds it impossible because B is so busy he can never find her alone. He seeks to make an opportunity by stratagem (163; 91) (352a)

188

(a) (85a) (114) (189)
B, impelled by an unusual motive, agrees to marry A if she loses to him in a certain contest of skill [archery, shooting at a mark with rifle or revolver, solving a mystery] (1343) (1364) (1384) * B has the ability to defeat A in a certain contest if she so desires ** (355) (1243) (234b)

(b) (162b) (968) (98 ch A to A-8) (926)
B, about to commit suicide, is restrained by a stranger, A. A is informed by B that life is too bitter, since there is no name for her unborn child * A, a stranger, offers to marry B and so save her from a crowning disgrace ** (411a, b) (963) (365d ch BX to B)

189

(188a) (164)
B, asked by A to marry him, wants a little more light on A's character before making up her mind * B challenges A to a contest of skill, her acceptance or rejection to be determined by the result ** (234b) (355) (615)

190

(641) (645) (659)
B, not in love with A, for certain reasons proposes to A, not in love with B (230) (365a)

(44) Seeking by Unusual Methods to Conquer Personal Limitations

191

(185) (187) (145)
A, seeking desperately his chance to propose marriage to B, rescues her from drowning, and proposes while they are clinging to an overturned boat (124) (227)

192

(a) (106) (99; 9a; 201)
A, lacking courage to propose to B face to face, proposes over the telephone (172) (182a tr A & A-3) (182b)

(b) (139) (160 ch A-3 to A-2)
A sends his friend, A-2, to B with a proposal of marriage * A-2 proposes to B for A; and B, thinking A-2 is speaking for himself, accepts him ** (266 ch A-3 to A-2) (300 ch A-3 to A-2) (318 ch A-3 to A-2)

193

(203) (609)
A, in love with B but too backward an diffident to propose marriage, is horrified to hear a child, CH, who knows of his passion, propos to B on his behalf. * But A is overjoyed when B accepts ** (754; 163) (801) (842a) (893)

194

(a) (38) (56) (196)
B, thinking A loves her and lacks the courage to make an avowal, proposes marriage to him after he has rescued her from a tragic accident (191 tr A & B) (264) (307) (325)

(b) (260b) (325a; 261)
B sends a telegram to A-3 accepting his offer of marriage * B, accepting A-3's proposal of marriage by telegram, through error sends the telegram to A, the lover from whom she is estranged ** (343) (381)

195

(9a, b) (160) (162a) (235)
B, out in a storm on a pitch-dark night, receives a proposal of marriage. Unable to see her lover, and scarcely able to hear him, she nevertheless accepts—and meets with a disagreeable surprise (182a) (182b tr B & B-3)

(20) Becoming Involved With Conditions in Which Misfortune is Indicated

196

(1061) (1132)
A, because of timidity, is unable to ask B's hand in marriage (127a; 628) (97) (179a, c) (194a)

197

(686) (687) (689) (691) (714) (937) (959)
A, threatened with death by savages, is offered his life by B, the ruler of the tribe, if he will marry her (904) (973)

198

(941) (905)
A, of a proud old Southern family, impoverished in fortune, feels that he cannot ask wealthy B, with whom he is in love, to marry him (93a, b) (1155)

199

(680a) (680b) (715b)
A is poor and crippled, and his pride will not suffer him to ask B, the woman he loves, to marry him (93b) (264) (257b; 345 tr B & B-3)

200

(675)   (1131)

A, in love with B and eager to win her in marriage, procrastinates as a matter of habit in making the marriage proposal (215b)   (221b)   (1075a ch B to B-3)

201

(1a, b, d, f, g)

A, fearing that B will refuse him, finds it impossible to propose marriage (324) (323; 325)

202

(24a, b)

A, in love with B, has reasons for not proposing marriage (211)   (214)   (227) (245)   (257a)   (272)   (287)   (288)

203

(1061)   (1132)

A and B, in love, are each too diffident to make an avowal to the other (179a, b, c) (193)   (352b)

204

(265b)   (1389b)

A is absent-minded * A asks B to marry him and forgets that he has done so ** (1075a ch B to B-8)   (1101)

(21) Falling Into Misfortune Through Mistaken Judgment

205

(214) (219) (221a)
A, winning the love of B (23a, b) (34) (250) in his youth, and casting it aside,
goes searching for it in later years (207) (148) (361b) (377-*; 378 ch B to B-3)

206

(260a) (280a)
A, in love with B, discovers that his rival, A-3, is unworthy. B seems to favor
A-3 (97) (266) (236; 267)

207

(34) (55) (71b ch B to A) (1095)
A suffers remorse for telling B that he was married when he was not * A did not
think that he loved B, but later finds that he does ** (46) (205) (220)

208

(1c, d) (10a)
A, in love with B, discovers that B is a confirmed coquette and is merely playing
with him (176a, b, c) (320) (244; 421 tr B & B-3)

209

(110) (112) (180)
A carries out successfully a very difficult enterprise when promised the hand of B
in marriage by F-B, father of B * A, discovering secretly that B loves a rival, A-3,
refuses to hold B to a promise of marriage made by F-B ** (267) (281b) (313)
(345 tr B & B-3)

210

(101b) (1389b) (968)
A, under abnormal conditions, falls in love with B; on returning to normal conditions, he sees B as she really is and his love fades. [1] A's imagination errs in
a high, mountainous country; on returning to sea level, the error is manifest, and
he renounces it (148) (150). [2] A's imagination errs on the romantic side in
spring; but, as summer advances, he corrects his mistaken fancy (149) (151).
[3] A believes B wealthy; on discovering that she is poor, his ardor cools (1e;
(59; 93a). [4] A's romantic success is won with a love "charm"; on discovering
that the charm is a humbug, romance evaporates (7a; 8a; 161)

211

(1075a, b) (898; 1075a ch B to b-3) (205) (315; 1075a ch B to B-3)
A, who has long cherished B in his heart as the loveliest and most perfect of her
sex, returns home after a long absence and discovers that B has become an immoral
character (921; 946; 97) (27; 359)

212

(a) (126) (176c)
A is pledged by B, the woman he loves, to undertake an enterprise that will bring
him serious misfortune * B pledges A to an enterprise which, unknown to B, will
bring him serious misfortune ** (50) (212b)

(b) (212a) (342)
A, having carried out successfully an enterprise instigated by capricious B, renounces her love (225) (746) (892 ch B-3 to A) (946)

213

(274) (597) (612) (623)
A and B are in love; but one of A's employees, A-7, tells B of a (seeming) trans-
gression that A has committed. B credits the story * A-7 is a mercenary of A-3,
A's rival in love ** (249) (262a) (315)

214

(24a, b, c) (22a)
A, in love with B, is persuaded by Old Dry-as-Dust, the sage, AX, to turn from
love as from something evil (82a, b) (205) (352a, b) (363a)

215

(a) (239)   (256)   (494 ch B to B-3, A to A-3 & A-3 to A)
A, because of the wiles of B-3, a coquette, breaks his engagement to marry B,
whom he loves (94a, b)   (220 ch B to B-3)   (361a)

(b) (218b)   (215a)
A is in love with both B and B-3 * While A debates within himself whether he
shall propose marriage to B or B-3, B and B-3 engage themselves to marry other
lovers (233)   (224)

216

(218a)   (170)
A is about to marry B-3, who has deceived him into thinking B, the woman he loves,
is unfaithful (220 ch B to B-3; 865; 880a)   (238)

217

(158)   (160)   (75a)
A's rival for the love of B, A-3, basely deceives B with false suspicious of A (213)
(220; 233)   (266)

218

(a) (1083)   (1088)   (34)   (292 ch B to B-3)
A, although he loves B, is a conceited person * B-3 flatters A's vanity and so man-
ouvers him into an engagement to marry her **(256)   (237 ch B to B-3)

(b) (153)   (1461d)
A sends a gift to B, the woman he loves; B-3 intercepts the gift, and craftily replaces it with a photo of herself, lovingly inscribed to A (82a, b)   (82a; 61; 364b)

219

(718b)   (24a, b)
A, influenced by his maiden sisters, SR-A, SR-A, renounces his affair with B, the
woman he loves (226)   (236)   (364b)   (261)

220

(3a)   (218b ch B to B-3)   (305)   (647)   (948)
A's friends, A-2, A-2, believe that B, whom A is about to marry, is a woman of
immoral character and that A should be restrained (1095; 953)   (870; 851; 364b)
(865)

221

(a) (24a, b)   (22a)
A, in love with B, renounces his love when told by his friend, A-2, that it is unwise
(139)   (601; 163; 91)   (117)   (716)   (671)

(b) (660b ch A-5 to A-3)   (664)
A's rival in love, A-3, abducts A and holds him a prisoner as a means of preventing
him from marrying B (233)   (280b)   (875b)

222

(a) (1f)   (6b)   (8a)
A, in love with B, becomes estranged from B through mistaken judgment (41a, b)
(40)   (62)   (85a, b)   (153)   (215a)   (225)   (228)

(b) (14a, b, c)   (15a)
A, in love with B, secretly discovers B in the arms of A-4 * A, secretly discovering
his sweetheart, B, in the arms of A-4, leaves in anger, unaware that A-4 is B's
brother (708-* ch A to BR-B) just returned after a long, mysterious absence **
(172)   (681a; 705; 879)

223

(641)   (676)
B's father, F-B, a religious fanatic, sends B away from home because she falls in
love with A (6a)   (14a), who is not of their religious belief (741; 738; 743a; 673;
817)   (993-*; 125c)

224

(263)   (284)
B, the woman A loves, proves false to him; and A fears B will reveal a secret (126;
1159; 1192)   (1165 ch A to A-8 & A-5 to A)   (923) that will cause him trouble if
it becomes known (338)   (665 ch B to A)   (797-*; 818a)

225

(114)   (125a)
B awakens her lover, A, from his apathy by arousing his ambition to get ahead in
the world—which results in disaster to her love (237)   (281c)

226

(38)   (242)
B, finding her supposed ideal lover, A (688; 307)   (296)   (324) discovers that A
has "feet of clay" like all the rest.

227

(1e)   (8a)   (9a)
B is unable to marry A because her father, F-B, in using B for his subject in a
scientific experiment, has instilled a poison into her blood (43)   (47)   (57; 742;
758 ch A to A-8; 627 ch A to A-8)

228

(38)   (148)   (171)
B wears a rose in her hair to reveal her love for A, as A has requested * B wears a
rose in her hair to reveal her love for A; but the rose, unnoticed by B, falls from
its place; and when A sees her, he turns without a word and goes away ** (105) (172)

229

(23b)   (331)   (332)
B, of an inferior race, in seeking to win the love of A, of a superior race, learns
how hopeless is the task of challenging racial conventions (241)   (247)   (248)

(50)   Being Impelled by an Unusual Motive to Engage
in Crafty Enterprise

230

(656; 860)   (155)   (186)
A, impelled by an unusual motive, pretends to fall in love with B * A pretends to
fall in love with B, and ends his make-believe by really falling in love ** (182b)
(217)   (223)

231

(71-*)   (131)   (1078)   (1356-*)
A hopes, by a surgical operation on nis skull, to be made immune from the "master
passion" (182b)   (1330)   (1351)   (1363)

232

(24b, c, d, e)
A is an aristocrat; and B, the woman he loves, is a "daughter of the people" and
hates the aristocracy * A, an aristocrat, in love with a working girl, B, pretends to
be a toiler ** (245)   (251)   (262a, b, c)   (336a, b)

233

(27)   (30)   (31)
A is in love with B, and they are to be married; but A leaves town mysteriously,
no one knows what has become of him, and he does not return until after the time
set for the wedding (1368)   (1387)   (1389a)   (1040)

234

(a)   (114)   (164)
A loves B and would like to marry her, but B considers A a weakling and keeps
him dangling * A, in order to prove his "courage" to B, stages a mock rescue **
(81)   (1227b, c)

(b)   (260a, b)   (266)
A, an aviator, is a person of masterful character * A, an aviator, in love with B and
in disfavor with B's parents, F-B and M-B, induces B to take a ride in his airplane;
and then A elopes with B along the sky lanes ** (364b)   (249)

235

(595)   (680a)   (1065)

A and A-3 (158) (160) are rivals for the hand of B. B secretly favors A, but because A is self-effacing and less enterprising than A-3, B pretends to favor A-3 in order to spur A into proving his worth and ability (77)   (78)   (111)

236

(1059-*)   (1093-*)

A and A-3 (59 ch A to A-3) are in love with B. B is about to marry A-3, whom A knows to be a crook * A induces his rival in love, A-3, to send B a certain gift, X; then, after X is sent, A proves that it was stolen by A-3 ** (206)   (260a)   (267)

237

(750)   (915-*)

A, discovering that he is not a fugitive from justice as he had supposed, returns to his native country, secretly abandoning B, for whom he had declared his love (12a) while thinking himself a transgressor (205)   (404)

238

(4b)   (6a, b)

A is engaged to marry B. B-3, a designing woman, seeks to compromise A (218a, b) so B will give him up. B-2 is a generous woman who seeks by secret enterprise (844b) to rescue A from the wiles of B-3 and restore him to B (15a ch B to B-2) (128 ch B to B-2)   (364b)

239

(291 ch A to A-3)   (659)   (261 ch A-3 to A)

B, poor, would marry wealthy A, whom she does not love, for the freedom from care his money would give her (253)   (403)   (405)

240

(31; 70)   (275)   (276)

B, revealing the fact that she is in love with A, of a family at war with her own, is denied further intercourse with A by her father, F-A * B meets A clandestinely ** (73)   (154a)   (362)

241

(220)   (648)   (946)

B, in love with A, and disapproved of by F-A, the father of A, seeks as an Unknown to impress F-A with her character and charm (616 ch A to F-A)   (666 ch A to F-A, 1010 ch A to F-A)

242

(13a)   (947)   (976)

B disapproves of the men she meets in her own social and business world * B, disapproving of the men she meets in her own social and business world, envisions her ideal, the man she would like to meet, and fares forth secretly in search of him (9a, b)   (29)   (31)   (226)

243

(15a)   (34)

B, in love with A, rejects his love when she learns that he jilted B-2 (277) B's dearest friend, to pay attentions to her (251)   (325)

(13) Seeking by Craftiness to Escape Misfortune

244

(687)   (688)   (937)   (942)

A fights against the blandishments of B (945-*), a morally inferior woman who is in love with him (627)   (682)   (901)

245

(697b)   (389 ch A to F-A)

A is accused by A-3, his rival in love (157), of having been born under a "bar sinister" (75a)   (1051)   (1054)

246

(a)   (244)   (31)   (229)   (331)   (332)
A, in love with B, of an inferior race, seeks to abandon B secretly in order to uphold a lofty conception of duty (348)   (1328)

(b)   (248)   (259-3)   (315)   (322b)
A, victim of an apparently hopeless love affair, seeks contentment in befriending all who are in need, especially those who are unjustly treated * A, by his enterprises in altruism, finds that his hard nature undergoes a beneficial change ** (368e) (360a)

247

(15a)   (13a)
A betrays B, thinking mistakenly that there is no one to take her part and avenge the wrong (1326 ch A to A-8; 1237a ch A to A-8 & A-3 to A)   (1253 ch A-3 to A-8) (1262)   (1266 ch A to A-8 & A-3 to A)

248

(255)   (271)   (272)   (288)   (732)
A, recognizing a relentless obligation, renounces B, with whom he is deeply in love (718; 705)   (246b-*)   (363a)   (964a)   (842a)

249

(1163b)   (1167)   (1186)   (1187)
B, in love with A, rejects his love because she thinks him a man of evil mystery (367b)   (635)   (859)   (1163c)

250

(10b)   (28b)
B is in love with A, but A avoids women, believing them all tempters of Satan (45a, b)   (55)   (71a)   (101a)   (363a)

251

(32)   (36-*)   (264)   (285)   (325)
B, denied love, seeks happiness in a mental personification of love (58a, b, c) (271)

252

(a)   (1g)   (16b)
B refuses A's offer of marriage because she feels that A is too model a man for her to be happy with (1c)   (1227b, c)   (1237-*)

(b)   (204)   (1d)
B refuses A's offer of marriage because she feels that A is so absent-minded he might forget he has married her (179a, c)   (260b)   (265b)

253

(291 ch A to A-8)   (659)   (261 ch A-3 to A)
B is loved by wealthy A. B does not love A, but, for certain reasons, she yields to his importunities and marries him (376)   (403)   (557b)   (593)

254

(15a)   (34)
B, although she loves A, realizes that she is not the intellectual equal of A, and that their marriage would prove a hindrance to him (358)   (367b)   (680a; 361a, b)

(22)   Following a Wrong Course through Mistaken Judgment

255

(718a)   (959)
A, with a taint of negro blood in his veins—known only to himself—loves and is beloved by B, a white girl (681a)   (705)   (951)

256

(215a)   (218a)
A, in love with B, leaves B for B-3, a woman who flatters his vanity and whose bold beauty has an appeal for him (94a, b)   (238)   (361b)

257

(a)   (6a)   (9a, b)
A falls in love with B; but love, in A's case, is a transgression (255)   (732)   (231a)

(b)   (680a, b)   (681a)
A loves B; but, after A meets with misfortune, B gives her favor to A-3. A's rival in love (266)   (263)   (267)

258

(124 tr A & B)   (149)   (332)   (335)   (990)   (1074)
A, in spite of the fact that there are reasons why he should not marry, nevertheless plans to do so (374)   (500b)   (579b)

259

A, when B, the woman he loves, refuses to marry him, becomes [1] blasé and cynical, a misyogonist (224)   (230)   (243)   (245): [2] reckless, "goes to the dogs" or loses his mental balance in other ways (263)   (636)   (638) or [3] seeks to forget his unhappiness by indulging in a love for adventure (109)   (917)   (246b)

260

(a)   (59 ch A to A-3)   (280a)
A loves B, but is rejected for a rival, A-3, who, known to A but unknown to B, is a transgressor (236)   (265a)   (266)

(b)   (204)   (252b)
A loves B, but is estranged from her because he is so absent-minded and forgetful; he writes B a letter, assuring her that he has cured himself of his great failing— and forgets to post the letter (81)   (265b)

261

(262a, b, c)
B, her life's romance apparently wrecked, decides to marry the man, A-3 (284) (290), she does not love (81)   (236)   (351a)   (315; 318)

262

(a)   (262b, c)
B receives a letter from an unknown source * B, influenced by an anonymous communication, breaks her engagement to marry A ** (261)   (340)   (870a ch B to A)

(b)   (98 ch B to B-3)   (68 ch B to B-3)
B, in love with A, receives an unsigned letter in which the writer states that she is the mistress of A and begs B not to take A away from her (364b)   (1154b)

(c)   (415 ch B to B-3)   (481 ch B to B-3)
B, in love with A, receives an unsigned letter in which the writer states that she is the wife of A by a secret marriage, and asks B to use her influence in persuading A to return to her (249)   (312-1)   (326-4)

263

(958)   (1146a ch A to A-3)   (1181 ch A to A-3)
B rejects A, an honorable lover, and accepts A-3, who is a knave * A becomes a crook ** (819 ch A-5 to A-3)   (818a tr A & A-4)

264

(194a)   (199)
B, in desperation and out of her great love, proposes marriage to A, and is rejected (57)   (251)

(15) Finding a Sustaining Power in Misfortune

265

(a) (300) (1342a) (1389b)
A, while in a psychic state, has a prophetic vision of his rival in love, A-3, discredited, and of himself achieving happiness in love (1361b; 326-3) (290; 266)

(b) (260b) (1389b)
A is very absent-minded * A, absent-minded, forgets that B has rejected his love and continues to pay court to her (182a tr A & A-3) (182b) (189-*; 125b)

266

(206) (217)
A would save B, the woman he loves, from marriage with a rival, A-3, when he discovers A-3 to be a scoundrel (351a) (1222a; 1222b) (1232 tr A & A-3)

267

(59 ch A to A-3) (260a) (97)
B, discovering the perfidious nature of A-3, the man she has promised to marry, turns from him to accept A, by whose shrewdness A-3 was unmasked (280b) (367b)

268

(243) (248 tr A & B) (992) (993)
B refuses marriage with A, the man she loves, because of an obligation * B sacrifices happiness when, faithful to an obligation, she refuses marriage with A, the man she loves. Her sacrifice, in time, brings the consolation of spiritual joy for a hard duty nobly done (893) (976)

269

(177) (301b; 1260b ch A to A-3 & A-8 to F-B)
B's father, F-B, bankrupt, refuses to give B in marriage to wealthy A-3, a man she does not love, in discharge of his debts (993; 88) (993; 1207)

270

(30) (32) (34)
B adores A (327b) in secret; and when A disappears and reappears with a bride, B still finds her happiness in the great, unselfish love she still has for him (496b tr B & B-3; 367b) (555b tr B & B-3) (368e tr B & B-3)

(2) Falling in Love at a Time when Certain Obligations Forbid Love

271

(694; 31) (255) (282b)
A and B are in love; but A realizes that if he, of an inferior race, should marry B, of a superior race, the result would be disastrous to both of them (286-*) (240*-**) (87; 61; 264; 705)

272

(250) (259-1) (22b ch B to B-3)
A falls in love with B, after taking vows that forbid marriage, or love of woman (55) (134a, b)

273

(139) (24b)
A falls in love with B, who is betrothed to his friend, A-2 (122 ch A-3 to A-2) (157 ch A-3 to A-2) (211) (294a, b)

274

(1a, c, d, g) (22a)
A becomes involved in a love affair at the same time that he becomes involved in a divorce proceeding (45a) as the "other man" (129; 170) (226)

275

(24a, b, c, d, e) (25) (29)
A and B, their families at enmity, fall in love with each other (53) (70) (73) (24J)

276

(4b)   (5)   (8a)
A and B fall in love; but their fathers, F-A and F-B, are bitter political enemies (118 ch GF-A to F-A)   (117)

277

(15a)   (34)
B falls in love with A, who jilts a friend of B's, B-2 (98 ch B to B-2)   (324 ch B to B-2 & B-3 to B) in order to pay suit to B * B-2 grieves so terribly over losing her false lover, A, that B's heart is wrung ** (243)   (307)

278

(18)   (281a)
B suffers persecution and sorrow by falling in love with A, who is married but is unable to tell her that he is married (279)   (368e tr B & B-3)

279

(420 ch B to B-3)   (464 ch B to B-3)
B, unmarried, falls in love with A, married * B, unmarried, falling in love with A, husband of B-3, is overcome with remorse. B flees from A and from the world to a solitary spot where she seeks to do penance and obtain a spiritual victory over her evil nature (921)   (945)   (946)   (956)

(20)   Becoming Involved with Conditions in which
.   Misfortune is Indicated

280

(a)   (245)   (265a)
A discovers that A-3, his rival for the love of B, is a defaulter (97)   (206; 157; 80a, b)

(b)   (280a)   (158)
A discovers that A-3, his rival for the love of B, is a transgressor. In order to prevent the truth from becoming known, A-3 kills A (951 ch A to A-3; 1461a ch A to A-3)   (1344 ch A to A-3 & A-2 to A)

281

(a)   (509 ch B to B-3)   (486a tr B & B-3)
A wishes to marry B, but is already united to B-3 (365b ch B to B-3)   (354b) by a secret marriage (279)   (415 ch B to B-3)   (426 ch B to B-3)

.   (b)   (313)   (211)   (209)   (271)   (288)
A, overwhelmed by misfortune in love, commits suicide

(c)   (225)   (176c)
A, poor, in love with B, suddenly puts forth a great effort and secures a large sum of money (1354b)   (1394) * A renounces his love for B and seeks to win wealthy B-3 ** (287)   (324)

(39)   Forsaking Cherished Ambitions to Carry out an
Obligation

282

(a)   (276)   (282b)
A's sense of filial obligation is so strong that, when ordered by his father, F-A, not to marry B, the girl he loves, he gives her up (205)   (241)   (330b)

(b)   (257a)   (171)
A, an Indian, in love with B, a white girl, is commanded by his father, F-A, and by the head men of the tribe, to renounce B (266)   (271)   (248)

283

(295a)   (310)   (334a, b)   (325)
B loves A, but rejects his love because of petty differences, and because her father, F-B, is an enemy of A's father, F-A (234b)   (293)

284

(283)   (290)   (291)
B, in love with A, is compelled by her parents, F-B and M-B, to marry A-3 (81)
(234b)   (206)

285

(992)   (995)
B cannot marry A, the man she loves, because of her promise to live with her
widowed father, F-B, and make a home for him (641)   (676)

286

(250)   (275)
B is ordered by her parents to have nothing to do with A * B allows herself to be
governed by filial duty when her parents, F-B and M-B, order her to have nothing
to do with A, the man she loves ** (284)   (261)   (325)

(40) Embarking upon an Enterprise in which One Obligation
is Opposed by Another Obligation

287

(302)   (334a)
A finds that he cannot do justice to his chosen career if he marries B, the woman he
loves (258)   (256)   (248)

288

(720)   (732)   (1061)
A fears he has inherited the evil traits of an ancestor * A, because he fears he has
inherited the evil traits of an ancestor, dares not ask B, the woman he loves, to
marry him ** (258)   (264)   (705)

289

(850b)   (288)
A, in love with B and engaged to marry her, has almost wrecked his life with dissipation and feels that he should give B up (367a)   (1126; 779)

290

(280a)   (245)
B is in love with A, but the sentiment of her family is against A and ranged on the
side of A-3, A's rival in love (104)   (261)   (284)

291

(334a)   (322a)
B loves, and is beloved by, A, a man who is poor but of admirable character; but
B, accustomed to luxury, shrinks from the idea of poverty, even with love (134a, b)
(239 ch A to A-3)   (253 ch A to A-3)   (341)

(35) Becoming Involved in a Complication that Challenges
the Value of Cherished Ideals

292

(220)   (330a)
A considers B the acme of womanly perfection * A considers B the acme of womanly
perfection; yet B, on the contrary, is a woman of doubtful character ** (302)   (313)
(314)   (328)   (211)

293

(24a, b, c, d, e)   (25)*
A is an aristocrat; and B, the woman he loves, is a "daughter of the people" and
hates the aristocracy (232)   (283)   (336b)

(41) Finding an Obligation at Variance With Ambition, Inclination or Necessity

294

(a) (287 ch A to A-2) (282a ch A to A-2) (274 ch A to A-2) (256 ch A to A-2)
A discovers that his friend, A-2, is cruelly fickle in his love affair with B * A, discovering that his friend, A-2, is cruelly fickle in his love affair with B, takes him to task for it ** (294b) (294b; 232)

(b) (294a) (96 ch A to A-2)
A, in order to arouse the jealousy of his friend, A-2, and cure him of fickleness in love, pretends to be in love with B, A-2's sweetheart (230) (232)

295

(a) (295b) (313) (350-*)
A is in love with B; and he sues F-B, father of B, for damages sustained in a certain proceeding (41a, c) (345 tr B & B-3) (363b)

(b) (299) (283)
A, in love with B, and disapproved of by F-B, father of B, is forcibly ejected from the home of B by F-B. A brings suit for damages against F-B (41b, c) (343)

296

(220) (263-*) (266)
A tells B, with whom he is in love, that he has killed A-3 * A tells B, the woman he loves, that he has killed A-3, and asks her to call the police ** (750) (787)

297

(403 ch A to A-8) (448 ch A to A-8)
A is the presiding magistrate at the trial for murder of B (10c) (14a) (27), the woman he loves (108 tr A & B) (727)

298

(a) (24e) (22b)
A, an eligible young man, is mystified by discovering in a newspaper the announcement of his betrothal to BX, a woman he does not know (4a ch B to BX)

(b) (1432 ch A to U-A & NW to A) (606)
A is left a fortune by a deceased relative provided he will marry BX, a woman he does not know (117) (19a)

(c) (669 ch B to BX) (470 ch B to BX) (1154a ch B to BX)
A is appealed to for aid by BX, a woman he does not know * A, appealed to for aid by a stranger, BX, refuses aid, and regrets the refusal when BX mysteriously disappears. A considers himself under an obligation to find BX (1410) (885a ch B to BX)

299

(43-*) (276)
A is in love with B; but F-B, father of B, orders A to keep away from the house and away from B (70) (73) (352a, b)

300

(299) (284) (301a)
A is in love with B; and B is plighted to A-3—a fact which A suddenly discovers (280a; 97) (146) (81)

301

(a) (137a) (157)
A's rival in love, A-3, is favored by F-B, father of B (64) (73) (75a, b) (79)

(b) (165) (162a tr A & B)
A's rival in love, A-3, finds a certain object B has lost, an object, X, that proves B's love for A. A-3 appropriates X and says nothing about it (220) (257b) (280a, b)

302

(96) (117) (118)
A, if he marries B, the woman he loves (305), will be disinherited (241) (244) (366)

303

A's love for B meets with obstacles because: [1] A is poor (291)   (127a)   (125a)
(313); [2] too old (1d); [3] too young (37)   (124); [4] of inferior family (171) (245);
[5] of superior family (3a, b)   (232); [6] one of the "idle rich" (98)   (924b); [7]
inherits a mental or physical taint (255)   (288); [8] is of questionable character
(59)   (108)   (152a); [9] is divorced (334b)   (377a ch B to B-8)   (388); [10]
is an ex-convict (338) (695b); [11] is "under a cloud" (80a)   (237)   (274); or
[12] wealthy (239)   (330a)

304

(285)   (288)   (289)   (292)
A is resolved to marry B, but relentless duty stands in the way (211)   (220)   (248)

305

(697b ch A to B)   (818c ch A to A-8 & CH to B)
B is a white woman who knows nothing of her birth and parentage * B's rejected
lover, A, spreads the report that there is negro blood in B's veins ** (323)   (364a)
(255; 364c)

306

(308a)   (299)
B, in love with A, is detained by her father, F-B, when she seeks to keep an appointment with A (316)   (64)   (73)

307

(31)   (36-*)   (38)
B, compelled by circumstances to be a companion of A (898-*)   (925-*) in an
isolated place (688), alters her rosy views of love and marriage when she discovers,
through A, the selfishness of men (322b)   (325)

308

(a)   (306)   (299)
B is locked in her room by her father, F-B, in order to prevent her from meeting
her lover, A, and telling him of her love (316)   (308b)

(b)   (1461d tr A & B)   (290)
B sends a letter to her sweetheart, A, but it is intercepted by B's father, F-B,
who does not approve of A (295a)   (256)   (43)

(c)   (63)
B sends a gift to A, the man she loves * Unknown to B, AU-B, an aunt of B's who
does not approve of A, secretly alters or marks the gift in such a way as to make
it offensive to A, or exchanges the gift for some other object which will offend A
(81)   (93b) **

309

(453 ch A to A-8; 468 ch A to A-8)   (470 ch A to A-8)
B and A are in love; but B, unknown to A, is already married (397 ch A to A-8 &
A-3 to A)   (400 ch A to A-8 & A-3 to A)   (402 ch A to A-8 & A-3 to A)

310

(908)   (1105)
B breaks her engagement to marry A because she feels unequal to the responsibilities of married life (315)   (345 tr B & B-3)

311

(958)   (1062)
B's parents, F-B and M-B, disapprove of A, B's lover, because of his lack of enterprise (311)   (114)   (125a)

312

B's love for A encounters obstacles because: [1] Either B's father, F-B, or mother,
M-B, knows a secret supposedly infamous regarding A (98 ch B to B-8)   (918a);
[2] M-B and F-B are jealous of B and do not want her to marry any one (286)
(299); [3] B is the sole support of M-B and F-B (992)   (1032); or [4] B has a career
before her which marriage would render impossible (335)   (1119)

(5) Becoming Involved in a Hopeless Love Affair, and Seeking to Make the Best of a Disheartening Situation

313

(110) (111) (112)
A has been promised B in marriage by F-B, father of B; but F-B, false to his promise, compels B to marry A-3, a wealthier man than A (234b) (315) (351a)

314

(233) (220) (330)
A, in love with B and about to marry her, is detained and does not reach B's house in time for the wedding (130) (154a) (664) (711a) (719a) (1040) * A, prevented by circumstances from marrying B, as planned, discovers the unworthiness of B (27) and decides not to marry her at all ** (337b tr B & B-3) (421 tr B & B-3)

315

(286) (310)
A's love is rejected by B; and A, in an effort to forget, buries himself in an isolated part of the country (24a, b, c, d, e tr B & B-3) (345 tr B & B-3) (246b)

316

(146) (308a) (40b)
A, when B fails to keep a tryst with him, considers the failure a rejection of love (341) (360a)

317

(316) (319) (286) (341)
A is in love with B, but B proves false to him (404) (177) (208; 421 tr B & B-3)

318

(284) (291)
A sees in a newspaper the announcement of the engagement of B, the woman he loves, to A-3 (280a; 97) (236)

319

(221a) (599)
A, in love with B, secretly discovers that B is about to marry his friend, A-2 (168) (157 ch A-3 to A-2)

320

(56) (62) (85a, b)
A, in love with B, thinks B is a confirmed coquette, and is merely playing with him (421 tr B & B-3) (352b) (364b)

321

(a) (898) (899-*)
A tries philosophically to make the best of fate when B, the woman he loves, refuses him (917) (922-*) (246b-*)

(b) (220) (330a)
A falls in love with B and intends to marry her. A's parents, F-A and M-A, do not approve of B, and A is shipped off to South Africa to get him out of danger and give him a chance to do some serious thinking (321a; 364b) (325 ch B to A)

322

(a) (85a) (736)
A, in love with B, finds her unresponsive, reserved and distant (176b) (234b) (253)

(b) (781) (924b)
A's love is rejected by B because, as she frankly tells him, he is hard-hearted and has made money his god * B advises A to go away somewhere and try to develop the generous side of his character ** (246b) (963) (964a) (971)

323

(23a, b) (331) (332)
B, of alien blood and inferior race, is abandoned by A, a white man with whom she is in love (229) (347a)

324

(238) (256)
B loses the love of A when B-3 comes into his life (94a) (325)

325

(286)   (307)   (324)
B, suffering disappointment in love, resigns herself philosophically to her fate
(14a, b)   (31)   (976)

326

(20a)   (24a)   (22a)
B loves A with all her heart but refuses his proposal of marriage because [1] she
is so much older than A (37)   (124); [2] she discovers that A does not love her
(142)   (162a); [3] she considers A an impractical dreamer (958)   (136b); [4]
she feels herself under a compelling obligation (268)   (993)   (995)

327

(a)   (322a tr A & B)   (317 tr A & B)
B loves A, but A, apparently, does not return her love (45b)   (55)   (57)   (68)
(71a)   (82a)

(b)   (15a)   (23a, b)
B loves A; and A, who is kind to B but not in love with her, does not even suspect
that he is the object of her affections (270)   (264)

(23) Becoming Involved in a Complication that has to do with Mistaken Judgment and Suspicion

328

(770a)   (777)   (797-*)
A and B are in love and betrothed; A, supposed dead by B, returns and finds B
arrayed for marriage with A-3 (284)   (339) and accuses her of faithlessness (64)
(336a; 351a)

329

(273)   (330a)   (292)
A falls in love with B in spite of the fact that his friend, A-2, has warned him against
her (139)   (314)   (318 ch A-3 to A-2)

330

(a)   (149)   (3a)   (10b)   (27)
A, wealthy, is in love with B.   A's friends, A-2, A-2, think that B is a designing
fortune hunter (239)   (253)

(b)   (276)   (117)
A's father, F-A, disapproves of B, A's sweetheart * B, by secret enterprise (241),
proves her charm and worth to A's father, F-A, and he withdraws his objections
to her marriage with A ** (330a; 135)   (347b)

(6) Challenging, in a Quest of Love, the Relentless Truth that "East is East, and West is West, and never the twain shall meet"

331

(31)   (34)
B, a Polynesian woman, challenges racial conventions by falling in love with A
(687)   (689), a white man (324)   (336c tr B & B-3)   (347a)

332

(23a)   (23b)
B, of alien blood and inferior race, seeks to marry A, the Caucasian with whom she
is in love (323)   (324)   (327b)

(7) Becoming Involved in a Love Affair that Encounters Unforeseen Obstacles

333

(59)   (236 tr A & A-3)   (1175a)
A makes a gift to B, the woman he wishes to marry—a gift of value, X, which
is proved to have been stolen (267 tr A & A-3)   (1200)

334

(a)   **(8a)**   **(4b)**
A's profession is a hazardous one—aviator, automobile racing driver, steeple jack, "human fly"—and B considers this fact an obstacle to their marriage (287)   (1006b) (1356)

(b)   **(379 ch B to B-8)**   **(377a ch B to B-8)**
A, in love with B, was divorced from his first wife.   B's parents, F-B and M-B, have religious scruples against B's marrying a divorced man (73)   (80a, b) (134a, b)

335

(1099)   **(1119)**   **(312-4)**
A, in love with B, discovers that B's desire for a career is an obstacle to their marriage (237)   (1203)

336

(a)   **(284)**   **(313)**   **(328)**
B loves A and is about to marry A-3.   Accused of faithlessness by A, B shows a dagger, and declares that she intends to kill herself at the altar steps before A-3 can claim her for a bride (267)   (351a)

(b)   **(232)**   **(2c)**
B believed that her lover, A, was what he seemed to be, poor and humble; but he reveals himself as a man of wealth and station, incognito. * B, who considered A poor and humble, discovers that he is a man of wealth and station; and, oddly enough, in B's mind A's deception outbalances the wealth and rank, and she makes his high estate an obstacle to their love (340)   (983 ch A-8 to F-B)

(c)   **(331 ch B to B-3)**   **(332 ch B to B-3)**
B, a white woman, is in love with A, also white.   B-3, a woman of alien race, seeks to win A away from B (238)   (688; 31; 244 ch B to B-3)

(12) Falling into Misfortune through Disloyalty in Love

337

(a)   **(256)**   **(324)**
A, in love with B, meets with misfortune when he leaves B for B-3, a woman who flatters his vanity (126 ch B to B-3; 623)   (126 ch B to B-3; 70!)

(b)   **(94a)**   **(324)**
A, engaged to marry B-3, abandons her and marries B * B-3 sues A for breach of promise ** (393)   (406)

338

(1175a)   **(1180)**   **(1181)**
A is told by B-7, a maid in the home of B, A's sweetheart, that B has informed the police of A's criminal operations (1192)   (1194), and that he is an ex-convict (1195)   (1201)   (568a change "married to" to "sweetheart of")

339

(233)   **(719a)**   **(750)**   **(917)**
B, supposing A, the man she loves, to be dead, yields to the wishes of her parents, F-B and M-B, and consents to a marriage with A-3 (334a)   (336a)

340

(41a) (218a) (218b)
B, who loves A and is beloved by him, loses him to B-3 through the wily strategy of B-3 (94a)   (256)

341

(261)   **(239)**   B's mother, M-B, is determined that B shall marry wealth; so, rejecting the man she loves, who is poor, to marry the man she does not love, who is rich, B is plunged into unhappiness (373)   (376)   (393)

(21)   Falling into Misfortune through
Mistaken Judgment

342

(175)   (176a, b, c)
A is sent into desperate danger by capricious B, on the very eve of their marriage *
B, capriciously sending her lover into desperate danger, drains the bitter cup of
remorse ** (212b)   (1445)

343

(41a, b)   (85a)   (334a, b)
A is estranged from B, the woman he loves, because of a difference of opinion over
a trivial matter * A discovers B was right, acknowledges his error, achieves a reconciliation, and presently they are married ** (408)   (412)   (424)

344

(145)   (153)   (170)
A is estranged from his sweetheart, B, and B refuses to return money A had given
her to save for him * A falls into misfortune (601) (604); and his sweetheart B, from
whom he is estranged returns money she has been saving for him, effects a reconciliation, and their marriage follows ** (539a)   (548a)

345

(322b ch B to B-3)   (326 ch B to B.3)
A, his love rejected by B-3, goes to a distant part of the country and meets B (9a, b)
(22a).   A falls in love with B * B-3, filled with remorse because she rejected A's
love, goes searching for him, finds him, and is informed by him that he is presently
to marry B ** (372)   (458a)

346

(23a, b)   (34)
B, of an inferior race, rescues A, of a superior race, and falls in love with him.   A
is engaged to marry B-3, a girl of his own people * A, telling B of an inferior race
who is in love with him, that he is going away but will soon return, never returns,
but marries B 3, a girl of his own people ** (261)   (264)   (323)   (325)

(50)   Being Impelled by an Unusual Motive to Engage
in Crafty Enterprise

347

(a)   (287)   (288)   (289)   (293)   (305)   (323)
A, seeking to uphold a lofty conception of duty, secretly abandons B (23c)   (331)
(332), a woman whom he loves dearly * A's enemy, A-3, as a means of persecution,
by subtlity (348)   compels A to marry B ** (377a)   (379)

(b)   (98)   (117)
A is compelled by F-B, father of B, to marry B * F-B believes he is fully warranted
in compelling A, at the point of a gun, to marry B ** (373)   (385a)

348

(347a-*)   (346-*)
A's enemy, A-3, is captain of a ship on which A has taken passage, and on which
B (87) is a stowaway * A-3, knowing a secret of A's (347a-*), compels A to marry
B, A-3 performing the ceremony ** (372)   (376)

349

(283)   (335)   A's gift to his sweetheart, B, is returned by B to A on account of a
lovers' quarrel * A's gift, returned by B on account of a lovers' quarrel, is sent
back to B, unknown to A, by A-2, a friend of both B and A; and attached to the
gift is a note requesting B to keep it until A calls for it in person ** A, estranged from
B, is influenced by A-2 to call on B; and the result of the call is reconciliation and
marriage *** (501)   (504b)

350

(1223a ch A to F-B & A-4 to A)   (1223b ch A to F-B, A-4 to A & A-8 to A-3)
A and A-3, rivals for the love of B, are put to a secret, gruelling test of worthiness by F-B, father of B * A and A-3 are lured into a secret ordeal to prove their merit; A-3 flunks completely, but A succeeds almost at cost of his life ** F-B approves of A, and he marries B *** (572)   (574a)

351

(a)   (266)   (313)
A kidnaps his sweetheart, B, (284)   (300) while she is on her way to marry A-3, A's rival in love, and marries her himself (379)   (381)

(b)   (311)   (335)
A and B, lovers, are innocently thrown into a compromising situation (134a, b) (876b) * A, in order to safeguard B's good name, has a marriage ceremony performed by a wandering circuit rider, A-8 ** (391)   (411a, b)

352

(a)   (299)   (311)
A masquerades as a servant in the household of F-B, father of B, the girl he loves * A, enacting the role of a servant, rescues B from an accident by heroic bravery (181a-*) (851a-*) not at all in the manner of a menial ** A stands revealed as the lover of B whom F-B has not favored *** F-B approves of A, and A and B are married **** (375)   (14)

(b)   (300)   (313)
A rescues B, the woman he loves, from a villainous rival in love, A-3 (154b).   A marries B (449)   (451)

353

(169)   (139)
A is supposed by B's parents, F-B and M-B, to be A-2, to whom B is betrothed * A elopes with B and marries her; A then returns B to F-B and M-B, tells them that A-2, to whom B was betrothed, is dead, and asks and receives the parental blessing ** (424)   (430)

354

(a)   (32)   (36)
B, impelled by an unusual motive, invents a fictitious character, AX-* AX, a fictitious character invented by B, "comes to life," falls in love with B (4a ch A to AX) (298 ch A to AX), and they marry ** (452)   (462)

(b)   (10c)   (36)
B must be married when she reaches a certain age if she would receive a rich inheritance * B has no lovers, but a "marriage of convenience" is arranged with A, on the understanding that it is to be secret, and that A is never to see B after the marriage ** (230)   (379)

355

(189)   (188a)
B, capable of winning a contest against her lover, A, deliberately suffers defeat— because it has been agreed that she shall marry A if he wins (375)   (419)

356

(104)   (330a ch A to A-3)
B could easily win a contest, but she deliberately allows herself to be defeated, thereby losing wealth, but winning in marriage poor A, the man she loves (410) (455a)   (469)

357

(49)   (105)
B, knowing that her sweetheart, A, believes her to have perished in a tragic accident discovers by secret enterprise (82a) (87) that A has remained true to her (497 ch "wife" to "sweetheart") reveals her identy and they marry (442)   (515)

358

(232)   (2c)
B, a working girl, discovers that her lover, A, is wealthy and only pretending to be a toiler * B pretends to be wealthy, and merely masquerading as a shop girl ** In order to win B, A is compelled to confess his true rank and station *** B, having given A a Roland for his Oliver, reveals to A her own rank and station **** (391) (399)

359

(3a, b) (27)
B, unworthy, wins the love of worthy A; and B, by pretending to be worthy, presently achieves worthiness * —and a reward of married happiness ** (3ઠ1; 39ö)
(401)

(15)   Finding a Sustaining Power in Misfortune

360

(a) (177) (276) (316)
A, thinking his love rejected by B, receives a letter from B telling him how much she loves him, and that her father, F-B, has consented to their marriage (5ö2) (571)

(b) (20a, b) (24a, b)
A loves B, but he is uncertain of her affections and is too timid to propose marriage * A finds an object, X, which B has lost, an object that proves her love for him (165) ** A joyfully proposes to B and is accepted *** (380) (405)

361

(a) (215a) (256)
A proves false to B, the woman he loves, and has a disastrous affair with B-3 * B-3 abandons A after he loses his money (606) (630) and is injured and sent to a hospital (655) (710) ** B, still loyal, returns to A, and there is reconciliation and marriage *** (585a) (589)

(b) (282a) (287)
A proves false to B, the love of his youth * A, middle-aged, goes searching for B, the sweetheart of his earlier years ** (205) A finds B patiently waiting for him, and they marry *** (428) (431)

362

(70) (73)
A and B are lovers, their families at enmity.A and B elope and are pursued by their rival kindred * A and B, eloping and hotly pursued by their rival kindred, are suddenly plunged into terrible danger.   A makes a heroic rescue of B under the very eyes of their anguished relatives ** Out of A's heroic rescue of B is born a reconciliation of opposing houses, and married happiness for A and B *** (419) (460)

363

(a) (55) (287) (302) (329) (330a)
A revolts against opposing restrictions and achieves happiness in marriage with B (473) (484a)

(b) (295a, b) (118)
A renounces an enterprise against F-B, father of B, the girl he loves, when F-B withdraws his objections to A as a son-in-law and allows him•to marry B (517) (532a)

364

(a) (245 ch A to B & A-3 to B-3) (305)
B, a white woman, contemplates suicide when a mystery of her birth and parentage apparently yields an evil secret * A, B's loyal lover, working in secret, secures proof of B's unsullied lineage (1051) (1052-*); and they marry ** (431) (43)7

(b) (316) (320)
B, in love with A and estranged from him, after various misadventures (82a) (89) discovers that A still loves her * A reconciliation is effected, and they marry ** 540) (561)

(c) (255) (282a)
A, with a taint of inferior blood in his veins, is in love with B, supposedly a white girl.   He is about to give B up when he discovers that B also has a taint of inferior blood (255 tr A & B) (1051) * A marries B ** (551) (575)

(d) (850a, b) (1075a, b)
A, with the help of B, overcomes an ignoble weakness * A's gratitude to B blossoms into love; and, when A is sure he has rehabilitated his character, he proposes marriage to B and is accepted ** (826) (828)

(20)   Becoming Involved with Conditions in which Misfortune is Indicated

365

(a)   (9a-*)   (190)
A and B, not in love with each other, nevertheless marry because it seems the logical outcome of their long, friendly association (230)   (373)

(b)   (101b)   (599)
A and B, unknown to each other, in a spirit of fun at a masquerade ball, go through with a supposedly mock marriage ceremony. It later appears that the marriage was legal (167a)   (432a)

(c)   (24a, b ch B to BX)
A is married to an unknown woman, BX, by an insane clergyman, A-8, at the point of a gun (432a, b ch B to BX)   (437 ch, B to BX)

(d)   (188b ch B to BX)   (365a, b, c)
A marries BX, a woman he does not know * A and BX, husband and wife, go their different ways immediately after the marriage ceremony ** (167a ch B to BX) (432b ch B to BX)

366

(302)   (117)
A refuses an inheritance because of a restriction that he must not marry; then he marries B (117; 116; 167a)   (370)

367

(a)   (289)   (1075a)   (1079)
B offers to marry A and, as his wife, help him to rebuild his wasted life (469) (524a

(b)   (24a, b, e)
B doubts A when he tells her he loves her; then, having convinced herself of A's love (97)   (116), B accepts A and they are married (369)   (428)

368

(a)   (285)   (641)
B, having rejected A, the man she loves, because of an obligation she feels herself under to her father, F-B, is informed by F-B that he is going to be married—and B finds herself turned out on the world (205; 361b **-***)   (325)

(b)   (659)   (1260 ch A-8 to F-B)
B marries wealthy A, a man she does not love, in order that she may have money with which to help a parent who is in desperate need (403)   (558)

(c)   (171)   (162a)
B accepts her lover, A, and A secures a marriage license; then, before B and A can marry, B suddenly marries A-3, A's rival in love (312-1)   (313)

(d)   (818d ch A to A-8 & CH to B)   (1051)   (1054)
B, a foundling, has the secret of her birth and parentage revealed to her by A. A rich estate awaits B's claim and proof of parentage * A, in love with B, is poor and feels that he may not aspire to the hand of wealthy B; but B proposes marriage to A, and happiness is the result ** (449)   (458a)

(e)   (270 ch B to B-3)   (278 ch B to B-3)   (528)
A, unhappily married to B and in love with B-3, is too high-minded to seek a divorce * A's unworthy wife, B, is killed in an accident, and A is free to marry B-3, whom he has long loved ** (241 ch B to B-3)   (254 ch B to B-3)   (307 ch B to B-3)

(21) Falling into Misfortune through Mistaken Judgment

369

(107) (367a)
A and B, married and devotedly in love with each other, are hasty and intolerant *
A and B quarrel (372)   (373), and an estrangement results ** (457)   (460)   (501)

370

(366) (367b)
A, husband of B, loves B devotedly, but he is so constituted that he never shows
his true feelings and often masks them with something that suggests their exact
opposite * B mourns over the mistaken belief that she has lost A's love ** (581)
(586)   (575; 918b)

371

(59) (368b)
A is suspected of having murdered (416)   (417) his wife, B (385a)   (1070 ch B to
B-8)

372

(345) (348)
A and B, devotedly in love with each other, through failure to understand each
other's ideals (898) (899-*) (908) (976), develop an incompatability which
results in frequent quarrels (369)   (394)

373

(341) (365a)
A is so much older than B that, after their marriage, the discrepancy in their ages
(808b) becomes the cause of quarrels and, finally, of estrangement (418)   (429a)

374

(9a, b) (190)   (239)
A believed B was of an artistic nature * After marriage, A is sorely disappointed
on discovering that B is indolent in the pursuit of a career ** (413)   (441)

375

(114) (491a)   (1060 ch A to B)
A is more capable than his wife, B, although B thoughtlessly treats him as mentally
inferior (419)   (427)

376

(253) (341)
A, husband of B, holds B in subjection * A is a religious fanatic who makes B miserable with his petty domination ** (403)   (410)

377

(n) (347a)   (421)
A divorces his wife, B * B is devoted to A, and he owes much of his prosperity to
her loyalty and shrewd advice ** (496a)   (499a)

(b) (656)   (781)
A marries B, thinking she is wealthy; after marriage, he discovers that B is not
wealthy * A, bankrupt, divorces B and plans to marry wealthy B-3 ** B-3, whom A,
divorced, seeks to marry, marries another man *** B, just divorced by A, falls
heir to a large estate **** (388)   (638)

378

(59) (234a)
A, marrying a widow, B, discovers that he has "caught a tartar" and has wedded a
domestic tyrant (417)   (473)   (480)

379

(351b) (354b)
A suffers the loss of happiness in carrying out honorably a distasteful obligation
to divorce his wife, B (388-*)   (460)   (483a, b; 352b)

380

(553) (561)   (562-*)
A is jealous of his wife, B * A embarks upon an ill-considered enterprise of gambling
and loses money that is not his to lose ** A gambles with A-3, the man with whom
A believes his wife has an "affair" *** (434a)   (445a)   (568d)   (396)

381

(359)   (367a)
A finds a note (561)   (562)   (582 tr B & A), somewhat ambiguously worded, which
leads him to a wrong conclusion regarding the conduct of his wife, B * A is fired to
seek revenge ** (396)   (420)   (464)

382

(1002; 988)   (1285b)   (422a)
A, in order to restore to B, without a confession of culpability, wealth of which he
has secretly defrauded her, marries her * Then he falls in love with B-3 ** (440)
(465)   (572)

383

(8a)   (148)   (234a)
A's wife, B, has a birthmark which mars her beauty * Influenced by the thought,
A grows discontented, and his love begins to wane ** (386)   (391)   (416)   (475)

384

(574b)   (1009a, b ch B to M-A & SN to A)
A and B, married, live with A's mother, M-A * B quarrels with M-A, and with A
on account of M-A ** (1067)   (1067 ch B to M-A)   (1068)   (518)

385

(a)   (341)   (365a)   (368b)
A and his wife, B, have frequent and violent quarrels * B is mysteriously murdered
(387) and A, innocent, is suspected of the crime ** (520)   (526)

(b)   (812a ch A-4 to B-2)   (836 ch A to B & A-2 to B-2)
A is asked by B-2 a friend of his deceased wife, B, for a bundle of love letters which
B-2 had given to B for safe-keeping * A, husband ot B, suspects B of receiving love
letters—and discovers that the letters were merely being held by B for B-2 for
safe-keeping ** (552b; 1441b)   (576a, b)

386

(539a)   (542)
A leaves his devoted, loving wife, B, to take up with B-3, a woman who flatters
his vanity * B-3 is wealthy, but shallow; and A, in following her advice, fails miserably in all his undertakings ** (391)   (393)

387

(484a; 490a)   (370)
A presents his wife, B, with a gift as a testimonial of his love * (1333a)   A finds B
dead. slain by the gift he had presented to her ** (385a)   (474)   (497)   (576a; 498)

388

(464)   (486a)   (509)   (573b)
A divorces B, then seeks a second marriage with her * B's health was declining and
beauty fading when A secured his divorce from her ** B, her health restored,
considers herself well rid of A *** (305)   (319)   (322b)

389

(23c, d)   (27)   (365b)
A, thinking his first wife is dead (49)   (400)   (486a), marries again and has children by his second wife * A learns that his first wife was living at the time of his
second marriage, but that she has died since his second marriage ** This invali-
dates the second marriage *** A seeks to make a new will and go through another
marriage ceremony with his second wife, but is killed in an accident on his way
to his lawyer's **** Thus the children of A's second marriage are illegitimate, and
A's property descends to the relatives of A's deceased first wife ***** (245 ch A to
SN-A, son of A)   (305 ch B to D-B, daughter of A's second wife)

390

(709-*)   (808a-* ch B to A-2)   (1044b)
A, through accident (711b) loses an object, X, belonging to his friend, A-2, at the
door of a woman whose character is not of the best * X, an object belonging to A-2,
is lost by A in a place of evil character, and, found, is sent by a mischief maker to
A-2's wife with a note stating where it was found (478) ** A-2, falsely suspected
of transgression, finds himself in a most unhappy position until A, by a statement
of the facts, clears A-2 of suspicion *** (506b ch A to A-2)

391

(369)   (539a)   (542)
A, through mistaken judgment, becomes estranged from his loving wife, B * A has
a foolish escapade with B-3 (386)   (540), whereby his eyes are opened to his error
and folly ** A, enlightened and transformed by the revelation of his error, returns
humbly to his wife, B *** (449)   (499a)

392

(116; 53)   (498)   (515)
A believes he sees the apparition of his dead wife, B * A struggles to overtake the
fleeing apparition of B, falls from a cliff and meets his death **

393

(421)   (422a)
A, married to B, is haunted by memories of a former sweetheart, B-3 * Because of
his memories, A's married happiness is not what it should be ** A finds B-3, his
love of other days, and discovers that her beauty and charm have faded (244 ch
B to B-3)   (211 ch B to B-3) A knows at once that his emancipation from the evil
influence of B-3 is complete, and he returns to B a better and a wiser man *** (409)
(454)

394

(372)   (395)   (408)   (462)
A, married to B, escapes from B on plausible pretexts (443-*) and lives in a furnished room for a few days each month * B discovers A's deceit (443 *-****), trails
him, and learns how A is merely seeking home comforts denied him by B ** (417)
(478) B, realizing suddenly the injustice her exacting nature has been causing A,
promises to be different—and there is a reconciliation ***

395

(378)   (475)
A's ideal of married happiness is tranquility and comfort * A's wife, B, proves
herself a termagant, and quarrels are frequent ** (385a)   (394)   (427)   (440 *-**)
(471)   (473)

396

(380 -**)   (449)   (553)   (561)   (562) A learns that his wife, B, has been true to
him * A-3, the man with whom A thought B had eloped, A discovers, was married
several days before the date of the supposed elopement ** (563a)   (506b tr A & B)

397

(398a, b)   (418)
B, married to A, has a flirtation with A-3, unmarried * Married B is away with un-
married A-3 when A-3 suddenly dies ** (738)   (1069 ch "daughter D-A" to "lover
A-3")   (1151)

398

(369)   (370)
(a) B fancies herself neglected by her husband, A * A-3, the "other man," appears
and, by flattering married B, and sympathizing with her, causes her to imagine
she is in love with him ** (380)   (400)   (418)   (507a, b)

(b)   (369)   (370)
B fancies herself neglected by her husband, A * B, in order to win back her husband,
A's, love by arousing his jealousy, flirts with A-3 ** (397)   (445a)   (478 tr A & B)

399

(508)   (524a)
B is the sensible, devoted wife of A * A is the victim of egotistical self-deception **
A, advised wisely by B, thinks B is jealous of his great abilities *** An estrangement
results **** (438)   (457)   (460)   (482)

400

(444)   (454)
B deserts her husband, A, for another man, A-3 * B, deserting her husband, A, for
A-3, discovers that A-3 is in love with another married woman ** (418 *-**)   (496a)
(499a)

401

(538-*)   (581)
B's husband, A, has failed to return home and B is worried about him * B, thinking
her husband A is in danger, plunges into danger herself on the chance of finding
him and helping him ** (538 *-***)   (545)   (546a)

402

(49 ch "lovers" to "man and wife")   (437; 548)   (572)
B, married to A, supposes A is dead and marries A-3 (339) * A, supposed to be
dead, returns mysteriously as from the grave ** A seeks to force B to give up A-3,
the man she has married *** (573b)   (1390)

403

(368b)   (376)   (407)   (454)   (493)
B's husband, A, is brutal and tyrannical * Goaded beyond her powers of endurance,
B puts poison in a glass and gives it to A ** B, giving her husband, A, poison, flees
before the poison has time to take effect *** (453; 468)   (16a)   (946)

404

(261)   (290)   (291)
B, after a loveless marriage with A-3, obtains a divorce and begins searching for
A, the man she loves and from whom she became estranged (261 ch B to A & A-3
to B-3)   (327a; 325)   (345 tr B & B-3)

405

(486 tr B & B-3; 474 ch B to B-3)   (578b tr B & B-3)
B is the second wife of A, a widower * A, thinking he has been disloyal to his first
wife, B-3, makes B unhappy by his brooding ** (496a)   (504b)

406

(261 ch A-3 to A)   (284 tr A & A-3)
B, just married to A, tells A she does not love him * B informs her husband, A,
that she married him from pique and because A-3, the man she loves, married B-3 **
(462)   (489)   (499b)

407

(376)   (493)
B is flogged by her husband, A, for a transgression (445a-*)   (483b)   (553)   (381-*)
she did not commit (403)   (438)   (470)   (516)   (557a, b)   (558)

408

(378)   (500b)
B, wife of A, keeps their house so well-ordered, and is so tyrannical and unreasonable about it, that A's home life becomes a hell   (417)   (429a)   (464)   (486a)
(473)   (533)

409

(414)   (422a)   (436)
B, wife of A, informs A that she is in love with A-3 (423a)   (457)   (460)

410

(469; 532a; 1293a)   (469; 532a; 583b ch A-3 to A-5)
B has committed a secret transgression in order to help her husband, A * B finds
herself in the toils of A-5 ** (411b ch A-3 to A-5)   (669)

411

(a) (445a-**) (434a-*) (414)
B, happily married to A, commits an indiscretion (469; 532a; 1293b) (445*-***)
(442) (446a, b) (449)

(b) (469) (492b)
B, wife of A, secretly borrows money from her old lover, A-3, for a certain purpose *
A-3 seeks to use his power over B to advance his own selfish aims ** (476b) (483b)

412

(376) (378) (405) (413)
B, wife of A, is annoyed by the little mannerisms of A: The crook of his elbow as
he lifts a cup or glass, his endless repetition of what he considers humorous stories,
his old carpet slippers, his habit of snoring when he takes his afternoon nap, etc.
These trifling banalities so work on B's nerves that bitter quarrels result (404 tr
A & A-3) (411a) (418) (557a)

413

(190) (261 ch A-3 to A) (253)
B marries A, a man much older than herself * B does not love A but thought when
she married him that he would help her realize her consuming ambition ** B's
great desire is to become an actress *** A, husband of B, proves a brutal tyrant
and gives B nothing but harsh and inconsiderate treatment **** (373) (404 tr
A & A-3) (409)

414

(376) (916 ch B to B-2; 765 ch B to B-2)
B, wife of A, admires the personal independence of B-2 and would pattern after
her * A has no admiration at all for B-2 and her ways ** (407) (441) (442) (452)

415

(472-*) (365b, c, ch BX to B)
B learns that her supposed legal marriage to A was a farce * B is abandoned by A
and left penniless and alone ** (479) (481) (647) (870a) (14b ch A to A-3)

416

(227) (441-*) (475-*) (558) (761b)
B, wife of A, dies as the result of an enterprise undertaken for her supposed benefit
(576a) (578a, b) (587) (588)

417

(378) (408) (420)
B, while too severely reprimanding her husband, A, bursts a blood vessel and expires (371) (526) (560)

418

(530) (543) (582) (592)
B, married, quarrels with her husband, A, and runs away from home in an attempt
to find peace and contentment * B has an experience with A-3 which proves to her
that running away from her husband, A, was a mistake ** (483b) (507b) (583b)

(50)   Being Impelled by an Unusual Motive to Engage in Crafty Enterprise

419

(372) (375)
A must have his abilities recognized by his wife, B, in order to be happy (432a)
(463) * A leaves B to run their joint business enterprise alone, and goes to a distant place, knowing that his absence will cause B to discover his business worth **
(501) (519a-*) (1395) (1445)

420

(395) (406) (408) (494)
A lives unhappily with his wife, B * A's marital discontent prompts him to reckless
and questionable adventures ** (429a) (848 ch B to B-3) (876 ch B to B-3)
(1209b) (246-*)

421

(131 ch B to B-3; 208 ch B to B-3) (176a ch B to B-3)
A marries B in order to emancipate himself from the evil influence of B-3 * B-3 is
a heartless coquette whom A loves ** (386) (393) (528)

422

(a) (1002; 1285b) (988)
A secretly defrauds B of a large sum of money * A (701 ch A-2 to B) marries B in order to make a crafty restitution of property which, before marriage, he had stolen from her ** (429a) (465) (486a)

(b) (59) (263 tr A & A-3) (284 tr A & A-3)
A has married B for her money * A, having secured B's money, grows tired of her ** A tells B he is a criminal, and will presently be arrested by the police *** A induces B to enter into a suicide pact with him **** B, carrying out a suicide pact with A, kills herself; A does not kill himself, but craftily explains that B commited suicide ***** (371) (392) (425; 1290b ch A to SN-A & F-A to A)

423

(a) (418-*) (426-*) (430) (400)
A and B, man and wife, each secretly leaves home on the same day * A believes he has deserted B, and B believes she has deserted A ** (394) (487) ₳(500a)

(b) (429b) (484a-*)
A and B, man and wife, are wealthy and socially popular * A and B are so occupied with social engagements that they have no time for the enjoyment of each other's society ** A and B seek solitude where they can be alone together *** A and B find the solitude they crave in [1] a lonely lighthouse, [2] on a desert island or [3] by pretending they leave for an extended trip abroad, closing their magnificent home and living secretly in humble furnished quarters **** (49) (688-*) (897 add B)

424

(461) (484a-*) (523)
A, an artist, works secretly as a day laborer in order to help his wife, B, who is also an artist * A tells B he is "realizing money on his art" ** (546a) (532b) (582) ₋ (574a)

425

(349) (363a)
A has a son by his white wife, B. B dies * A, while traveling abroad (917), marries B-3, a woman of inferior race (347a ch B to B-3) (901 ch B to B-3), abandons her and returns to his own country ** This secret A craftily keeps from his son, SN-A *** (881) (934)

426

(378) (464) (539a)
A, married to B and desiring his freedom, resorts to craftiness * A persuades his friend, A-2, to elope with B ** (377b) (489) (466a ch A-3 to A-2) (550 ch A-3 to A-2)

427

(378) (430) (432a) (438) (463) (513)
A, married to B, is impelled by an unusual motive to furnish a suite of bachelor lodgings in another town. He does this unknown to B * A secretly retires to his bachelor apartments and lives a hermitlike existence ** (423a) (385; 520 ch B-3 to to B) (502)

428

(354a) (356)
A and his wife, B, are artists. Their art does not prosper * A and B encounter dire misfortune. Each seeks some secret method of recouping their joint finances ** (124) (455b) (532b) .

429

(a) (420) (422a) (430-*) (471) (473)
A, married to B, is impelled by an unusual motive to drop out of sight, lose his personality and go adventuring in the under-world (1225) (1233) (1275)

(b) (423b-*) (471) (473)
A and B, married and devotedly in love with each other, are impelled by an unusual motive to drop out of sight, leave the world they know and search for an environment more to their liking (423b *-****) (484a)

430

(455b)   (461)   (491b)
A, husband of B, is heavily in debt * A disappears mysteriously ** (572)   (719)
(770a; 540)

431

(748; 700)   (924a)   (997b)
A, wealthy and desiring to be poor, has married B in order that she may spend his
money (484; 929)   (488a)

432

(a)   (375)   (378)   (382)   (383)
A, married to B, seeks by secret enterprise to effect a change in unpleasant marital
conditions (377b)   (393)   (394)   (419)

(b)   (354b)   (365b)   (155 ch AX to A)
A's wife, B, is a mystery woman * A does not know B, and has not seen her since
the day of their romantic marriage ** (167 ch AX to A)   (486)

433

(a)   (1316)   (1317 ch A-8 to A-3)
A's enemy, A-3, who wronged A grievously, is dead * A seeks to revenge himself
upon B, the wife of A-3, for a grievous wrong committed by A-3 ** (1310)   (1311)
(1323a ch B-3 to B)

(b)   (434a)   (450)   (494)
A's wife, B, is loved by A-3 * A-3 seeks craftily to win B, the wife of A ** (444)
(434a, b)

434

(a)   (553)   (561)   (562)
A's wife, B, seems to have an "affair" with another man, A-3 * A is manoeuvered
by A-3 into gambling with money not his own, and losing it ** (434b)   (445a)
(572)

(b)   (433b)   (171)
A is craftily manoeuvered into misfortune by A-3 * A, in the power of A-3, is compelled to divorce his wife, B ** (378 ch A to A-3)   (385 ch A to A-3)   (403 ch A
to A-3)

435

(a)   (402 ch A to A-3)   (451)
A marries B, a woman who, unknown to A, is already married to A-3, a husband
who is living and undivorced * A-2, a friend of A's, sends A-3 to A, B's second
husband, and exposure of deceitful B follows ** (743b; 921)   (738)

(b)   (466b)   (510)
A's wife, B, is untrue to him, a fact of which A is in ignorance. A-2 discovers B's
unfaithfulness, and informs A, who is on his death bed obstinately refusing treatment that would heal him * A, desperately ill, fired by tales of his wife, B's, unfaithfulness, makes up his mind to live and takes treatment that cures him ** (487) (489)

436

(458b)   (1061)
A, husband of B, a very beautiful woman, persuades B to pretend that she is his
sister * A fears that he will be killed by some admirer of his wife, B, so that the
admirer may marry B ** (584b)   (554)   (557a)

437

(681b)   (683)   (734)   (1368)
A, married to B, loses his identity * A assumes a fictitious identity and marries B-3*
(402)   (548a)   (571)

438

(503a)   (521; 1177 or 1178 or 1185)   (525)   (568b)
A seeks to achieve the refinement of cruelty in persecuting his wife, B * A secretly
and mysteriously sequestrates himself and fosters the deception that he is dead **
(402)   (559)   (884a ch A to B & A-5 to A)

439

(376)   (403-*)
B's friend, A-3, seeks to save her from persecution at the hands of her brutal husband. A * B's friend, A-3, forces a quarrel on B's brutal husband, A, hoping A will kill him, thus entangling himself with the law and freeing B of his tyranny.   A-3 accomplishes his heroic sacrifice **

440

(488b)   (1211; 422a)
A is impelled by an unusual motive to marry B, a woman he does not love * A succeeds by a stratagem in leaving his unloved wife, B (1204 ch B to A & B-8 to A-8) (952) and, under a fictitious name, marries B-3, the woman he loves ** (917) (963)

441

(33 ch B to D-B & M-B to B; 258 ch A to B)   (421)   (422a; b-*)
B, wife of A, is a drug addict * B keeps her husband, A, in ignorance of the fact that she is a drug addict ** (435b) (440)   (442)   (446a)

442

(376; 642-*)   (376; 646)   (403-*; 739)
B is forbidden by her husband, A, to do a certain thing * B, ordered by her husband, A, not to do a certain thing, does it anyway, during A's absence from home ** (642 *-**) (599; 534)

443

(386-*)   (408)
B's husband, A, leaves for town, as he declares, to meet a friend, A-2 * A's friend, A-2, sends a letter to A; it arrives during A's absence, and B opens it ** A-2, friend of A, is in a foreign country; and B conceals the letter from A-2 and, the next time A leaves home "to meet A-2," B trails him *** (394)   (486a; 552a tr A & B; 404 tr A & A-3)

444

(433b)   (492b)
B elopes with A-3, who has artfully inspired doubts of her husband, A's (213-*) (176b)   (540) loyalty (507a)   (568a)   (568b)   (573b)

445

(a)   (553)   (561)
B, wife of A, is mistakenly supposed by A to have an "affair" with A-3 * B, wife of A, detests A-3, but calls on him at night (483b)   (583b) ** B forces A-3, at the revolver point, to return to her money which he has taken craftily from A *** (380 *-***)   (396)   (499a)

(b)   (284)   (573a)
B, wife of A, seeks desperately to escape disaster * B drinks a potion which throws her into a condition resembling death, having been assured that A will appear and rescue her when she revives ** (105)   (576b)

446

(a)   (494)   (495)   (580)
B, wife of A, is guilty of an indiscretion * B, in order to escape consequences of personal culpability, falsely accuses innocent A-2 ** (446b ch "lover" to "friend") (507a)

(b)   (411b ch A-3 to A-2)   (433b ch A-3 to A-2)   (449 ch A-3 to A-2)
B, wife of A, calls on her lover, A-2 * A calls on his friend, A-2 ** A-2 conceals B so A will not see her *** A discovers his wife, B, concealed in the apartment of his his friend, A-2 **** (400 ch A-3 to A-2)   (418 ch A-3 to A-2)   (446a)

447

(90 ch A to A-5)   (59 ch A to A-5)
B, in her extreme youth, was lured into marriage with a criminal, A-5 * A-5 a criminal, is killed, and B, his widow, leaves home and goes to a distant country ** B marries A (20a, c)   (24a, b), a man of wealth and high social standing, and keeps her black past a close secret *** (669 ch A-5 to "a pal of A-5's")   (669 ch A-5 to "a pal of A-5's"; 738)   (870b ch A-5 to "a pal of A-5's")   (870a)

448

(450; 550)   (450; 1204; 502 tr B & A)
B kills her husband, A, in order to prevent A from revealing an evil secret (557a)
(1258)   (1294)

449

(398b)   (411b-*; 445*-**)   (433b; 583b)
B is happily married to A * B, wife of A, impelled by an innocent motive, clandestinely meets an old lover, A-3 ** (411a-*; 410)   (434a)

450

(492b-**)   (494)
B seeks by secret enterprise to be free of A, her husband who is poor, in order that
she may marry wealthy A-3 (451)   (557a)   (1204)

451

(450)   (418-*)   (470)
B, married to A and neither widowed nor divorced, pretends to be single * B,
married, assumes another name and marries A-3 ** (448)   (471 ch A to A-3)   (550)

452

(376)   (383; 403-*)   (521)
B seeks by secret enterprise to emancipate herself from fear of her husband, A
(470)   (475)   (516)

453

(403)   (448)
B believes she has killed her husband, A * B seeks to save herself from the consequences of transgression by taking to flight ** (46S)   (502)

454

(1a, b, d, e, f, g)   (421)   (422a)   (440-*)
B's husband, A, married her under false pretenses * B seeks by secret enterprise
to be revenged upon her husband, A ** (400)   (408)   (451)   (467)   (477)

455

(a)   (428)   (455b)   (490a-*)
B secretly disposes of a dearly prized possession in order to buy her husband, A,
a Christmas (or birthday or wedding anniversary) present (430)   (532b)   (1293c)

(b)   (428)   (522)
B, and her husband, A, have fallen upon evil days * B, in order to "keep the wolf
from the door," finds work in a laundry, but tells A she is working as an "art director" ** (424)   (69)   (579a)

456

(422b-*)   (430-*)   (525)
B bears a close physical resemblance to B-8 * B marries A. B has property in
her own name which, by a marriage settlement, is to descend to A if he outlives B **
B-8 dies, and A contrives to make it appear that it was B who died *** B, as B-8,
is immured in an insane asylum, and A inherits the money belonging to B ****
(732)   (1447a tr A & A-8)   (1461a)

(13) Seeking by Craftiness to Escape Misfortune

457

(463)   (485) A and B, married, finding they cannot live together happily, agree
to the secret and honorable expedient of living apart, undivorced. [1] They
have a child, CH, and, on CH's account, refuse to seek a divorce. [2] Religious
convictions will not allow them to seek a divorce. [3] Inability to reach a satisfactory settlement of their joint estate prevents a divorce. [4] Determination
on the part of husband or wife to prevent the other's re-marriage acts as a bar to
divorce. [5] Fear of scandal and gossip prevents the estranged pair from seeking
their legal freedom (475)   (484a)   (499a)   (501)

458

(a) (260b; 367b) (326-1; 363a)
A and B, just married, start by train on their honeymoon * B, the bride, seeks to
escape annoying experiences when A, the groom, leaving the train to send a telegram, is left behind ** (445a-*; 396-*) (583c) (589)

(b) (423b-2) (687 add B) (601 add B)
A and B, married, find themselves cast away among a strange, half-barbarian
people * A, finding the beauty of his wife, B, a source of danger to himself, seeks
to avoid the danger by a stratagem ** (436)   (688-*; 307 or 197 ch B to B-3
or 973)

459

(376) (434a-*) (495) (503a) (559)
A, husband of B, is cruel and tyrannical * A seeks craftily to kill A-3, an unmarried
man with whom B is in love ** (439) (503b; 403)

460

(463) (553)
A is estranged from his wife, B, whom he dearly loves * A flees to a distant part
of the country and tries to bear his hard lot with fortitude ** (396) (501) (539b)
(1395)

461

(239) (341) (585b)
A is deeply in love with his wife, B * A faces failure in business (491b) (606)
(631) (747)—a failure which, he knows, will bring disaster to his married happiness ** (484b; 770b, c) (505)

462

(461) (491b)
A is unhappy with his wife, B * A seeks with firmness to achieve cherished ambitions ** (905) (907) (913) (928a) (492b)

463

(408) (420) (491)
A revolts against the injustice he is compelled to suffer at the hands of his beloved
wife, B (419) (427) (429a) (460)

464

(437) (509) (525)
A, married to B, is impelled by an unusual motive to lead a double life (486b)
(548a, b) (1200)

465

(422a; 486a) (1295)
A seeks to escape difficulties, restore property and be free of an unloved wife, B,
all by secret enterprise (572)   (952)   (1172 ch B to A & B-5 to A-5; 1204 ch B to
A & B-8 to A-8)

466

(a) (482) (493)
B is married to A and they have one child, CH * B loves CH but she does not
love A ** B loves A-3, and elopes with him, leaving her child, CH, with her husband,
A *** (507b; 499a) (500a)

(b) (503b ch A-3 to A-7) (495 ch A-3 to A-7)
B, young wife of elderly A, has an intrigue with a servant of A's, A-7 * A is ill and
about to die; B, his wife, could save him, but she will not ** (435b) (524b)

467

(1339) (1341)
B has seen her husband, A, secretly as he thought, exchange a pair of muddy shoes
for the clean shoes of A-8 * A's evident purpose is to shift the responsibility for a
crime to the shoulders of innocent A-8 ** (521) (540) (569-*)

468

(403) (486b) (488b)
B attempts to poison her husband, A * B, attempting to poison her husband, A,
mistakes a bottle of harmless white powder for the poison and gives A some of its
contents ** (453; 502) (539b tr A & B)

469

(428)   (430-*)
B, seeking to aid her husband, A, by secret enterprise, finds poverty a bar (411b)
(449)   (455a, b)   (532a, b)

470

(407)   (412)
B seeks to escape from her tyrannical husband, A, by running away (400)   (418)
(451)   (743b)

(14)   Falling into Misfortune through the Wiles
of a Crafty Schemer

471

(450 tr A & A-3)   (451 tr A & A-3)
A, after his marriage to B, discovers that B, who ..ad professed to be single, was
a married woman and neither divorced nor widowed (473)   (480)   (489)

472

(476a)   (488b)   (503a)   (521)
A, married to B, has not been divorced from a former wife, B-3 * A discovers that
B has married another man, A-3 ** (540)   (568a, b, c, d)

473

(378)   (420)   (548a tr B & B-3)   (572 ch A to A-3)
A becomes the second husband of B, whose first husband, A-3, had mysteriously
disappeared and was supposed to be dead * After A and B are married, B's first
husband, A-3, appears secretly to A ** (533; 594b)   (486a)

474

(376)   (378)   (420)
A's wife, B, dies * Tricky so-called spiritualists pretend to materialize the spirit
of deceased B in order to influence A to give them money by advice of the supposed
B ** (392)   (830)   (880a)

475

(383)   (454)
A finds himself under a weird psychic spell because of a birthmark on the face of
his wife, B * B craftily gives a birthmark a peculiar significance, and holds A under
its power ** (1334a)   (1342a)   (1374)   (1375)

476

(a)   (389a, b)   (405) B, wife of A, is craftily persuaded by A-3, the "other man"
in a "love triangle," to elope with him (397)   (400)

(b)   (398b)   (449)   (483b)
B, wife of A, finds herself in the power of an old lover, A-3 * A-3 threatens to reveal
to B's husband, A, a fateful secret (441)   (447)   (455b)   (492b) unless B will
agree to a certain proposition A makes to her ** (446b ch A-2 to A-3)   (483b)
(507a)

477

(398b ch A-3 to A-2)   (446b)   (580)   (589)
B, wife of A, persuades A-2, a friend of A's, to elope with her (418 ch A-3 to A-2)
(423a)

478

(540)   (589)
B falsely accuses her husband, A, of transgression (506a, b)   (507a)

479

(382) (386) (426)

B suffers betrayal at the hands of A, her husband by a secret marriage * B is accidentally killed by a series of manoeuvers set in motion by her husband, A ** (545)
(557b)

480

(426-*) (575)

B, wife of A, desperately ill, sends A for a doctor * A, sent for a doctor by B, who
is seriously ill, does not return (634) (655) (711c) (438)—and he does not
send the doctor **

481

(64; 415) (386)

B is abandoned by A, her husband by a secret marriage * B is unable to prove her
secret marriage to A; the marriage records disappear and the priest who performed
the ceremony dies ** (188b ch A to A-8) (738)

482

(528) (566a)

B, wife of A, sees happiness and beauty in everything and evil in nothing until
A accuses her of causing his downfall (539a) (542) * B's bright outlook on life
changes to one of darkness and despair when she is falsely accused of evil by her
husband, A ** (546a) (581) (587) (588)

483

(a) (410 ch A-5 to A-3) (433b) (436)

B, wife of A, falls into misfortune * A-3, a man of evil character, seeks by violence
and while intoxicated, to dishonor B, wife of A ** (476b) (483b; 519a, b) (433a
ch B to B-8)

(b) (398b) (433b) (583b)

B, wife of A, is by subtlity made a prisoner by A-3, a rejected lover, in his apartment (411b) (519b)

(22) Following a Wrong Course through Mistaken Judgment

484

(a) (429b) (436) (563c)

A and B, man and wife, struggle to realize a cherished ideal * A and B discover
that their cherished ideal is a mistaken one ** (420) (457)

(b) (375) (491b) (524a)

A tries in vain to pay the debts incurred by his extravagant wife, B, whom he
idolizes * A, facing ruin, seeks to save himself by committing a transgression **
(753) (754) (770b)

485

(395) (464)

A, husband of B, is wealthy, cultured and of high social standing * A indulges a
taste for low companionship and questionable adventures ** (429a) (499a) (500a)
(501)

486

(a) (378) (382) (383)

A, married to B, falls in love with B-3 (386) (368e) (555b)

(b) (395) (420) (464) (525)

A has two wives, B and B-3, two homes several miles apart, two names by which
he is known in two different communities, two circles of acquaintances, and practices two professions (548b) (1148a) (1248)

487

(373) (412)

A is estranged from his wife, B * A. estranged from his wife, B, seeks a reconciliation, and then quarrels with B as to which of them caused the estrangement—and
the estrangement continues ** (391) (400) (429a)

488

(a) (93a) (431)
A marries B because he thinks she is poor * A discovers, after his marriage with
B, that she is wealthy in her own right ** (429b) (563c) (929)

(b) (367a) (368b)
A marries B, a woman he does not love * A has committed a transgression (1290a)
(1301) (1304); B knows of the transgression, and A marries her in order to safeguard his evil secret ** (528) (1291a)

489

(486a) (472)
A begins divorce proceedings against his wife, B * A seeks to divorce B, thinking
to find happiness in a new love ** (496a) (556) (886; 563a)

490

(a) (484a-*) (966-*)
A and B, man and wife, keep themselves in poverty by spending all their money
for rich furnishings to put in a mansion they are going to build when they become
wealthy * A and B keep themselves poor by buying rich furnishings for the mansion
they are some day going to build; but the furnishings, inadequately housed, fall
into ruin before A and B are able to build their air castle ** (484a*-**) (576a)
(770a)

(b) (484b) (461)
A, and B, man and wife, are to inherit money from a rich relative, A-2, when a
child shall bless their union * A and B, childless, write a rich relative, A-2, that a
son has been born to them ** A-2 writes A and B that he is coming to see their
child; and A and B find it necessary to resort to further simulation *** (1057b)
(1430b)

491

(a) (372) (461)
B is the wife of A, and loves him devotedly * B insists on dominating A in business
affairs ** (419) (420) (463)

(b) (510) (585b)
B, wife of A, insists on living beyond her husband's means * B, through foolish
extravagance, brings A close to ruin ** (461) (505)

492

(a) (370) (372) B's husband, A, loves her devotedly * A is of a parsimonious
nature and gives B little money ** (492b) (593)

(b) (370) (372) B's husband, A, is a poor man * B loves jewels and fine clothes
which her husband, A, is unable to give her ** B is persuaded to accept a valuable
piece of jewelry from an old admirer, A-3 *** B tells A, her husband, that a valuable
piece of jewelry, given her by A-3, is set with imitation stones and that she bought
it for herself **** (476b) (483b)

493

(485) (486b)
B's husband, A, is affectionate and kindly and puts on his "Sunday manners" in
company; but when he and B are alone, he is cross-grained, petty and tryannical
(477) (495)

494

(508) (547)
B, wife of A, is shallow, foolish and faithless * B, married to A, flirts with an unmarried man, A-3 ** (503b) (568c)

495

(492a, b) (494)
B, wife of A, falls in love with young and reckless A-3 (503b) (505-*) (507a, b)

(15)   Finding a Sustaining Power in Misfortune

496

(a)   (489)   (509)   (539a)   (553)
A falls ill * A's wife, B, from whom he is seeking a divorce, nurses him back to
health ** (396)   (379)   (500a)

(b)   (420)   (478)   (486a)
A's wife, B, deserts him and obtains a divorce * A falls ill.   B-3, who loved A before he married B, nurses A back to health ** (22b; 22a ch B to B-3)   (515 ch B
to B-3)

(c)   (473)   (594b)   (395)   (435a)
A. hen-pecked husband of B, discovers that B has an undivorced husband, A-3,
living * A secretly abandons B and leaves her to A-3. B's undivorced former husband ** (548a ch A to A-3)   (573b tr A & A-3)

497

(546a)   (575)
A has recently lost his wife, B * A finds his memories of his deceased wife, B, an
inspiration and a sustaining power ** (498)   (1433b; 504a)   (578a, b)

498

(576a)   (567-*)   (579a; 578a)
A seeks to find his deceased wife, B * A believes that his deceased wife, B, has returned to earth to comfort him ** (392)   (474)   (526)   (560)

499

(a)   (463)   (460)   (563a)
A and B, husband and wife, are estranged from each other * A and B, estranged,
undergo a character transformation through love for their child, CH, and become
reconciled ** (494; 505-*)   (507b)

(b)   (406)   (510)   (547)
A dearly loves his wife, B, but B does not love him * A wins the love of his wife,
B, by patience, forbearance, kindliness and devotion ** (588)   (591)

500

(a)   (549)   (553)   (561)
A is seeking a divorce from B * A becomes reconciled with B when she nurses him
through a serious illness ** (396)   (575)   (956 ch A-8 to A; 578a)

(b)   (606)   (656)
A, failing in business and almost a bankrupt, nevertheless marries B, a shrewd
and thrifty woman * B so reorganizes and manages A's affairs that he becomes
prosperous ** (419)   (491a)

501

(369)   (373)   (457)
A and B are estranged and living apart, their married happiness in a sad tangle *
A receives a letter from B (1395) calling him home ** A learns that a child, CH,
has been born during his absence.   Result, reconciliation with B, and happiness ***
(532a)   (565)

502

(572; 402-*)   (430)
B supposes that her husband, A, is dead * B reads in a newspaper that her husband,
A, whom she had supposed dead, is alive ** (548a)   (550)

503

(a)   (582)   (590)
B's husband, A, is brutal and tyrannical * B. married to brutal and tyrannical A,
loves and is beloved by, A-3 ** (503b)   (544)

(b)   (503a)   (554)
B discovers that her husband, A, is seeking the life of her lover, A-3 * B seeks
desperately to save her lover, A-3, from the vengeance of her husband, A ** (507b)
(557a)   (568c, d)

504

(a) (405) (485) (492a) (490b tr A & B) (579a; 565) (1133)
B seeks to win her husband, A, to a certain enterprise * B, with the help of the
elements during a devastating storm, succeeds in winning her husband, A, to an
enterprise long cherished by B ** (534) (546a) (884b)

(b) (493 ch B to B-3) (528) (578b tr B & B-3)
B is the second wife of A * A's sorrow for his deceased wife, B-3, causes B, his
second wife, much unhappiness ** B, second wife of A, discovers that B-3, A's
first wife, was unfaithful *** (389) (391 ch B-3 to B-8)

505

(544) (563b) (585b) (580) (484b) (908)
B, wife of A, suffers a critical illness at childbirth and her character is completely
transformed * B lives for her children, gives all to them, and loses her moody despondency ** B loyally helps her husband, A, recoup his financial losses *** (474)
(455b)

506

(a) (540) (541) (571) (582) (561 tr A & B, ch A-3 to B-3)
B thinks her husband, A, has committed a moral transgression (563a) * B discovers
through a friend, B-2, that the moral transgression of which she has accused her
husband, A, was never committed ** (496a, b) (506b) (536) (546a)

(b) (485) (506a) (770a)
B, through false suspicion, is estranged from her husband, A * B becomes reconciled
with her husband, A, when a suspicion is proved to be false ** (1451a ch A to B)
(1462)   .

507

(a) (398a, b) (411b) (433b) (444)
B is eloping with A-3, the man who destroyed her faith in her husband, A * B,
wife of A, eloping with A-3, meets A-2, A's friend, and is rescued by A-2 from an
act of folly ** (536) (568d)

(b) (466a) (543)
B, married to A, elopes with A-3 * B's love for her child, CH, left with her husband,
A, when she deserted him, draws her back to CH and A ** (568c, d)

(39)   Forsaking Cherished Ambitions in order
to Carry out an Obligation

508

(512) (513) (521) (528) (539a) (579b)
A finds his marriage to B a bar to his contentment (510) (529b)

509

(382) (420) (500b)
A finds his marriage to B a hindrance in his love affair with B-3 (377a) (385a)
(386) (393) (426) (556)

510

(372) (375) (378)
A is unhappy in his married life with B * A, unhappily married to B, proves true
to his obligation to run a charted course as a family man, even though he must
sacrifice cherished ambitions ** (385a) (393) (435a) (511)

511

(513) (484b-*)
A, married to B, finds the necessity of supporting his wife and family a bar to
cherished ambitions (484b *-**) (991)

512

(513) (991) (1073)
A is prevented by family and business obligations from embarking upon a cherished
enterprise (900) (917) (952)

513

(511) (768
A, married to B, is compelled to lead a prosy, middle-class life, drab and monotonous * A, married to prosy B, treasures in his heart of hearts dreams of knightly
exploits and chivalrous adventures, himself the star of each performance ** (771a)
(773 ch B to B-8) (774) (1077) (1330) (1335)

514

(581) (565)
B, married to A, her second husband, finds her domestic happiness imperiled by
the obligation to care for CH, a child by her first husband (516) (503b ch "lover
A-3" to "child CH") (507b) (594b)

515

(585b) (1106) (1119)
B, wife of A, forsakes cherished ambitions in order to carry out the desire of A that
she bear him a son * B dies in childbirth ** (425) (576a) (578b)

516

(514) (521) (1341; 467 ch A-8 to CH) (896 ch SN to CH) B deliberately
sacrifises her life at the hands of her husband, A, in order to save their son, CH,
who is falsely accused of transgression by A, the real transgressor.

(40) Embarking upon an Enterprise in which one Obligation is Opposed by Another Obligation

517

(525) (925-*) (957a)
A, husband of B, is discovered by honest and high-minded B to be planning a transgression that will work untold hardship to the public * A, rich and powerful, is
determined to use all his wealth and influence in carrying out an iniquitous project.
His wife, B, seeks in vain to persuade him against it ** (403) (553) (557a -*)

518

(384) (543) (574b)
A and B are married, and A's mother, M-A, lives with them * A and B quarrel
regarding M-A, and A is forced to choose between M-A and B ** (551) (568c)
(578b)

519

(a) (483a, b) (519b-*)
A learns that his wife, B, is in terrible danger * A, if he leaves his post of duty to
save his wife, B, who is in terrible danger, will sacrifice lives and property he is in
duty bound to safeguard ** (519b *-**) (576b)

(b) (519a (591)
A, over the phone, receives an agonized call from his wife, B, for help. B is in
terrible danger * A rescues B **

520

(371) (449 tr A & A-3) (537)
A, innocent, is arrested on a murder charge * A could prove an alibi and win freedom of a murder charge, but only by involving B-3, another man's wife ** A's
obligation to save himself, is opposed by an obligation to protect B-3, another
man's wife *** (535-* ch B to B-3, A to A-8 & A-3 to A) (1204 ch B to B-3) (1151
ch B to B-3)

(41) Finding an Obligation at Variance with Ambition, Inclination or Necessity

521

(382) (441 tr A & B) (464) (467)
A, B's husband, pretends to be innocent of a transgression, but B knows he is guilty
(454) (594c)

522

(574a)   (601)   (620)   (631)
A is unable to find a job and support his wife, B * A and his wife, B, find themselves
face to face with starvation ** (523)   (532a)   (532b)   (579a)   (583b)   (628)

523

(585b)   (680a)   (681a)
A, because of extreme poverty, finds it impossible to remember his wife, B, with
a Christmas present (or a gift on her birthday, or on their wedding anniversary)
(398a)   (400)   (411b)   (455a)   (628)

524

(a)   (500b)   (1079)   (1132)
A, husband of B, has a dangerously reckless passion for gambling in stocks * A,
husband of B, is a lawyer with trust funds in his possession; and B fears that he
will be tempted to use the trust funds for gambling purposes ** (380)   (443)
(474)   (566b)

(b)   (408)   (466b)
A, elderly husband of youthful B, will die if a limb is not amputated * A refuses
to have a limb amputated, preferring "to die in one piece."   B, his wife, upholds
him in his determination ** (403)   (474 tr A & B)

525

(420)   (421)   (461)   (509)
A, married to B, attempts to carry out an infamous project in spite of family obligations (426)   (438)   (465)   (486b)   (548b)   (555a)   (556)

526

(474-*)   (497)   A struggles to carry out an obligation to his deceased wife, B,
which he considers sacred (474*-**)   (198)   (578b-*)   (588)

527

(317a)   (579b)
A seeks to be loyal to his wife, B * B, wife of A, is of alien blood and inferior race **
(585a)   (588)   (593)

528

(365a)   (382)
A is the husband of worthy B, whom he does not love * A, married to B, whom he
does not love, is haunted by memories of a former sweetheart, B-3, whom he still
loves ** (393)   (420)   (555b)   (246b)   (368e)

529

(a)   (530)   (531)   (540)   (541)
A, deeply in love with his wife, B, is made defendant in divorce proceedings started
by B (568a)   (573a)   (594c)   (496b)

(b)   (378)   (395)   (408)
A dominates his wife, B, a nagger and a scold, by petty tyrannies that are more
masterful than any B has at her command * B, when properly subdued by her
husband, A's, pretended tyrannies, finds A gentle, kindly and considerate ** A,
by being cruel in order to be kind, insures the married happiness of himself and B
*** (545) (546a)

530

(1132 ch A to B)   (1334a ch A to B)
B, wife of A, refuses to live with A in a house beside which there is a mysterious
grave (918b ch A to B)   (1358 ch A to B)   (1366 ch A to B)   (1375 ch A to B)
(529a)

531

(574b)   (1009b ch B to M-A & SN to A)
B, wife of A, is compelled to live with A's mother, M-A * B finds the conditions of
her married life with A unpleasant ** (529a)   (543)   (557b)

532

(a) (469) (583a)
B must have money in order to save her husband, A * A, husband of B, is desperately ill, and will die unless he can have a change of climate ** (410) (583b) (1293a, b, c)

(b) (469) (522)
B's long, beautiful tresses are greatly admired by her husband, A * B, in order finance a certain enterprise involving her husband, A, sells her long hair ** (455a) (739)

533

(378) (395)
B, A's tyrannical wife, goes out for the evening and orders A not to leave the house while she is away (420) (426) (435a) (471) (473)

534

(376) (378 tr B & A) (413)
B is forbidden by her husband, A, to engage in a certain enterprise * B engages in a certain enterprise which her husband, A, condemns and forbids her taking part in (442) (449*-**) (452) ** B, engaging in an enterprise forbidden by her husband, A, discovers that A has a part in it (599); and, because of this discovery, B comes to an agreement with A which enables them to go forward happily in life with a better understanding of each other's rights and privileges ***

535

(667) (449; 537 ch A to A-3, B to B-3 & B-3 to B; 1070 ch A to A-3)
B, wife of A, saves A-3, a supposed transgressor, from the law by a public confession of her delinquency * A, because of his great love for his wife, B, forgives her delinquency and glories in her moral courage in making a confession of it ** (695a ch A to A-3) (557b ch A-2 to A-3)

536

(370) (372) (398a, b) (433b)
B, married to A, is about to elope with A-3 * B, wife of A, is eloping with A-3 when they meet a stranger, A-2; and A-2, in the presence of both B and A-3, tells about a man, AX, who broke up a home by eloping with a friend's wife and then abandoning her. A-2 has recognized A-3 and, in order to save B, tells this story about him, hiding A-3's identity under a fictitious name. But it is enough. A-3 sneaks away, and B never sees him again ** (391 tr A & B & ch B-3 to A-3) (396)

(29) Aiding Another to Hide from the World a Fateful Secret

537

(378) (385a) (395)
A's wife, B, is murdered at a certain hour of the night * A is suspected of having murdered his wife, B; but, at the hour the murder was committed, A was with B-3 (411a ch B to B-3) (411b-* ch B to B-3, A to A-8 & A-3 to A) a woman of spotless reputation and happily married ** (520) (667 ch B to B-3) (535 ch B to B-3, A to A-8 & A-3 to A) (1070 ch B to B-3)

(23) Becoming Involved in a Complication that has to do with Mistaken Judgment and Suspicion

538

(438) (561)
A, husband of B, enroute to his home in the country, is caught in a storm and is out all night * A, absent from home all night, finds on reaching home in the morning, that his wife, B, is missing ** A mistakenly supposes that his wife, B, has eloped with A-3 *** (401) (545) (546a)

539

(a) (399) (954) (966-*)
A, husband of B, is the victim of egotistical self-deception and thinks himself a great man * A believes that he is prevented from becoming famous by the jealousy of his wife, B ** (386) (391)

(b) (429a) (430) (460) (540)
A reads in a newspaper that his wife, B, has divorced him * B divorces A on the grounds of desertion ** (388-* tr A & B) (496b)

540

(719) (770a) (743b ch B to A)
A, husband of B, vanishes mysteriously * A, husband of B, and B-3, both vanish mysteriously at the same time ** Gossip has it that A, husband of B, has eloped with B-3 *** (506a, b) (571) (573b)

541

(1383) (1389b) (1397) (1400) (1401) A, whenever he attempts to have X, a certain object of mystery, explained to him, meets with misfortune * A, showing X, a mysterious object of mystery, to his wife, B, is astounded when B, without explanation, begins divorce proceedings (1357) (1425)

542

(405) (420)
A labors under the mistaken belief that the altruism of his wife, B, is prompted by selfish motives (377a) (386) (391) (555a, b)

543

(531) (574b) (994 ch B to M-A & SN to A)
B, wife of A, is jealous of the attentions A gives his mother, M-A * B has a mistaken idea that her husband's mother, M-A, is trying to interfere between her and A (507a ch A-2 to A's mother, M-A) (518)

544

(462) (547)
B labors under the mistaken belief that her husband, A, receives all the praise for her own kindly acts (457) (646; 594d) (644; 594d) (572; 573b) (540; 506a, b)

(11) Confronting a Situation in which Courage and Devotion Alone can save the Fortunes of One Beloved

545

(528) (539a; 553)
B's husband, A, fails to return home. A blizzard is raging, and B fears that A has suffered misfortune in the storm * B meets her death while searching vainly in a storm for her husband, A ** (576a) (577) (578a)

546

(a) (706a, b, c)
B, wife of A, during A's absence, sees destruction threatening A's life work * B, at the cost of her own life, heroically saves from destruction the life work of her husband, A ** (497) (576a)

(b) (828) (885a)
B, homely, marries a blind man, A, who thinks her surpassingly beautiful * B hires a noted eye-specialist to perform an operation on the eyes of her blind husband, A, whereby A's sight is restored ** (489) (581) (933)

(12) Falling into Misfortune through Disloyalty in Love

547

(369) (406) (529a)
A dearly loves his wife, B; and her ﹍ove, which he does not possess, is necessary to his happiness (499b) (563a) (573b)

548

(a) (681b) (734; 402-*)
A, married to B, suffers a memory lapse and marries B-3 * A, husband of B, suffers an attack of amnesia and marries B-3; his memory returns, and he forgets B-3 and goes back to B ** (548b) (550)

(b) (548a) (486b)
A is a bigamist; and his two wives, B and B-3, meet by chance and compare notes (472) (705)

549

(492a) (494 ch A-3 to A-2)
A is married to B, and his ideal is faithfulness * A's wife, B, elopes with his friend, A-2, a man more successful in business than A ** (496a, b) (507b ch A-3 to A-2)

550

(540) (548a) (681b) (770a)
A, married to B, after a long, mysterious absence returns to find B married to A-3 (568b, c, d) (571) (573b)

551

(515) (397 ch A-3 to A-2) (549) (588) (764) (79 ch A to A-2 & A-3 to A)
A discovers that his wife, B, is the mother of A-2's son, CH (585a) (392) (474)

552

(a) (510) (547) (561)
A, husband of B, discovers that B is unfaithful (551) (568a, b, c, d)

(b) (510) (554)
A finds a bundle of love letters in a locked drawer of his wife, B's, desk—letters written after B's marriage to him, but not by him * A, discovering that his wife, B, is unfaithful, strangles her while she sleeps ** (385b) (568a)

553

(410) (411a) (547)
A believes that his wife, B, is in love with A-3 (396) (418) (496a)

554

(405) (412)
A secretly discovers that his wife, B, has an affair with A-3 (380) (400) (434b) (438) (503b)

555

(a) (464) (481) (486a)
A abandons his loving, devoted wife, B, to elope with B-3, a younger and prettier woman * A, abandoning his wife, B, to elope with B-3, pays a penalty of remorse and unhappiness ** (377b; 408 ch B to B-3) (556) (552a ch B to B-3)

(b) (486) (1073)
A, unhappily married to B, falls in love with B-3, a girl much younger than himself * A, married to B and in love with B-3, takes a long journey in an attempt to forget B-3 ** (528) (1379)

556

(485) (486a) (494 ch A to A-8 & A-3 to A)
A, married to B, pretends to be single in making ﹍ove to B-3 * A, husband of B, is killed in an accident while on the way to elope with B-3 **

557

(a) (398a) (413) (433b) B's husband, A, has a weak heart, and is lured into over-exertion by A-3, B permitting * A dies as the result of a conspiracy between B and A-3, and B suffers remorse ** (665) (669) (738) (743b) (946) (956)

(b) (470; 477) (441; 477) (503a ch A-3 to A-2) B, wife of A, elopes with A's friend, A-2 * B, wife of A, and A-2 with whom B is eloping, meet death in an automobile accident **

(26) Seeking Secretly to Preserve Another from Danger

558

(368b; 403-*) (376)
B, wife of brutal and tyrannical A, has a loyal friend in A-3. A-3 seeks to help B escape from A * A, the brutal and tyrannical husband of B, is a huge man and as powerful and determined as he is brutal; and A-3, who would save B from A, is a coward ** (1061 ch A to A-3; 1075a, b ch A to A-3) (857 ch A to A-3; 557a) (568d) (403 *-**)

559

(376) (403-*)
B's husband, A, is a tyrannical, churlish person whose dislike for his attractive wife inspires in his small mind a desire to persecute her * B, wife of brutal and tyrannical A, is loved by A-3. B, although she loves A-3, is too high-minded to consider an elopement, or to be a party to any sort of intrigue ** (403 *-**) (438) (568d)

(57) Seeking to Unravel a Puzzling Complication

560

(371) (474) (498) (576a) (577) (578a)
A finds that a delusion regarding the apparition of his deceased wife, B, is entangled with truth * A hears the voice of his deceased wife, B, and there seems absolutely no doubt that it is her voice ** (392) (587)

561

(428) (433b) (562)
A, husband of B, receives anonymous communications regarding B and A-3 (434a) (445a) (538) (553)

562

(381) (434a-*) (445a-*)
A, husband of B, receives each morning a mysterious communication regarding B (1383) (1397) * A finds an anonymous communication regarding his wife, B, on a sheet of paper in his typewriter (1381) (1389a) ** A receives through the mails, "poison pen" letters (564b-*) regarding his wife, B *** (377a) (396) (397) (398b)

(37) Seeking Against Difficulties to Realize
a Cherished Ideal

563

(a) (460) (547)
A, estranged from his wife, B, whom he dearly loves, seeks a reconciliation (487) (499a, b) (500a) (501)

(b) (378) (395)
A marries B, a beautiful woman notorious for her vicious temper and scorpion tongue * A is deeply in love with his wife, B, a virago, and plans to transform her nature by a method of his own ** (443; 394) (529b)

(c) (423b) (429b) (954 add B) (974 add A)
A and B, man and wife, deplore the insincerity and the mercenary spirit of modern city life * A and B, man and wife, leave the city and search in the country for their ideal of what life should be ** A and B, man and wife, discover that they are searching for an ideal that does not exist *** (900 add B) (963 add B)

564

(a) (557a) (569-*) (572)
B, young and attractive, has recently lost her husband, A * B, a young and attractive widow, resolves to remain faithful to the memory of her deceased husband, A, and never marry again ** (14b ch A to A-8; 405 ch A to A-8)   (564a tr A & B; 14c) (20a ch A to A-8)   (31 ch A to A-8)

(b) (373) (376) (450) (452)
B, wishing to be free of her husband, A, writes anonymous "poison pen" letters regarding herself, and sends them to A * B writes anonymous "poison pen" letters regarding her husband, A, and sends them to herself ** (385a)   (418)

565

(975a) (957a) (976) (1133; 1120)
B cherishes a dear desire that her husband, A, shall become religiously inclined (504a)   (1427b)   (1445 ch B to A)

566

(a) (472-*) (473)
B seeks to aid her husband, A, who is morose and discontented (410)   (445a) (469)   (481)   (482)

(b) (524a) (579a)
B, fearing her husband, A, will commit a transgression, pretends herself to commit a transgression * B pretends to be a shoplifter, but has honestly purchased the goods which her horrified husband, A, finds in her possession ** (504a)   (1050)

(46) Seeking Retaliation for a Grievous Wrong that is Either Real or Fancied

567

(483a, b) (492b) (583b)
A's wife, B, is dishonored (and slain?) by A-3 * A's wife, B, is dishonored and slain, during the war, by an enemy officer, A-3 ** A seeks to find A-3 and be revenged on him for a grievous wrong committed against A's wife, B *** (1318)   (1319)   (1322) (1323)

568

(a) (397) (398a) (444) (451) (494) (551) (554)
A, married to B, discovers the unfaithfulness of B * A, discovering that his wife, B, is unfaithful, kills her and himself **

(b) (466) (503a; 554)
A seeks craftily to be revenged upon his wife, B, for falling in love with A-3, the man who has befriended her (438; 550)   (503b)

(c) (446b ch A-2 to A-3) (476a) (483b) (495)
A, husband of B, discovers the unfaithfulness of B * A kills A-3, the lover of his wife, B ** (594e ch A-5 to A & last A to A-3)   (610)

(d) (503a, b) (550) (554) (558)
A, husband of B, attempts to kill B s lover, A-3 * A-3, murderously assaulted by A, husband of B, slays him in self-defense ** (705 ch A to A-3)   (712 ch A to A-3) (738)   (895 ch A to A-3)

569

(730 ch A-3 to A-5) (483a ch A-3 to A-5; b, ch A-3 to A-5)
B's husband, A, is killed by A-5 * B's husband, A, is killed by A-5; and A-5, through the law's delay and technicalities, escapes with only a light sentence ** B invokes the Mosaic law in seeking revenge upon A-5 for the murder of her husband, A *** (594e)   (1244b ch A to A-5)   (1325 ch A to A-5)

570

(992 ch F-B to A; 641 ch F-B to A; 378 ch B to SM-B)   (948 ch F-B to A & M-B to SM-B)
B is the daughter of A and step-daughter of A's wife, SM-B * B seeks revenge upon her step-mother, SM-B, because she thinks SM-B has stolen the affections of her father, A, away from her ** (909 ch BR-B to SM-B)   (933)

(20)   Becoming Involved with Conditions in which Misfortune is Indicated

571

(548a)   (660a)   (719a)   (750)   (770)
A, mysteriously missing, returns to his home and his wife, B, in a dazed condition, unable to give any explanations (540)   (550)   (572; 402)

572

(664)   (681b)   (1389a)
A, husband of B, mysteriously disappears * B's husband, A, mysteriously disappears, and B mourns for him as dead ** (402)   (502)

573

(a)   (70)   (290)
A and B, for certain reasons, keep their marriage a close secret * B's father, F-B, insists that B, already united to A by a secret marriage, shall marry A's rival in love, A-3 ** (445b)   (477)   (481)   (483b)

(b)   (572)   (734; 1368; 548)
A, missing and supposed to be dead, returns secretly and finds his wife, B, married to A-3 * A, discovering that his wife, B, dearly loves A-3, whom she has married thinking A to be dead, secretly goes away and takes himself out of her life ** (913) (918b)

574

(a)   (601)   (606)
A, a toiler, seeks to support his wife, B, and family by honest enterprise; but he is out of work, his wife is ill and his family in need (549)   (579a)

(b)   (522)   (574a)
A, husband of B, is in dire financial straits * A, and his wife, B, are compelled to live with A's mother, M-A, and avail themselves of her slender resources ** (518) (531)   (543)

575

(421)   (429b)   (464)
A becomes aware of the impending death of his wife, B (576a, b)   (578a, b)

576

(a)   (567)   (591)
A suffers overwhelming sorrow because of the death of his wife, B * A's sorrow over the death of his wife, B, culminates in hallucination ** (53)   (498)   (1334a) (1345)

(b)   (49)   (445b)   (460)
A, mistakenly supposing his beloved wife, B, is dead, kills himself * B, discovering that her husband, A, is dead, commits suicide **

577

(55)   (376)   (377a)   (386)   (492a)
A suffers remorse and overwhelming sorrow—remorse for broken vows, and sorrow because of the death of his dearly beloved wife, B * A, goaded by sorrow for the death of his wife, B, goes into seclusion ** (474)   (497)   (971)

578

(a)   (420)   (464)   (485)
A, because of the death of his wife, B,suffers great sorrow and undergoes a character transformation (918a)   (922a)   (923)

(b)   (382)   (421)   (486a)
A's wife, B, dies.   B, A's wife, on her death bed, has A promise that he will marry B-3, B's best friend * B-3 loved A before he married B ** (526)   (378 ch B to B-3) '405 tr B & B-3)

579

(a)   (574a)   (566a)
B is convinced that all the misfortunes of herself and her husband, A, are due to
A's irreligious nature (504a)   (565)   (884b)   (1353)

(b)   (347a)   (508)   (527)
A's wife, B, is racially, morally and mentally A's inferior * B, wife of A, proves a
hindrance to him socially and in a business way ** (371)   (386)   (398b)   (407)
(491b)

580

(421)   (462)
B is the wife of A, a friend of A-2's * A's friend, A-2, discovers that A's wife, B, is
a "vamp" ** (505)   (508)   (443)   (457)

581

(370)   (482)   (514)
B desires the love and consideration of her husband, A, which she believes she has
lost (410)   (445a)   (515)

582

(427)   (461)   (464)
B, opening a letter addressed to her husband, A, discovers that A has lied to her
(394)   (443)   (499a)

583

(a)   (376)   (413)
B, if discovered doing something she has in mind, will find herself at odds with
her husband, A (442)   (534)

(b)   (532a)   (561)   (585b)
B, wife of A, is desperately in need of money for a certain purpose * A-3, a rejected
lover of B's, promises to help B, wife of A, if she will come to his apartment for
an interview ** (476b)   (483a, b)

(c)   (458a)   (470)
B, wife of A, is desperately in need of money for a certain purpose * B, wife
of A, happens to meet an old lover, A-3, and is forced to borrow a sum of money
from him ** (418)   (476a, b)

584

(a)   (395)   (403-*)
B, just married to A, discovers in a secret place her obituary notice (written by A?)
the date of demise alone left blank (403*-***)   (590)   (1346; 1462)

(b)   (421)   (436)   (1061)
B, wife of A, loses her love for A when she discovers his cowardly nature (409)
(1082a)   (1104)

585

(a)   (553)   (561)
B, wife of A, leaves home suddenly on important business while A is absent * B,
leaving home suddenly during the absence of her husband, A, writes a line to A
explaining her departure, but the wind whisks the note out of an open window and
away. B's absence is accounted a mysterious disappearance ** (396)   (538)
(572 tr A & B)   (755)

(b)   (488b)   (522)   (523)
B, wife of A, is a butterfly of fashion * B, wife of A, must have rich clothes and
luxurious surroundings in order to be happy ** (484b)   (492b)

586

(1377b ch B to B-3)   (1383)   (1384 ch B to A)   (1389b)   (1440 ch A to A-8)
B believes that her husband, A, loves her less than he does a certain small statue,
X, that stands on his desk (1352)   (1408)   (1425)   (1444)

86

587

(537) (539a) (577)
B, the deceased wife of A, appears to a relative of A's and describes her mortal reactions to A's lack of affection for her (922) (984)

588

(376) (420) (515)
B, dying, reveals to her husband, A, a closely guarded secret which he finds greatly perturbing (441) (451) (467) (492b) (503a ch A-3 to A-2) (551)

589

(540) (555b)
B is convinced that her husband, A, has eloped with B-3 (496b) (506a) (539b)

590

(426-*) (584a)
B, fourth wife of A, discovers shortly after her marriage that A's other wives have all died suddenly and mysteriously (387) (403) (422b) (552b)

591

(483a, b) (1137a; 179a)
B, alone, helpless and in terrible danger, sends to her husband, A, a despairing call for aid (519a, b) (851)

592

(398a-*) (405) (486a) (485)
B revolts against certain unpleasant conditions involving her husband, A (398a*-**) (398b*-**) (403)

593

(441) (454) (492a) (503a)
B secretly takes money from her husband, A, for her own use (450) (484b) (491b)

594

(a) (542) (566a) (581)
B, undemonstrative in her affections, surprises ner husband, A, and arouses his suspicion by bringing his breakfast to him in bed (403) (582) (593)

(b) (378) (471) (473) (550 tr A & A-3) (533)
B, a termagant, supposes herself a widow and marries A * A-3. B's undivorced husband, appears secretly to A, B's present husband, and tries craftily to get A. to pay him money for not claiming B as his wife ** (417) (496c)

(c) (485) (493) (555a, b)
B divorces her husband, A, and is awarded the custody of their child, CH * A steals his child, CH, from his divorced wife, B ** (499a) (500a)

(d) (410) (532a; 1293a) (1293b)
B, wife of A, innocently commits a transgression * A, in order to save his wife, B, declares that he is guilty of a transgression committed by B ** (499a,b) (500a) (695a, b)

(e) (568d ch A-3 to A-5) (569)
B, wife of A, takes the law in her own hands and shoots A-5, who has murdered A (738) (743b) (801 ch A to A-8)

(f) (528) (486a)
B, wife of A, dons the mask and custume of B-3, A's paramour, and meets A as B-3 at a masquerade ball (534) (1309b ch A-3 to B-3)

(g) (475 ch A to A-2 & B to B-2) (510 ch A to A-2 & B to B-2)
B uses her weird powers of mental telepathy in reshaping the destiny of an unhappily married couple, A-2 and B-2 * B, having succeeded in reconciling A-2 and B-2, married and estranged from each other, discovers herself to be in love with A-2 ** (57) (279)

(21)   Falling into Misfortune through Mistaken Judgment

595

(935)   (1065-*)
A exercises mistaken judgment in forwarding a certain undertaking * A loses his
initiative, his enterprise and his ambition, and becomes merely a cog in the wheels
of his employer ** (85a)   (114)   (235)   (1065*-**)   (1088)   (1243)

596

(612)   (646 ch B to A & AX to A-5)   (1114)
A secures knowledge of a closely-guarded secret * A, securing knowledge of a closely-
guarded secret, is hounded by a guilty persecutor, A-5, until his life is made miserable ** (705)   (854 ch A-9 to A-5)   (884a)

597

(898)   (925-*)   (1159 ch B to A-8 & A-4 to A)
A's chauffeur, A-7, driving A's car by A's orders at a high rate of speed, apparently
injures a pedestrian, A-8 * A, when his car apparently injures a pedestrian, seeks
to evade legal consequences by having his chauffeur, A-7, drive on at speed **
(669 ch B to A & A-5 to A-7)   (750)   (775)   (783)   (1064)

598

(1074)   (1090)   (1092)
A, an author, impersonates the crook hero of a story he is writing for the purpose
of obtaining situations and "local color" * A, a novelist, impersonates the hero of
a story he is writing and becomes involved in an unpleasant complication ** (2b)
(786;   803a)   (815a)   (817)   (822)

599

(442;   534-**)   (793a)   (838)   (1168)
A, in order to oblige his friend, A-2, acts contrary to his own principles and experiences unpleasant results * A dons A-2's mask and costume and assumes A-2's
role at a carnival, A-2 being called away suddenly on pressing business and promising to return shortly. A is against masquerades on principle and, when A-2 fails
to return, he is in a dilemma ** (534**-***)   (365b)   (603a)   (594f)

600

(647)   (1198)
A, in a foreign seaport and seeking to return at night to his steamer, loses his way
and finds himself in the lawless slums (848a; 664)   (12a)   (31)   (1218)   (1226)
(1230 ch A to A-8)

601

(111)   (704)   (981)
A, seeking to help his friend, A-2, lends him all his money * A's friend, A-2, fails
to repay money borrowed from A and A is left penniless ** (257b ch A-3 to A-2)
(574b)   (621 ch A-5 to A-2)   (656)   (1337)

602

(176c)   (225)   (1338)
A, a pugilist, loses a ring battle and all the money he has wagered on himself (361a)
(500a)   (850b)   (874)   (918a)

603

(a)   (1273; 174 ch A-3 to A-2)   (426)   (446b)   (601)   (607)
A suffers defeat because his friend, A-2, does not efficiently carry out his part in
a certain enterprise (568c, d ch A-3 to A-2)   (280b ch A-3 to A-2)   (601)

(b)   (169)   (779)
A and his friend, A-2, are attacked by robbers in a lonely wood * A's friend, A-2,
receives a wound from which he dies ** (168)   (701)   (754)

(c)   (770b)   (793a, b)
A and his friend, A-2, on horseback, are swimming a flooded river. A-2 is struck
by a piece of floating drift, but A rescues him and gets him to the river bank *
A-2 is so badly injured that he dies ** (794)   (868)

(d)   (906)   (913)   (1174)   (1013 ch A-6 to A-2)
A and his friend, A-2, are wandering afoot in the desert. A-2 is injured and their
water supply fails * A's friend, A-2, dies from injuries and hardships ** (997; 1007)
(1160)   (1168)

604

(299 ch F-B to A-8)   (409 ch A-3 to A-8)

A is in the employ of A-8, a man in whom he has implicit confidence * A, employed
by A-8, comes to work one morning and finds the office in the hands of federal agents,
A-6, A-6 ** A's employer, A-8, has been "using the mails to defraud" *** (750)
(1279b ch A to A-8)

605

(652a)   (1248)

A, stricken with fever in a wilderness country, is attended by an old woman, B *
A, falling ill in a wilderness country, is attended by an old woman, B, to whom
years before, he had taught a fake method of healing ** (1220)   (1228-*)   (1325)

606

(114)   (461)   (574a)   (602)   (958)

A has invested all his money in a certain enterprise * A, investing all his money in
a certain enterprise, sees the enterprise fail and himself plunged heavily into debt **
(500b)   (574b)   (700)

607

(937)   (1115)

A and his friend, A-2, explorers, are alone in the jungle * A's friend, A-2, goes insane
from eating the berries of a strange plant, and makes a murderous attack upon A **
(972)   (1007)

608

(652a)   (731)

A, in a strange part of the country, is arrested by the police as a criminal "suspect" *
A, arrested by the police as a criminal "suspect", has in his possession a satchel,
innocently come by (804)   (1044a,b)   (1046).   The satchel, X, is found to contain burglar's tools ** (91) •(109)   (163)   (635)   (695a)

609

(196)   (201)   (982b)

A, temporarily in charge of two mischievous children, CH-1 and CH-2, finds himself in more dilemmas than he can successfully manage (193)   (728-**)

610

(654)   (750)   (754)

A is a fugitive from justice, hunted by A-6, an officer of the law * A is in a trap in
the town of X.   He can escape only by passing through the towns of Y or Z,
and detectives, A-6 and A-6, are watching for him in both places ** (651)   (707)
(717)   (1176)

611

(a)   (249)   (623)   (695a)

A's youthful escapades, committed thoughtlessly and not with malice, constitute
the wrong which has given him a bad name among the people of his native place
(864)   (1275)

(b)   (949a)   (954)

A induces his father, F-A, to advance him his patrimony * A leaves his native
place, squanders his substance in riotous living, comes to want and experiences
remorse ** (815b)   (818b)

612

(658)   (704)

A receives A-5 on a forged letter of recommendation from a friend, A-2, and introduces A-5 into his own social circle * A, standing sponsor for A-5, discovers
that A-5 is a crooked gambler who uses A's sponsorship for the purpose of mulcting A's friends ** (635)   (725)   (859)

613

(926)   (927)   (928a)

A, given to altruistic enterprises, befriends a tramp, A-5 * A befriends a tramp,
A-5; and A-5, taking advantage of A's hospitality, steals valuable property from
him ** (894)   (998 ch A-4 to A-5)

614

(709)   (763)   (778)   (1166a)

A loses a valuable diamond, X * A loses a valuable diamond, X, in a place where
there is a flock of chickens, and he insists that the chickens must be killed, one by
one, until the diamond is found.   The chickens are all killed ** A loses a valuable
diamond, X, and has his suspicions as to where it can be found, but discovers that
his suspicions are unfounded *** (771a)   (1200)   (1222b)

615

(1g) (78) (857) (1061) (1150) (1219 ch A to A-8)
A, a coward and a braggart, is manoeuvered into a dangerous test, and must either eat his words or acquit himself with credit * A, a coward who has been manoeuvered into a dangerous test of courage, is almost beside himself with fear as he sets forth to meet the test ** (1104) (1227b, c)

616

(679) (743b) (946) (1244b)
A has confided to B the combination of his safe, X * A, confiding to B the combination of his safe, X, brings danger to B ** (144) (666) (801)

617

(2a) (59) (412) (768) (1187)
A shows his ignorance of the usages of high society by unpacking his satchel when a servant, A-7, is expected to do it for him * A, annoyed by a faux pas he has committed, seeks to "save his face" ** (709; 786) (814)

618

(1063) (1071) (1094) (1126)
A is bored by certain duties he is obliged to perform * A, bored by certain duties he is obliged to perform, finds a way out—with unpleasant results ** (1163a, b) (1184) (1164 ch A to A-2)

619

(601) (602) (606) (212a) (461) (1343) A loses all his life's savings * A plans to take his own life, but fate intervenes ** (621) (365) (879) (1373) (1388)

620

(113) (131) (726a)
A loses his job * A suffers misfortune because he departs from the strict line of duty in order to carry out a cherished ambition of his own ** (628 ch B to A-9 "A's employer") (753) (779) (836) (832) (902) (903)

621

(127a) (522) (619) (246b ch A to AX)
A is swindled out of his life's savings by A-5 * A, swindled out of his life's savings by A-5, is about to take his own life when his lost money is returned to him by a mysterious person, AX ** AX, a mysterious "righter of wrongs," at the point of a gun takes from A-5 money out of which A-5 has swindled A and restores the money to A *** (1455b) (1424a)

622

(611 ch A to SN) (928b)
A mistakenly supposes his son, SN, to have perished in a tragic accident (698) (628 ch A to SN & B to A) (297 ch B to SN) (674) (734 ch A to SN) (1053) (1056)

623

(109) (163) (513) (611a) (798) (815a)
A, innocent, is supposed to be a transgressor * A is supposed to be a transgressor because he is found with contraband goods in his possession ** (859) (1168) (1228) (1264 tr A & A-2) (1265a tr A & A-3)

624

(597) (699a) (712) (750) (777) (787) (857) (1449)
A considers himself a transgressor until he discovers that his supposed transgression was never committed (635) (1448) (1451a) (1456)

625

(1202a) (1220a) (1227b, c)
A awakens in B a consuming desire to leave the city and return to her home in the country to live. All of which was farthest from A's plans, since he seeks a business engagement from B which can only be carried out in the city, and with B's help (641) (1155)

626

(959; 966c)   (925-*)
A, in making a scientific experiment, has unintentionally caused his daughter, D, a grievous injury (627 ch B to D)   (227 ch B to L. A to A-8 & FB to A)

627

(416)   (626 ch D to B)
A unintentionally causes the death of B * A, seeking to save B by giving her an antidote for a certain poison, causes her death ** (578a, b)   (633; 634)

628

(111)   (522)   (523)   (615)   (838)   (1086)   (1101)
A, in need of money to finance an enterprise, holds up a stage * A, robbing a stage, discovers that B, who knows and recognizes him, is one of the passengers ** (651) (699a, b)

629

(711a)   (726a)   (1162 ch A-5 to A)   (1163a ch A-4 to A-2)   A has his "double," A-2, take his place in an important enterprise * A finds himself ruined, and his reputation gone, when his double, A-2, bungles an important enterprise while posing as A ** (635 ch A-5 to A-2)   (1337)

630

(1226)   (1214; 1227a-**)
A seeks to defeat a grafter, A-5, at the grafter's own game * A, seeking to defeat the schemes of a grafter, A-5, is betrayed by a confederate, A-2, whom A asks to help him ** Through A-2, A's confederate in an enterprise, A suffers loss *** (1268) (1269 tr A & A-2)

631

(461)   (602)
A is ruined when his appeal to his supposed friend, A-2, for financial aid, is denied (505)   (619)

632

(687)   (692)
A, in desperate danger, appeals for rescue to A-4 * A's appeal to a selfish power, A-4, for rescue, is denied because commercial interests would be imperiled by the delay necessary to save A's life ** A is abandoned and left to die by A-4 *** (898 ch A to A-4)   (899-* ch A to A-4)   (957c tr A & A-4)

633

(1338)   (1342a)   (1344)   (1347)   (1356)   (1357)   (1360)
A mixes truth with delusion in an earnest investigation of a psychic problem * A, mixing truth with delusion in an earnest investigation of a psychic problem, finally loses his reason ** (1391)   (1428)

634

(130)   (480)   (732)   (776)   (1350)
A, imagining he sees a fast motor car almost upon him, leaps in front of a car that is not imaginary and is instantly killed (762)

635

(249)   (608)   (612)   (624)   (629 ch A-2-a to A-5)   (859)
A suffers false suspicion as a transgressor * A, mistakenly supposed to be a transgressor, is finally cleared of suspicion by a confession of the real transgressor, A-5 ** (854)   (884a)

636

(763)   (1166a)   (1196)   (1267a)   (1335)
A is a professional burglar who throws caution to the winds in one of his burglaries * A, a burglar, breaks into a house that is quarantined ** A contracts a contagious disease *** (681b)   (705)

637

(778) (1023) (1024) (1027) (1029) (1268) ˙
A robs a heathen temple of jewels and proceeds about his work with reckless audacity * A, committing a robbery, is caught red-handed and turned over to the law for punishment ** (866) (1209c tr A & A-2)

638

(259-2) (377b) (681a) (732) (753)
A, ruined financially, takes to drink and "dies in his cups"

639

(758-*) (768) (898) (925-*)
A is abducted by A-5 and held for ransom * A, abducted by A-5 and held for ransom, is a meddlesome, disagreeable person and his family and friends are glad to be rid of him and will not pay the ransom ** A, abducted by A-5 and held for ransom, makes A-5's life so miserable that he pays a round sum to have A taken off his hands *** (781) (880) (918a, b)

640

(126) (488a, b) (904) (1278a)
A is tricked by B in a certain enterprise * A, tricked by B in a certain enterprise, dies when the trickery is discovered ** (557a)

641

(285) (992)
B, trying to make a home for her widowed father, F-B, is neglected and cruelly treated by F-B (14a) (223) (368a) (676) (993)

642

(491b) (585b) (766)
B, as a sop to her vanity, borrows a valuable ornament from her wealthy friend, B-2 * B loses a valuable ornament she borrowed from her friend, B-2 ** B, and her husband, A, poor, are compelled to labor hard and deny themselves every confort for years in order to replace a valuable ornament B borrowed from B-2, and lost *** (767) (792a) (870a)

643

(60) (470) (1416)
B, tired, and unable to get a room in a hotel in a large city, wanders about the lobby and neighboring rooms. It is very late; and B, unfamiliar with her surroundings, finds a dark, deserted room with comfortable chairs and large mirrors, and falls asleep in one of the chairs. She does not awaken until morning; then, to her horror, she discovers that she has spent the night as no respectable woman ought to have done (645) (870a)

644

(147) (544)
B innocently befriends a stranger, A-4; and it later develops that A-4 is a political offender whom government officials, headed by A-6, are straining every nerve to capture * If A-6 knew that B had befriended A-4, she would be considered a confederate of A-4's and suffer accordingly ** (179a, c) (594c) (824)

645

(737b-*) (737c; 737b*-**)
B finds herself, innocently and through error, a prisoner at night in a bedroom not her own * B, caught innocently in a compromising situation, discovers a state of affairs that renders her dilemma tragic ** (648) (669 ch A-5 to A) (1135b)

646

(147) (544)
B befriends an Unknown, AX, in a spirit of altruism * B discovers that AX, an Unknown whom she has befriended, is a notorious criminal who is being hunted by the police ** (660b) (669) (743b) (211)

647

(279)   (470)
B, a respectable working girl, seeking employment, follows the advice of a supposed friend, A-5, and finds herself in an immoral dance hall where she is compelled to dance with patrons and serve drinks (14a)   (738)

648

(645)   (647)   (1050)
B is accused of being a transgressor because she is found in an environment, or because she has property in her possession, which indicates transgression * B is accused of transgression, but the accusation is unjust ** (21)   (69)   (186)   (817)   (822)   (828)

649

(628 ch A to BR-B)   (770b, c ch A to BR-B)   (977)
B, sister of BR-B, in order to prevent BR-B from bringing dishonor to their family, unintentionally causes his death (746)   (909)

(13)   Seeking by Craftiness to Escape Misfortune

650

(687)   (689)   (690)   (691)
A, a white man cast away among bloodthirsty savages, has his life spared because he is a ventriloquist and supposed to be a god (714)   (244)   (878a)

651

(1193)   (1282)   (1298)
A, a fugitive from justice seeking to avoid capture, finds himself in a tight corner with sheriffs, A-6, A-6, A-6, apparently approaching from every direction * A, a fugitive driven to bay by officers of the law, takes refuge in a house which is a place of mystery ** (699b)   (74a)   [1] A house built squarely on the dividing line between two states, so that one may pass from California into Navada by crossing the living room. The serving of legal processes from one state or the other is thus avoided or delayed. Similarly [2], a cabin built where four states "corner," a cabin with one room: the stove in Arizona, the cupboard in New Mexico, the bed in Colorado, the trunk in Utah. [3] A room in an ancient house, sealed up for two hundred years, with an inscription over the door threatening death to any one attempting to enter

652

(a)   (651-*)   (153)   (321b)   (385a)   (639-**)
A is caught in an unpleasant complication, and disaster threatens him unless he is crafty enough to devise plans for his own safety (651*-**)   (639**-***)   (650)   (658)

(b)   (180)   (212a; 726b)   (793a)
A, the idol of his people, is about to lose a wrestling match to A-3, his rival * A, wrestling in the open with A-3, a rival wrestler, prevents A-3 from winning a victory by falling from a cliff, apparently by accident, and losing his life **

653

(651-*)   (652b-*)   (655-*)   (661)   (1267a)   (1419b)   (662 ch A-2 to A-5)
A is a captive, held by his captor, A-5, in a physical environment which constitutes a trap, and from which there seems absolutely no means of escape * Nevertheless, A, with desperate determination, seeks to free himself by subtle enterprise ** (651*-**)   (652b*-**)   (655*-**)

654

(40a)   (182b)   (208)   (385a)   (610)   (615)   (655-*)   (732)   (787)   (826)   (853)   (1016a)   (1176)
A, facing misfortune, seeks desperately to evade disaster (655*-**)   (656)   (657)

655

(600)   (758-*)
A, faced by a robber, A-5, with a gun, tries craftily to delay yielding up his valuables * A is shot and seriously wounded by a robber, A-5 ** (619)   (681a)   (724)   (763; 655 ch to "A is shot and killed")

656

(751) (961) (1000) (1079) A's ancestral estates have been heavily mortgaged and he is about to lose the property * A, by hook or crook, seeks to save his mortgaged paternal acres from foreclosure ** (500b) (860) (874) (1029)

657

(23c) (245) (718a)
A is a person of ability but of a race considered inferior * A takes part in a football game and falls innocently under a suspicion of treachery ** A, innocent of transgression, seeks to prove his innocence by subtle enterprise *** (771b) (1222a, b)

658

(612) (1038) (1130) (1177) (1247) (1306) (1233-*) (1275-*)
A, a man of high standing in his community, fears that through unusual conditions his character will be discredited * A seeks to safeguard his reputation, which is threatened by unusual conditions ** (652b) (1233*-**) (1275*-**)

659

(10a, b, c)
B's mother, M-B, is a widow in poor health * M-B's life hangs on a change of climate, but she and her daughter, B, are penniless ** B is desperately determined to do something, anything, to raise money to help her mother, M-B *** (88) (253) (368b) (1293b, c)

(14) Falling into Misfortune through the Wiles of a Crafty Schemer

660

(a) (1248) (1130 ch AX to A-4)
A, a professional man, is captured in his office at night by mysterious strangers. A-4, A-4, A-4, blindfolded and taken to a secret place * A, spirited away by A-4, A-4, A-4, is compelled to perfom a professional service ** (571) (635 ch A-5 to A-4) (653 ch A-5 to A-4)

(b) (646; 147) (252a, b)
A, captured by enemies of B, is threatened with death by A-5 in an attempt to extort from him a secret of B's * A, threatened with death by A-5 in an attempt to force him to reveal a secret of B's, defies A-5 to do his worst ** (875b) (884a)

661

(898) (957a)
A, wealthy and powerful, goes alone to bathe in a mountain stream * A is robbed by AX, who secretly puts on A's clothes, takes his horse and flees ** (715a) (1146 ch A to AX)

662

(1394 ch A to A-2) (1436)
A helps A-2 secure treasure in a secret place * A, helping A-2 secure treasure in a secret place, is abandoned to die in a deep pit by A-2 who makes off alone with the treasure ** (653 ch A-5 to A-2) (701 tr A & A-2) (704)

663

(654) (883-*)
A's deadly enemy, A-3, has A at his mercy, and there seems nothing for A to do but to make the best of his hard lot (628 ch B to A-3) (883*-**)

664

(130) (314-*) (572) (600) (752) (786) (863a)
A finds himself unexpectedly locked and barred in a room in a strange house * A, suddenly finding himself a helpless prisoner, tries to bear his fate with equanimity ** (799) (824) (856)

665

(557a) (946)
B is leading an exemplary life and trying honestly to live down an unfortunate past * B, a reformed transgressor; going about doing good, has her transgression revealed by A-3, who knew her in the old days ** (669 ch A-5 to A-3) (945)

666

(27) (152b) (616) (679) (1244b)
B knows the combination of A's safe; and she knows, also, that there is a small fortune in jewels in the safe * Crooks, led by A-5, threaten B with violence in an attempt to force her to open the safe ** (144) (885a)

(29) Aiding Another to Hide from the World
a Fateful Secret

667

(50) (446a-*) (449 ch A to A-8 & A-3 to A) (520 ch B-3 to B)
B, unless she conceals a personal delinquency, will seriously compromise herself * B, unless she reveals a personal delinquency, will cause an innocent man, A, to suffer for transgression ** (535 ch A to A-8 & A-3 to A) (1461a ch A to B)

668

(285 ch F-B to M-B) (976) (978)
B's mother, M-B, is a drug addict * B makes a heavy personal sacrifice in order to help her mother, M-B, hide from the world a terrible secret ** (33) (368b) (785) (892 ch B-3 to M-B)

669

(410) (447 ch A-5 to A-8) (557 ch A-3 to A-5) (597 ch A to B) (667-*)
B commits a secret transgression * B, committing a secret transgression, has her secret discovered by A-5 ** B's secret transgression is discovered by A-5, who seeks to use his knowledge for purposes of blackmail *** (784) (870b)

670

(641 ch F-B to M-B) (740)
B's mother, M-B, is subject to recurring periods of temporary insanity * B helps her mother, M-B, hide from the world a terrible secret ** (33) (659) (720 ch A to B)

(26) Seeking Secretly to Preserve Another from Danger

671

(663 ch A to A-2) (672; 764-*)
A's friend, A-2, is helpless against the persecutions of a powerful enemy, A-3 * A decides to undertake a secret enterprise for the purpose of protecting helpless A-2 from a powerful enemy, A-3 ** A's friend, A-2, commits suicide before A can help him overcome his misfortunes *** (672; 671-**; 764) (671-**; 807) (841)

672

(671-**) (853) A's friend, A-2, is the owner of a flock of sheep. A-3 is a cattle baron, rich and influential. A-3's men kill nearly all A-2's sheep, and A-3 is scheming to take A-2's land away from him. A-2, deep in debt, scarcely knows which way to turn * A plans a secret enterprise in an effort to help A-2 ** (671) (805 ch A-4 to A-2) (807) (809 ch A-5 to A-2) (839)

673

(743a) (1298)
A finds a motor stage wrecked and the U. S. mail it was carrying scattered from the broken pouches. The stage driver, A-4, has gone for help. A picks up a torn letter, reads it, and discovers that B is in misfortune * A, a fugitive from justice, seeks to rescue B from her misfortunes ** (817) (869) (1209a)

(18) Rebelling against a Power that Controls Personal Abilities and Holds them in Subjection

674

(622)   (755)   (1450)
A loses his son, SN, in whom all his ambitions were centered * A struggles against an overwhelming sorrow that proves an obstacle to enterprise and holds his abilities in subjection ** (1053)   (1056)

675

(200)   (1108)
A is a confirmed procrastinator, and the habit inhibits enterprise and circumscribes his abilities * A is taught a lesson which shows him how reprehensible a pet failing may become ** (215b)   (1134)   (1163a)

676

(285)   (641)
B is intellectual and of an artistic temperament * B rebels against the authority of her father, F-B, who compels her to do all sorts of rough farm work ** (14a; 223)   (741)   (743a)   (871)

677

(145)   (455b)   (679)
B is engaged in forwarding an important undertaking * B fights against insomnia brought on by overwork ** (28a)   (183)   (239)

678

(668 ch M-B to SR-B)   (670 ch M-B to SR-B)
B is compelled to live with a sister, SR-B * B rebels against the tyranny and selfishness of her sister, SR-B, which make B's life miserable ** (14a)   (137b)   (737a)   (743b)

679

(1121)   (1244b)
B is overshadowed and dominated by her mentally inferior employer, A * B rebels against A's method of appropriating as his own the brilliant achievements which B accomplishes at his command ** (616)   (677)

(36) Undergoing an Experience which Results in a Remarkable Character Change

680

(a)   (654)   (734)
A was in the World War * Before the World War, A was a successful business man; after the war, a physical wreck, and a bankrupt ** (199)   (608)   (1188)

(b)   (680a)   (715b)   (257b)
A undertakes an enterprise when he is prosperous; and then, suffering loss and becoming a bankrupt and a cripple, he has not the heart to go on with the enterprise (199)   (345)   (690)

681

(a)   (49)   (211)
A, happy and optimistic, undergoes a critical illness which makes of him a morbid, melancholy, superstitious pessimist (106)   (900)   (918b)   (963)

(b)   (313)   (572)
A undergoes a critical illness * A recovers from a critical illness but loses all remembrance of his personal identity ** (548a)   (879)   (1308)

682

(687)   (689)   (690)   (937)   A, a white man of brilliant intellectual attainments, battles for existence in an isolated, primitive, savage wilderness * A, battling for existence in a savage wilderness, suffers a deterioration of character until, after some years, he sinks to the level of his primitive surroundings ** (244)   (728-**) (728**-***)   (901)

683

(385a; 918a)　(732)　(857)　(897)
A is a telegraph operator at a lonely railroad way station * A is a sheep herder, isolated with his flock of sheep ** A is a lighthouse keeper on a lonely coast *** A gradually, because of loneliness, becomes demented **** (560)　(1344)　(1345)

684

(930)　(921 ch B to F-B)　(1209a ch A to F-B)
B's father, F-B, is an unworthy character, long mysteriously missing * B's father, F-B, long mysteriously missing, returns to his old home as an Unknown and discovers that his daughter, B, thinks him dead, believes his character to have been noble, and holds him in hallowed remembrance ** F-B renounces his intention to disclose his identity to his daughter, B, and shambles away as an Unknown, leaving B happy with her mistaken ideals *** (922a)　(681b)

(19) Meeting with Misfortune, and Being Cast Away in a Primitive, Isolated, and Savage Environment

685

(130)　(176a, c)　(212a)　(438)　(711c)
A, traveling alone, is caught in a snowstorm　A is caught in a snowstorm in the mountains, becomes snowbound, marooned, and finds it impossible to reach a place of safety ** (713)　(762)

686

(109)　(718b)
A, of gentle birth and breeding, is isolated in a primitive, uninhabited wilderness, and compelled to battle with Nature for his very existence (197)　(918b)　(904)

687

(650)　(689)
A finds himself the only white man in a tribe of half-savage natives * A, finding himself the only white man in a tribe of half-savage natives, is compelled to struggle against their primitive superstitions ** (682)　(901)　(915)

688

(49)　(690 add B)
A and B find themselves cast away in a desolate, primitive environment where they must fight for their very existence * A and B, strangers to each other, are together thrown into misfortune ** (226)　(244)　(307)　(458b)

689

(691)　(926)　(937)
A is traveling through a savage wilderness * A, traveling through a savage wilderness, is captured by natives and threatened with death ** (197)　(331)　(650)

690

(109)　(957a)
A takes a sea voyage in the hope of recovering his health * A, taking a sea voyage, is shipwrecked and cast away on a desert island ** (682)　(686)

691

(1379)　(1388)　(1394)
A, an explorer, loses his way in a trackless wilderness (650)　(689)　(1426b)

692

(690-*)　(719b)　A, without food or water, is adrift in a small boat at sea (632)
(690*-**)　(878b)

693

(1082a, b)　(1408)
A, wandering alone among the mountains, is trapped and held powerless * A, caught in a trap, faces death ** (713)　(728**-***)　(728-** ch A to A-2 & CH to A)　(1419a)

694

(470) (676) (740) (916) (1033) (1207)
B is riding alone through a wilderness country * B, riding alone through a wilderness country, is thrown from her horse and sprains her ankle. The horse runs away, and B is left helpless in an uninhabited region ** (31) (179a, c) (885a-*)

(20) Becoming Involved with Conditions in which Misfortune is Indicated

695

(a) (385a) (787) (822) (829)
A's neighbors persist in thinking A guilty of a crime for which he was tried and acquitted * A, tried for a crime and acquitted seeks happiness in freedom from suspicion ** (635) (833) (1064)

(b) (608) (623)
A suffers imprisonment for a crime he did not commit * A, finishing a term of imprisonment for a crime he did not commit, finds that his character as an ex-convict seriously hampers him in his honest enterprises ** (299) (1183)

696

(715c) (695b)
A, a patriot, but a wanderer and an outcast, is deprived of all news of his native land (823) (826) (859)

697

(a) (990) (1006b)
A's parents, F-A and M-A, insist that he study to be a doctor, while all his soul is yearning to make another profession his life work (756) (791) (950-*)

(b) (818c ch A to A-8 & CH to A) (818d ch A to A-8 & CH to A)
A is a foundling who knows nothing of his birth and parentage * A knows nothing of his birth and parentage, and he finds this a serious and humiliating handicap ** (245) (944) (1051)

698

(622) (898)
A seeks to live down his bitter grief over the loss of his only child, CH, but finds it impossible (674) (705) (732) (746 ch B to A) (1068 ch B to A)

699

(a) (608) (610) (623) (1298) (1300)
A is a fugitive from justice, who discovers that a relative, A-8, has died and left him a rich estate * A is a fugitive from justice who dares not show himself to receive a rich estate that has been left to him, for he knows he will be arrested ** (624) (635)

(b) (651) (652a) (653)
A, driven to bay by pursuers, takes refuge in an old house * A is rescued from pursuers, A-6, A-6, when the old house in which he has taken refuge is blown away by a tornado ** (1142b) (1209a)

700

(748) (958) A is a man who believes that poverty is the true source of contentment * A, against his wish and inclination, has been left a fortune by a deceased relative, A-8 ** (431) (924a)

701

(1249) (1296) (1304)
A seeks wealth by craftily defrauding his friend, A-2 * A, seeking wealth by craftily defrauding A-2, is tortured by conscience ** (832) (987) (1461a)

702

(863b, c)
A invites a number of guests to meet A-4, a celebrity * A has invited a number of hero-worshipers to meet A-4 a celebrity. The hero-worshipers arrive, but A-4 does not ** (178 ch A to A-4) (1162 ch A-5 to A-4) (1164)

703

(68) (96) (486a)
A is a minister of the gospel * A, a religious teacher of the people, errs secretly on his human side and becomes the prey of conscience ** (279 tr A & B, ch "husband of B-3" to "wife of A-8") (348) (393) (951) (1461a)

704

(139) (601) (607) (716)
A finds happiness in being loyal to his friends * A, because of a disturbing experience, is compelled to turn against his friend, A-2 ** (770b tr A & A-2) (790a) (840) (1227a) (1402) (1216 tr A & A-2)

705

(150) (248) (255) (288) (548b) (568c) (698)
A, unable to conquer his misfortunes, seeks to escape them by committing suicide (868 tr A & A-2) (879)

706

(a) (115) (793a)
A, an engineer, has flung a span of steel across a mountain gap, backing his ingenuity and judgment with a bridge in a spot where other engineers have declared no bridge is possible * A's life work, nearing completion, is threatened with destruction by a great storm ** (546a) (603a) (726b) (779)

(b) (810) (898)
A, a scientist, has spent years in research work and has the result of his labors in manuscript form * A's priceless manuscript is threatened with destruction by fire ** (918b)

(c) (959) (966-4)
A is an artist who has spent years painting a certain picture which he considers his life work * A's life work is threatened with destruction by a mob during a political outbreak ** (1233 ch A to A-2) (808a tr A & B)

707

(610) (866)
A asks A-4, a stranger, to remove a pair of handcuffs from his wrists (1066) (1311 ch A to A-4 & A-3 to A)

708

(770a) (797) (859) (918a) (952) (864) (611a)
A, after a mysterious absence of many years, returns to his old home town * A, returning as an Unknown to his native place, discovers that no one recognizes him ** (1275) (1453)

709

(836) (1021a) (1058)
A assumes charge of a valuable object, X, for a friend, A-2 * A, custodian of a valuable object, X, misses X and believes it has been stolen ** (774) (807)

710

(130) (180) (726a) (1356)
A is expected by a large crowd of people to appear and carry out an obligation of professional duty * A is forced to give up an enterprise when he is taken suddenly so ill he cannot leave his bed ** (757) (1162 ch A-5 to A) (1163a) (1163a; 1163c)

711

(a) (130) (188a) (525)
A, engaged in an important enterprise, suddenly finds himself in quarantine because of an outbreak of a contagious disease (856) (875a tr A & A-2 and eliminate "prison cell")

(b) (798) (985)
A, engaged in an important enterprise, becomes involved in an automobile accident * A is removed in an unconscious condition from the scene of an accident ** A loses an important object, X, on the scene of an accident *** (808a) (1161 tr A & A-4)

(c) (154a) (185) (209-*) (347a) (382) (598) (603a) (607)
A, seeking to carry out an important enterprise, meets with obstacles that defeat his plans (826) (209*-**) (827) (828) (866)

712

(1248)   (1282)
A, a doctor, is a fugitive from justice * A, a doctor who is fleeing from A-6, an officer of the law, by his skill restores sight to A-6, who is temporarily blind ** (1011 ch A to A-6 & A-5 to A)   (1013)

713

(662)   (685)   (692)   (693)
A, deprived of food through misfortune, faces slow death by starvation (878b) (878c) * A dies of starvation **

714

(650)   (687)   (863a; 690)   (878a)
A, because he is a ventriloquist (a conjuror or a magician?) saves his life among savages; then he loses his voice (197)   (244; 878c; 904)

715

(a)   (661)   (925-*)
A, wealthy and influential, loses his clothes, personal belongings and all other means of identification (658) * A, wealthy, finds that his pretentions to place and power are treated as a joke ** A cannot convince others of his identity, and undergoes the hardships and evil treatment accorded an upstart imposter *** (635) (963)   (1348a; 1455b)

(b)   (680b)   (113; 257b)
A cripples himself for life in rescuing a child, CH, from death (842b) * A loses his small fortune in trying to help a friend, A-2 (601) ** A, a poor man and crippled, finds his life in a sad tangle *** (345)   (690)   (944)

(c)   (212a)   (1323b)
A is found guilty of a political conspiracy (793b) * A, convicted of being a traitor to his country, is expatriated and forced to live abroad ** (696)   (826)

716

(830 tr A & A-2)   (865 tr A & A-2)
A and A-2, before the war, were fast friends (1021b)   (662-*) * A is captain in the army, and his men capture and bring before him A-2, a bosom friend of A's who is one of the enemy and a spy ** (790a)   (1016a ch A-5 to A-2)   (1016b)

717

(866)   (1162 tr A & A-2 & ch A-5 to A-6)   (1180 ch A-4 to A-6)
A is impersonating an officer, A-6 * A, impersonating A-6, meets A-6's sweetheart, B, and she recognizes him as an imposter ** (885a-*)   (1173-*)   (1176)

718

(a)   (255)   (257a)
A knows something others do not know, something that proves the greatest obstacle to his enterprising and capable nature (1061) * A, believed by all to be a white man, knows there is negro blood in his veins ** (248)   (657)   (959)

(b)   (800 ch SN to A)   (928b-* ch SN to A & A to A-8)
A is a youth who, sheltered from the world and pampered by doting parents, has no true conception of life and no ability to face its rugged issues * A, callow and inefficient, learns some real truths through hard experience ** (759)   (768)   (769) (783)   (918b)

719

(a)   (130)   (314-*)   (430)   (770a)
A disappears mysteriously * A, set upon by mysterious persons, AX, AX, AX, in the cellar of his own home, is spirited away through a concealed passage ** (540) (571)

(b)   (690-*)   (1116-*)
A, passenger on a vessel on the high seas, is made a prisoner when the vessel is captured by mutineers, A-5, A-5, A-5 * A, captured by mutineers, A-5, A-5, A-5, is placed in a small boat and cast adrift on the high seas ** (692)   (878b)

720

(288)   (1061)
A's fear that he has inherited the evil traits of an ancestor, A-8, paralyzes his will in enterprise (862)   (1374)

721

(706a, b, c)   (903)

A's whole future is wrapped up in a mighty work which he has brought almost to successful completion * A's life work is threatened with destruction ** (546a) (1256)

722

(833)   (834)   (1298 ch A to A-5)

A is an officer of the law, hot on the trail of a fleeing criminal, A-5 * A, an officer of the law, while pursuing a fleeing criminal, A-5, meets with misfortune ** (634) (664)   (693)   (711a)   (712 ch A to A-5 & A-6 to A)   (1013 ch A to A-5 & A-6 to A)

723

(998 ch A to A-5 & A-4 to A)   (1016a-*)

A, a police officer, owes a debt to A-5, a criminal, but has no money and cannot pay (1011)   (983 ch A to A-5 & A-8 to A)

724

(1227a-**)   (1377a)

A has recovered a stolen object, X, and is on his way to return it to its owner * A, on his way to return to the owner a stolen object, X, which he has recovered, loses the object and again seeks to recover it ** (614)   (711b)

725

(833)   (1303 ch A-9 to A-5)   A seeks to reveal to the authorities the identity of a criminal, A-5, who, so far, has been unsuspected * A, in trying to lodge information with the police against a criminal, A-5, meets with misfortune ** (1228 ch A-3 to A-5)   (1232 ch A to A-3 & A-5 to A)

726

(a)   (1060)   (1082a)

A, a matador, is getting ready in his room to appear in the bull ring * A, making ready to undertake an enterprise, has his plans suddenly interfered with ** (710) (809-* tr A & A-5)

(b)   (180)   (782)

A, ill, and worn by a long journey, is suddenly called upon to undertake an enterprise which would be difficult if he were physically at his best (652a, b)   (793a)

727

(3a)   (297)   (425; 813; 821)   (800 ch B to A; 821)

A, a judge presiding at a murder trial, finds himself unexpectedly confronted with a circumstance that makes his work a torture to his soul (790b)   (833)

728

(686)   (687)   (1319b-*)

A digs a pit for a tiger trap and baits it with a quarter of bullock meat * A constructs a concealed trap, and a person dear to him, CH, falls into the trap and cannot escape (622 ch SN to CH)   (591 ch B to CH; 179a ch B to CH) ** A constructs a deadly trap and, by accident, falls into it himself *** (875b)   (1319b ch A-2 to A)

729

(601)   (1334a)   (1382b)

A, desperately in need, is offered a large sum of money for a diamond, X, which he knows is an imitation * A, desperately in need of money, can recoup his finances at the expense of his integrity. He resists the temptation ** (778 ch A to A-5; 1144 ch A to A-5; 1166 ch A to A-5)   (803b)   (944)

730

(918a)   (959)   (1014 ch A-5 to A-3)

A fights with A-3 in safeguarding valuables, X, of which A is custodian * A is slain by A-3, who takes valuables, X, of which A is custodian ** A-3, having slain A, places a revolver in A's stiffening fingers in order to make it appear that A is a defaulter and a suicide *** (569 ch A-5 to A-3)   (802b tr A & B)   (977a)

731

(109) (608) (708) (808a)
A is honest, but he is a stranger and regarded with suspicion * A is arrested as a criminal "suspect" because he happens to be in the vicinity when a crime is committed ** (695b) (815a ch A to A-8 & A-4 to A)

732

(288) (654) (683) (698)
A has a conviction that he is going insane and that, sooner or later, he will be confined in an asylum (634) (638) (1365) (1374) (1375)

733

(718b) (723)
A finds a bank note of large denomination * A finds a valuable paper, X, between the leaves of the family Bible ** A, poor, comes into possession of a bank note of large denomination. There is no bank in the village in which he lives, and he can find no one who can, or who would if he could, change the bill for him *** (652a) (655) (731)

734

,222b, (315) (430) A is mistakenly reported dead during the World War * A, in the World War, is shell-shocked and loses all knowledge of his identity ** A, victim of amnesia in a foreign land, wanders back to his native country *** (437) (548a) (1128a-*; 918b)

735

(912 & a ch A to A-8) (913 ch A to A-8; A-2 to A)
A is annoyed by a person, A-8, who constantly crosses his path with the most untimely intrusions * A rids himself of a meddlesome person, A-8, and later regrets his harshness ** (762 tr A & A-8) (815a ch A to A-8; & A-4 to A) (822 ch A to A-8 & B to A)

736

(322a) (737a) (740)
B inherits the trait of disguising her affections, a trait that proves an obstacle to her success and happiness (162a) (594a) (742)

737

(a) (12b) (36) (60) (62) (162a) (182a) (225) (226) (643)
B is greatly discontented because of an unfortunate state of affairs * B, discontented, seeks to gain contentment, but the obstacles seem insuperable ** (93a) (114) (346) (403) (785)

(b) (470) (976)
B, in a large city hotel, returns at night from her bath and, through error, enters through an unlocked door into a room which proves to be not her own * B finds that the knob and lock on the door of a hotel room are in disrepair: the lock apparently locks itself, and the knob will not turn ** (645) (885b) (890)

(c) (470) (1154a)
B, near-sighted, unsophisticated, on leaving her room in a big city hotel, ties a black ribbon to the doorknob so she can easily find the door on her return * CH, a child, playing in the corridor of a big city hotel, transfers a black ribbon from the knob of B's door to that of A ** (645) (792b)

738

(60) (223) (397) (435a) (647) (665)
B, a victim of certain unpleasant conditions, seeks to escape them by self-destruction (879 ch A to B) (188b) (880 ch A to B & A-2 to B-2)

739

(947) (1293b)
B, owing to financial difficulties, has been compelled to pawn an object, X, dearly prized * B is unable to redeem an object, X, necessary to her happiness, which she has pawned ** (806 ch B-4 to B) (792a; 21) (1384 ch B to A)

740

(15a)   (327a)   (736)   (848b ch B to M-B)
B is a strange, wild creature, marked at birth by an unfortunate experience of her
mother, M-B's * B is shunned and ostracised because of a misfortune for which
she is not responsible ** (221a; 264)   (221a)   (738)   (746)   (872)   (892 ch B-3
to A)

741

(223)   (676)
B is forced by her father, F-B, to leave home and become a domestic drudge in a
distant town (183)   (743a)   (869)

742

(57)   (585a)   (743a)   B writes a note, and the note contains a very important
secret * B writes a note; and it is picked up by a gust of wind, carried across a narrow court, through an open window, and deposited in a neighboring apartment **
B writes a very important note, then loses it. If the note is found and read by other
persons, B will be greatly humiliated *** (758)   (955)

743

(a)   (223)   (435a)   (676)
B becomes the victim of such desperate misfortunes that she plans to take her own
life * B writes a letter explaining her reasons for committing suicide ** (742)   (673)

(b)   (403)   (594e)   (646)
B commits a transgression. B, in order to escape the consequences of a transgression, flees secretly to a distant place and assumes a fictitious name (750 ch A
to B)   (921)

744

(816b)   (844a)   (1105)
B goes to a restaurant to keep a dinner engagement with A. A does not appear
(1240 ch A-3 to A)   (1391 ch A to B)

745

(947)   (948)
B's father, F-B, pursuing rustlers who have stolen his cattle, is shot down and
killed * B, elder daughter of F-B, is the sole support of the family when F-B dies **
(14a)   (1207)

746

(89)   (212b)   (649)   (698 ch A to B)   (740)
B, who was thought by the people of her community to have supernatural powers,
is discovered to have been insane—a condition caused by a great sorrow (766)
(1328)   (1441a ch A to B)   (1373 ch A to B)

(21) Falling into Misfortune through Mistaken Judgment

747

(41a) (125a) (111)
A, believing that a certain proposition has merit, buys stock in it himself and sells stock to his friends, A-2, A-2 * A honest and high-minded, recommends a certain proposition, and then discovers that it is a swindle ** (604) (606) (619) (979)

748

(941) (958)
A, poor, is happy in the belief that poverty is the source of contentment * A, believing poverty the source of contentment, refuses to develop resources in his possession that would give him wealth ** (111) (700) (929)

749

(965) (966-1) (1074)
A, a writer, is happy in producing a literary masterpiece * A, a writer, unconsciously plagiarizes from the work of another author in producing a literary masterpiece ** (1238) (1357*-**) (1391; 1461b)

750

(224) (597)
A flees to escape the consequences of a crime * A believes he is guilty of a crime, but no crime has been committed ** (108) (237) (624)

751

(1061) (1210) (1102)
A, informed that he has only a few months to live, undertakes an unusual enterprise [1] A seeks to spend all his money before he dies [2] A hurls himself recklessly into perilous situations in the hope of losing his life * A, told that he has only a few months to live, discovers that the doctor was in error and that he still has a long life ahead of him ** (811) (918b) (1104) (1134*-**)

752

(113) (126) (923)
A is discovered burglarizing a house * A, an intruder in a strange house, is discovered; he flees through the nearest door into a windowless closet and is trapped by a spring lock ** (801 tr A & B) (856)

753

(484b) (524a)
A, seeking to finance himself, gambles with money not his own—and loses it (620) (638)

754

(380) (484b) (807)
A gambles with money he is holding in trust (829) (832) (865)

755

(49) (585a) (622)
A resigns himself to fate and seeks to bear patiently a supposed bereavement; but the bereavement is imagined, not real (357) (576b)

756

(697a)
A, desiring a musical career, defers to the wishes of his parents, F-A and M-A, and becomes a doctor; but, all his life long, he feels that he has made a mistake (1153 ch B to A; 1248) (1388) (1434) (949a)

757

(114) (710) (126a, b)
A, confronting a hard and dangerous duty, is suddenly taken very ill and compelled to go to bed (1163a) (1163c) (1164 tr A & A-4)

758

(57) (742)

A is a hard-hearted man of the world, seeking gain by exploiting the misfortunes of others * A finds a mysterious note. It contains a woman's fateful secret—the secret of B, in desperate misfortune ** A, attempting to exploit B's troubles for his own gain, ends by yielding his sympathy and befriending B *** (21) (817) (955)

759

(718b) (898)

A, a tenderfoot in the West, takes offense at the slurs of a cowboy, A-8 * A and A-8 proceed to settle their differences with their fists ** (782) (820 ch A-2 to A-8) (830 ch A-2 to A-8)

760

(954) (925)

A accomplishes his work so completely that his success results in failure (1d, f, g) (231) (44b) (207) (377b) (595) (625) (751)

761

(a) (1126; 779) (793a) (836)

A, through the influence of a reckless friend, A-2, comes to his death (601; 705) (793a; 603d tr A & A-2)

(b) (383) (837)

A removes a birthmark from the beautiful face of his wife, B, with chemicals * A, seeking to help B, falls into tragic error ** (385a) (416)

762

(735 tr A & A-8) (845 ch A-2 to A-3) (1430a)

A struggles in vain for the friendship of A-8 * A meets with a fatal accident (634) (705) ** A, after his death, receives the friendship of A-8—for which he had vainly struggled in life *** (868 ch A to A-8 & A-2 to A) (1423 ch A to A-8; & AX to A)

763

(1146) (1175a)

A, a crook who has acquired wealth, in a quest for happiness returns to his native place to foregather with pals of his younger criminal day * A, a crook, discovers that his pals are all married and "going straight" ** (868 ch A to A-8 & A-2 to A) (963) (1087)

764

(671-**) (672)

A, in order to save his friend, A-2, picks a quarrel with A-2's enemy, A-3, and slays him * A, in order to protect A-2, slays A-3, quondam enemy of A-2's, unaware that A-2 and A-3 have composed their differences, and that A-3 has become A-2's friend and financial backer ** (671**-***) (1344 ch A-2 to A-3) (1355)

765

(376 ch B to B-2; 414 tr B & B-2) (916)

B, a school teacher, unknowingly violates the rules set up by the school board by * going to dances and by taking long walks at night (31) (870a) (891)

766

(56) (1106) (1121)

B, a plain woman, believes herself surpassingly beautiful * B has a character weakness which proves a bar to many of her enterprises ** (642) (746) (893) (1067)

767

(1152 ch B to B-2; 642-**)

B, poor, borrows a supposedly valuable object, X, and loses it * B, borrowing a supposedly valuable object, X, and losing it, labors for years to earn the money with which to replace it; only to discover that X was a counterfeit, and of trifling worth ** (642**-***) (918b ch A to B)

(22) Following a Wrong Course through Mistaken Judgment

768

(718b) (1060-*)
A, with no social distinction whatever, entertains the grandiose delusion that he
will be greatly missed if he drops out of society (617) (639)

769

(675) (718b) (1060-*)
A is mistakenly convinced of his great business ability * A seeks to manage A-2's
languishing business and place it on a paying basis ** (606 ch A to A-2; 1058)
(672; 906)

770

(a) (430) (461)
A is heavily in debt * A, in order to secure money to pay off his pressing obligations,
leaves home to take a position at a distance; and he leaves suddenly and mysteriously without telling his creditors he is going ** (540) (550) (571) (708)

(b) (490b) (601)
A, heavily in debt, seeks to save himself from ruin by forging the name of a friend,
A-2, to a note (649 ch BR-B to A) (704 tr A & A-2)

(c) (524a) (606)
A, heavily in debt, seeks to save himself by fraudulently using trust funds in his
possession (701) (753) (754)

771

(a) (513) (614) (1337) (1386a)
A thinks a certain crime has been committed and lodges information with the
police, A-6 * A thinks a crime has been committed, but he is mistaken ** (780)
(802a)

(b) (299) (657-**) (798)
A finds a paper containing the signals of his football team * A finds and keeps an
incriminating document, X, with the intention of discovering the author of it at
a later time ** A is accused of transgression by his rival, A-3, and an incriminating
paper, X, is found in his possession *** (820 tr A & A-2) (657**-***) (829)

772

(600) (608) (612 ch A-5 to A-4)
A befriends a needy stranger, A-4 * A befriends a needy stranger, A-4, who proves
to be a criminal ** (613 ch A-5 to A-4) (623) (635 ch A-5 to A-4)

773

(817) (837) (1154a) (1159) (1173)
A, in a spirit of altruism, befriends B * A befriends B, who proves to be a transgressor who has lied to A regarding her identity ** (828) (1171)

774

(513) (709) (772)
A pursues a stranger, A-4, to recover from him an object, X, which has been stolen *
A, pursuing a stranger, A-4, and taking from him a valuable object, X, which, A
thinks, was stolen from him, later discovers that X, which he supposed was stolen,
has all the time been in his own possession ** (780 ch A to A-4 & A-8 to A) (859)

775

(1144 ch A to A-7) (1212c ch A to A-7 & A-9 to A)
A trusts his servant, A-7, and makes a confidant of him * A discovers that his
trusted servant, A-7, is a thief ** (1166b ch A to A-7) (1008ch A to A-7 & A-9 to A)

776

(732) (711b-*)
A is seriously injured by a motor car * A, seriously injured by a motor car, ever
afterward has a weird delusion while he is in the streets that motor cars are trying
to run him down ** (634) (1078)

777

(624) (783) (787) (1199-*) (1342a) (1389a)
A, although not really a criminal, has become convinced that he is one * A conceals
his identity, avoids people, and leads a furtive, hermit-like existence ** (681b)
(705) (1199)

778

(1143a ch A to A-8) (1152)
A is a thief who plans to steal what he believes is a very valuable gem, X * A, believing that a counterfeit gem, X, is genuine, plans to steal it ** (1144) (1217a)

779

(289) (840-*)
A's bibulous friend, A-2, influences A to take to drink, scoffing at the doctor who
has forbidden A to indulge in spirituous liquors (840*-**) (620) (761a)

780

(771a) (1317) (1386a)
A discovers, as he supposes, plain circumstantial evidence of a crime, and informs
the police where A-8, the criminal, can be found * A-8, arrested as a criminal on
information furnished by A, easily proves that no crime has been committed **
(802a) (1340 ch A-4 to A-8)

781

(898) (983)
A looks upon others as people to be exploited * A, grasping and relentless, and
sparing no one in his greed for gain, encounters an experience which transforms
his character ** (377b) (639) (811)

782

(718b) (759)
A, aristocrat, endeavors to pound a comprehension of class distinction into the
thick skull of A-8, a plebian * A, an aristocrat, and A-8, a plebian, fight a drawn
battle. ·Equal prowess spells equality, and A and A-8 become fast friends **
(807 ch A-2 to A-8) (830 ch A-2 to A-8) (839 ch A-2 to A-8)

783

(597) (718b) (777)
A allows himself to be blackmailed by A-7, because he is convinced that he unintentionally committed a crime * A, supposing himself a criminal, discovers that no
crime has been committed ** (775) (1456 ch A-5 to A-7)

784

(403) (669) (787 ch A to B)
B, thinking herself a criminal, seeks to evade the law by various makeshifts * B
discovers that she is innocent of a crime she supposed she had committed ** (468)
(635 ch A to B) (870b)

785

(668; 33) (670; 33)
B's mother, M-B, is a widow in desperate misfortune * B's mother, M-B, is planning
a move which B knows will have unhappy consequences, but B cannot persuade
M-B against it **(420 ch B to M-B; 453 ch B to M-B) (892 ch B-3 to A & B to M-B)

(23) Becoming Involved in a Complication that has to do with Mistaken Judgment and Suspicion

786

(598) (833) (1389a)
A., week-end guest at a country house, prowls about the place at night on a perfectly honest enterprise * A is mistaken for a burglar ** (664) (828) (1188-*)

787

(1291b) (1449)
A, through circumstantial evidence, believes himself guilty of a crime which he
cannot remember of having committed, and which he did not in reality commit
(296) (624) (695a, b) (1064)

788

(21)   (1127 ch CN to B)
A believes B is an adventuress, seeking unlawful gain by pretending to be the
daughter of A-8 * B proves that she is the daughter of A-8 ** (422b)   (647 ch A-5
to A)

789

(633)   (1331-*)
A, seeking information as to his proper course, is under the delusion that everyone
is giving him false directions (759)   (1331*-**)

790

(a)   (830)   (865)
A, before the war, had a friend, A-2, who had rendered him a very great service *
A-2, during the war, is captured as an enemy spy and brought before Captain A **
Captain A allows an enemy spy, A-2, to escape, and ever afterward is regarded as
a traitor to his country *** (919a)   (921 ch B to A)   (1183)

(b)   (838)   (1115)
A, a judge, has a friend, A-2, brought before him for trial and sentence * A, a judge,
presiding at the trial of his friend, A-2, so manipulates proceedings in favor of A-2
that A-2 is acquitted ** A, a judge, proving false to his high duty, ever afterwards
bears a "crooked" reputation *** (949b)   (952)

791

(697a)   (926)
A, a doctor, comes of a proud old Southern family * A, a doctor, considers it his
duty to give medical assistance to outcasts and the morally inferior ** A, a doctor,
in following his ideals loses caste with his friends and neighbors *** (1434)   (1447)

792

(a)   (642-**)   (739; 1401)
B mistakenly supposes A to be a thief when he restores to her an object, X, which
she has lost * A, restoring to B an object, X, which she has lost, mistakenly supposes her to be a thief because X seems too valuable to be honestly owned by one
in B's straitened circumstances ** (21)   (822)

(b)   (737c)   (1154a)   (1172 ch B-5 to B-8)
B places an identifying mark on the door of her hotel room. The mark is changed
in an unusual manner to another door; and B-8, occupant of the other room, is
found to have been murdered (645)   (1204**-***)

(20)   Becoming Involved with Conditions in which
Misfortune is Indicated

793

(a)   (599)   (603c)
A is persuaded by his friend, A-2, to engage in an enterprise * A is persuaded by
his friend, A-2, to undertake an enterprise which A knows to be extremely difficult
and which his judgment warns him to let alone ** (653)   (761a)

(b)   (79 ch A-3 to A-2)   (809 ch A-5 to A-2)
A is influenced by his friend, A-2, to take charge of some important papers * A,
obliging his friend, A-2, by taking charge of some secret documents, is arrested,
and accused on the strength of the documents, of having a part in a criminal conspiracy ** (108)   (715c)

(24)   Becoming the Victim of Mistaken Judgment in
Carrying out an Enterprise

794

(603d)   (671)   (1291b)
A supposes his friend, A-2, is dead * A is astounded when his friend, A-2, whom he
supposed to be dead, suddenly appears before him ** (1344)   (1371)

108

795

(110-3)   (182b)   (431)
A, by trickery, is mistakenly convinced that he has achieved a cherished ambition
(313)   (488a)   (918b)

796

(687)   (973)   (976 ch B to A)   (1038 ch A-8 to A-3)   (1274-*)
A, by prayer, achieves success in an enterprise * A's success is mistakenly credited
to A's enemy, A-3 ** (1163c ch A-4 to A-3)   (1289b**-***)   (1274*-**)

797

(930 ch F-B to A & B to D-A)   (919b)   (1298)
A is a transgressor, long mysteriously missing from his home * A, a transgressor,
returning as an Unknown to his home, finds his daughter, D-A, reverencing his
memory as of a great and noble person ** (964b)   (1461c ch B to D-A)

798

(1319a ch A to A-8 & A-3 to A)   (1438b)   A finds an object of mystery, X, seemingly of great value * A highly prizes an object of mystery, X, carries it about with
him, and is unaware of the fact that his possession of X is fraught with terrible
danger ** (623)   (711b)   (1382a)

799

(24b)   (58a ch AX to A)   (185)   (737b ch B to A)   (773)   (786)
A commits a fault against propriety * A forces his way into the room of an unmar-
ried woman, B (766) ** B, in order to protect herself from A, calls a policeman,
A-6 *** (249)   (347b)   (658)

800

(514 ch CH to SN)   (594c ch CH to SN)   (551 ch CH to SN)
B has a weird delusion regarding her son, SN * B considers her son, SN, brilliant
and highly talented, whereas he is less than mediocre in mentality ** (718b ch A
to SN)   (821 ch A to B)   (853 ch A to SN)   (896)

801

(24a, b, c, d, e)   (27)
B wins the respect and protection of A * B reveals herself to A in the character of
a transgressor ** (45a)   (61)   (69)   (147)   (648)   (665)

(61) Becoming Aware of an Important Secret that
Calls for Decisive Action

802

(a)   (771a)   (780)   (1444 ch B to B-8)
A discovers that B, supposed to have been murdered, really committed suicide
(669; 738)   (741; 738)   (324; 738)

(b)   (833)   (841 ch A-2 to B)   (1417)
A discovers that B, supposed to have committed suicide, was really murdered
(422b)   (568a ch A to A-8)   (1154a)

803

(a)   (1337)   (1444)
A discovers that a coroner's verdict of "accidental death" should have been one
of cold, premeditated murder (79 ch A to A-8)   (568c ch A to A-8)   (568d ch A
to A-8)   (1456)

(b)   (606)   (729)
A, in desperate need, discovers that a gem, X, which he supposed to be worthless,
is in reality genuine and immensely valuable (792a)   (1166 ch A to A-8)

(21) Falling into Misfortune through Mistaken Judgment

804

(926) (928a) (709 ch A-2 to A-4)
A, tramping along a country road, sees a satchel, X, drop from a passing automobile and takes possession of it * A, finding a satchel, X, in the road, picks it
up and carries it on with him, in the hope of returning it to the stranger, A-4, who
lost it ** A finds a satchel, X, which, unknown to him, contains evidence of an
incriminating nature *** (608) (623) (808a)

805

(600) (613-* ch A-5 to A-4) (772-*)
A seeks to help A-4, an old man in misfortune * A, seeking to help a stranger, A-4,
meets with an unpleasant experience ** (613*-** ch A-5 to A-4) (6J8) (623)

806

(162b) (1157 ch B to B-4 & A to A-5) (1241a, b) (1244b) (1220b ch A to A-8)
A, walking in the street, sees B-4, a stranger, weeping * A, giving aid to a stranger,
B-4, later regrets his impulsiveness ** (801) (152b) (1159) (1208 ch B tc B-4)

807

(906-*) (913)
A, trying to be of service to his friend, A-2, is suspected of treachery by A-2 (906*-**)
(603a, b, c, d) (867)

808

(a) (804-** ch A-4 to B) (778-* ch A to A-5; 1214 ch A-2 to B; 1227 ch A-2 to B)
A takes possession of B's property in order to save it for her * A, taking possession
of B's property in order to save it for her, is falsely suspected by B of trying to
steal it ** (21) (706c ch A to B)

(b) (747 ch A to B & A-2 to B-2) (773) (766) (800)
A is older and more experienced than B and seeks to advise her wisely and help
her avoid making mistakes * B resents the superior attitude assumed by A **
(747*-** ch A to B) (799) (812a) (870a) (828)

809

(599 ch A-2 to A-5) (612-*) (662-* ch A-2 to A-5) (793b-* ch A-2 to A-5)
A seeks to help A-5 in a certain enterprise * A, seeking to help A-5, does not know
that A-5 is a crook ** (612*-**) (662*-** ch A-2 to A-5) (793b*-** ch A-5 to A-2)

810

(461) (619) (695a) (929-*)
A is old, believes he is slipping in his work, and considers himself a failure * A's
son, SN, wins for his college in a gruelling contest; and SN tells A, who is gloomy
and despairing and considers himself a failure, that his success was inspired by
the thought that his father had never been beaten ** A is inspired to carry on
successfully in his profession because of the faith his son, SN, has in him *** (674)
(729*-**)

811

(751-1) (781)
A, a miser, is lured into a charitable enterprise by the prospect of death * A, undertaking charitable enterprises when he thought he was soon to die, regrets the enterprises when he finds he still has a long life ahead of him ** A, a miser, would
recover money given in charity until he discovers how popular his bounty has made
him. Charmed by his popularity, he continues to be generous, and so consummates a most remarkable character change ***

812

(a) (646-* ch AX to A-4) (808b)
B, sympathetic and generous, befriends a needy stranger, A-4 * B, through befriending a needy stranger, A-4, becomes involved in an unpleasant complication ** (646*-** ch AX to A-4) (669 ch A-5 to A-4)

(b) (982a ch A to F-B & NW to A) (997a ch A to F-B)
B's father, F-B, fails in his attempt to subdue and control A, a "wild" and unmanageable youth left in his charge * B, when her father, F-B, fails in an enterprise, takes the enterprise off his hands ** (22a) (115) (367a)

(50) , Being Impelled by an Unusual Motive to Engage in Crafty Enterprise

813

(425) (551 ch CH to SN) (594c ch CH to SN)
A seeks to protect his son, SN, from what he conceives to be disgrace and dishonor on his own part (821) (881)

814

(114) (176b) (225)
A succeeds in an enterprise secretly devised by B as a test for his abilities (281c) (367b)

(15) Finding a Sustaining Power in Misfortune

815

(a) (598) (985; 623) (890 ch B to A-4 & A-4 to A)
A is overtaken by A-4, a fugitive who is being pursued by A-6, an officer of the law * A's sympathy goes out to A-4, a fugitive from the law, and he attempts to rescue him ** (866) (998) (1161) (1163 tr A & A-4)

(b) (611b) (631)
A, a dissolute son, in want, returns to his home and his father, F-A, a better and a wiser man than when he went away * A, a dissolute son, is freely forgiven his transgressions by his father, F-A ** (821 ch A to F-A & SN to A) (1166b ch A-9 to F-A)

816

(a) (174) (834)
A is on his way to keep an important engagement * A finds a stranger, A-4, ill, exhausted and unconscious, lying in the road ** A subordinates his own affairs to those of a stranger, A-4, who is ill, and helps him to a place where he can receive medical attention *** (772) (1265b)

(b) (647) (669)
A's friend, B, is in a foreign country, alone, homesick and discouraged * B, in a foreign country, unexpectedly meets A, a friend from "home" ** (744) (817) (850a)

817

(598) (610) (955)
A is an outlaw, hunted by the authorities and dodging about to escape capture * A, under ban of the law, runs the risk of capture in order to aid B (647) (57), a stranger who is in critical misfortune ** (801) (837) (870b ch A-6 to A) (885a)

818

(a) (598) (610) (1169)
A, well-to-do and of good family, is impersonating a person who is "down and out" * A has been hired by A-4 to circulate an infamous slander against B (60 ch A to A-4) (339a ch A to A-4) ** A, hired by A-4 to injure B, meets B, his sympathy goes out to her, and he revolts against A-4's scheme and warns B *** (14a) (828) (870a; 870b ch A-6 to A & A-5 to A-4)

(b) (887b) (1329)
A, a hoodlum, rescues B from an attack by footpads * B befriends A, picks him out of the gutter and makes a man of him ** (837 tr A & B) (1075b) (850b)

(c) (905) (914)
A finds a small child, CH, on the beach after a shipwreck * A takes CH, a foundling, into his heart and his home and rears her as his own child ** (305 ch B to CH) (1089)

(d) (898) (926)
A rescues a baby, CH, from death in a shipwreck * A, unable to learn anything about a foundling, CH, adopts the child as his own ** (245 ch A to CH) (948 ch B to CH) (1106 ch B to CH) (1458 ch B to CH)

819

(646 ch AX to A) (844a) (850a) (263 ch A-3 to A-5)
A, a burglar, seeks to aid B, who was his friend before he "went to the bad" * A, friend of B, breaks into a building for the purpose of committing a robbery, and finds a trusted employee, A-5, B's husband, dead at his desk, a defaulter and a suicide. A-5 has left a note explaining his guilt (753 ch A to A-5) ** A, in order to save his friend B from disgrace, destroys a letter that would have proved B's husband, A-5, a defaulter and a suicide, "blows" a safe and pretends to have committed a robbery *** (1075b; 918b) (922a) (952)

(25) Seeking to Save a Person who is Accused of Transgression

820

(898) (913) (949b)
A learns that his friend, A-2, is accused of a crime * A, learning that his friend, A-2, is accused of a crime, seeks to prove his innocence ** (790b) (906)

821

(623 ch A to SN) (628 ch A to SN) (718b ch A to SN; 770a ch A to SN)
A's son, SN, is arrested for committing a crime * A seeks to save his son, SN, from misfortune and becomes involved in an unpleasant complication ** (1290b ch A to SN & F-A to A) (601 ch A-2 to SN)

822

(648) (737b) (792a) (876a) (1172)
A supposes that B is a transgressor * A, honest, poses as a transgressor in order to help B ** (1167) (1171) (1192)

823

(918a) (955) (972)
A is a ne'er-do-well who has a friend, A-2, of worth in the world * A's friend, A-2, is unjustly condemned to death (715c ch A to A-2) (793b ch A to A-2 & A-2 to A-3); and A, by subtlity, takes A-2's place in the prison cell and dies in his stead ** (875a)

(27) Refusing to Betray Another's Secret and Calmly Facing Persecution Because of the Refusal

824

(644; 147) (1016a-* ch A to A-6 & A-5 to A)
A is a prisoner of A-6, and A-6 seeks to secure from A information inimical to B (878c) (943b)

(26) Seeking Secretly to Preserve Another from Danger

825

(641 ch B to D & F-B to A) (1285a ch A to NW-A)
A, aware that his end is approaching, seeks to protect his adopted daughter, D, by making a will (1041) (1270)

826

(793b) (1228) (1323b)
A is thrown into prison through false evidence in a political conspiracy * B, working secretly, rescues A from prison by proving his innocence ** (1244b ch A to A-3) (1278b ch A to A-3, B to B-3 & B-3 to B)

827

(711c) (603b, c, d; 1334b) (855)

A. a sprinter, is on the point of losing a footrace because he believes he hears the voice of a dead friend, A-2, calling for help (1160) * A, superstitious, is on the point of suffering defeat in an enterprise because he thinks he hears the voice of a dead friend, A-2, calling to him; but he is saved when A-8, one of the spectators, turns the tragic call into a mere incident by a counter-call which allays A's superstitious fears ** (918b) (1365)

828

(16a) (818a-**)

A, working "under cover," contrives to prove B's innocence of a certain crime (648) (1154a) (1172) * A, proving B innocent of a certain crime, proves also the guilt of B-5, a criminal whom B physically resembles ** (818a**-***) (851-*)

829

(75a; 163) (663) (793b ch A-2 to A-3) (1228) (1323b)

A is arrested for transgression on charges trumped up by a jealous rival, A-3 * B, working in secret, proves A's innocence of a certain transgression ** (352b tr A & B) (1244b ch A to A-3)

830

(474 ch A to A-2) (1021b)

A, friend of A-2, exposes A-5, a spiritualist charlatan who is mulcting A-2 of large sums of money * A, threatening A-5 with arrest, forces him to return money out of which he has swindled A's friend, A-2 ** (1323c-2 ch A to A-5 & A-8 to A) (1337 ch A-8 to A-5)

(16) Being Delivered from Misfortune by One who in Confidence Confesses a Secret of Transgression

831

(1024) (1027)

A, ill and starving, receives food and money from his friend, A-2 * A-2 tells his friend, A, in confidence, that he is a bootlegger ** (815-* ch A-4 to A-2) (824 ch B to A-2) (1269)

832

(754) (809 ch A-5 to A-2) (1085)

A steals money from his employer. A-9, to help his friend, A-2, over a financial crisis (753 ch A to A-2), intending to make good the shortage when A-2 gets back on his feet and repays the loan * A tells his friend, A-2, that he has stolen money from A-9 in order to help A-2 ** (601; 631) (601; 654; 628) (730 ch A-3 to A-2)

(57) Seeking to Unravel a Puzzling Complication

833

(1334c) (1337)

A sifts the circumstantial evidence of a crime in an attempt to discover the perpetrator (1371) (1413a) (1449)

(53) Opposing the Plans of a Crafty Schemer

834

(1214) (837 ch B to A-2)

A, becoming secretly aware of the plans for a holdup, endeavors to prevent it (865 ch A to A-8 & A-2 to A) (1227a)

(43) Seeking to Overcome Personal Limitations in Carrying Out an Enterprise

835

(115) (1074) (1090) (1096) (1111a)

A overhears a chance conversation and secures information of the utmost value * A, by chance, overhears a conversation that gives him material for a literary masterpiece ** (281c) (749)

(28) Facing a Situation in which the Misfortunes of One Greatly Esteemed Call for Courage and Sagacious Enterprise

836

(601-*)   (671-**)   (716)
A meets with unhappy experiences when he tries to help his friend, A-2, who has fallen into misfortune (601*-**) (671**-***) (704) (764) (790a, b)

837

(179a, b, c) (188b-*) (230-*) (382-*) (773-*) (851-*)
A tries to help B—with results that are wholly unexpected (45a, b) (188b-**) (230*-**) (382*-**) (773*-**) (851*-**)

838

(220 tr A & A-2) (716) (793a)
A, in order to help his friend, A-2, puts aside his principles and engages in distasteful enterprise (790a, b) (807) (840)

839

(1061 ch A to A-2) (1062 ch A to A-2) (1063 ch A to A-2)
A seeks to correct a character weakness in his friend, A-2 * A seeks to correct a character weakness in his friend, A-2, by telling him a story which subtly suggests a method of self-correction ** (607) (918a ch A to A-2) (922a ch A to A-2) (1104 ch A to A-2) (The story: 1082b) (The story: 1330)

840

(126 ch A to A-2) (619 ch A to A-2) (1314 ch A to A-2)
A seeks to prevent his friend, A-2, from committing a reckless act that would have fateful consequences * A plies his friend, A-2, with drink until he is intoxicated and helpless in order to prevent him from committing a reckless act that would have fateful consequences ** (779 tr A & A-2) (880a tr A & A-2)

841

(313 ch A to A-2; 705 ch A to A-2) (720 ch A to A-2; 705 ch A to A-2)
A discovers secretly that his friend, A-2, has committed suicide * A seeks to save the family of A-2 from shame and disgrace because of a reckless act committed by A-2 ** (868) (1160)

842

(a) (847) (911) (923) (963) (1061)
A tries to rescue a child, CH (842b-*), makes a heroic attempt, and both die

(b) A rescues a child, CH from [1] a burning house. [2] a speeding train, [3] a racing automobile [4] or a cattle stampede * A, in performing a rescue, cripples himself for life ** (257b) (715b)

843

(59 ch B to B-2) (239 ch B to B-2)
B is convinced that her friend, B-2, is making a mistake * B, convinced that her friend, B-2, is making a mistake, resolves to correct the mistake in secret, since B-2 will not do it ** (294b ch A to B, A-2 to B-2 & B to A) (849 ch B-4 to B-2)

844

(a) (850a, b) (1083)
B, an attractive married woman, clever and influential, seeks diversion by helping her friend, A (17a, b) (257a)

(b) (256) (324)
B's friend, B-2, seeks to save A, B's fiance, from the wiles of a designing woman, B-3, and restore him to B * B's friend, B-2, seeks to save B's lover, A, from a designing woman, B-3, by winning A away from B-3 ** (243 ch B-2 to B-3) (24a, b, ch B to B-2)

(30) Enlisting Whole-Heartedly in the Service of a Needy Unfortunate and Conferring Aid of the Utmost Value

845

(755 ch A to A-2; 922b ch A to A-2)   (926)
A, poor and humble, at great self-sacrifise helps A-2, an old man poorer than A himself * A, through his enterprise, restores A-2 to friends and fortune ** (876a ch B to A-2; 850b ch B to A & A to A-2; 880b tr A & A-2; 601)

846

(710 ch A to A-2)   (1145 ch A to A-2; 1161 ch A-4 to A-2)
A's friend, A-2, falls from exhaustion while engaged in an enterprise * A completes a task for A-2, his friend, which A-2 was unable to finish ** (662)   (1058)

847

(911)   (914)
A, a rough frontiersman in a rough frontier camp, undertakes the care of an orphan baby, CH (842a, b)

848

(a)   (74b)   (928a)   (970)
A, seeking to help B, who is in distress, meets with unpleasant complications (772 ch A-4 to B)   (773)   (792a)

(b)   (974)   (1118)
A rescues B, who has been attacked by a huge snake * B, attacked by a huge snake, suffers a psychic shock ** (505-*)   (740 ch B to D-B & M-B to B)   (872)   (1445)

849

(173)   (1343 ch A to B)
B, in charge of a booth at a charity bazaar, seeks to prevent B-4 from buying a certain object, X, on which she seems to have set her heart (1245)   (839 ch A to B & A-2 to B-4)

850

(a)   (85a, b)   (114)   (115)   (718b)   (812a-* ch A-4 to A)
B discovers in backward A a promise of great things, and attempts to guide him to a high goal (801 tr A & B)   (814)   (844a)

(b)   (818b-*)   (1075a)   (1126)   (1329)
B seeks to rescue A from a life of dissipation and make a man of him * B picks A out of the gutter and gives him employment ** (818b*-**)   (1075b)

(21)   Falling into Misfortune through Mistaken Judgment

851

(87)   (176b)   (232)   (375)   (600)
A rescues B from imminent danger, but only by bringing the danger upon himself * A is unable to extricate himself from the peril from which he rescues B ** A rescues B from [1] a ferocious wild animal, [2] from a burning steamer, [3] from the undertow while ocean bathing, [4] from a train wreck, [5] from an automobile accident or [6] from a landing airplane on a flying field (31)   (367b)   (500a)   (885a)

852

(1366)   (1428-*)   (1433a, b, c)
A dreams of danger, but discredits the dream and believes the danger real (1428*-**)
(1358)   (1375)

853

(1374-*)   (1377b)   (1389b)   (1418b-*)
A, a mediocre person, undergoes a weird experience (1342)   (1082b) * A, a mediocre person, undergoes an experience which inspires him with grandiose ideas of his power and ability ** (1418b*-**)   (1374*-**)   (1060)   (1134)   (1330)

854

(1346 ch A to A-9; 596 ch A-5 to A-9)   (1303)   (1290a ch A to A-9; 596 ch A-5 to A-9)
A discovers a fateful secret of his rich and powerful employer, A-9 * A, because he has knowledge of A-9's guilty secret is persecuted, spied upon and thrown into prison on a trumped-up charge ** (884a ch A-5 to A-9)   (887a ch A-3 to A-9)

855

(661)   (681a)   (1347)   (1391)
A struggles against an hallucinary enemy, AX, who fights with superstition as a weapon (732)   (1348a)   (1375)

856

(690)   (693)   (1419b)
A, caught in a trap that holds his body powerless but leaves his mind alert, seeks to achieve physical freedom (682)   (1419a)

857

(858)   (862)   (1061)   (1078)   (1110)
A seeks to achieve emancipation from a fear which dogs his life, shows in his face and manner, and plunges him into misfortune (951)   (1104)   (1350)   (1374)
(1375)

858

(558 tr A & A-3)   (1061)
A is made miserably unhappy by the fear of death * and would emancipate himself from it ** (439 tr A & A-3)   (1082a)   (1104)

859

(249)   (385a)   (623)   (786)
A, falsely accused of crime, seeks to clear himself of the accusation (828 tr A & B & ch B-5 to A-5)   (829)   (1291a ch A to A-5)   (1447)

860

(601)   (606)   (656)   A, impoverished, seeks to recoup his fortunes by a wealthy marriage (230)   (378)   (422b)

861

(718a)   (332 tr B & A)   A, of an inferior race, rescues B, of a superior race, from accident * A, when he rescues B, becomes involved in an unpleasant complication, due to mistaken judgment ** (31)   (282b)

862

(288)   (937)   (1064)   (1075a)
A fears he will commit a transgression * A, fearing he will commit a transgression, seeks to emancipate himself from the fear, and from the possibility of doing evil ** (963)   (1075b)

(50) Being Impelled by an Unusual Motive to Engage in Crafty Enterprise

863

a) (618) (726a) (954) (1071) (1094)
A's popularity becomes so great that it annoys him * A desires a place of seclusion where he can be absolutely alone, away from cables, wireless, mails and the public ** (690) (719b) (897)

(b) (768) (965)
A seeks to enhance his social prestige * A invites a celebrity, A-4, to be guest of honor at a reception in his home, and A-4 accepts ** (702) (1164)

(c) (461) (606)
A, keeper of a hotel at a summer resort, faces failure in business through lack of custom * A, a hotel keeper facing failure, invites A-4, a celebrity, to be a guest at his hotel, and A-4 accepts ** (1161 ch A to A-8) (1162 ch A-5 to A-4)

864

(611a) (770a) (952)
A is a man of wealth and high character whose conscience is troubled by a transgression committed in his earlier years * A, under a fictitious name, returns to his native place, where he had committed a youthful transgression, and, as an Unknown, seeks to discover: [1] Whether his youthful escapades have been forgotten and forgiven; [2] whether the person whom he wronged has suffered any lasting injury. Also, he wishes [3] to make reparation in an assumed character for wrong done in his true character; and [4] to establish a reputation for good behavior and lofty aims in the community before revealing his real identity ** (708) (1199)

865

(216) (314-*) (619)
A, about to commit an act of folly, is abducted by his friend, A-2, and held a prisoner as the only means of restraining him (314*-**) (880a) (867 tr A & A-2)

866

(92) (637)
A is arrested and is being taken to prison by A-6 * A's captor, A-6, an officer of the law, is killed in an accident, and is supposed to be A; consequently, A secures his freedom ** (707) (717)

867

(807) (865 tr A & A-2) (808a ch B to A-2) (709) (1319a) (1214)
A, suspected of treachery by his friend, A-2, in a daring rescue saves the property and perhaps the life of A-2, and proves his faithfulness by a revelation of the danger to which A-2, unknown to himself, was exposed (1227a) (839)

868

(601 ch A to A-2 & A-2 to A-8; 705 ch A to A-2) (838)
A, destroying a letter in which his friend, A-2, declares he is about to commit suicide, makes it appear that A-2 died of a contagious disease (906) (944)

869

(949a) (955) A, a fugitive from justice with a price on his head, prevents B from committing suicide (641; 743a) (647; 743a)

870

(a) (62) (134a) (220) (415) (447)
B, harrassed by gossip that reflects on her integrity, seeks deliverance from false suspicion (83) (86) (870b) (1151)

(b) (669) (784) (817 ch A to A-6) (818 ch A to A-6)
B, her integrity seriously compromised, finds a friend in A-6, a detective * A-6 proves that B's enemy, A-5, is a crook, and has him sent to prison **

871

(313)   (676)
B's father, F-B, is compelling B to take a step which she believes will be fatal to her happiness * B, compelled by her father, F-B, to take a step which she believes will be fatal to her happiness, escapes the catastrophe by a stratagem ** (1241b) (1244b)

872

(740)   (1334a ch A to B)   (1342a ch A to B)
B fears she is going insane * B, fearing she is going insane, seeks emancipation from the demoralizing fear ** (1067)   (1069)   (1445)

873

(227)   (305)   (1458)
B discovers an evil secret of her past * B, discovering an evil secret of her past, meditates suicide ** (802a)   (870b)   (893)   (1051)   (1055)

(15)   Finding a Sustaining Power in Misfortune

874

(430)   (606)   (680a)
A is heavily in debt and facing bankruptcy * A seeks to escape financial disaster by undertaking an honest but secret enterprise (1394)   (1399)   (1408) that will bring him in enough money to discharge his pressing obligations ** (540)   (770a)

875

(a)   (823-*)   (824 ch A to A-2)   (731 ch A to A-2)
A, visiting A-2 in his prison cell, exchanges clothes with him and A-2 leaves the prison as A (823*-**)   (1344 tr A & A-2)

(b)   (233)   (660a)   (662)   (664)   (719a)   (179 tr A & B)
A is rescued by B * B makes use of A's hound dog in tracking A ** (367b)   (850a)

876

(a)   (3a)   (949b; 801)
A sees a policeman, A-6, watching B, who is about to pick a pocket (724 ch A to B) * A warns B of danger from A-6 ** (69)   (359)

(b)   (85b)   (97)   (134b)
A and B find themselves prisoners in a deserted house * A and B, trapped in a deserted house, seek some method of escape (170). A hurls himself from an upper window and, his arm broken, secures aid and rescues B ** (140)   (360a)

877

(895 ch A to A-2)   (1070 ch A to A-2)
A, a sheriff, is by duty compelled to hang a condemned man, his friend, A-2 * A, a sheriff, believes A-2, the man he is about to hang, innocent of the crime for which he was sentenced ** A, a sheriff, delays hanging a condemned man, A-2, in the hope that a Higher Power will intervene to save A-2 *** (535 ch A to A-8 & A-3 to A-2)   (826 ch A to A-2)

878

(a)   (691)   (687)
A, a ventriloquist, is captured by savages and threatened with death * A, a ventriloquist, captured by savages and threatened with death, makes an animal talk—and is given his freedom and loaded with honors ** (714)   (714; 197)

(b)   (692)   (719b)
A, adrift at sea in a small boat and near death from exposure, lands on an unknown coast (686)   (690)

(c)   (244)   (331)   (714)
A, a prisoner, bound, helpless and facing death, is rescued by resourceful B (347a) (901)

879

(188b ch B to A & A to A-4)   (705)
A, attempting to commit suicide, is prevented from doing so by A-4, who comes to the same place to make an attempt on his own life (840 ch A-2 to A-4)   (850a ch B to A-4)   (865 ch A-2 to A-4)

880

(a) (216)   (314)   (840 tr A & A-2)   (865)
A, by a stratagem of his friend, A-2, is saved from an act of folly * A, saved by a
stratagem of his friend, A-2, from an act of folly, comes to realize his intended
folly, forgive the stratagem, and thank A-2 **

(b) (805 ch A-4 to A & A to A-2)   (894 ch A-5 to A & A to A-2)
A, an old man, a homeless outcast and a "bum," is restored to relatives and to
fortune by a friend, A-2 (831; 1269)   (1264)

881

(813)   (928b-*)
A has turned his back upon happiness because of an obligation he fancies himself
under to his son, SN * A's son, SN, discovers a fateful secret of A's (425), and
persuades him to correct an error and regain lost happiness ** (928*-**)   (499a)
(790b ch A-2 to SN)

882

(946 ch B to A)   (914)   (1239)
A's philanthropic enterprise is about to fail * A's philanthropic enterprise faces
financial failure; and A, a reformed gambler, keeps the enterprise going with crooked card games ** (665 ch B to A)   (963)

883

(1209a)   (1298)   (955)
A, a hunted outlaw in disguise, takes refuge with an enemy, A-3 * A, a hunted
outlaw, takes refuge with an enemy, A-3; and A-3, considering himself bound by
the laws of hospitality, conceals A and saves him from his pursuers, A-6, A-6 **
(923 ch A-5 to A-3)   (1022)

884

(136 ch A-3 to A-5)   (596)   (660b)
A is bitterly persecuted by a relentless enemy, A-5 * A, bitterly persecuted by a
relentless enemy, A-5, sees no possible escape from the coil; then, suddenly, A-5
is killed in an accident ** (1344-* ch A-2 to A-5)   (1132)

(b) (579a)   (976)   (1427b)   (1133)
A, an agnostic, is caught in a terrific storm * A, an agnostic, is persuaded into a
belief in God by B when, together, they escape a terrible danger through prayer **
(1375)   (1128a-*)   (922a)

885

(a) (666)   (837)   (879 ch A to B & A-4 to A)
B, while carrying out an enterprise, is rescued from imminent danger by A * A,
unable to rescue himself from danger incurred in saving B, is in turn rescued by B **
(31)   (191)

(b) (144)   (146)   (306)   (483b)   (737b)
B is a prisoner in one of the upper floors of a tall building * B, a prisoner in a room
on one of the upper floors of a tall building, saves herself by making use of the fire
escape ** (31)   (870a, b)

886

(676 ch F-B to M-B)   (739)   (741 ch F-B to M-B)   (908)   (996; 1105)
B's mother, M-B, is in straitened circumstances and estranged from B * B's mother,
M-B, inherits a large sum of money unexpectedly, and becomes reconciled with B,
from whom she was estranged ** (785)   (1067)   (1246)

(20)   Becoming Involved with Conditions in which
Misfortune is Indicated

887

(a) (677 ch B to A; 1309a ch B to A & A to A-3)   (677 ch B to A; 568c)
A, held on a murder charge, wins freedom by an unusual plea of his attorney, A-7 *
A, held on a murder charge, is released from custody when his lawyer, A-7, proves
that A, "drunk with sleep," had believed his victim, A-3, was trying to kill him **
(870a ch B to A)   (695a)

(b)   (682; 880b)   (937)
A, once a cultured man but now a barbarian, is rescued from an unfortunate situation by his old friend, A-2 * A, a barbarian, is compelled to deal with a civilization which he once knew but now has forgotten ** (1093) (1132) (1291b; 1195) (1291b) (1345)

888

(1418a; 1427a)   (1436; 1427a)   (1441a; 1427a)   (1426b-*)
A undergoes a strange experience among people hypnotically deluded * A, undergoing a strange experience among people weirdly deluded, discovers the secret of the delusion written in a notebook belonging to A-8, one of the victims who had died. By means of information obtained from the notebook, A succeeds in rescuing the other victims of the delusion ** (1366)   (1368; 1061)

889

(115)   (591)   (633)   (681a)   (708)   (1082b)
A, recovering his reason after it has long been obscured, relates a strange story of his experiences, a story which his friends find it difficult to believe (888)   (1411) (1418a; 1422a)

890

(87; 1100)   (470)   (1154a)   (1172)
B, engaged in carrying out a secret enterprise, finds herself in danger and calls upon a stranger, A-4, for aid (1025)   (1417)

891

(32; 35 ch A to A-3)   (765)   B's escort to a dance, A-3, gets into a fight with another man, A * B saves A from a knife in the hands of his enemy, A-3 ** (31 tr A & B)   (94a)

892

(220)   (218a)   (340)   (946)   B dies of pneumonia brought on by exposure while rescuing B-3 from an accident (53)   (405 tr B & B-3)

893

(27)   (124)   (227)   (514)   (594c)   (665)   (800 ch SN to CH)   B performs an act of great heroism in rescuing a child, CH, from death, but sacrifices her own life in making the rescue

(25)   Seeking to Save a Person who is Accused of Transgression

894

(613)   (926)   (939)
A, robbed by A-5 and wishing to save him from the law, declares to A-6, the officer who has arrested A-5, that he gave A-5 the stolen property in his possession (918a ch A to A-5)   (918b ch A to A-5)   (923 ch A to A-5 & A-5 to A-8)

895

(568d ch A-3 to A & A to A-5)   (667)   (1070)
B implores A-9, the governor of the state, for a pardon for A, a condemned prisoner * B knows that A is innocent of the crime for which he was convicted ** (108)

896

(467 ch A-8 to SN)   (623 ch A to SN)
B learns that her son, SN, is suspected of having committed a crime * B knows that her son, SN, is innocent of the crime of which he is accused, and she knows who is guilty, but this knowledge makes the task of protecting SN dangerous and difficult ** (516 ch CH to SN)   (725 ch A to B & A-5 to A)   (1291a)

(21)   Falling into Misfortune through Mistaken Judgment

897

(618)   (954)   (1094)

A's popularity becomes so annoying that he seeks what he conceives to be ideal seclusion (865; 664)   (689)   (690) to escape from it * A, seeking seclusion because his popularity annoys him, becomes hungry for the old applause and suffers remorse because of his flight from it ** (682)   (900)

898

(106-*)   (492a)

A is a selfish person, constantly looking out for "Number One" * A, selfish and miserly, finds that his methods are mistaken and that he is making no progress towards happiness ** (106*-**)   (307)   (372)   (597)   (632)   (661)   (698)   (918b)

899

(99)   (902)

A is wealthy and avaricious, and happy only when adding to his riches * A, wealthy and avaricious, loses all by grasping for trifling gains ** (322b)   (377b)   (747)

900

(1330)   (1350)

A's imagination leads his mind astray, and in seeking emancipation from fancied misfortunes he is plunged into real misfortunes * A, given all he thought necessary for his happiness, finds there is still something lacking—something in himself ** (150)   (634)   (1348a)

901

(687; 244)   (878a).   (937)

A is a white man who seeks to make his white civilization a pattern for half-savage peoples * A "goes native" and marries a native woman, B ** (682)   (922b)

902

(675)   (718b)   (913)   (991)   (1079)   (1124)   (1148)   (1150)

A has a passion for a certain pastime: [1] card games, [2] billiards, [3] tennis, [4] bowling, and he becomes so absorbed in his trifling game that big events, demanding his immediate attention, are neglected with disastrous results (620)   (629)   (753) (957b)

903

(850a)   (1143b)

A is a conscientious artist, whose ideal is Truth * A, hired by B to paint her portrait, puts so much character and so little beauty into his work that B is deeply offended ** (1143b; 1386b; 1408)   (1386b)

904

(197)   (244)

A, a morally superior person thrown into a savage environment, is conquered by moral inferiority in the person of B, a native girl (347a)   (901)

905

(656;927)   (768)

A's pride will not allow him to discontinue benefactions for which his family has long been noted, although his poverty forces him to many shifts of simulation, demands pinching sacrifices, and taxes his ingenuity (628)   (1213)

906

(157 ch A-3 to A-2)   (836)   (838)   A discovers that his friend, A-2, is a defaulter * A-2 has important responsibilities, which A has not, and A flees, thus making it appear that he is the defaulter ** (80a ch A-3 to A-2)   (603b, c, d)   (807)   (841)

907

(918a)   (922a)

A, unable to find the noble ideal for which he has long and vainly searched, dies * A, after searching in vain for a noble ideal, dies unaware of the fact that he himself, because of his earnest search, has come to exemplify the ideal ** (943a)   (944)

908

(65-*)   (372)   (585b)
B is a selfish, hard-hearted, worldly-minded woman who seeks to live for herself alone. She wonders why she is not happy and contented (65*-**)   (310)   (505)

909

(649)   (628 ch A to BR-B)   (977a, b)
B indirectly causes the death of her brother, BR-B, by opposing a discreditable enterprise he was attempting to carry out * B dies a broken-hearted victim of her own high ideals **

(31) Living a Lonely, Cheerless Life and Seeking Companionship

910

(736 ch B to D-A)   (1105 ch B to D-A)
A seeks happiness in being the pal of his daughter, D-A, and in making her happy * A is ultra old-fashioned, and his daughter, D-A, is ultra modern ** (1067 ch B to D-A)   (1151 ch B to D-A)

911

(698)   (914)   (914; 918a)
A seeks happiness in his love for a child, CH, but for certain reasons finds it difficult to realize his desire (912a)   (842a, b)   (922a; 923)

912

(a)   (695a)   (695b)
A's consuming desire is for friendship, for some one with whom he may associate and converse; but he is old and ugly, and no one pays him any attention (735 tr A & A-8)   (762)   (911)   (1059)

(b)   (1311)   (1314)
A becomes reconciled with an enemy, A-3, when A-3 renders him a service (815a ch A to A-3 & A-4 to A)   (829 ch A-3 to A-8 & B to A-3)

913

(379)   (457 ch A to A-2)
A, suffering misfortune, seeks happiness in the companionship of A-2 and in playing golf (157 ch A-3 to A-2)   (603b, c, d)   (807)   (820)   (981)   (1007)   (1035)

914

(817 ch B to CH)   (911)
A is a gambler pursuing his blackleg vocation * A handicaps himself by taking charge of an abandoned baby, CH ** (847)   (963)   (1087)

915

(623)   (1186)   (1282)   A flees to a foreign country to escape the consequences of a transgression * A, a fugitive in a foreign land, becomes so homesick for his own country that he has to return ** (237)   (635)   (635; 708)   (864)   (1199)   (1209a)

916

(60)   (816b)   B, her lot cast in a lonely place, craves excitement as a condition necessary to happiness (88)   (143)   (414)   (694)   (765)   (844a)

(32) Seeking to Conceal Identity Because of a Lofty Idealism

917

(512)   (952)   (971)
A mysteriously disappears from his own community; and, when he reappears among strangers, he bears a fictitious name * A, seeking to forward an enterprise which those who know him might consider absurd or unworthy, changes his name and goes secretly to a place where he is unknown ** (259-3)   (967)

918

(a) (80a) (150) (312-1) (602)
A seeks to rebuild his life wasted in dissipation, along the lines of exemplary ideals *
A, in carrying out a worthy enterprise, changes his name and goes to a place where
he is unknown ** (683) (708) (864)

(b) (718b) (898)
A undergoes a tragic experience which results in a beneficial character change
(639) (686) (751) (767 ch B to A) (819) (894 ch A to A-8 & A-5 to A)

919

(a) (940) (949a) (960) (1082a)
A, a soldier, disappears from the ranks * A, a soldier, disappears from the ranks
and dies secretly and heroically for an ideal of duty; but he is reported "a deserter
under fire" ** (919c) (928b ch A to F-A & SN to A)

(b) (930 ch B to D-A & F-B to A) (734) (967)
A, a soldier, is a deserter under fire but falsely reported "missing in action" * A,
after long years of wandering as an outcast, returns as an Unknown to his own
home ** (548a) (550) (684 ch F-B to A) (797)

(c) (615) (1061)
A, a soldier, is reported "a deserter under fire" * A, a soldier facing a large force
of the enemy, fights against overwhelming odds until he is killed ** (930 ch F-B to
A & eliminate "whom she mistakenly thinks is dead") (928b ch A to F-A & SN
to A) (958) (963)

920

A, humble and supporting himself by menial tasks (718a) (748) (749-*), loses
a work of art (709 tr A & A-2) (711b ch A to A-2) about which there are no marks
of identification. The work of art, X, is found and pronounced by connoisseurs
to be the production of a master. In the public prints the unknown artist is invited to come forward and receive the honors and wealth to which his genius entitles him. But A's ideal is "art for art's sake," and he will not be tempted (1275)
(931 ch B to A & M-B to F-A)

921

(279-*) (435a)
B realizes that her happiness and her duty lie in rehabilitating her character; in
establishing, under an assumed name, an exemplary character and thus to make
amends for a grievous wrong committed under her real name (279*-**) (743b)
(665)

(35) Becoming Involved in a Complication that Challenges
the Value of Cherished Ideals

922

(a) (578a) (819) (894 tr A & A-5) (918b) A has low ideals, but changes
them abruptly for high ideals * A searches everywhere for a Good Man, whom he
envisons and personifies, but who evades him ** (963) (964a)

(b) (158) (606)
A has high ideals but, on suffering misfortune, he changes his high ideals for low
ideals * A becomes a "bum," an outcast and a wanderer ** (259-2) (263)

923

(224) (578a)
A, a crook, is trying to "go straight" * A, a crook trying to "go straight," is compelled by A-5, the leader of his old gang, to take part in a criminal enterprise **
(894) (998 ch A to A-5 & A-4 to A)

924

(a)   (700)   (1062)
A, wealthy, d•sires with all his heart to live as a poor man * A, wealthy and desiring to live as a poor man, finds that his wealth makes it impossible ** (431)   (929)

(b)   (898)   (899)
A, wealthy, seeks to lead a life of idleness and luxurious leisure * A is wealthy, and his ideal life is a life of leisure—but he meets with an experience that challenges his ideal ** (322b)   (751)

925

(139; 245 ch A to A-2 & A-3 to A)   (433b ch A to A-2 & A-3 to A; 411b ch A to A-2, A-3 to A)
A is a "man of the world," relentlessly looking out for "Number One" and having little regard for others * A grievously wrongs his friend, A-2, and is taught a beneficial lesson when A-2 freely forgives him ** (922a)   (963)

926

(954)   (970)
A's lofty aim is to be a benefactor of mankind * A, trying to realize his ideal of being a benefactor of mankind, meets with a disturbing experience ** (188b)   (613)   (791)   (804)

927

(926)   (928a)
A seeks to throw open his home to friends and strangers alike, and be generously hospitable, but certain unpleasant conditions make it difficult (613)   (905)

928

(a)   (764-*)   (769)   (772-*)   (773-*)   (805)
A, in a spirit of altruism, befriends all in need * A is never too busy to give aid to others and, because of it, he has an unpleasant experience ** (764*-**)   (772*-**) (773*-**)   (807)

(b)   (800 ch B to A)
A is proud of his son, SN * A's son, SN, dies a shameful, inglorious death, bringing dishonor and sorrow to A ** (568c ch A to A-8 & A-3 to SN)   (821)   (919a)

929

(431; 488a)   (924a)
A, believing poverty the key to happiness, changes his ideals when he finds himself wealthy, and happy as he had never been in the days of his poverty

930

(919b-* ch A to F-B)   (1142b ch A to F-B)
B builds a monument to her father, F-B, whom she mistakenly thinks is dead, and whose memory is to her a source of pride and honor (684)   (797 ch A to F-B & D-A to B)

931

(65-*)   (83)   (143)   (766)   (1105)   (1106)   B is happy in her mistaken ideals * B is compelled to challenge the value of her ideals when she sees her mother, M-B, pursuing them ** (1246)

(50) Being Impelled by an Unusual Motive to Engage in Crafty Enterprise

932

(1111a)   (1074)
A is a writer who plans to work up a pet idea into a story * A, a writer, before he begins work on a story, wishes to make sure that the tale he has in mind will be interesting to the general public. He plans to settle the question by secret enterprise ** (598)   (835)   (1460)

933

(104)   (189)
B decides that there is more to be gained by suffering defeat in an enterprise than by being successful (356)   (931)

124

(17) Bearing Patiently with Misfortunes and Seeking to Attain Cherished Aims Honorably

934

(181b-*) (425-*)
A, father of SN, renounces happiness in order to uphold a lofty conception of duty and save SN from disgrace (881) (181b*-**) (425*-***) (330b ch F-A to A & A to SN)

935

(718b) (948 ch B to A)
A, penniless, exchanges ten years of servitude for a college education (595) (756) (918b)

936

(512) (513) (1006b) (1073)
A's cherished ideal is the sea, and far-flung adventures * A cannot realize his cherished ideal because he is compelled to work at a desk job in order to support himself and his dependents ** (991) (1148a)

937

(687) (689) (690)
A is a morally superior person * A, a morally superior person, is cast away in a vicious, isolated, primitive environment where moral inferiority assails his high idealism on every side ** (197) (244) (682) (901) (973)

938

(941) (1122)
A is a clever craftsman who struggles to earn a living while upholding his ideals * A, if he chooses, could win vast wealth by sacrificing his high principles ** (943a) (944)

939

(485) (922a) (926)
A seeks good in evil by culling lessons in good out of his association with transgressors—inspiration for contentment out of his misfortunes (907) (772) (1167)

940

(939) (900-*)
A is a man of wealth and influence who feels that the gold of his true worth is obscured by the dross of his riches * A enlists as a private in the army when he might easily have secured an officer's commission ** (918b) (919a, c)

941

(171) (748)
A seeks, through idealism, to be content with life in spite of a grinding poverty that makes life wretched (942) (943a) (922b)

942

(903) (941)
A has fallen upon evil days and luck goes against him in every way * A clings to his lofty ideals through all his vicissitudes of fortune ** (601) (632) (944)

943

(a) (700) (715b) (729)
A starves to death in holding fast to a lofty conception of duty * A starves to death rather than amass wealth by shattering his ideals **

(b) (824) (987) (1014) (1022)
A, a prisoner, dies holding fast to a lofty conception of duty rather than win freedom by shattering his ideals of loyalty (80b) (136)

944

(171) (549) (715b) (729) (938) (942)
A is a gentleman of the "old school," who comes through life enduring with patient fortitude every manner of misfortune; and then, at last, poverty stricken and pronounced a failure according to all the material standards of the world, he still clings to his high ideals and counts his vicissitudes, which could not overcome his ideals, as blessings in disguise (907)

945

(121)   (244)   (179-*)   (162b-*)   (665)
B, as the world regarded her, was a moral transgressor; but, in her own estimation, she was seeking the best and noblest in life * B, considered a moral transgressor, through her magnetic personality and the sincerity of her convictions, disarmed criticism in life and was praised by all after she died ** (211)

946

(162b)   (211)   (279)   (403)   (557a)
B, a transgressor, tries to live down her unfortunate past by exemplary conduct (665)   (669)   (892)

947

(96)   (745)   (647)   (976)
B seeks to remain a good woman in spite of a vicious, morally inferior environment (242)   (645)

948

(947)   (978)
B's parents, M-B and F-B, are "just poor white trash," but lowly B struggles for an education that will lift her out of her squalid environment (745)   (935 ch A to B)   (993)

(34) Embarking Upon an Enterprise of Insurrection in the Hope of Ameliorating Certain Evil Conditions

949

a)   (395)   (420-*)   (915)
A's capricious fancy, groping toward happiness, leads him to depart from the strict line of duty (148)   (155)   (420)   (628)

(b)   (246b-*)   (322b)
A is a police magistrate with lofty humanitarian ideals * A, a police magistrate who wishes to know more of the private lives of those who are brought before him for judgment, disguises himself as a "bum" and plunges into the underworld ** (833)   (834)   (838)   (876a)   (1209b)

950

(1082b)   (1090)   (1111b)   (1131)
A's half-knowledge of the world constitutes his handicap * A believes he can be happier and more successful as a lawyer than as a doctor, as a general than as a private, as his own "boss" than by working for somebody else ** A feels that he can do more good outside the priesthood than as a priest *** (900)   (1091)   (1098)   (1104)

951

(68)   (255)   (703)   (1304)   (1306)
A's happiness lies in freeing himself of a torturing conscience * A will suffer ruin and disgrace if he carries out his plan to free himself of a torturing conscience ** (1295)   (1461a)

952

(465)   (601; 1277b)   (606; 1277b)
A's ambition, one that is necessary to his happiness, is to fall out of the world that knows him * A leaves his coat on a cliff at the seaside, drops his hat in a stunted tree below the brink, and vanishes from the scenes that know him ** (440)   (864)

953

(74a-*)   (604)   (651)
A, for reasons of his own, craves peace and quiet * A, desiring peace and quiet, finds his ideal retreat in a vacant house, and there he secretly takes up his quarters ** (664)   (719a)   (1409)   (1423)   (1225)

954

(106-*)   (539a)   (863a)
A, through erring imagination, becomes discontented with his life and surroundings * A, discontented, in a spirit of revolt seeks to achieve contentment ** (106*-**) (391)

955

(1298)   (1300)
A, a highwayman, is robbing the mails * A, a highwayman, opening a letter that
falls into his hands, secures information (738)   (742)   (743a) that sends him away
on an altruistic undertaking—all by the way of proving that there "is good in
the worst of us" ** (817)   (869)

(20)   Becoming Involved with Conditions in which
Misfortune is Indicated

956

(279)   (669 ch A-5 to A-8)   (557a)   (377a ch A to A-8)
B volunteers to nurse a sick person, A-8, when no one else will undertake the work *
A-8 is ill of a disease that is contagious and deadly ** B, nursing A-8, contracts a
contagious disease and dies ***

957

(a)   (898-*)   (899-*)   A becomes so wealthy and powerful that, in the overweening pride of his mistaken ideals he voices the query: "Is there any god greater
than I?"   (517)   (565)   (661)

(b)   (902)   A is a general in the army * A, a general in the army, is engaged in
an unimportant enterprise, and he is so absorbed in it that he gives no attention
to the attacking enemy.   A's troops are defeated ** (919b, c)

(c)   (692 ch A to A-4)   (719b ch A to A-4)
A is captain of a steamship, racing across the Atlantic in an attempt to cut down
the time of the passage * A refuses to delay his important enterprise long enough
to rescue A-4, a person in distress and facing death ** (632 tr A & A-4)

(33)   Resisting Secretly and from an Honorable Motive
a Mandate Considered Discreditable

958

(748)   (918a)
A takes issue with the accepted belief that poverty is the source of discontent,
and conceives it to be the true source of happiness * A struggles against difficulties
in seeking to avoid wealth ** (127b)   (311)   (326-3)   (700)   (905)

959

(861)   (954)   (1088)
A, with negro blood in his veins, aspires to all the opportunities of the white race
(255)   (271)   (579b tr B & A)   (919c)

960

(a)   (922a-*)   (928b ch A to F-A & SN to A)
A is a soldier, eager to fight but who is commanded to retreat before a superior
force of the enemy * A receives orders from his superiors which he considers discreditable ** (919b)   (919c; 928b ch A to F-A & SN to A)

(b)   (902)
A is a general in the army * A, a general, when the enemy attack, is engaged in an
unimportant enterprise, and he is so absorbed in it that he will not give it up.
A's troops are defeated ** (705)   (919b, c)

961

(606)   (1079)
A's pride rebels against the loss of his ancestral acres through poverty (628)   (656)

962

(740)   (946)
B, who finds her happiness in a beautiful garden, learns that the garden is about
to be destroyed (737a)   (975)   (848b; 1445)

(36) Undergoing an Experience that Results in a Remarkable Character Change

963   •

(322b) (715a) (763) (862) (914) (922a)
A discards low ideals for high ideals * A, discarding low ideals for high ideals, struggles in vain to realize his high ideals; but, although baffled in realizing his cherished ambition, he effects a beneficial change in his character ** (188b) (563c)

964

(a) (839 tr A & A-2) (888) (898) (1418b-*)
A, becoming aware of an old prophecy, unconsciously seeks to become like the exalted protagonist of the prophecy (963) (1418b*-**)

(b) (540) (797) (1209a)
A, a transgressor, returns to his home as an Unknown after a long absence, and meets his daughter, D-A * A, a transgressor, learning that his daughter, D-A, thinks he is dead, and that his character was high and noble, does not reveal his identity but leaves D-A happy in her mistaken ideals ** (963) (964a)

(37)· Seeking Against Difficulties to Realize a Cherished Ideal

965

(1060) (1088) (1091)
A's one desire is to achieve a high honor, an honor that is unmerited, and to enjoy that honor is a condition necessary to happiness (749) (863b) (1101) (1103)

966

(539a) (965) (1150)
A has set his heart on accomplishing something beyond his powers, and his happiness depends upon his success * As [1] writing a great poem, [2] becoming famous as a composer of music, [3] demonstrating the power of science to set aside the laws of heredity, [4] painting a great picture or [5] performing an act of great daring (1058) (1065) (1075a)

967

(770a) (917) (919b) (864) (797) (763) (918a)
A has been mysteriously absent from his home for long years * A, for many years mysteriously absent from his home, seeks a happy renewal of old ties by returning suddenly and unheralded to his native place ** (869) (923) (1199)

968

(926) (939)
A is a young man of lofty ideals * A, a young man of lofty ideals, craves all sorts of experiences in order that he may find the best and noblest in life ** (773) (786) (937) (74a, b) (188b)

969

(620; 962 ch B to A) (620; 974 ch B to A)
A, a city toiler, cherishes a dear desire for the open fields and the song of the lark (608) (625) (683)

970

(922a-*) (926) (927) (928a)
A befriends any strangers who may be in need of assistance, often neglecting his own family in carrying out his generous enterprises (848a) (613) (612) (707 tr A & A-4) (772)

971

(322b) (577) (681a) (863a) (969)
A believes solitude the greatest of human blessings * A, believing solitude to be the greatest of human blessings, encounters difficulties in his search for it ** (664) (683) (686) (690)

972

(922b; 820)   (922b; 859 ch A to A-2)   (922b; 824 ch B to A-2)
A is a worthless ne'er-do-well, while his friend, A-2, is a man of worth in the world *
A resolves, at any cost to himself, to save his friend, A-2, from threatening misfortune ** (823)   (833)   (836)

973

(650)   (687)   (689)   (937)
A, a white man battling against the superstitious frenzy of a half-savage tribe stricken with the plague, upholds the highest ideals of the white man's civilization (888)   (796)

974

(969 ch A to B)   (921)
B, reared in the slums of a large city and seeking her ideal of happiness in the woods and open fields, comes finally to live in a drab, cheerless countryside (31)   (31; 763)   (563c)   (848b)   (916)

975

(741)   (743b)   (873)
B is in failing health and her days numbered * B, in failing health and her days numbered, feels that she cannot die happy until she sees again her native place, and re-visits the well-remembered haunts of her childhood ** (893)   (945)

976

(145)   (268)   (325)   (372)   (565)
B believes that the practice of the religious virtues is the crying need of the world, and seeks by her own life to exemplify her convictions (242)   (737b)   (796 ch A to B & A-3 to B-3)

977

(a)   (992 ch F-B to M-B)
B is determined to protect the honor of her family, but she can do so only by following the path of relentless duty (668)   (649)   (993)

(b)   (977a)   (976)
B's brother, BR-B, has committed a crime * B, apprised of a crime committed by her brother, BR-B, informs the police and has BR-B arrested ** (730 ch A to BR-B) (909)

978

(668)   (670)   (948)
B's mother, M-B, cherishes the fixed desire to give B a good education * B and her mother, M-B, are penniless, and B has to work to support the two of them ** (647)   (659)   (935 ch A to B)

(21) Falling Into Misfortune Through Mistaken Judgment

979

(747; 606)   (769)   (898)
A has innocently caused a number of people to invest money in a worthless enterprise * A, having innocently caused a number of people to lose money in an enterprise, feels that he cannot rest content until, by his own efforts, he recovers the money for the losers and restores it ** (610)   (635)   (1148b)

980

(1382a ch A t o A-4; 985)   (718b)
A, by undertaking an obligation finds himself threatened by misfortune * A, by concealment and stratagem, transfers a dangerous obligation to A-8, a stranger ** (608 ch A to A-8)   (623 ch A to A-8)   (709 ch A to A-8 & A-2 to A)   (1161 ch A to A-8)

981

(830 tr A & A-2)   (865)
A, in return for a service A-2 has rendered him, agrees to grant any favor A-2 may ask that is within his power (601)   (836)   (838)

982

(a)   (611a ch A to NW)   (999 tr A & A-2)
A agrees to take in hand and control an incorrigible youth, NW, who has proved too hard a problem for his uncle and guardian, A's friend, A-2 (658)   (701 ch A-2 to NW)   (812b ch A to NW & F-B to A)

(b)   (193-*)   (926)
A, a bachelor, undertakes to care for CH, the child of his married sister, SR-A, while SR-A is away on a vacation (609)   (193*-**)   (639 ch A to CH)

983

(433b ch A to A-8 & A-3 to A)   (1251-*)
A, in order to get A-8 into his power, craftily manoeuvers him heavily into debt * A hopes to secure A-8's help in an undertaking by offering to free him from debt ** (313 ch F-B to A-8, A to A-2 & A-3 to A)   (380 ch A to A-8 & A-3 to A)   (1251*-**)

984

(1001b-*)
A, after B dies, carries out honorably the distasteful obligation to travel (1001b*-**) (1019)   (1044a)   (1001b-*; 1041 ch A to U)

985

(793b-* ch A-2 to A-4)   (805)   (809 ch A-5 to A-4)
A is threatened with misfortune because of a mysterious parcel (1382b-* ch A to A-4), which he has obligingly taken from A-4, a stranger, and promised to deliver (608)   (1438b)   (793*-**)

986

(16a)   (1258)   (1293a)   (1293b)   (1309b)   (403 ch A to A-8; 468 ch A to A-8)
A, a detective, returns B, a criminal, to the scene of her crime for trial and punishment * B, a criminal who has undergone a character change and become an honest woman, is given her liberty by the jury before whom she is tried ** (363a)   (359)

(38) Committing a Grievous Mistake and Seeking in Secret to Live Down Its Evil Results

987

(1319a)   (1214)   A, influenced by a compelling idea of responsibility, finds it necessary to protect his friend, A-2, from a secret danger * A is indirectly the cause of danger to his friend, A-2—danger of which A-2 is ignorant and of which A cannot tell him ** (867)   (1227a)

988

(1023)   (1027)
A's friend, A-2, was the father of B; and, when A-2 died, A promised him he would care for B as though she were his own child * A is disloyal to B, his ward ** (1211) (1285b)

(39) Forsaking Cherished Ambitions to Carry Out an Obligation

989

(697a)   (990)   (991)   (996 ch B to A & M-B to M-A)
A's promise to his mother, M-A, prevents him from undertaking a cherished enterprise (936)   (1097a)

990

(258)   (697a)
A's family all worked in order that he might be helped to a technical education * A conceives it to be his duty to work at a calling he dislikes so that he may repay his family for their sacrifices ** (991)   (1130)   (1434)

991

(513)   (990)
A, unable to realize a cherished ambition because of family obligations, comes as near realizing the ambition as he can * A seeks theoretical adventure, "armchair" adventure—the thrill of high emprise caught second-hand from travel books ** (1433b; 719b; 878b; 650; 714; 197; 957a)   (1433b; 1082b; 24a; 181c; 1363)   (433b; 109)

992

(268-*)   (976)
B makes a great personal sacrifise in order to carry out a filial obligation to live with her father, F-B, and make a home for him (368a)   (641)   (993)

993

(601 ch A to F-B; 705 ch A to F-B)   (606 ch A to F-B; 705 ch A to F-B)
B's father, F-B, dies heavily involved in debt * B, the only child of her father, F-B, considers herself in honor bound to pay the debts of the deceased F-B, and undertakes a strange enterprise in order to carry out the obligation ** (88)   (1032)

994

(574b ch A to SN & B to B-8 & M-A to B)   (1009a)
B, a widow, finds her happiness in being independent * B, a widow, is compelled by family obligations to live with a married son, SN ** (543 ch B to B-8, A to SN & M-A to B)   (800)   (1067)

995

(747 ch A to F-B; 705 ch A to F-B)   (770a ch A to F-B; 634 ch A to F-B)
B labors for years at a lonely task * B labors for years at a lonely task in order to clear the name of her father, F-B, from dishonor ** (828 ch A to B, B to F-B & B-5 to A-5)   (993)

996

(285 ch F-B to M-B)   (948)
B's mother, M-B, denies herself the necessities of life in fulfilling her duty to educate B (659)   (670)   (785)   (1151 ch B to M-B & D-B to B)

(20) Becoming Involved with Conditions in Which Misfortune is Indicated

997

(a)   (830 tr A & A-2)   (865)   A, on his sacred honor, has promised his friend, A-2, that he will do whatever A-2 shall require of him (139)   (820)   (846)   (906) (1003)   (1007)

(b) (925-* ch A to U) (926) (958) (700)
A has $500,000. A rich relative, U, bequeaths a million dollars to A, provided
he shall spend his half-million within a year * A, with a half million dollars must
be "broke" within a year, and he must not give away any money nor spend a cent
foolishly ** (431) (865)

998

(613 ch A-5 to A-4) (1277a ch A to A-4)
A secretly discovers a delinquency A-4 wishes to conceal * A, secretly informed
regarding a transgression A-4 wishes to conceal, threatens to inform the authorities
unless A-4 does something A wants him to do ** (923 ch A to A-4 & A-5 to A)
(1232 ch A to A-4 & A-3 to A) (1267a ch A to A-4)

999

(611a ch A to NW) (1024 ch A to NW)
A's nephew and ward, NW, is wild and reckless and A is unable to manage him *
A passes his unmanageable nephew and ward, NW, along to a friend in the West,
A-2, who declares that he will either kill NW or tame him ** (793a tr A & A-2) (982a
tr A & A-2)

(41) Finding an Obligation at Variance with Ambition, Inclination or Necessity

1000

(905) (925-*)
A is the scion of a proud old line whose greatest pride has been to keep its estates
intact * A, in desperate need, ignores a family obligation ** (1260a tr A & A-8)
(1291c)

1001

(a) (127a) (1123) (1127)
A finds it necessary to carry out a certain distasteful enterprise if he would attain
wealth (1201) (1290b)

(b) (117 ch F-A to U) (1432 ch A to U & NW to A)
A is to inherit a fortune from his uncle, U, on condition that he shall never leave
his native land * B, an enemy of U who has left a fortune to A on condition that
he shall never travel abroad, wins a promise from A that he will travel abroad
after she dies ** (984) (116 ch B to B-8)

1002

(106-*) (988-*)
A is a woman-hater * A, against his wish and inclination, becomes the guardian
of a beautiful young woman, B ** (140) (106*-**) (988*-**)

1003

(818a-**) (983 tr A & A-8) (997a)
A is under an obligation to commit a crime * A, under an obligation to commit
a crime, is not a criminal at heart and cannot meet the obligation ** (818a**-***)
(1014)

1004

(249) (263) (1194-*) (1248)
A, a doctor who is also a crook, is returning at night from a successful burglary
job, when he is hastily summoned to attend a very sick person, A-8 (1194*-**)
(1196) (1221)

1005

(913 ch A-2 to BR-A) (137a ch A-3 to BR-A) (1021b ch A-2 to BR-A)
A and BR-A are twin brothers with the same likes and dislikes * A and BR-A,
brothers, carry out honorably the distasteful obligation of living apart ** (157 ch
A-3 to BR-A) (446a, b ch A-2 to BR-A)

132

1006

(a) (446b ch A-2 to A-5; 1291a ch A to A-5) (1290b ch A to A-5)
A, a lawyer, honorably discharges the distasteful duty of defending a criminal, A-5
(828 ᶜh B to A & A-5 to A-8) (1311 ch A-3 to A-5)

(b) (287) (334a) (756) (936)
A, in order to carry out an obligation, gives up his chosen profession and enters
another line of work (900) (942) (950)

1007

(132) (607) (997a)
A carries out honorably the heart-breaking obligation of killing his friend, A-2,
hopelessly ill and tortured with suffering * A-2 begs relief at A's hands as an act
of mercy ** A-2 is the brother of B, who is very dear to A *** (296 ch A-3 to A-2)
(315)

1008

(775) (1212c) (775 ch A to A-9 & A-7 to A)
A, trusted butler in the household of A-9, is really a crook * A, using his position
in the household of A-9 as a "cover" to his black designs, loots the jewel box of
A-9's wife, B, and departs secretly between two days ** (610) (614) (1209a)

1009

(a) (908) (574b ch A to SN-B, "son of B", M-A to B & B to B-8)
B, a widow, wishes to be independent and to have a home of her own; but there
are certain obligations at war with her desire (384 ch B to B-8 & M-A to B) (933)
(1009b)

(b) (531 ch B to B-8 & M-A to B & A to SN) (994) (1009a)
B, a widow, has given all her money to her son, SN * B, penniless, is compelled
to live with her son, SN ** (543 ch B to B-8, M-A to B & A to SN) (738)

1010

(152b) (666)
B, ordered by thieves, A-5, A-5, A-5, to open a safe belonging to A, refuses in
spite of threats against her life (144) (1309a ch A to A-5)

(40) Embarking Upon an Enterprise in which One
Obligation is Opposed by Another Obligation

1011

(723) (712 ch A to A-5 & A-6 to A) (1013 ch A to A-5 & A-6 to A)
A, an officer of the law, is under a personal obligation to a criminal, A-5 * A, an
officer of the law, is compelled by duty to arrest a criminal, A-5, to whom he is
under an obligation ** (1016a) (1284)

1012

(276 ch A to GCH & F-A to A) (288 ch A to GCH and "ancestor" to A)
A's impecunious grandchild, GCH, buys A a birthday present, X, on credit * X,
a birthday present, will not be delivered until it is paid for ** A pays for X, a birthday present, which his impecunious grandchild, GCH, is giving him *** (118 ch
A to GCH & GF-A to A) (628 ch A to GCH & B to A)

1013

(722 ch A to A-6 & A-5 to A)
A, a fugitive in the desert, discovers that the officer who is pursuing him, A-6, is
sunblind and dying from thirst * A, a fugitive from justice, will be arrested if he
rescues A-6, the officer who is pursuing him, from misfortune; and if A abandons
A-6, A-6 will die ** (712) (817 ch B to A-6)

1014

(171 ch A-3 to A-5) (959)
A, a cashier responsible for the funds of the firm employing him, is ordered by A-5 (1079 ch A to A-5), junior partner of the firm, to give him secretly a large sum of the firm's money (730 ch A-3 to A-5) (884a) (1003)

1015

(1174 ch A to A-5 & A-2 to A-8) (1175a ch A to A-5)
A is a United States consul * A lives on an island, and on the same island are two other white men, A-2 and A-5, both friends of A's * A-6, an officer of the law, calls on A to help him arrest A-5 ** (1175b ch A to A-5) (1174 ch A to A-5;,1222a ch A to A-6 & A-3 to A-5) (1282 ch A to A-5)

1016

(a) (817 ch A to A-5 & B to A; 1011) (1013 ch A to A-5 & A-6 to A; 1011)
A, a police officer, has captured a criminal, A-5 * A, a police officer, is under an obligation of professional duty to arrest A-5, and he is under a counter-obligation of a personal nature to help A-5 ** A cuts a Gordian knot by taking poison ***

(b) (972 tr A & A-2) (1021b)
A, an army officer, has a friend, A-2, one of the enemy and a spy, brought before him for punishment by court-martial * A's friend, A-2, rescues A from a heart-breaking situation by killing himself **

1017

(712 ch A to A-5 & A-6 to A) (816a ch A to A-5 & A-4 to A)
A, an officer of the law, and A-5, his prisoner, are lost in the desert, afoot, without food and with only a small supply of water—not enough for the two of them * A, an officer of the law, is old; and A-5, his prisoner, is young, and there are extenuating circumstances in his case (1309b ch B to A-5) (1291b ch A to A-5) (747 ch A to A-5) ** A and A-5, officer of the law and prisoner, are lost in the desert with only a small supply of water between them. They draw lots to see which shall take the water and make his escape. A cheats in the drawing so that A-5 may win. A-5 picks up the water canteen and abandons A to die *** (713 ch A to A-5) (918b ch A to A-5)

(42) Falling Into Misfortune While Seeking Honorably to Discharge an Obligation

1018

(606 ch A to F-A; 705 ch A to F-A or 638 ch A to F-A)
A, the son of F-A, feels it his duty to sell all his property in order to help pay the debts of the deceased F-A (268 tr B & A) (943a) (944)

1019

(791) (1434)
A is the recipient of anonymous threats of violence if he tries to carry out an obligation * A, threatened anonymously with violence if he carries out an obligation, proceeds boldly with what he believes to be his duty ** (1287) (1351) (1414a) (1422a) (1424a) (1427a)

1020

(70) (445b) (1075a, b) (1125b)
A, pledged to die if B dies, learns that B has committed suicide (576b) (802b)

1021

(a) (769) (836) (265b-*; 836)
A, as a favor to his friend, A-2, promises to undertake a certain enterprise * A promises his friend, A-2, to undertake a certain enterprise, and then forgets his promise ** (603a tr A & A-2) (807) (744 ch B to A-2)

(b) (716) (782 ch A-8 to A-2)
A and A-2 are as Damon and Pythias, David and Jonathan * A and A-2 have their ideal of friendship challenged by an unusual experience ** (1016b) (1021a)

1022

(136-*) (883)
A's life is saved by his enemy, A-3 * A's life, saved by his enemy, A-3, is mutually agreed to be forfeit to A-3 whenever A-3 so desires ** (136*-**) (280a; 136*-**)

(21) Falling Into Misfortune Throu~h Mistaken Judgment

1023

(113) (461) (606)
A is desperately in need of money * A, desperately in need of money, undertakes a rash enterprise and becomes involved in an unpleasant complication ** (637) (753) (860) (1290a) (1373)

1024

(718b) (1297)
A is young, and had considerable money, but by a wild life he impoverishes himself and comes to want * For A, beating back to Easy Street has its difficulties ** (628) (1084) (1101) (1144) (1386a)

1025

(470) (890) (1033) (1100) (1154a) (1172)
B is carrying out a secret enterprise and falls into danger * B, carrying out a secret enterprise and falling into danger. appeals for aid to a stranger, A-4; but A-4 is wary and refuses assistance ** (933) (1309a) (1417)

(20) Becoming Involved with Conditions in Which Misfortune is Indicated

1026

(622 ch A to F-A & SN to A) (1024)
A is an outcast son, sorely in need of money * A seeks to borrow a large sum of money from A-8, a money-lender, on his prospects of inheriting the estate of his wealthy father, F-A ** (1217b) (1226 ch A to A-8 & A-5 to A)

1027

(770a) (1023)
A, hard-pressed for money, is beguiled by the devil into an unwise proceeding (637) (1341) (1354a) (1373)

1028

(113) (114)
A, in needy circumstances, acts as a tailor's dummy for a young millionaire, A-9, who dislikes the annoyance of trying on his new clothes * A, for services rendered, receives the cast-off clothes of a young millionaire, A-9 ** (1146 ch A to A-9) (1163a ch A to A-9 & A-4 to A) (1168 ch A to A-2 & A-9)

1029

(522) (523) (620) (656) (1257)
A, a man of ability who has fallen upon evil days and is almost bankrupt, meets with unpleasant complications in seeking to recoup his fortunes (1217a) (1236) (1254) (1256)

1030

(608) (623)
A, innocent, is in the hands of the police on a groundless charge * A, in the hands of the police, must be free at once in order to carry out a certain enterprise, and cannot wait to prove his innocence ** (73) (130) (174)

1031

(926) (1248) A, a doctor, while taking an evening stroll, is summoned hurriedly to attend a sick person. He meets with evil experiences (1194) (1447)

1032

(745) (993) B seeks employment, but her sex is against her * B, in order to carry out an enterprise, resorts to a stratagem ** (1207) (1454)

1033

(532a) (659) (739) B, sorely in need of money, undertakes a rash enterprise (368b) (1159) (1293a)

(21) Falling Into Misfortune Through Mistaken Judgment

1034

(957c ch A to A-8) (1107a ch A to A-8)
A, an inventor, is secretly testing out an invention * A, an inventor secretly testing out an invention, so delays in mid-ocean a ship carrying a fabulous cargo of bullion that fears are entertained for the ship's safety ** (1052b ch A to A-8) (1116 ch A to A-8)

1035

(139) (1021b) (1234 tr A & A-2)
A, thinking he has a robber to deal with, by mistake shoots his friend, A-2 (794) (786 ch A to A-2)

(20) Becoming Involved with Conditions in Which Misfortune is Indicated

1036

(702 ch A to A-8) (1187)
A is a plain man of mediocre abilities * A, of an humble station in life, is mistaken for A-4, a celebrity ** (1161) (1173)

1037

(1146) (1164 ch A to A-9, A-4 to A-8 & A-8 to A) (1224)
A is impersonating A-8, when he is confronted by A-8 in person (998 ch A-4 to A-8) (1232 ch A-3 to A-8)

1038

(1170) (1177)
A, highly placed, wealthy and influential, has exactly the same name as a characterless individual, A-8, who lives in the same community (1146 ch A to A-8) (1448 ch A to A-8, A-5 to A & A-8 to A-4)

1039

(1314) (1316)
A is seeking the life of A-3, an enemy * A, seeking the life of A-3, follows A-4 with murder in his heart; for A-4, by chance, is wearing the hat and coat of A-3 ** (1035 ch A-2 to A-4) (1311 ch A-3 to A-4)

1040

(130) (174) (599 tr A & A-2)
A is on his way to keep an important engagement * A is injured in an accident and taken unconscious to a hospital ** (500a) (681b) (711b)

1041

(118 ch A to A-8 & GF-A to A) (825) (389-***) (899) (1433a)
A, on his way to execute a new will disposing of his estate, meets death in an accident (389***-*****) (1432)

1042

(a) (619) (1195)
A carelessly leaves a door unlocked while engaged in a secret enterprise * A, engaged in a secret enterprise, suffers a chance intrusion and discovery owing to his own carelessness ** (879) (1448 tr A & A-5)

(b) (153) (63 tr A & B)
A has a jewler, A-9, send to his friend, A-2, a silver whiskey flask, and to B (976) an expensive "slave" bracelet * A's presents to A-2 and B are in packages, and the packages are transposed by A-9 with unfortunate results ** (321a) (635 ch A-5 to A-9)

1043

(601) (606) (652a) A sells a gold mine of little value tentatively to A-8 at a bargain price. A-8 delays turning over the money and getting the deed * A's gold mine, seemingly of little value, is turned into a "bonanza" b-- a lucky strike ** (1255b) (1255b; 1040) (1255b; 1040 ch A to A-8)

1044

(a) (513) (923) (1167) (1177) (1186)
A unwittingly takes a suit case belonging to a stranger, A-4, when leaving a train, leaving his own suitcase in place of A-4's * A's suit case is in the hands of a stranger, A-4. The train is wrecked and A-4 is killed. A, on the evidence of his own suit case, is reported a casualty ** (550) (608) (917)

(b) (370 ch A to A-2) (378 ch A to A-2)
A unwittingly takes an object, X-1, belonging to his friend, A-2, leaving for A-2 a similar object, X-2, in place of X-1. Close inspection is necessary to discover the difference between X-1 and X-2 (390) (390-**; 594c ch A to A-2)

1045

(1444; 1364a) (1444; 1384)
A, in a half doze, overhears a chance conversation that concerns a transgression; but he is in doubt as to whether he overheard a real conversation, or was deceived by a dreaming mind (828) (1453)

1046

(677 ch B to A) (664 ch A to A-4) (1389b)
A is strolling through the streets of a large city at dead of night * A is suddenly arrested by an object, X, that drops in front of him from the upper window of a house ** (1364a ch B to A) (1369) (1394) (1400) (1425) (1435)

1047

(666 ch A to A-8) (848a)
A, a blind man, is groping his way along the street * A, a blind man, answering a wild call for help, stumbles into a nest of crooks, A-5, A-5, A-5, who are engaged in a criminal enterprise ** (27) (801) (1220b ch A to A-5) (1128) (1253 ch A-3 to A-5)

1048

(1304) (1296) (1298)
A, years after he has stolen money from A-2, by merest chance and unwittingly happens to stop for the night with A-2 and his wife, B * B, and her husband, A-2, meeting A, by chance discover secretly that A has with him a bag of unset diamonds ** (1279b) (1291b) (1325) (1309a)

1049

(675) (747-*) (815-*)
A, when in doubt regarding his course of action in any enterprise, flips a coin to let chance decide. This has always been his custom, and it has invariably been successful; but there comes a time when the coin proves unreliable (747*-**) (815a*-**) (836) (837) (848a)

1050

(3a) (524a)
A is disagreeably surprised when, by chance, he finds stolen jewels in the possession of B (69) (566b) (623 ch A to B)

(15) Finding a Sustaining Power in Misfortune

1051

(245) (364a-*) (697b) (1089)
A, finding by chance an aged nurse, B-7, learns from her a secret of birth and parentage which means happiness for him (364*-**) (368b)

1052

(a) (1369 ch A-4 to A-8) (1371) (1437)
A, by chance. meets A-8 who. under the influence of liquor, reveals an important secret * A learns from A-8 whether a man or his wife died first in an accident—a secret of tremendous importance ** (845 ch A-2 to A-8) (1451b)

(b) (692) (719b) (1367b)
A is abandoned to die in mid-ocean by A-9, captain of a steamship, who refuses to delay his vessel to make the rescue * A is rescued from a boat adrift in mid-ocean when an accident delays the steamer of which A-9 is captain ** (1034) (1116b ch A to A-8)

138

1053

(622)   (755)   (1378 ch A to SN & FA to A)
A hears by chance a familiar name, and the name solves a riddle of the past * A,
hearing by chance a familiar name, finds his long-lost son, SN ** (928b)   (1291a
ch A to SN; 1461c ch A to SN & B to A; 928b)

1054

(245)   (870a)   (1089)   (1458)
A solves a mystery involving his happiness * A solves an important mystery when
falling plaster reveals the place where some old love letters are concealed ** (448)
(1451c)

1055

(245; 1051)   (245; 1054)   (801; 828)
A and B achieve happiness when a questionable story is proved to be false (366)
(367b)

1056

(622; 674; 953)   (750; 953*-**)   (755)   (1378)
A, hiding in a place where there is no food, steals from the larder of his nearest
neighbor, A-4 * A-4, missing food from his larder, half believes it was taken by
a "ghost" ** A, a supposed ghost, is caught in a trap set by A-4; and A-4 proves
to be A's missing son, SN***

(21)   Falling Into Misfortune Through Mistaken Judgment

1057

(a) (152a) (937-*)
A, young and unmarried, assumes temporary charge of an infant, CH, for a woman stranger, B-4 * A, volunteering to care for an infant, CH, for a woman stranger, B-4, finds himself with CH on his hands when B-4 fails to return ** (249) (914) (1229)

(b) (490b) (1224)
A borrows an infant, CH, from a married friend, A-2 (594c ch A to A-2) (1057a ch A to A-2) in order to carry out an unusual enterprise (1218 ch A to CH & A-2 to A) (1289c)

1058

(982a) (985 ch A-4 to A-2)
A lightly assumes a task to oblige his friend, A-2 * A, assuming an enterprise to oblige his friend, A-2, finds it completely beyond his powers ** (980) (812b ch F-B to A & A to A-8)

1059

(912a) (177 ch F-B to A-4)
A, although simple minded and genuine, is awkward in speech and forward and uncouth in manner * A, in spite of certain character defects, seeks the friendship of A-4, but succeeds only in annoying A-4 and so fails of his purpose ** (43 ch F-B to A-4) (762 ch A-8 to A-4)

1060

(768) (1134-*) (1418-*)
A, a young man of mediocre abilities, is happy in considering himself a very superior person * A attempts audacious enterprises, but his confidence has a way of leaving him "flat" before the enterprises are carried through to completion ** (769) (1134*-**) (1187)

1061

(115) (203) (436)
A is told by a clairvoyant that he has inherited the trait of cowardice * A's belief in the statement that he has inherited the trait of cowardice, makes a coward of him ** (584b) (615) (839 tr A & A 2) (842a) (888) (919a)

1062

(115) (311) (1063)
A is so content with what he has that any impulse toward enterprise is throttled (839 tr A & A-2) (1444; 1093)

1063

(311) (1131)
A's mistaken ideals are an obstacle to his advancement * A's ideal of labor is to do just enough to "get by" and hold his job ** (595) (604) (620) (839 tr A & A-2)

1064

(787; 1461b) (1291b; 1291a ch A to A-5)
A makes the mistake of thinking himself a criminal; then he discovers that he is not a criminal * A has assumed the furtive manner of a criminal for so long that it has become habitual with him and he cannot act like an honest man ** (952) (1075a) (1101) (1334a)

1065

(114) (235) (595) A, giving ten years of his life to a miserly uncle, U, in exchange for a college education, loses his ambition and enterprise * A's uncle, U, has promised A all that he has when he dies, but U dies a bankrupt; and A is thrown upon the world with abilities obscured and enterprise strangled ** (814) (839 tr A & A-2) (1354b) (1374)

1066

(610) (707)
A, an escaped prisoner, finds it impossible to free himself of his handcuffs; and when, in desperation, he appeals for help to a stranger, A-4, A-4 notifies a police officer, A-6, and A is recaptured (866) (1309 ch B to A & A-3 to A-6; 1142b)

1067

(384)   (872)   (908)

B fails to understand how her fretful disposition makes herself and all around her unhappy * B, overhearing a conversation which brings home to her a bitter truth regarding her unpleasant disposition, alters her mental attitude and undergoes a beneficial character change ** (921)   (956)   (976)

1068

(384)   (908)

B comes to understand the evil of her selfish outlook upon life when one of her children, CH, dies (581)   (1069 ch D-A to CH)   (1240)

1069

(378)   (466a ch CH to D-B)

B, over the dead body of her daughter, D-B (557b ch B to D-B)   (842 ch CH to D-B)   (945 ch B to D-B), experiences a psychic revelation that transforms her whole character (401)   (410)

(29)   Aiding Another to Hide from the World ' a Fateful Secret

1070

(371 ch B to B-8)   (1163c)

A, on trial for murder, could establish an alibi and prove his innocence—but only by a dishonorable act * A could save his life by revealing a secret that would compromise the good name of B ** (535 ch A to A-8 & A-3 to A)   (877 tr A & A-2) (635)

(43)   Seeking to Overcome Personal Limitations in Carrying Out an Enterprise

1071

(1072)   (1073)   (1094)   (1095)

A finds that the duties of his position are so numerous it is physically impossible for him to carry them out (863a)   (1163a)

1072

(926)   (963)

A's high official position makes it impossible for him, in his own person, to acquire information which he thinks of first importance (949b)   (1167)   (1170) (1184)

1073

(512)   (991)

A, a successful business man, has an overwhelming desire to break away from commercial affairs and go adventuring in quest of Romance * Only the fear of public opinion restrains him (555b)   (690)   (917)

1074

(114)   (258)   (675)

A, a writer, discovers that he is losing his grip on his reading public and is becoming unable to write salable material (598)   (749)   (835)   (1103)

1075

(a)   (850b)   (902)

A, struggling hopelessly against a character weakness, forms a platonic friendship for B (838 ch A to B·& A-2 to A)   (850a, b)   (1075b)   (364d)

(b)   (857)   (862)

A's admiration for his friend, B, and his desire to please her, inspires him to bring out the best in his nature (819)   (844a)

1076

(837 tr A & B)   (818b)
A, supposed to be a hoodlum, is transformed into a gentleman in an astonishingly short period of time * A, transformed almost over night from a hoodlum into a cultured gentleman, imparts to B, his friend, the secret of his surprising rehabilitation ** (1209a)   (1329)

1077

(1385)   (1403; 1400)   (1440 ch A to A-2)   (1283)
A calls at a pawnshop to redeem an object, X, pawned by his friend, A-2, who has died leaving the pledge unredeemed * A has lost the ticket of a pawned object, X, and the pawnbroker will not give up the pledge without the ticket ** (1166b) (1384)

1078

(776)   (857)   (1111a)   (1332)
A is obsessed with fear of a pursuing peril * A, obsessed with fear of a pursuing peril, seeks to gain contentment of mind ** (888)   (1350)   (1351)

1079

(127a)   (656)
A's character weakness is betting; and he seems unable to conquer the failing although he invariably suffers loss (367a)   (524a)   (902)

1080

(1092)   (1101)
A, a reporter, assigned to "cover" a certain story and finding it impossible, decides to write up an imaginary interview, pretending it is bona fide (979 ch A to A-4)   (1301 ch A to A-4; 1340)

1081

(1129c)
A finds it beyond his power, in any ordinary manner, to secure a man of proven courage for a dangerous piece of work * A proceeds by secret enterprise to find a man of courage ** (1219)   (1223a, b)

1082

(a)   (115)   (584b)   (858)
A is a man who finds cowardice an obstacle to enterprise * A, a craven at heart, deliberately forces himself into danger as a method of developing his courage ** (918b)   (1082b)   (1104)

(b)   (289)   (1061)
A lives in a strange lost community which is ruled by an idol of Fear * A seeks escape from a community ruled by Fear, but finds it difficult to develop sufficient courage to accomplish his purpose ** (1082a)   (181c)

1083

(114)   (1075a)   A lacks initiative, and the ability unaided to advance his material fortunes * A secures the help of B, a woman friend, to aid him in a difficult enterprise ** (225)   (844a)   (839 ch A to B & A-2 to A)   (850a)   (963)   (1278a)

1084

(113)   (126)
A seeks to forward an honest enterprise but lacks the means to finance it * A, in order to secure means to forward an honest enterprise, becomes a bootlegger for a time ** (92)   (1309b ch B to A & A-3 to A-6; 699a)

1085

(606 ch A to A-2)   (639-* ch A to A-2)   (672)
A would like to save his friend, A-2, from disaster, but money is necessary—and A has no money (832)   (1277b)   (1281 tr A & A-2)

1086

(905)   (914)   (927)
A would like to achieve a lofty enterprise, but is so poor he cannot finance the undertaking (628)   (1027)   (1028)

1087

(763)   (894 tr A & A-5)   (898)
A, a crook, would like to restore some of his ill-gotten gains, but finds it difficult without revealing his culpability (923)   (1097a)   (1239)

1088

(959)   (965)
A's happiness is wrapped up in his ambition * A lacks ingenuity and the power to force circumstances to contribute their utmost in forwarding his undertakings ** (85a)   (595)

1089

(914)   (818c)
A seeks to find the relatives of CH, a foundling, of whom he has taken charge * A writes to government authorities sending a copy of a coat of arms found on a foundling, CH's, coat, but receives no information regarding CH ** (818d)   (697b ch A to CH)

1090

(115)   (950)
A is hampered in his work, and his success imperiled, by a lack of new ideas (598) (835)

1091

(950-*)   (965)
A's knowledge of the profession he seeks to follow has been obtained solely by reading stories about it; he has had no practical experience (1111b)   (1444)

1092

(1060)   (1071)   (1074)
A reaches a point in his chosen work where his ingenuity and enterprise grow stale and will not help him onward (598)   (1073)   (1075a)

1093

(1444)   (115)   (887b)   (1062)
A is considered a very inferior person intellectually * A, considered an inferior person intellectually, seeks to solve a mystery that has puzzled the most sagacious [1]   A cipher message in which the key word, or phrase, suggests its complement, as "abide" suggests "with me," "silver threads" suggests "gold," "when you and I were young" suggests "Maggie," etc. [2]   A message written in bars of music, the music suggesting words of a song that yield the message. (1076)   (1174 ch A to A-5; 1282 ch A to A-5 & A-6 to A)   (1283)

1094

(900)   (1071)
A is a celebrity; and the written requests for his autograph become so numerous that they interfere seriously with his work (618)   (863a)

1095

(71a-*)   (101a)   (1002)   (1094)
A seeks to free himself from certain meddlesome influences that interfere seriously with the practice of his profession (71a*-**)   (83 ch B to A; 207)

1096

(1074)   (1090)   (1092)
A, a playwright, having no new ideas for a play, goes forth in quest of them (598) (711a)   (835)

1097

(a)   (990)   (991)   (1018)
A has a cherished ambition which he cannot realize because he is hampered with certain obligations * A's obligation, which prevented him from realizing a cherished ambition, passes, but the habit of excusing himself from enterprise on account of the obligation remains, and his cherished enterprise is never undertaken ** (1374)   (1375)

(b)   (1021b)   (1376)
A, for worthy purposes, poses as a criminal * A, posing as a criminal, finds that he is arrayed against some of his friends of the elite, A-2, A-2, A-2, who are engaged in a swindling enterprise and are fortified with police protection ** (807) (834)   (836)

1098

(115)   (1396)   (1444)
A is a subordinate, and considered mentally inferior * A, a subordinate, attacks
a problem that defies solution by his superiors, and solves it, thereby winning
just recognition and preferment ** (1426b; 181c) (1376; 1097b) (1435) (1413a, b)

1099

(32)   (102)   (145)   (325a)   (335)
B is too young, too attractive, too modern for the scholarly position she occupies;
and her success, which means happiness to her, is endangered * B, young and attractive, in order to win success in her chosen work, dresses the part of a spinster,
and makes herself appear prim and old-fashioned ** [1] B is a professor of higher .
mathematics in a large college [2] B has charge of the book department in a large
department store [3] B is the librarian in a large public library [4] B has been elect-
ed to a political office usually filled by some one of the opposite sex (818a)   (358)
(870a)   (1154a)

1100

(82a)   (87)   (1207)
B's happiness and success hang upon her successful impersonation of a boy * B,
impersonating a boy, is subjected to the rough pranks of her male companions,
who do not suspect her true sex ** (61)   (1451)

(44)   Seeking by Unusual Methods to Conquer Personal Limitations

1101

(111)   (1024)
A seeks to overcome personal limitations in an honest enterprise by a resort to
dishonest methods (628)   (1080)   (1084)

1102

(751-1-*)   (1024 ch A to A-2)
A, wealthy and too old to have his "fling," gives A-2, a spendthrift, a large sum
of money to squander as he sees fit * A hopes to enjoy A-2's spendthrift experiences
second-hand ** (751*-**)   (1023 ch A to A-2)

1103

(1074)   (1090)   (1092)
..., an elderly writer who runs out of ideas, copies material which his friend, A-2,
another writer long dead, wrote in his younger days (669 ch B to A)   (1238)

1104

(584b)   (615)   (839 tr A & A-2)   (857)   (858)   (1082a)
A's ignoble weakness is lack of courage in investigating events that have great
news value; for A is a newspaper reporter, and news is his stock in trade * A, a
coward, by deliberately forcing himself into risky situations in order to acquire
first-hand information, develops courage, transforms his character, and becomes
a "star" reporter ** (1407)   (1408)   (1409)

1105

(910 ch D-A to B)   (916)
B is young and pretty, and believes that Youth, seeking self-expression, is warranted in overriding any and all conventions (86)   (182a)   (252a)   (310)   (931)

1106

(740)   (766)   (948)
B, of an humble station in life, yearns for social prestige * B pretends that she
is entertaining a duke, AX** (58a)   (642)   (931)

(37) Seeking Against Difficulties to Realize a Cherished Ideal

1107

(a) (117)   (1432 ch A to U & NW to A; 1201 ch A to A-8 & CN to A)
A, on one side of the Atlantic, must arrive on the other side at a certain time or he will lose a rich inheritance * A, pursuing an important enterprise, catches a swift steamer for a hurried trip across the Atlantic ** (1034 ch A to A-8) (1414b)

(b) (606)   (1129a ch A-4 to A-9)
A applies for the position of butler in the home of wealthy A-9 * A, applying to A-9 for a job, is asked for references as to character and ability, and is referred by A to wealthy A-4 ** (805 tr A & A-4)   (809 ch A to A-4 & A-5 to A)

1108

(675)   (1149-* ch A to SN)
A is so preoccupied with business affairs that, while he intends writing to his son, SN, he somehow never gets around to it (622; 674)   (821)   (1149*-** ch A to SN)

1109

(1314)   (1315)
A, a simple mountaineer, comes to a large city in pursuit of an enemy, A-3 * A, from the mountains, seeking his enemy, A-3, in the city, is so overawed and impressed by his unfamiliar environment that his enmity fades away **   (857) (831-* ch A to A-3 & A-2 to A)   (832 ch A to A-3 & A-2 to A)

1110

(68)   (1178)   (1306)   A has committed a crime but has never fallen under suspicion * A's guilty conscience handicaps him in the field of enterprise ** (857) (1291a, b)   (1259)

1111

(a) (675)   (749)   (1074)   (1090)
A, an author, becomes suddenly aware of deterioration in his creative work (1391; 1455b) (1391; 1461b)   (1103)

(b) (1091)   (125a; 1444)
A, reading detective stories, is fired with a desire to become a detective * A, highly confident of his own ability, takes up a line of work with which he has had no practical experience ** (1426a, b)   (1435)   (1418b; 1433b; 1330)   (1397)

1112

(756)   (1060)   (1091)
A finds that his obligations as a "quack" doctor are too difficult for his powers (605)   (627)   (1004)   (1031)

1113

(934)   (959)   (966)   (1389b)
A has a theory that the perfume of flowers may be blended into musical conceptions (1333a)   (1363)   (1375)   (1422b)

1114

(949a)   (1060)
A, private secretary to A-9, knows that A-9 is jealously guarding some weighty secret * A's curiosity gets the better of him and he meddles with the personal affairs of A-9 ** (718a ch A to A-9; 596 ch A-5 to A-9)   (1194 ch A to A-9)

1115

(1021b)
A seeks to be loyal to his friend, A-2, but certain conditions render it difficult (221a; 139)   (601)   (607)   (662)   (1269 tr A & A-2)

1116

(97)   (100; 1209a)   (1107a)
A is hastening across the ocean on a fast steamer in order to carry out an important enterprise * A, engaged in an important enterprise, is delayed in mid-ocean by an accident to his steamer; the vessel's wireless is out of commission and A faces failure in a pet undertaking ** (793a; 623)   (1034 ch A to A-8)

1117

(1389a, b)
A, a somnambulist, deceives himself in a certain enterprise by opposing, in an unconscious state, all the efforts of his waking moments (562)   (1111b)   (1438a)

1118

(974)   (1137b)
B, a banker's wife, trying to subscribe to the socia. conventions of a farming community, finds her efforts embarrassing and distasteful (848b)   (1151)   (1172)

1119

(335)   (676)
B, who lacks every qualification of a successful writer, nevertheless believes herself highly gifted as a novelist (364b)   (743a)   (749 ch A to B)   (1153)

1120

(565)   (1133)
B, unhappy because of A's sins, appeals to God to save him (1353)   (1433b; 1353)
(918b)

1121

(766)   (1099)   (1119)
B is ambitious to "get ahead," to advance herself in her chosen line of work; but she has difficulties that are disheartening (679)   (1067)   (1100)

(20)   Becoming Involved with Conditions in which Misfortune is Indicated

1122

(926)   (941)   (964a)
A manufactures a hand-made product in a worthy manner no machinery can duplicate * A, by manufacturing a hand-made product by machinery, on a large scale, and so keeping up with the demand, will amass wealth; but the standard of quality will be lowered ** (938)   (943a)

1123

(111)   (31 ch B to SR-A & A to A-8)
A, brother of SR-A and her only living relative, is poor, while SR-A is wealthy and unmarried * A, poor, will not inherit the money of his wealthy sister, SR-A, if she marries, as she seems likely to do ** (213 ch A to A-8, B to SR-B & A-7 to A)   (892 ch B to SR-A & B-3 to A)   (1001a)

1124

(1177)   (1178)   (1291a, b)
A, in his absent-minded moments, mechanically draws odd designs on a piece of paper, unaware of what he is doing, or that it may have an adverse effect upon some of his secret enterprises (1289d)   (1282)

1125

(a)   (56)   (61)   (176a)   (736)   (744)   (808a)   (850a)
A rejects unfeelingly the friendship of B because he finds her too capricious (261) (843 tr B & B-2)   (893 ch CH to A)

(b)   (73)   (422b-****)
A and B, impelled by unusual motives, enter into a suicide pact * A and B pledge each other that he or she will die whenever the other dies ** (573b)(422b****-*****\
(1020)

1126

(98)   (289)   (850b)
A is a bibulous person, and his ultimatum from his doctor is this: "Either quit drinking, or resign yourself to die within a few months" (761a)   (779)   (1326; 779)   (364d)

1127

(1299)   (1432 ch A to A-8 & NW to CN)
A is a cousin of CN, and CN is to inherit the wealth of a deceased relative, A-8.
If CN were out of the way, A would be the legal heir (50)   (1162 tr A & A-2 &
ch A-5 to CN)   (1195)

1128

(a)   (607)   (446b)
A, suffering a terrible mental shock, seemingly falls dead * A, apparently dead,
is really in a cataleptic state and sees and hears everything that takes place around
him although powerless to move a muscle ** (856; 878c)   (1142a)

(b)   (898)   (1043)
A is in a mine when a charge of giant powder explodes prematurely * A loses his
eyesight in a powder explosion ** (918b)   (1047)

1129

(a)   (1217a)   (1152 ch B to B-4)
A desires a certain object, X; but X is in the hands of A-4, who guards it carefully (1144)   (1191)   (1197 ch A-8 to A-4)   (1166a, b ch A-9 to A-4)

(b)   (1298 ch A to A-5)   (1304 ch A to A-5 & A-2 to A)
A's cattle have been stolen by A-5, a notorious "rustler" whose very name inspires fear in the law-abiding * A seeks a courageous person who will recover property that has been stolen from him ** (1081)   (1219)   (1129c)

(c)   (1165)   (1304 ch A-2 to A-5)
A has been robbed of valuable property, X, by A-5, a notorious criminal, and A
tries to secure a courageous man who will recover X for him (1081)   (1219)

1130

(926)   (1073)
A a doctor, who is about to leave his office on a night emergency call, is made a
prisoner by mysterious strangers, AX, AX, AX, and spirited away (660a ch A-4
to AX)   (1447)   (660b ch A-5 to AX)

1131

(158)   (1062)   (1063)
A's obstacle to enterprise is laziness; and he submits to it cheerfully (114)   (225)

1132

(887b)   (1061)
A's character weakness is superstition * A is so superstitious that it prevents him
from winning success in his enterprises ** (1075a, b)   (1332)   (1334a, b)   (1350)

1133

(565)   (1120)
A is an agnostic who, in his arrogance and presumption, defies a Higher Power
(1353)   (1443b)   (1445 ch B to A)

1134

(1418b-*)   (718b; 1061; 839 tr A & A-2)
A. a very ordinary young man, suddenly becomes afflicted with megalomania,
and his character is completely changed * A, who was timid and shirked enterprise,
undergoes a character change which impels him to rush audaciously into the most
difficult undertakings ** (111)   (768)   (769)   (1418b*-**)

1135

(a)   (737a)   (1010)
B, in the hands of crooks, A-5, A-5, A-5, and being forced to do their will, is tortured by having A, the man she loves, threatened with death by one of the crooks
who is "drawing a bead" on A from behind a window curtain (or, as it later developed, A was not outside the house at all, and not in any danger) (885a) (1309a
ch A to A-5)

(b)   (645)   (1335 ch A to B)
B, alone and in a strange bedroom, discovers a man, AX, dead in the bed * B is
forced to battle for her honor with A-5 when finding herself trapped in a room **
(885a, b)   (1448 ch A to B, A-8 to AX)

1136

(41a, b, c)   (335)   (460)
B sends a telegram to her maid, B-7, to "Come at once" * B (677), intending to send a telegram to her maid, B-7, through error addresses the message to A ** (499a, b)

1137

(a)   (890 ch A-4 to A)   (1389b)
B. in a small boat, has lost her oars and is drifting out to sea in a fog * B, in great danger, seeks to apprise A, at a distance, of her danger by occult methods—methods with which they have often experimented ** B, ocean bathing, is caught in the undertow and is being swept out to sea *** (179a, c)   (1433c)   (1451c)

(b)   (677)   (872)
B, in poor health, is ordered by her docter to leave the city and live in the country * B, city bred, undergoes unpleasant experiences when she goes to the country to live ** (916)   (962)   (1118)

(45) Seeking to Forward an Enterprise and Encountering Family Sentiment as an Obstacle

1138

(1129a ch A-4 to B)   (1333b ch A to A-8 & B to F-B)
A seeks professionally to secure a desired object, X, from B * A, seeking to secure a desired object, X, from B, finds the object so dearly prized because of family associations that B will not part with it at any price ** (20a)   (739)   (1217c)

1139

(1023)   (1026)
A is a profligate son who seeks to borrow money of A-8 on the prospect of inheriting the estate of his wealthy father, F-A.   A-8 is skeptical regarding A's inheriting the estate (1162 ch A-5 to F-A)   (1226 ch A to A-8 & A-5 to A)   (1217b)

1140

(898-*)   (899-*)
A, publicly, is honest and prosperous, but privately he is a transgressor * A desires a piece of ground on which to build a mansion.   The ground is owned by A-8, a poor man, in whose family it has been for generations.   Influenced by family sentiment, A-8 refuses to sell ** (1220b ch B to A-8)   (1260a)

(50) Being Impelled by an Unusual Motive to Engage in Crafty Enterprise

1141

(1095) (1133) (1427b-*)

A has a violent distaste for ghost stories and stories of the supernatural * A pretends to be ill in order to avoid listening to ghost stories ** (1427b*-**) (1343) (1360) (1365) (1366) (1375) (1377a) (830)

1142

(a) (557a) (601; 638) (1128a; 1455a) (1128a)

A, in his coffin and just before burial, revives from a cataleptic trance * A, just before burial, revives from a cataleptic trance, puts weights in the coffin, closes it, and secretly escapes from the house ** (918a) (1313b)

(b) (651) (699b)

A is mistakenly supposed to have met his death in a storm * A, a fugitive from justice, supposed to be dead, assumes an alias and escapes to a distant place ** (699a) (923) (930) (1066)

1143

(a) (778 ch A to A-5; 1217a ch A to A-5 & A-8 to A) (1144 ch A to A-5)

A is a connoisseur of precious stones and has a valuable collection * A, in order to protect his collection of valuable stones against robbery, displays replicas of them, comparatively worthless, to would-be customers ** (729) (1166a ch A to A-5)

(b) (903-*) (1370b ch A to GF-B) (1370c ch A to F-B)

A, an artist, is hired by B to paint a miniature; and into the miniature he is to weave an intricate series of lines which constitute a concealed map of great importance (903*-**) (1444)

1144

(778; 729 ch A to A-8) (1143a ch A to A-8)

A, a crook, seeks by substituting a worthless counterfeit for the valuable original, to secure an object carefully safeguarded (1166a) (1217a)

1145

(1181)

A, a crook, seeks unlawful gain by selling A-8 an object, X, which A-8 already owns (1165 ch A to A-8 & A-5 to A)

1146

(59) (1152)

A, a crook, in order to carry out a crafty enterprise, disguises himself as a person of wealth and social standing (763) (661 ch AX to A) (1144) (1166a)

1147

(758-* ch A to A-8) (899-* ch A to A-8; 1129a ch A to A-8)

A, poor, at the request of a rich man, A-8, leaves with A-8 a valuable object, X, which he has in his possession and wishes to sell * A calls on A-8 for a valuable object, X, which A had left with A-8, in the hope of making a sale; but A-8 declares A never left X with him, and has A ejected from the premises ** (1433a) ch A to A-8; 1443b ch A to A-8) (1439b)

1148

(a) (486a) (1184-*) (1185) A desires to get away frequently to the city and have his "fling" with boon companions but fears the gossip of the rural community in which he lives * A, wishing to carry out an enterprise that would cause gossip, puts gossip to sleep by inventing a fictitious relative, AX, who is always in trouble and always calling on A to help him out ** (1170) (1216 tr A & A-2)

(b) (979) (770a) (1377b)

A, an innocent transgressor under ban of the law, owes a large sum of money which he must pay * A, a fugitive from the law, assumes a fictitious character and an alias and wins a large sum of money in a certain enterprise ** (1451a, b) (1408)

1149

(466a ch CH to A, B to M-A & A to F-A)   (1108 ch A to F-A & SN to A)
A is a lad away from home, very unhappy because he does not receive letters from
home as all his other young friends do * A, lonely, and never receiving any letters
from his home folk, writes letters to himself and shows them to his friends ** (499a
ch CH to A, A to F-A & B to M-A)   (622 ch A to F-A & SN to A)

1150

(1061)   (1132)
A is a coward who seeks, by arrogant boasting, to convince everybody that he
is a hero (615)   (1433b; 1330)   (1336)   (1433b; 1363)

1151

(644)   (669)   (737b)   (1240)
B simulates ignorance regarding a certain compromising event in her life * B, in
order to avoid slander and evil gossip and protect a daughter, D-A, who is about
to marry a man of wealth and social position, seeks to hush up a possible scandal
in her own life ** (870a)   (870b)

1152

(778)   (1129a ch A-4 to B)
B is the owner of a gem so valuable that she fears to wear it in public; so she keeps
it in a strong box and wears a replica of it which is of comparatively little value.
The fact that she owns the real stone is well known, and the counterfeit is supposed to be the original (767 ch B to B-2)   (1144)

1153

(335)   (413)   (739)   (850a tr A & B)   (1099)   (1119)   (1121)
B fails in an undertaking dear to her heart * B, failing in an undertaking dear
to her heart, seeks to make others think she has succeeded ** (364b)   (1203)

1154

(a)   (179a, b, c)   (470)
B, mistaken for another woman who is under ban of death by a strange secret
society (1438c-1), seeks to escape from her pursuers (792b)   (1025)   (1446b)

(b)   (138; 94a-*)   (1229 ch B to B-3)   (1265a ch A to B-3 & A-3 to A)
B masquerades as an Unknown in order to prove or disprove an evil story about
A * B discovers that B-3 has told an untruth about A ** (844b)   (944)

1155

(163)   (606)
B, the friend of A, learns that A is desperately involved in debt * B, unknown to
A, settles with A's creditors and frees A from debt ** (93a)   (801)   (850a, b)

1156

(645)   (646)   (647)
B innocently commits a transgression * B, innocently committing a transgression,
for fear of the law keeps the transgression a close secret ** (665)   (669)

1157

(1159)   (1220b)   B is forced to weep at an appointed time; and A strikes her
in order to make her grief more realistic (806 ch B-4 to B)   (1192)

1158

(766)   (870a)   (947)   (1242a)
B, traveling alone, invents a fictitious aunt, AUX, as a chaperone (801)   (1309b
ch A-3 to AUX)

1159

(1033)   (1220b)
B pretends she has been injured by an automobile in order to collect damages
from the owner of the car, A-4 (801 ch A to A-4)   (1192)   (1192; 224)

(29) Aiding Another to Hide from the World a Fateful Secret

1160

(841)　(1021b)　(1291b)
A's friend, A-2, is the sole support of his parents, F-A and M-A * A's friend, A-2, the sole support of his parents, dies (603b, c, d), and A withholds the knowledge from the needy parents, writes them in A-2's name, and continues sending money for their support ** (1461a)　(1462)

1161

(724 ch A to A-4; 816a)　(707 tr A & A-4)　(787 ch A to A-4; 816a)
A, falling in with A-4, a stranger who has been injured in an accident, agrees to take over an enterprise which the accident prevents A-4 from finishing * A, in in order to help A-4, poses as A-4 ** (711a, b, c)　(1168 ch A-2 to A-4)

1162

(793a tr A & A-2)　(981 tr A & A-2)
A induces a friend, A-2, to play the role of A-5 in order to carry out an enterprise in which the presence of A-5 is necessary (1148a ch AX to A-5)　(1164 ch A-8 to A-2 & A-4 to A-5)

1163

(a)　(615)　(618)
A finds his "double" in A-4, and he hires A-4 to attend to certain duties which devolve upon himself 'A)　(1424b; 249)　(639-* ch A-5 to A-4)　(1163b, c)

(b)　(101a)　(1095)
A unloads upon A-4 (101b ch A to A-4) certain romantic affairs which he (A) finds distasteful (72 ch A to A-4 & A-2 to A)　(182a ch A-3 to A-4)

(c)　(1163a)
A's "double", A-4, carries out an enterprise as A which A finds disastrous to his own fortunes (1180 tr A & A-4)　(1192 ch A to A-4 & A-4 to A-8)　(1197 ch A to A-4 & A-8 to A)

1164

(710 ch A to A-4)　(711a ch A to A-4)
A, having invited friends to meet a celebrity, A-4, who does not arrive, persuades A-8 to impersonate A-4 in order that the guests may not be disappointed (603a ch A-2 to A-8)　(610 ch A to A-8)　(717 ch "officer A-6" to "celebrity A-8")

(47) Finding (Apparently) an Object Greatly Coveted, and Obtaining (Apparently) the Object

1165

(1145 ch A to A-5 & A-8 to A)　(1161 ch A to A-8 & A-4 to A-5)
A is an art collector * X1 and X2 are very rare and valuable art objects, the only two in the world ** A owns an objet d'art, X1; and he buys X2, as he supposes, which is an exact duplicate of X1, from A-5, only to discover that he has repurchased X1 which the scheming A-5 had stolen from his collection *** (224 ch A to A-5)　(1146 ch A to A-5)

1166

(a)　(1129a)　(1144)
A is a thief who has a real gem, X1, which he thinks is a counterfeit * A, a thief, has a real gem, X1, which he thinks is a counterfeit; and, adroitly, he substitutes X1 for X2, a counterfeit which A thinks is a genuine stone ** (614)　(1166b)

(b)　(1166a-*)
A, adroitly, secures an object greatly desired, X2, from A-9, who willl not dispose of it * A, making a replica, X1, of a valuable original, X2, secures X2 by leaving X1 in its place ** (1166*-**)　(1343)

(48) Assuming the Character of a Criminal in a Perfectly Honest Enterprise

1167

(598) (939)
A, for worthy purposes, plays the role of a fictitious criminal, A-5 * A, for worthy purposes playing the role of a fictitious criminal, A-5, is sought by the police for a crime committed by the real A-5 ** (249) (635) (1044a)

1168

(599) (1161 ch A-4 to A-2)
A, inspired by altruistic motives, assumes the name and character of A-2, using A-2's clothes and other belongings, and seeking to carry out an enterprise begun by A-2 * A, posing as A-2, does not know that A-2 is a transgressor ** (603a) (822 ch B to A-2) (1044a)

1169

(1073) (1096) (818a-*)
A seeks to demonstrate his ability to enact a certain role in a forthcoming play * A, in order to prove his ability to enact a certain role in a forthcoming play, assumes the role off the stage ** (818a*-***) (625)

1170

(485) (513) (949b) (1072) (1073) (1148a)
A, wealthy and of high social standing, desires adventures in the underworld * A, desiring adventures in the underworld and unable to realize his desire in his own character, assumes a fictitious character ** (773) (786) (876a) (1148a*-**) (1209b)

1171

(623 ch A to F-B) (773 ch A to F-B & B to B-5) (822)
B's father, F-B, is suspected of a certain crime * B, in order to save her father, F-B, who is suspected of a certain crime, confesses that she is the culprit ** A, B's best friend, in order to save B, who is suspected of a certain crime, declares that he alone is guilty *** (635) (1291 ch A to A-5)

1172

(890) (1025) (1118)
B's striking physical resemblance to B-5, a criminal, causes her to be suspected of a crime (69) (792b) (822) (828) (1154a)

(49) Assuming a Fictitious Character When Embarking Upon a Certain Enterprise

1173

(2b, c, d, e, g, h) (1187; 2f) A, a pretender, encounters B, who is also a pretender * A and B are pretenders, yet neither knows that the other is not what he or she seems to be ** (773; 772 ch A to B & A-4 to A) (806 ch B-4 to B) (1462)

1174

(1165 ch A to A-8, A-5 to A & add A-2) (1311 add A-2)
A and A-2 are crooks, seeking escape through the closing net of the law * A and A-2, crooks trying for a "get-away" after a successful "job," slip through the police net, A-6, A-6, A-6, when A disguises himself as a woman ** (603c, d) (1015 ch A to A-8 & A-5 to A) (1282)

1175

(a) (59) (1146)
A is a fugitive from justice who has assumed an alias and is posing as an innocent and worthy member of society (69) (90a) (333) (338) (763)

(b) (1021b) (1168)
A and A-2 are friends, but one of them is a criminal and a fugitive from justice. Which of the two is the criminal? (1015 ch A to A-8 & A-5 to A) (1282 ch A to A-5)

1176

(610)   (654)

A, a crook, is trapped and surrounded by officers of the law, A-6, A-6, A-6 * A, a crook trapped and surrounded by officers of the law, A-6, A-6, A-6, escapes by pretending to be another A-6 who is hunting for **himself ** (963) (1142b) (1209a)

1177

(263 ch A to A-8 & A-3 to A)   (438)   (658)

A, a banker, has juggled with the bank's funds * A, a transgressor, covers up his criminal acts by a painstaking simulation of honor and excellence ** (1038) (1044a)   (1124)

1178

(568c ch A-3 to A-8)   (1291b ch ʌ-2 to A-8)   (1309b ch B to A & A-3 to A-8)

A, highly respected in his community, has committed a murder * A buries the body of his murdered victim, A-8, in a swamp and, by his usual exemplary conduct, seeks to escape suspicion ** (1291a)   (1302)

1179

(866)   (1189)   (1316 ch A-3 to A-5)

A is a criminal who is posing as an officer of the law hunting for another criminal * A, a criminal, poses as an officer of the law looking for A-5, another criminal. Authorities pick up A-5, turn him over to A, and A starts with his prisoner for the scene of A-5's crime—and his own ** (923)ↄ(1209c ch A-2 to A-5)   (1309b ch B to A & A-3 to A-5)

1180

(1146)   (1181)

A, a crook, in order to overcome the difficulties of a certain enterprise, impersonates a celebrated novelist, A-4 * A, a crook impersonating a celebrated novelist, A-4, proceeds to a small town and becomes the lion of a ladies' literary society ** (338)   (717 ch A-6 to A-4)   (1163c)   (1173 ch A to A-4)   (1271)

1181

(126)   (1146)

A is a transgressor who poses as an honest man for the purpose of carrying out another transgression (1145)   (1180)

1182

(608)   (611a)   (623)   A, through no fault of his own, is estranged from his parents, F-A and M-A * A, estranged from his parents, F-A and M-A, effects a reconciliation with them by proving his worth in an assumed character as an Unknown ** (830 ch A-2 to F-A)   (1199)

1183

(695a)   (695b; 1160)

A, in order to achieve happiness, seeks to be free of suspicion * A drops his own name and assumes the name of a deceased friend, A-2 ** A-2, deceased, has a sister, SR; and SR, not knowing of A-2's death, corresponds with A, thinking him her brother *** (31; 1461a)   (1461a; 1461c)

1184

(420)   (1072)   (1073)

A's high place in society is at odds with an enterprise he wishes to undertake * A, in order to proceed with certain plans, finds it necessary to hide his identity ** (917)   (1181)

1185

(249)   (1177)   (1178)

A, to the public, is highly placeᴜ, ʌonest and successful.   This reputation is necessary as a "cover" for his private transgressions (98)   (438)   (1148a)

1186

(249)   (1184)

A seeks to rebuild his life, wasted in ᴜissipation, along the line of exemplary ideals * A, pursuing a worthy enterprise, changes his name and goes to a place where he is unknown ** (152a)   (818a)

1187

(513)   (768)

A is a poor clerk who, with a limited capital, dons a dress suit and takes a brief "fling" in high society (2a)   (617)   (1173)

1188

(680a) (1023) (1024)

A, to secure relief from desperate misfortunes, pretends to be a victim of lost identity * A, pretending to be a victim of lost identity, appeals to the police and is given food and shelter while the authorities try to discover who he is and where he comes from ** (1196) (1212b)

1189

(637) (664) (866)

A is a captured criminal who, when the detective who has him in charge, A-6, suddenly dies, appropriates the clothes and belongings of A-6 and seeks to escape by impersonating him (717) (923) (1173) (1179)

1190

(1169) (1170)

A, a tramp, in order to have more success in his "panhandling," pretends to be a missionary (1053) (1147) (1161) (1196) (1199)

1191

(1129a) (1132)

A, a crooked gambler, seeks to fleece a stranger, A-4, (1079 ch A to A-4) out of his money * A, a crooked gambler, pretends to be a friend of A-4, a stranger, in order to lure him into a card game ** (1255a ch A to A-4 & A-3 to A) (1276 ch A to A-4 & A-5 to A)

1192

(1159) (1220b) A, a confederate of B's, seeks damages from A-4, the owner of an automobile that apparently injures B (338) (822)

1193

(1076 ch A to A-3) (70; 1459 ch B to A) (70; 1459 ch B to A & A-3 to F-B)

A, assuming a disguise and an alias, secures employment from A-3, for the purpose of obtaining certain information * A, discovered masquerading under a false name and in disguise, is compelled to flee for his life ** (1451b ch A-8 to A-3) (1439a ch A-2 to A-3)

1194

(1004) (1031)

A is a thief who has an honest profession which he uses as a "cover" for his dishonest practices * A seeks to appropriate a large sum of money which a dying man, A-8, has in his possession ** (338) (636)

1195

(887b) (1127) (1290b-*)

A is a murderer who, for his own protection and gain, impersonates the man he has murdered (339) (1001a) (1290b*-**)

1196

(636) (1004 ch A-8 to B) (1188) (1190)

A is mistaken by B for her son, SN * A, mistaken by a dying woman, B, for her son, SN, altruistically fosters the delusion in order to give B a few last moments of earthly comfort ** (1197 ch A-8 to SN) (1201 ch CN to SN)

1197

(1163c ch A to A-8 & A-4 to A) (1129a)

A bears a striking physical resemblance to A-8 * A impersonates A-8 for the purpose of acquiring gain ** (1146) (1163a ch A to A-8 & A-4 to A)

1198

(598) (1167)

A, for the purpose of discovering what obstacles a certain person will meet and how he will react to them, assumes the role of a fictitious character and falls into very real misfortunes (608) (717) (786)

1199

(205)   (864)   (915)   (967)
A is a wanderer "under a cloud" who returns as an Unknown to his home town,
scene of his youthful transgressions * A, returning to his home town as an Unknown, prevents a bank holdup ** (211)   (1182)

1200

(59)   (1194)   (1196 ch SN to A-8)
A, a crook, assumes the role of an honest, cultured gentlemen, A-8 * A, a crook,
assuming the role of an honest, cultured gentlemen, A-8, undergoes experiences
which break down his nerve and exhaust his resourcefulness ** (236 tr A & A-3)
(333)

1201

(1414a ch A to CN)   (1414b ch A to CN)
A's cousin, CN, has long been mysteriously missing * A's uncle, U, dies and leaves
A's cousin, CN, a large estate. A impersonates CN ** (95)   (794 ch A-2 to CN)

1202

(a)   (1168-*)   (1169)
A plays the role of a "rube" so successfully that he defeats the purpose for which
he undertook the impersonation (625)   (1168*-**)

(b)   (926)   (928a)
A, wealthy, entertains his friends lavishly; consequently, he counts his friends
by scores * A, wealthy, as a test of his friends' loyalty, pretends to lose his wealth;
then he tries to borrow, but not one of his former friends will lend him so much
as a plugged nickel, or even notice him in the street as he passes ** (681a)   (922b)

1203

(335)   (1153)
B seeks to convince the home folks that she is a celebrity when she is really a
failure * B sends newspaper clippings regarding a celebrity, B-4, to the home folks,
and pretends that she is B-4 under a stage or pen name ** (364b)   (1208 ch
B-2 to B-4)

1204

(450)   (921)   (1172)   (1220b)
B's happiness requires a complete escape from her life and environment * B hires
B-8, a woman who has not long to live, to take her name ** B-8 dies and is buried
as B *** (435a)   (1244b)

1205

(1160 ch A-2 to BR-B & F-A and M-A to B)   (1168 ch A-2 to BR-B)
B does not know that her brother, BR-B, is dead. She corresponds with a man,
A, who pretends to be BR-B * B, after corresponding with A, whom she supposes
to be her brother, BR-B, calls on A unannounced and discovers A's deception **
(21)   (31)

1206

(784-*)   (946)
B, seeking to carry out an enterprise in a large department store, finds the enterprise endangered by A-6, a detective * B, faultlessly dressed, in order to escape A-6, a detective, steps into the show-window of a large department store and
poses as a life-size wax figure, one of several figures displaying the latest suits
and cloaks ** (784*-**)   (870a, b)

1207

(745)   (1032)   (1100-*)
B's sex prevents her from securing employment among men; so she disguises herself as a boy (61)   (1454)   (1100*-**)

1208

(1172 ch B-5 to B-2)   (1203 ch B-4 to B-2)
B is impersonating B-2. In the midst of the impersonation, B-2, at a distance,
is injured in an accident and expected to die. Great newspaper publicity is given
the incident (1151)   (1258).

(50) Being Impelled by an Unusual Motive to Engage in Crafty Enterprise

1209

(a) (100) (673-*)
A, a fugitive from justice, disguises himself and, as an Unknown, risks discovery and arrest to carry out a romantic enterprise (52b) (673*-**) (684 ch F-B to A) (915) (964b)

(b) (420) (485) (949b) (1170) (1184)
A, a Beau Brummel, wealthy and aristocratic, disappears inside a public wash room at a railway station with a suit case. When he reappears, he has transformed himself into a typical hoodlum. A checks his suit case and plunges into the underworld in quest of adventure (681b) (711b)

(c) (820) (1212a)
A, a fugitive from justice, succeeds by a stratagem in rescuing his pal, A-2, from the toils of the law (1179 ch A-5 to A-2) (1174) (1216)

1210

(898) (925-*) (858-*)
A is told by his doctor that he has only three months to live * A, wealthy miser, told by his doctor that he has only three months to live, decides to spend all his money before he dies so none will be left for his heirs ** (751) (865)

1211

(440-*) (988) (1087)
A, having committed a transgression, seeks to make restitution without betraying his guilt (440*-**) (422a) (1239)

1212

(a) (723 ch A to A-2 & A-5 to A) (981 tr A & A-2)
A, for his own selfish reasons, gives aid to his friend, A-2, who is suffering misfortune (1218 tr A & A-2) (1209c) (1264)

(b) (622 ch A to A-8 & SN to A) (1188) (1414b ch A to SN)
A, for his own selfish reasons, pretends to be the long-lost son of wealthy A-8 (1200 ch A-8 to SN) (1291a ch A to SN)

(c) (1107b) (1181) (1146 ch A to A-9)
A, seeking a job from A-9, refers A-9 to A-4 for a recommendation as to character and ability, telling him A-4 can be reached at a prominent hotel at a certain hour by phone * A, when A-4 is paged in a prominent hotel, answers the call, assumes the character of A-4 and gives himself such a flowery recommendation that he secures a job from A-9 ** (1008) (352a-*)

1213

(905) (927)
A invents a fictitious servant, A-7 * A invents a fictitious servant, A-7, on whom he pretends to depend, and whose unreliability, while seeming to occasion A much embarrassment, is really a convenience to A ** (1423 ch AX to A-7) (1424a ch AX to A-7) (1216 tr A & A-2 & ch AX to A-7)

1214

(1129a ch A to A-5 & A-4 to A-2; 1268 ch A to A-5)
A, friend of A-2, learns that A-2 is to be made the victim of a transgression. A discovers this too late to warn A-2, and determines to help him by secret enterprise (834) (1227a)

1215

(1231) (1212a)
A tries to make two pugilists, A-2 and A-8, who are fast friends, stage a spirited ring battle * A, for certain reasons, seeks to make enemies of two friends, A-2 & A-8 ** (273 ch A to A-8; 230-*) (1278a)

1216

(86)   (1148a ch A to A-2)
A's friend, A-2, has invented a fictitious character, AX, for personal reasons *
A, for personal reasons, impersonates the fictitious character, AX, invented by
his friend, A-2 ** (1146 ch A-8 to AX)   (1184)   (1187)

1217

(a)   (778)   (1129a ch A-4 to A-8)   (1144)
A is a bold thief who wishes to hide his identity and appear free of ulterior motives while carrying out an audacious robbery * A, a crook, pretends to be a lover
of precious stones while calling on a collector of gems, A-8 ** (1143a ch A to A-8)
(1166a)

(b)   (1026)   (1139)
A, the outcast son of F-A, seeks to borrow money of A-8 with the approval of
F-A *. A, seeking to borrow money of A-8 on the supposed approval of F-A, asks
A-8 to call on F-A and secure authority to make the loan ** (1195)   (1290b)

(c)   (1138)   (1129a ch A-4 to B)
A wishes to buy an object, X, in the possession of B. B will not sell X. A-5, a crook,
steals X from B and tries to sell it to A (20a)   (808a)

1218

(600)   (639-*)
A is captured by a brigand, A-5, and held for ransom * A's friend, A-2, plans
to rescue A from a brigand, A-5, who is holding A for ransom, and he plans to
make the rescue without paying the ransom ** (653)   (1281)

1219

(1081)   (1129c)
A, secretly searching for a man of courage, stages a crafty enterprise in order to
find a man of sufficient courage to face a dangerous test (1287 ch A to A-5)   (793a
ch A to A-5 & A-2 to A`

1220

(a)   (947)   (1138)   (1140 ch A-8 to B)
A, craftily seeking gain, overcomes the opposition of B with the use of strong
drink (738)   (951)

(b)   (1157)   (1220a)
A is a grafter who forces B to help him in his grafting enterprises * A compels
B to wander about the streets in rags, forlorn and weeping, with the idea of secur-
ing money from guileless strangers ** (1159)   (1192)   (1204)

1221

(600)   (652a)
A is secretly drugged by enemies, A-5, A-5, A-5 * A, secretly drugged by enemies,
A-5, A-5, A-5, is a drug addict and the potion has no effect; but A, realizing the
attempt has been made, simulates unconsciousness to discover why it was made **
(664)   (834)   (835)

1222

(a)   (266)   (657)   (1175b ch A to A-3)   A believes A-3 guilty of a crime * A,
as a means of forcing a confession of guilt from A-3, throws both himself and A-3
into a situation where death for both of them seems imminent ** (1461a ch A to
A-3)   (1456 ch A-5 to A-3)

(b)   (635-*)   (833)   (1222a)   A, by subtle enterprise, forces a confession of
guilt from A-3, and thus wins success in a difficult undertaking (635*-** ch A-5
to A-3)   (894 ch A-5 to A-3)   (887a ch A to A-3)

1223

(a)   (1090)   (1102 ch A-2 to A-4)   (1111b)
A tries to discover what obstacles a certain person will meet and how he will react
to them * A hires A-4 as a catspaw and sends him uninformed into various misadventures ** (1161 ch A to A-8)   (1162 ch A-2 to A-4)   (1163a)

(b) (77 ch A to A-4, A-3 to A-8 & F-B to A) (1081)
A, in order to forward a certain enterprise, contrives a test of merit for two men,
A-4 and A-8 * A pretends to disappear and to be in great danger, and so lures
A-4 and A-8 into real danger in a quest for him ** (295a ch A to A-4) (209 ch A
to A-4 & A-3 to A-8)

1224

(1146) (1162 ch A to A-2, A-2 to A & A-5 to A-8)
A seeks for his own gain to impersonate a widower, A-8, who has a child, CH.
A has no child but overcomes the handicap by a stratagem (1057b) (1167 ch A-5
to A-8) (1147-* ch A to A-4 & X to CH)

1225

(429a) (734) (953) (1378 ch F-A to A & A to SN)
A has taken up his quarters in a vacant house (74a-*) * A, taking refuge in a vacant house and desiring to stay on secretly in the place, moves into the attic when
the house is rented ** (719a) (1056)

1226

(79 ch A-3 to A-5) (600) (1275)
A learns that he has been cast, by A-5, for the role of victim in a confidence game *
A simulates guilessness in an attempt to lure designing A-5 to his own undoing **
(630) (1193 ch A-3 to A-5)

1227

(a) (252a) (704) (1214)
A's friend, A-2, is waylaid and robbed by three men; and one of the men is A *
A's friend, A-2, is robbed by A and A-5; then A, in turn, robs A-5 ** A robs A-5
of valuables stolen from A-2, and returns the property to A-2 *** (867) (808a
ch B to A-2)

(b) (234a) (252a)
A, in order to convince B that he is a man of courage, arranges with A-2 to stage
a fake holdup with B the supposed victim* A appears during a fake holdup and
"rescues" B ** (234b) (367b)

(c) (234a) (252a)
A hires a confederate, A-2, to abduct B * A hires A-2 to abduct B under pretense
that she is to be held for ransom ** A "rescues" B during a mock abduction ***
(367b) (81)

1228

(725 ch A-5 to A-3) (1447)
A possesses knowledge inimical to A-3 * A is manoeuvered into jail by the politically powerful A-3 in order to prevent A's information from causing A-3 any
injury ** (623) (826) (829)

1229

(1057a) (1430b)
A finds himself with a strange baby, CH, on his hands * A, with a strange baby,
CH, on his hands, secretly leaves CH in the care of B, who has other children **
(249 ch B to B-8) (1154b ch B to B-8)

1230

(1268 ch A to A-5) (1311 ch A-3 to A-5)
A is obsessed with a fear of burglars * A, obsessed with a fear of burglars, places
a wax figure, X, in his bed at night and sleeps in a locked closet ** (1252 ch A to
A-5 & A-8 to X) (1313b ch A-3 to A-5)

1231

(125a) (311)
A wagers all his money on a boxing bout * A, wagering all his money on a boxing
bout between A-2 and A-8, learns that the pugilists are fast friends and that neither
will fight to win ** (606) (1215)

1232

(725 ch A to A-3 & A-5 to A) (998 ch A to A-3 & A-4 to A)
A discovers that A-3 has knowledge of a secret that will bring disaster to A if revealed * A finds it necessary to abduct A-3 and hold him incommunicado ** (719a
ch A to A-3) (875b ch A to A-3) (1130 ch A to A-3)

1233

(79)　(804)　(980-*)　(985)　(1265a tr A & A-3)
A finds himself in danger because he has innocently undertaken the custodianship of a mysterious package, X * A, in danger because he is the custodian of a mysterious package, X, contrives a dummy package, X2, exactly counterfeiting X in appearance ** (980*-**)　(1226)

1234

(838)　(1046)　(1050)
A recovers property stolen from his friend, A-2 * A, recovering property stolen from his friend, A-2, seeks to restore it by stealth so A-2 will not know it has been out of his possession ** (786)　(808a ch B to A-2)　(1035 tr A & A-2)　(1337)

1235

(1216)　(1227a-*)
A attempts to deceive his friend, A-2, thinking to profit by the deception, but fails * A's friend, A-2, reaps a rich reward from a discovery he has made and offers to share with A; but A, knowing he is unworthy of such generosity, refuses it ** (1249)　(1295)

1236

(213-* ch A to A-8, B to SR-A & A-7 to A)　(1123; 126 ch B to B-3; 24a ch A to A-8 & B to SR-A; 262a ch B to SR-A & A to A-8)
A, by trickery, prevents his sister, SR-A, from marrying A-8 * A, through deception involving his sister, SR-A, wins a large estate ** (1291a)　(1295)　(1443b)

1237

(a)　(1314)　(1316
A pretends to lead a dissipated life * A pretends that he is "going to the dogs" in order to deceive his mortal enemy, A-3, and lead A-3 to believe he is not to be feared ** A, when his mortal enemy, A-3, is lulled by a false sense of security, strikes and kills *** (1039)　(1311)

(b)　(484b)　(606)　(631)
A kills himself, but contrives to make his death appear accidental * A kills himself in order that money, to be secured as life insurance, will take care of his pressing obligations ** (802a ch A to A-6 & B to A)　(952)
[1] A closes himself inside his garage, starts the engine of his car, inhales the exhaust gases, and dies [2] A pretends to stall his automobile on the railroad track and is killed by a limited train [3] A while in a profuse perspiration from violent exercise deliberately exposes himself to the wintry air [4] A, on a hunting trip, is killed when his gun is "accidentally" discharged

1238

(654)　(839 tr A & A-2)　(1074)　A, a writer, slipping in his work as the years advance, draws on the material of his earlier days to keep himself going. The material exhausted, A dies (868 tr A & A-2)　(Allegorical: 1348b)

1239

(1087)　(1211)
A, a crook, launches a benevolent enterprise as a means of making secret restitution of his ill-gotten gains (882)　(923)

1240

(449)　(583b)
B goes innocently with A-3, a friend, to pass a few days at a summer resort * B's friend, A-3, dies suddenly in his room in a summer resort hotel; and B, first to discover A-3's death, flees secretly in order that her name may not be compromised ** (410)　(1151)

1241

(a) (₡16) (1033)
B undertakes, for extravagant pay, to carry out a secret investigation (1267b, c ch A to A-8) in which it is necessary for her to pretend to be deaf and dumb, and in which she must have a knowledge of "sign" language (677) (802b ʈr A & B) (890) (933)

(b) (284) (871) (1220b ch A to F-B)
B, compelled by her father, F-B, to engage in a distasteful enterprise, evades the enterprise by pretending to have suddenly been stricken deaf and dumb (676) (741)

(c) (664 ch A to B) (1135b)
B, engaged in an enterprise that might cause gossip or censure, escapes from a room by picking the lock of a door with a bent hairpin (669) (1151)

1242

(a) (470) (1033)
B, a young woman engaged in an enterprise that might cause gossip or censure, defers to public opinion by a stratagem (84a) (86) (1025) (1158)

(b) (117 ch F-A to B) (118 ch GF-A to B & B to B-8)
B, wealthy relative of A, dies and leaves him a fortune provided he will not do a certain thing * A renounces an inheritance because of a distasteful obligation attached to it; and then, after giving up the inheritance, a codicil to the will restores it to him, stating that the supposed obligation was merely a "test of merit" ** (1041 ch A to B) (1462)

1243

(125a) (189)
B subtly places obstacles in the path of A; obstacles which, when overcome, will profit A and develop his moral courage (188a) (814)

1244

(a) (241) (812b)
B plans to forward an enterprise, but cannot do so openly and must resort to craftiness (806 ch B-4 to B) (1241a, b, c) (1242a) (1243)

(b) (152b) (946) (1220b-*)
B, in order to forward a certain enterprise, assumes a fictitious name and secures the position of private secretary to A (666) (679) (826)

1245

(849) (173) (1343 ch A to B) B prevents a stranger, B-4, from buying an article, X, which, B is convinced, will bring her only misfortune, by tying to Y a ticket labeled "sold" (89) (1400)

1246

(766) (908) (1105) B, daughter of M-B, falling into error, conducts herself unwisely and scorns admonition * B's mother, M-B, copies B's foolish conduct, thus giving B a visible demonstration of its absurdity ** (931) (933)

(13) Seeking by Craftiness to Escape Misfortune

1247

(98) (658) (1177) (1185)
A seeks craftily to keep the good opinion of the public * A closely guards an evil secret which, if known, would reflect upon his character and make impossible a cherished enterprise ** (1084) (1101) (1103) (1110)

1248

(756) (925-*) (1146)
A is a doctor, who follows his honest profession by day, and makes it a "cover" for his activities as a burglar by night (660a) (712) (1031)

1249

(701)   (1304)

A attempts craftily to clear himself of a suspicion of robbery * A explains that he invested money, belonging to himself and A-2, in an enterprise that failed ** (1160)   (1162)   (1235)

1250

(280a)   (655-*)   (663)   (607 ch A-2 to A-3)   (1255b ch A-8 to A-3)

A is helpless against an armed enemy, A-3 * A pretends to be hors du combat for the purpose of luring his enemy, A-3, within arm's reach ** (1189 ch A-6 to A-3) (1222b)   (1232)   (1237a)

1251

(983)   (998 ch A to A-8 & A-4 to A)

A is aware that A-8 knows too much for his (A's) good * A gives A-8 money with which to take himself out of the country ** (1239)   (1247)

1252

(1291b ch A-2 to A-8)   (1290a ch A-2 to A-8)   (1309b ch B to A & A-3 to A-8)

A, to rid himself of the body of his murdered victim, A-8, and escape suspicion, hides the body in an old tomb (1291a)   (1302)   (1344-* ch A-2 to A-8)

1253

(1255a-**)   (1265a)

A is lured into a trap by A-3 * A, lured into a trap by A-3, has set a counter-trap for A-3 ** (1255**-***)   (1261)   (1272 ch A-9 to A-3)

1254

(1085)   (1086)   (1297)

A, painting a house, finds the purse of B lying on a bench in the garden * A finds a purse which contains the key to B's strong box ** A rifles the safe of B, his employer, and returns the key of the strong box to the place where he found it. **But there is a smear of yellow paint on the key** *** (1295)   (1302)   (1447 tr A & A-8)   (1461a)

1255

(a)   (75a)   (1253)   (1278a ch A-8 to A-3)

A is inveigled into a gambling game by A-3 * A's enemy, A-3, lures A into a gambling game and arranges for a fake police raid * A's enemy, A-3, arranges for a fake police raid on a gambling game; but A, secretly informed, has the police make a real raid (236)   (280b)

(b)   (1029)   (1043)   (1128b)

A is in a wild race with A-8 for a fortune * A's fortune depends on winning a race with A-8, and in reaching town and securing a certain document, X, before A-8 can get his hands on it ** (711b-**)   (685)   (1250 ch A-3 to A-8)

1256

(903)   (1029)   (1257)   A has a valuable work of art destroyed by a lady, B, in a tantrum * B, a very great personage, snatches A's cane and belabors him with it. A auctions off the cane as a priceless piece for a collection ** (814)

1257

(721)   (938)

A, a sculptor, models a bust of B (908)   (1067-*) at B's order * B, displeased with the work of a sculptor, A, destroys a bust in an angry outburst ** (1256)   (1395)

1258

(448)   (1309b)

B, a woman criminal arrested by A-6, a detective, seeks to effect her escape by artful strategy (3b)   (10a)   (16a)

1259

(974)   (1267a ch A to A-5)

B traps A-5, a thief, by telling him ner valuables are in a clothes closet—and then locking the closet (1335 ch A to A-5)   (850b)

(14) Falling Into Misfortune Through the Wiles of a Crafty Schemer

1260

(a) (1140) (1000-* ch A to A-8)
A, rich and unscrupulous, has set his heart on acquiring a certain piece of ground * A desires property which A-8 refuses to sell; so A ruins A-8 financially and forces him to sell ** (1000*-**) (1443b) (1439b tr A & A-8)

(b) (380 ch A to A-8 & A-3 to A) (898-*)
A, rich and unscrupulous, craftily manoeuvers A-8 into debt * A, manoeuvering A-8 into debt, offers to cancel the debt if A-8 will agree to a certain proposition ** (48 tr A & A-8) (269 ch A-3 to A-8)

1261

(280a tr A & A-3) (1191 ch A-4 to A-3)
A's confederate, B, with a woman's wiles, lures A-3 into a trap that has been set for him (1253 tr A & A-3) (1255a tr A & A-3)

1262

(96) (98)
A represents guilt-masquerading-as-innocence * A is influenced to engage in an enterprise that will bring about his punishment for transgression ** (753) (628) (1261 tr A & A-3)

1263

(447 ch A to A-8) (1293a)
A discovers an evil secret of B's past * A decides to use secret information for blackmailing purposes ** (870b ch A-5 to A) (1309a)

1264

(1168-* tr A & A-2) (1277b ch A to A-2) (1288-*)
A persuades his friend, A-2, to undertake a hazardous piece of work—and does not tell him it is hazardous (1168 tr A & A-2) (1265a ch A-3 to A-2) (1288*-**) (1272 ch A to A-2 & A-9 to A) (1275 ch A to A-2 & A-5 to A)

1265

(a) (75a tr A & A-3) (1264 ch A-2 to A-3)
A, seeking to obtain unfair advantage of A-3, induces him to take charge of some contraband goods, knowing he will be apprehended (623 ch A to A-3) (1154b ch A to A-3 & B-3 to A)

(b) (174; 816a) (711a)
A's rival, A-3, when A fails to join him in an enterprise as agreed, carries out the enterprise alone (603a ch A-2 to A-3) (701 ch A to A-3 & A-2 to A)

1266

(98 ch A to A-3; 1326) (554)
A's enemy, A-3, is a connoisseur of wines * A, by working on A-3's pride as a connoisseur of wines, lures him into a wine vault where he is faced with death ** (1311-*) (1311) (1325 ch B to A & A to A-3)

1267

(a) (409 tr A & A-3) (1314 tr A & A-3)
A, influenced to carry out an enterprise, falls into a trap—a trap of mysterious dangers unknown to him (1264 ch A to A-8 & A-2 to A) (1265a ch A to A-8 & A-3 to A) (1266 tr A & A-3)

(b) (1241a) (1267c)
A, a miser who is deaf and dumb, is made a prisoner in his home by A-5, who seeks to force him to reveal the whereabouts of hidden wealth (885a) (890)

(c) (1278b ch A to A-8) (1438b)
A, deaf and dumb, is dying and desires to make a will. The lawyer who has been summoned, A-8, thinks chicanery is afoot, and hires B to go with him to read A's "sign language" (1432) (1461b ch A to B & AX to A)

1268

(1023)   (1024)
A's plan to commit a robbery becomes known, and a trap is laid for him at the scene of the intended crime (637)   (664)

1269

(831)   (832 tr A & A-2)
A discovers his friend, A-2's, secret transgression * A informs the authorities of his friend, A-2's, secret transgression and receives the reward for A-2's capture ** (1039 ch A to A-2 & A-3 to A)   (1313a tr A & A-2)   (1313b ch A to A-2 & A-3 to A)

1270

(825)   (1024 ch A to NW)
A disapproves of his nephew, NW; and A, sick unto death, sends for a lawyer, A-8, to draw his will * A's nephew, NW, tricks A into thinking that he is A-8, the lawyer who has come to draw A's will ** (117 ch A to NW & F-A to A)   (1432)

1271

(1180)   (1184)
A pretends to be a novelist, A-4, writing a burglar story * A, a crook, pretends to be a novelist, A-4, writing a burglar story; and a banker, A-8 (1177 ch A to A-8), obligingly gives A information about his own bank vaults ** (1174)   (1251 tr A & A-8)   (1253 ch A-3 to A-8)

1272

(604 ch A-8 to A-9)   (1267a)   (1264 ch A to A-9 & A-2 to A)
A, at the instigation of A-9, unknowingly commits a crime * A, innocent, is arrested for a crime; and his employer, A-9, testifies against him ** (866; 1322 ch A-3 to A-9)   (329 ch A-2 to A-9; 850a)

1273

(922b)   (1082b)   (1389b)   A is selling luck charms among a superstitious people * A, selling luck charms in a town, is denounced by the mayor of the town, A-9, as an imposter because A has not "crossed A-9's palm with silver" ** (1220a ch B to A-9)   (1278e ch A-8 to A-9)

1274

(689)   (937) · (1289b-*)   A, seeking to convert a savage people to Christianity, has all his efforts set at naught by A-3, a witch doctor * A smashes an idol, X. supposed by a savage people to be a god, and immediately good fortune comes to the tribe. A-3 is discredited ** (973)   (1289b*-***)   (1319b tr A & A-3)

(52) Encountering a Would-Be Transgressor and Seeking to Prevent a Transgression

1275

(572)   (708)
A, supposed to be dead, assumes a fictitious name * A, supposed dead, discovers an imposter, A-5, using his name and pretending that he is A ** (658)   (1226)

1276

(612)   (1191 ch A to A-5 & A-4 to A)
A detects A-5 cheating at cards, and denounces him; in the fight that follows, A-5 is killed (750)   (1017 ch A to A-6 & A-5 to A)

(51) Devising a Clever and Plausible Delusion in Order to Forward Certain Ambitious Plans

1277

(a)   (568c)   (1291b ch A-2 to A-3)   (1316)   (1341 ch A-4 to A-3)
A, to escape suspicion, places the body of A-3, the man he has slain, on a railroad track in an attempt to make it appear that A-3 was killed by a train (1247)   (1332)

(b) (952) (1085)
A craftily fosters the delusion of his own death * A, by a stratagem, fosters the delusion of his own death in an attempt to realize money on his life insurance ** (1211) (1222a tr A & A-3) (1239)

1278

(a) (125a) (126)
A, counseled by artful B, makes use of important papers belonging to A-8 (1054) in forwarding a certain enterprise (110-2) (1278c)

(b) (153-*) (1461d)
A sends a package to B, by messenger * B-3, lurking in the doorway of B, pretends to be B and receipts for a package delivered by messenger ** (218b) (153*-**) (826 ch A to A-3 & B to B-3)

(c) (125a) (1278a)
A, by chance, receives confidential information sent by A-4 to A-8 * A, by using confidential information, convinces A-8 of his supposed ability and secures a position at a good salary ** (225) (367b)

(d) (1143a ch A to A-4; 1144) (1188-*)
A, pretending to be seriously ill, is befriended by wealthy A-4. A-8, a doctor, is called in by A-4, and he informs A privately that he is an imposter * A is discovered by A-8, a doctor, to be shamming illness. By collusion, they foster A's pretensions, whereby A secures bed and board from wealthy A-4, and A-8 secures a fat fee ** (698 ch A to A-4; 1378 ch A to A-4; 1212b ch A-8 to A-4) (1166a)

(e) (1212a ch A to A-8 & A-2 to A) (1273 ch A-9 to A-8)
A, a confidence man selling "luck charms," finds his business languishing because miserly and influential A-8 has warned the people that his wares are a delusion * A agrees to go "fifty-fifty" with respectable and influential but miserly A-8; and A-8 recommends the luck charms A is selling, and A's business flourishes (1222a ch A-3 to A-8) (1232 ch A-3 to A-8)

1279

(a) (124-*) (135)
B, middle-aged, is so adept in the arts of the toilette, that she keeps her beauty youthful and blooming. Apparently in her early twenties, she is really in her late forties (11b) (103) (124*-**)

(b) (1048) (1304)
B seeks to recover, by stratagem, wealth which was stolen from her by A * B steals softly into the room of A, who is spending the night at her home, and appropriates a bag of jewels that is under A's pillow ** B fires a revolver and pretends she is shooting at a thief who got away in the night *** (701) (1309b ch A-3 to A) (1309a)

(53) Opposing tne Plans of a Crafty Schemer

1280

(1254 ch A to A-3) (1303 ch A-9 to A-3) (1305 ch A-5 to A-3)
A catches his enemy, A-3, red-handed in a transgression * A, who "has the goods" on A-3, keeps his information from the authorities and holds A-3 in his power and subject, through fear of the law, to his will ** (1265a tr A & A-3) (1323b)

1281

(1218) (1085)
A, captured by A-5 and taken to a secret place, is being held for ransom * A's friend, A-2, captures B, daughter of A-5, and makes overtures to exchange B for A, whom A-5 is holding for ransom ** (885a ch A to A-2) (3a-* ch A to A-2)

1282

(1093 ch A to A-6) (1174)
A, a crook, commits a robbery and escapes in woman's clothes * A had local fame as a female impersonator; and A-6, a detective, makes use of this fact as a clue in apprehending A for transgression ** (651) (712)

1283

(1181)   (1268)   (1440 ch A to A-2; 1077)
A discovers where a certain object, X, small but immensely valuable, has been
concealed *A, to secure a certain object, X, must proceed warily and without
arousing suspicion ** (1146)   (1166a, b)

1284

(983 ch A to A-5 & A-8 to A)   (997 ch A-2 to A-5)   (1011)
A, a detective, captures a criminal, A-5, who was once an old friend of his * A,
a detective, owes A-5, a criminal he has captured, a sum of money which he has
not been able to repay; and A-5 hopes to make use of the debt in securing his release from custody ** A, a detective, gives A-5, a criminal he has captured, a written order for the reward offered for A-5's apprehension; thus A, having paid the
debt, takes A-5 to jail *** (1209c ch A to A-5)   (1319a ch A-3 to A-5 & tr A & A-5)

(20) Becoming Involved with Conditions in which
Misfortune is Indicated

1285

(a)   (1123)   (1127)   (1289c-*)
A plans by crafty enterprise to secure a rich inheritance   (1289c*-**)   (1197)
(1201)   (1285b)   (1290a, b)

(b)   (988)   (1002)
A, unknown to B, holds a large sum of money in trust for her * A, desperately in
need, secretly appropriates to his own use money belonging to B ** (422a) (1295)
(647 ch A-5 to A)

(c)   (680a)   (1248)
A, a "dummy chucker," pretends to have a fit on the walk in front of the mansion of A-4, a wealthy man * A, a crook, pretends to have a fit, and is befriended
by A-4, who calls in a doctor, A-8, to attend to him ** (711c)   (1278d)

1286

(600)   (1451d)
A finds the fly leaf of the Bible owned by his father, F-A * A finds evidence to
prove that his father, F-A, is dead ** (802b ch B to F-A)   (1018)

1287

(1019)   (1219 ch A to A-8)
A is threatened with violence if he carries out an enterprise connected with his
profession * A, in the face of threats, carries out a certain enterprise and discovers
that the threats were merely a stratagem to prove his courage ** (1006a) (1223b
ch A to A-9 & A-4 to A)

1288

(245 ch A-3 to A-2)   (380 ch A-3 to A-2)   (1267a ch A to A-2)
A challenges his friend (really his enemy), A-2, to a mock duel, the pistols to be
loaded with blank cartidges—a performance ostensibly for the entertainment
of their friends * A, in what is supposed to be a mock duel with A-2, falls at the
first exchange of shots, craftily killing himself in such a way that it appears the
killing was done by A-2 ** (603a tr A & A-2)   (624 ch A to A-2)

1289

(a)   (830 ch A to A-2)   (1199-* ch A to SN)
A is a wealthy man whom sharpers, A-5, A-5, are seeking to influence to disinherit
a son, SN (1199*-** ch A to SN)   (1432 ch NW to SN)   (1432)

(b)   (687)   (689)   (1274-*)
A, a white man among savages, seeks to avert a calamity by prayer * A's enemy,
A-3, seeks to avert a calamity by an incantation ** A, by prayer, and A-3, by an
incantation, seek to avert a calamity. The calamity is averted *** (1274*-**)
(197)

(c)   (490b ch A-2 to U)   (1057b)   (1285a)
A's rich uncle, U, promises to leave his wealth to A when A and his wife, B, shall be blessed with a son and heir * A, seeking by strategy to secure a rich inheritance, fails in his plans when his uncle, U, discovers A's "son and heir" to be a girl ** (781 ch A to U)   (867 ch A-2 to U)

(d)   (1124)   (1337 ch A to A-6 & A-2 to A)   (1341)
A is so worried about a certain secret enterprise that, in his absent-minded moments, he pencils, on anything that happens to be convenient, diagrams that offer a clue to the enterprise * A's secret is discovered by A-6, who craftily makes use of clues furnished unwittingly by A himself ** (1011 ch A to A-6 & A-5 to A) 1284 ch A to A-6 & A-5 to A)

(21) Falling Into Misfortune Through Mistaken Judgment

1290

(a) (1001a) (1285a)
A kills A-2 who is about to marry his sister, SR-A, in order that he may inherit wealth possessed by SR-A (51a, b) (1252 ch A-8 to A-2)

(b) (1195) (1217b)
A, profligate son of wealthy F-A, cast off and disowned, murders F-A then poses as F-A in an attempt to secure F-A's property * A, posing as F-A, is unmasked when discovered removing F-A's clothes ** (705) (1006a ch A to A-8 & A-5 to A)

1291

(a) (1236) (1277a, b) (1278c) (1290a)
A commits a transgression and escapes unsuspected * A, committing a transgression and escaping unsuspected, is so tortured by conscience that he has to give himself up and confess ** (802b ch A to A-6) (803a ch A to A-6) (787 ch A to A-8)

(b) (1276 ch A-5 to A-2) (1269)
A, in a drunken brawl, quarrels with A-2 * A, recovering sense and reason after a drunken brawl, discovers A-2 dead at his feet and thinks he has killed him ** (1168) (1183) (1277a ch A-3 to A-2)

(c) (1000) (1432 ch A to F-A & NW to A)
A's estate has been in his family for hundreds of years and it is an unwritten law of the family that it is to be held intact * A commits a transgression when he sells a piece of woodland, part of an inherited estate ** (1353) (1358)

1292

(3a) (397) (448)
B seeks happiness as a retormed transgressor * B, seeking happiness as a reformed transgressor, has her old transgression discovered ** (359) (665) (669)

1293

(a) (179a, c) (532a)
B forges the name of her father, F-B, to a note in order to secure money for a certain purpose * B forges the name of her father, F-B, to a note. Unknown to B, F-B dies suddenly before the date of the note ** (69) (410)

(b) (668) (993) (1033)
B secretly borrows on property she is holding in trust in order to forward a certain enterprise (669) (743b) (801) (921) (946)

(c) (532a) (659) (1308)
B, in order to carry out a certain enterprise, sells a valuable heirloom, X, confided to her for safe-keeping by A (1440 ch A to B; 1384 ch B to B-4) (1204)

1294

(446a) (448) (1309b)
B commits a transgression in order to conceal a less serious transgression * B, committing one transgression in order to hide another, is apprehended for her crime, brought to trial and sentenced ** (1308; 1309a) (1293c; 1309a)

(20) Becoming Involved with Conditions in which Misfortune is Indicated

1295

(1110) (1236) (1254) (1285b)
A, suffering remorse because he has committed a transgression, seeks to make restitution (422a) (842a) (1160) (1211)

1296

(1021b) (923) A, a prospector, discovers gold * A, a prospector, makes a rich "strike". Of right he should share his discovery with his partner, A-2, but decides to exploit his discovery for himself alone ** (701) (1235) (1291b)

1297

(111)   (113)   (484b-*)   (723)
A, a poor man going about his honest duties, is suddenly afforded the opportunity
to commit a secret transgression whereby he will acquire great gain without incurring suspicion * A fights against the temptation to acquire gain through transgression ** (484b*-**)   (1278c)   (1254)

1298

(900; 31)   (922b)   (954)
A is a notorious outlaw, at large and craftily avoiding apprehension (52b)   (100)
(651)   (673)   (699a)   (722 ch A to A-6 & A-5 to A)   (883)

1299

(1123 ch SR-A to A-8)   (1127 ch CN to A-8 & A-8 to A-4)
A seeks to acquire a rich estate in spite of A-8's legal rights (1236 ch SR-A to B-8)
(1290a ch A-2 to A-8 & SR-A to B-8)

1300

(1277b)   (1291b)
A has committed a crime and fled to escape the consequences * A finds it important that he show himself where he is known; but it is also important that he remain in hiding ** (699a)   (955)   (1013)

1301

(1277a)   (1282)   (1285)   (1289b-*)
A seeks to evade the legal consequences of a crime he has committed (866)   (883)
(887a)   (923)

1302

(1291c)   (1340)   (1341)
A, a transgressor, seeks to forget a transgression, but a certain object, X, (or circumstance) continually reminds him of it (1344)   (1355)   (1360)   (1365)   (1366)

1303

(802b)   (803a)   (1114)
A discovers secretly that his employer, A-9, is   murderer and a fugitive from
justice (725 ch A-5 to A-9)   (596 ch A-5 to A-9)   (854)

1304

(1079)   (1085 ch A-2 to B)
A and A-2 are placer mining in partnership * A, under cover of night, takes all
the wealth belonging to both himself and A-2 and decamps with it ** (488b) (701)
(1048)   (1160)

1305

(968)   (970)   (1111b)
A captures a burglar, A-5, who is looting his house (1234)   (1451b ch A-8 to A-5)
(1460 ch A-4 to A-5)

1306

(68)   (658)
A, a minister of the gospel, errs secretly on his human side and commits a moral
transgression * A, highly placed and universally respected, protects his reputation by keeping a moral lapse a close secret (951)   (1110)   (1291a)

1307

(616)   (898)   A, in his safe, has a fortune in valuables. During his absence,
crooks, A-5, A-5, A-5, attempt to open the safe and loot it of its contents * B (666)
(152b)   (921), A's secretary, is made a prisoner by crooks, A-5, A-5, A-5, when
they fail to open A's safe ** (144)   (801)   (885b)   (1010)

308

(988) (1002)

B's guardian, A, appropriates to his own use the property of B * B, engaged in carrying out an enterprise, finds that she must give it up for lack of funds when her guardian, A, misappropriates her resources ** (642-*\ (739) (812a) (850 ch A to A-8)

1309

(a) (407) (890) (947)

B, seeking to protect herself from A, shoots and kills him (60) (887a ch A to B & A-3 to A)

(b) (400) (483b) (495) (126 ch A to A-3)

B's friend, A-3, mysteriously disappears (770a ch A to A-3) (1277b ch A to A-3) while in B's company * B is arrested on suspicion of having murdered A-3 ** (635 ch A to B) (648)

(21) Falling Into Misfortune Through Mistaken Judgment

1310

(66a, b, c)   (433a)   (1320 tr A & A-8)
A seeks by craftiness to be revenged on B * A, seeking revenge against B, over-reaches himself ** (647 ch A-5 to A)   (648)   (669 ch A-5 to A)   (818a tr A & A-4)

1311

(1237a)   (1317 ch A-8 to A-3)
A revenges himself upon an enemy, A-3 * A revenges himself upon an enemy, A-3, unaware of the fact that A-3 is his brother ** (1039)   (1319a)

(46) Seeking Retaliation for a Grievous Wrong that is Either Real or Fancied

1312

(695b ch A to A-8)   (696 ch A to A-8)
A's relative, A-8, has been grievously wronged by the authorities of their common country * A seeks revenge against his country for a grievous wrong ** (1372a, b)

1313

(a)   (139)   (446b)   (601)
A seeks revenge upon his friend, A-2 * A and his friend, A-2, are of high and hon-ored station; and A, seeking revenge against A-2, must conceal his purpose and proceed by indirection ** (1216)   (1260a ch A-8 to A-2)   (1264)   (1265 ch A-3 to A-2)   (1269)   (1288)
(b)   (79)   (557a)   (1142a)   (1275 ch A-5 to A-3)   (1277b)
A, supposed to be dead, plays the role of a ghost * A, supposed dead, plays the role of ghost and, as a method of reprisal, haunts his enemy, A-3 ** (1291a ch A to A-3)   (1334a ch A to A-3)   (1332 ch A to A-3)   (1344 ch A to A-3 & A-2 to A)   (1358 ch A to A-3)

1314

(1003)
A has no personal enmity against A-3, but he is caught in the toils of a family feud and his obligation requires that he kill A-3 (1109)   (1309a ch B to A & A to A-3)   (912b)

1315

(123 ch F-B to A-3)   (245)   (1109-*)
A seeks revenge against A-3 for a disrespectful remark against A's family (1109*-**)
(840 tr A & A-2)   (1222a)

1316

(1323c ch A to A-3 & A-8 to A)   (1333a ch A to A-3)
A seeks revenge against A-3 for a persecution that results in the death of A's par-ents and sisters (433a)   (1039)   (1237a)   (1277a)

1317

(313 ch F-B to A-8)   (171; 223 ch F-B to A-8)
A, a poor young man, inspired by anger and a desire for revenge, seeks to ruin wealthy A-8, a powerful captain of industry (780)   (1319 ch A-3 to A-8)

1318

(79)   (247 ch A to A-3)   (411b)   (567)
A seeks revenge against A-3 for a terrible wrong * A, seeking revenge against A-3, discovers after a long search that A-3 is dead ** (433a)

1319

(a)   (567-*)   (1269 ch A to A-3 & A-2 to A)   A, in order to be revenged upon his enemy, A-3, manufactures an infernal machine, X * A sends an infernal machine, X, to his enemy, A-3, and it falls into the hands of A's friend, A-2 ** (987)   (1344)
(b)   (887b)   (300; 887b)   A constructs a deadly trap in a place where, he thinks, his enemy, A-3, will fall into it * A sets a trap for A-3, but A-2 is caught in it ** (653 ch A to A-2 & A-5 to A)   (728 ch CH to A-2)

1320

(818a-*) (1138) (1310 ch A to A-8)
A is a malefactor of small pretensions, a down-and-outer of striking physical appearance masked by rags and squalor * A, down and out, is hired by A-8, a revengeful rich man, to wear evening clothes, appear at a social gathering and act as a catspaw in carrying out a vicious scheme of reprisal ** (818a*-** ch A-4 to A-8) (1217c ch A to A-8 & A-5 to A)

1321

(812a ch B to SR-A) (1326 ch B to SR-A)
A seeks revenge for a wrong committed against his sister, SR-A * A, seeking revenge for a wrong committed against his sister, SR-A, has difficulty in discovering the name of the wrong-doer ** (737c ch B to SR-A & A to A-8) (801 ch B to SR-A)

1322
(567) (1228)
A seeks to be revenged on A-3· but A-3 is powerful and constantly on his guard against A (1222a) (1237a)

1323

(a) (433a) (662 ch A-2 to A-3) (1323b)
A, seeking revenge against B-3 for a wrong committed by her husband, A-3, who is dead, finds that B-3 treasures A-3's memory most sacredly, unaware of his evil character * A could destroy the beautiful love and devotion of B-3, for her dead husband, A-3, by telling her the sort of man A-3 was ** A, in a spiritual victory, decides to forego a cherished enterprise and spare an innocent woman her happy but mistaken ideals ***

(b) (157) (260a)
A, prosperous and successful, is hated by a rival, A-3 * A is brought under suspicion as a political conspirator through the craftiness of a rival, A-3 ** (715c) (829) (1280)

(c) (1310 ch B to A-8) (1317)
A commits an act of reprisal against A-8 with more serious results than he had intended [1] A blows up a dam and sends a flood of released waters down on the home of A-8 [2] A sends an infernal machine to the home of A-8 [3] A sends a box of poisoned candy to the home of A-8 (797) (1298) (817)

1324

(a) (1324b-*) (1299 ch A to A-3) (1261 tr A & A-3)
A's enemy, A-3, craftily seeks to encompass the death of A * A, by subtle enterprise, brings upon A-3 the fate A-3 was seeking to bring upon him ** (1324b*-**) (1250) (1253) (1267a ch A to A-3)

(b) (1324a) (1310 ch A to A-3 & B to A) (1313a ch A to A-3 & A-2 to A)
A is sent abroad with a companion, A-3. A-3 bears a letter to a clique of powerful conspirators, A-5, A-5, ordering the death of A * A secretly examines a letter in the possession of A-3, his traveling companion, and discovers that the letter is his own death warrant. A carefully erases his own name and fills in the name of A-3 ** (1262 ch A to A-3) (1313b ch A-3 to A-8)

1325
(98) (605) (1422b)
B, suffering a grievous injury at the hands of A, seeks to kill him by making use of a certain odor which A regards with superstitious fear (1268) (1445)

1326
(162b) (225 ch A to A-8)
B, wronged, is helpless in reprisal; her friend, A, champions her cause (188b) (294a; 294b)

1327

(1324b-*)   (1323b)

A, high born, falls under the ban of death as a political conspirator in his native country * A evades a conspiracy aimed at his life and escapes to a distant land **
(1324b*-**)   (1329)

1328

(98)   (246a)

B seeks revenge as a lofty conception of duty—and comes to her death while seeking it (746)   (802b)   (893)

1329

(777)   (942)   (1327)

A, an aristocrat, is trailed and spied upon by enemies, A-3, A-3, A-3, seeking his life * A disguises himself as a hoodlum and lives in the underworld as a means of escaping enemies, A-3, A-3, A-3, who are seeking his life ** (1225)   (1275)   (1324a)

(21) Falling Into Misfortune Through Mistaken Judgment

1330

(853)   (900-*)   (1150)
A, dabbling in things he does not understand, seeks to accomplish wonderful results * A, involving himself recklessly in matters he does not understand, succeeds
only in making himself ridiculous ** (231)   (513)   (900*-**)   (1111b)

1331

(98)   (565)   (568b)   (1342a)
A, with a fearful oath declares: "I will see home to-night in spite of the storm, or
I will never see home!" * A, homeward bound, drives and drives; and he is still
driving, no nearer his home than he was when he first started ** (545)   (789)
(1345)

1332

(1061)   (1078)   (1132)   (1344)
A flees from a pursuer who is wholly imaginary (855)   (857)   (1104)

1333

(a)   (96)   (387-*)   (1113)   (1310)
A, a chemist, with the use of subtle poisons, develops a flower of unusual color
and beauty * A gives B, who loves flowers, some of his rare blooms—with unhappy results ** (387*-**)   (371)

(b)   (1410)   (1384 ch B to A)
A, with a hobby for collecting curios, presents B with an old, hand painted miniature * The miniature of a beautiful woman, framed in gold, containing a mechanism
by which a needle, steeped in poison, is thrown out of the painted face.   The
minature to be worn "next the heart" ** (1461b)   (1433c)   (1438b ch A to B)

1334

(a)   (475)   (576a)   (872 ch B to A)   (1064)   (1132)
A is haunted by a delusion that arouses superstitious fear and causes him to give
up an enterprise (1350)   (1351)   (1356)

(b)   (603b, c, d)
A's friend, A-2, is killed in an accident at A's side * A, superstitious, believes he
is haunted by the ghost of his friend, A-2 ** (827)   (830 tr A and A-2)   (839 tr
A & A-2)

(c)   (1277b ch A to A-2)   (1348b ch A to A-2)
A's friend, A-2, is mysteriously murdered * A seeks to discover the murderer of
his friend, A-2 ** (1222a)   (833)

1335

(74a)   (513)   (1248)   (1283)
A, seeking to carry out a certain enterprise, climbs into a building and suddenly
discovers that the room he has entered is a trap; all windows bar themselves, and
the stout door locks against him (636)   (1272)

1336

(922b)   (1150)
A, a needy person, picks up two pairs of cast-off shoes, one pair discarded by a
clergyman, and the other pair by a man of reckless nature and "shady" reputation *
A, in one pair of shoes, is meek and circumspect in his behavior; when wearing
another pair he is wild and profligate ** (What would happen if he wore one of
each pair?)   (1084)   (1134)   (1148a)

1337

(750)   (1234)   A stumbles over the body of a murdered man, A-8 * A, stealthily
entering the house of his friend, A-2, finds the body of a murdered man, A-8 **
(808a ch B to A-8)   (807)   (820)   (833)

1338

(1215 ch A-8 to A)   (1344)
A, a pugilist, believes that A-2, a friend whom he killed by a chance blow in a practice bout, is present in the ring every time he has a battle (602)   (1357)

1339

(1129b ch A to A-4 & A-5 to A)   (1129c ch A to A-4 & A-5 to A)
A is a transgressor posing as an honest man * A is hired by A-4 to recover stolen property which, unknown to A-4, was stolen by A himself ** (1193 ch A-3 to A-4) (1209a)

1340

(623 ch A to A-4)   (1080)   (1301 ch A to A-4)
A a reporter, writing up an imaginary interview as fact, quotes A-4 as being in town on a certain day * A-4, accused of a crime, establishes an alibi through an interview innocently faked by a reporter, A ** (635 ch A to A-4)   (1302)   (1203 ch A to A-4)

1341

(1027)   (1277a ch A-3 to A-4)
A murders a stranger, A-4, in a lonely wood where the soil is of a peculiar color, unlike any other soil for miles around. A sulks back home with the mud on his shoes (467)   (1302)

1342

(a)   (1357-*)   (1374-*)   (1389)
A, staring at a certain object, X, falls under a spell which leads him to believe certain events are transpiring—events that are partly true but mostly grotesquely false (265a)   (633)   (1358)   (1361b)   (1357*-**)   (1374*-**)   (1375)   Note: [1] X is a small image, a peculiar idol, that has such a strange fascination for A that he keeps it always before him on his writing desk; or [2] X is a mirror. A little cloud appears on the face of an old mirror, then disappears, leaving mysterious persons and scenes on the glass; or [3] X is a green stone, a beautiful piece of jade, on which are engraved characters signifying "Bakht," Persian for "good luck"

(b)   (1291a)   (1301)   (1311)   (1324a)   (1449 ch A-2 to A-3)
A supposes he has murdered A-3; then, suddenly, A-3 appears before him (1366) (1375)

1343

(1380)   (1282a-*)   (1383)
A carries in his pocket a queer object of mystery, X * A, apparently as the result of carrying in his pocket a queer object of mystery, X, experiences all sorts of misfortunes ** (595)   (596)   (597)   (1352)   (1377b)   (1382*-**)   Note: [1] X is a large silver watch, engraved with queer inscriptions, considered a tailsman by the tribe of wandering Arabs from whom it was stolen; or [2] X is a Chinese coin; or [3] X is a dried "button" of the mescal plant. See [3] 1342

1344

(683)   (1291b)
A has a delusion that he is haunted by A-2 * A believes that the blood öf A-2 is on his hands ** (633)   (794)

1345

(53)   (567a)   (683)   (887b)   (681a)
A is under the delusion that he lives in a chaotic world. such a world as is pictured by pessimists (1331)   (1332)   (1351)

1346

(723 ch A-5 to A-3)   (735-* ch A-8 to A-3)   (764)   (775 ch A-7 to A-3)
A, in early life, killed A-3 in the heat of passion by striking him with the weighted handle of a riding crop. A, unsuspected, escapes from the scene of the tragedy * A, a man of wealth and influence, holds his place in society by closely guarding a tragic secret ** (1263 ch A to A-7 & B to A)   (1269 ch A to A-7 & A-2 to A) (1114 ch A to A-7 & A-9 to A)

1347

(853)   (855)   (858)
A, seeking sincerely to investigate psychic phenomena, begins unconsciously to mix truth with delusion (633)   (1357)   (1375)

1348

(a) (899) (925) (715a-*)
A's mortal pride would transgress the Divine Power; so fate, seeking to discipline A, materializes a spirit, AX, in A's image * A's property and high place in the world are appropriated by AX, and when A would claim his earthly possessions, he is treated as an imposter ** (681b) (715a*-***) (918b)

(b) (1387) (1389b) (1418a; 1433b)
A invents a mechanical giant, AX, and endows it with life * A, inventing a mechanical giant, AX, and endowing it with life, is pursued by AX and brought to his death **

1349

(98; 1326 ch A to A-7) (1177) (1178) (1262)
A represents guilt-masquerading-as-innocence * A, representing guilt-masquerading-as-innocence, is influenced by his valet, A-7, through a curiosity-arousing suggestion, to visit a certain place where, unknown to A, a deadly trap has been laid for him ** (1266 ch A-3 to A-7) (1267a) (1266 ch A to A-7 & A-3 to A)

1350

(567a) (857)
A thinks himself obsessed with a fear of speeding automobiles, and that the cars that are trying to run him down are phantom cars * A, in order to disprove a fancied hallucination, deliberately throws himself in front of a speeding automobile which he supposes to be a phantom ** (634) (1375)

1351

(1019) (1078) (1334a)
A decides that what he has come to consider a danger is merely a fancied danger inspired by fear * A, in order to shatter his fear complex, plunges into a supposed fancied danger that proves to be real ** (1350) (1367a) (1374)

1352

(1343) (1347) (1380)
A is given a small object of mystery, X, by a stranger, A-4, and assured that its possession will bring misfortune* A, carrying in his pocket a small object of mystery, X, is harried by ill-luck and comes to believe in the malefic powers of X ** A, meeting A-4, a man who gave him a small object of mystery, X, which has brought A ill luck, is informed by A-4 that only A's belief in the misfortunes inspired them, and that he was merely the victim of suggestion *** (1375) (1400)

1353

(579a) (1120) (1134) (1291c) A, during a storm, defies the Supreme Power * A, during a storm, has a narrow escape when lightning strikes a tree under which he is standing, throwing A to the ground and injuring him severely** A, slowly recovering from injuries in a hospital, changes his views on certain important questions *** (918a, b)

1354

(a) (1027; 1421) (1441a) (1451b ch A-8 to AX) (1418b)
A discovers a magic method for realizing all his wishes (1384 ch B to A) but at the expense of years of his life for every wish granted * A, discovering a magic method for **wishing** and **having**, makes a last wish that he shall live forever; but his magic fails him, and he dies ** (1432) (1433b)

(b) (1444; 1377b) (125a)
A, spurred into putting forth an unusual effort by B, succeeds in winning a fortune [1] in an oil well or [2] in a gold mine (212b) (225) (307)

1355

(599; 1330) (830 tr A & A-2; 807) (1337; 820)
A is caught in a snare of superstitious delusion * A is haunted all his days by an act which he committed in an effort to help a friend, A-2 ** (732) (1302)

1356

(234a) (1344) (1352-*)
A's will is waging a psychic battle against fear * A is a performer whose specialty is a dare-devil act of great danger; but in A there is growing the feeling that he will fail, although he knows that death is sure if he even contemplates failure **; A is [1] a high-diver; [2] a "trick" bicycle rider with a "loop the loop" specialty; [3] an aviator whose specialty is airplane stunts; or [4] a "human fly" who climbs the walls of tall buildings (633) (710) (1334a) (1334b tr A & A-2) (1352*-***) (1375)

1357

(541) (1343) (1344) (1347)
A is investigating psychic phenomena * A meets with disaster when illusion becomes reality through the overthrow of his reason ** (1348a, b) (1351)

1358

(1433a, b) (1418a) (1427b)
A has a prophetic vision which _orecasts his death * A, taken ill, is haunted by a vision that forecasts his death, and he dies **

1359

(1325) (1326 ch A to A-8) (1422b)
A has a delusion in which a certain odor, manifesting itself during a tragic experience, fills him with superstitious dread * A, unreasoningly fearful regarding a certain odor, succumbs and dies, a victim of his own delusion **

1360

(586) (600) (1342)
A encounters seemingly supernatural experiences which have to do with a small idol, X * A has supernatural experiences which prove an obstacle to enterprise ** (1354a) (1356) (1357)

1361

(a) (171; 1433b) (1366)
A, in a dream, sees a person he hates, A-3, in his room * A has an evil dream which haunts his waking moments, works on his mind and has its effect on his behavior ** (1311) (1317 ch A-8 to A-3)

(b) (1142b; 1342a) (1377b; 1160)
A is sure that an occult experience he has had portends success in a certain enterprise * A is so sure of success in an enterprise that he puts forth no effort to win; and the enterprise fails ** (836) (1166a)

1362

(1124 ch A to A-5) (1247 ch A to A-5; 1289d ch A to A-5)
A finds that A-5, in absent-minded moments, beguiles his leisure with a trifling proceeding that has become habitual with him * A, investigating a crime, discovers the criminal, A-5, through a most unusual clue ** (1284) (1222b ch A-3 to A-5) (1289d*-** ch A to A-5 & A-6 to A-5)

1363

(1330) (1343) (1347)
A, plunged into misfortune through mistaken judgment and folly, is rescued by a devoted friend, A-2 * A, transformed into an ass by witchcraft when he was seeking to transform himself into a bird, is given a garland of flowers to eat and becomes his normal self—plus sorely garnered wisdom ** (1433b; 918b) (1375)

1364

(a) (1046 ch A to B) (1383 ch A to B)
B receives in a mysterious manner a photograph, not of herself but of some one greatly resembling her * B receives a photograph; and on the back of it is written: "You are in great danger! Beware!" ** (328) (1154a)

(b) (461) (1424b)
B finds a note, ostensibly written by A, which causes B great perturbation * B's friend, B-2, perpetrates a hoax by forging a note which has to do with B and A ** (1055) (1402)

176

(50) Being Impelled by an Unusual Motive to Engage in Crafty Enterprise

1365

(732)   (827-*)   (1361a)   (1344)
A believes that he hears strange voices talking to him * A counters the belief that
he hears strange voices talking to him with the auto-suggestion that he is merely
the victim of superstitious delusion ** (1357)   (1374)   (1375)   (827*-**)

1366

(852)   (1141)   (1361a)
A is influenced unduly by his dreams * A, influenced unduly by his dreams, strives
to master the ignoble weakness and control his dreams by sheer force of will**
(1374)   (1377)

1367

(a)   (1380)   (1382a)   (1383)
A, annoyed by a certain object, X, destroys it * A destroys a certain object, X,
but mysteriously it reappears; again and again A destroys X, but always it reappears ** (1342a)   (1375)   (1381)

(b)   (1083)   (1287)
A has invented a life preserver for the use of shipwrecked persons * A, in order
to prove the value of a life preserver he has invented, dons the rubber suit, inflates
it and secretly, by night, drops overboard from a steamer on the high seas **(1414b)
(1419b)

1368

(231)   (233)
A undergoes a memory lapse and forgets everything about himself * A, victim
of lost identity, assumes a fictitious name and character ** (7a, b)   (437)

1369

(1382a)   (1397)   (1143b ch A to A-8 & B to B-4; 739 ch B to B-4; 1384 ch B to A)
A receives half of an important message, X, and is looking for a stranger, A-4,
who has the other half.   The message cannot be read until both halves are joined
(1286)   (1436 ch A-2 to A-4)   (1451a)

1370

(a)   (793a)   (1093)   (1212a)   (1427b)
A's friend, A-2, is in the dark regarding an important secret that surrounds X,
an object of mystery that has been stolen from him * A knows the secret of X, an
object of mystery stolen from A-2, and seeks to use his knowledge in recovering
X ** (833)   (1234)   (1453)   (1456; 1377a)

(b)   (1354b-2)   (1374)
A, a Fortyniner, returning with a wagon train from California, has with him a
fortune in gold dust * A and his companions are attacked by Indians, A's companions are killed and A is mortally wounded ** A, alone and near death, buries
his store of gold dust and draws a map of the cache on a water canteen, X ***
(1394 ch A to A-8)   (1369 ch A to A-8)   (1401 ch A to A-8)

(c)   (1298)   (1358)
A, discovering a "pocket" of gold in the desert, dies before he can take out the
gold * A, near death, draws a cryptic map on the page of a note book, locating
the spot where a store of gold may be found ** (1143b ch A to A-8)   (1383 ch A
to A-8)   (1384 ch B to A-8)

1371

(1290a ch A to A-5)   (1334c)
A is positive, in his own mind, that his friend, A-2, has been murdered by A-5 *
A suspects A-5, seemingly an honest man, of a crime, and tries to prove him guilty **
(1222a ch A-3 to A-5)   (1413a)   (1456a)   (1413 ch A-3 to A-5)

1372

(a) (695b) (696) (1312) (1323b)

A, as a method of reprisal against his country, seeks to sell important government information to a foreign country: [1] blue prints of a new instrument of war, [2] a diplomatic code or [3] a plan of coast fortifications (711c) (1372b)

(b) (1312) (696)

A, as a method of reprisal against his native land, turns traitor in time of war and joins the forces of the enemy (919c) (1021b; 1016 tr A & A-2)

(13, Seeking by Craftiness to Escape Misfortune

1373

(1027) (1418a; 1433b)

A sells his shadow for an inexhaustible purse (1354a) (1357)

1374

(475) (720) (857) (1064)

A has a character weakness that prevents him from achieving success in enterprise * A has a dream, or an unusual experience, psychic or otherwise, which enables him to conquer a serious character weakness and become successful in his undertakings ** (853) (1418b)

1375

(53) (475) (732) (853) (855)

A, in a desperate mental conflict with a superstitious obsession, succeeds in scoring a victory for sense and reason—all by his own unaided powers (1141) (1365) (1366)

1376

(485) (598) (820) (822) (1098-*) (1161) (1209b)

A, seeking evidence against a gang of crooks, A-5, A-5, A-5, assumes the character of a burglar in order the more successfully to achieve his aims * A, a detective, is falsely suspected of being a professional crook by those unaware of his secret motives ** (635) (658) (854)

1377

(a) (1141; 1377b ch A to A-2) (1384 ch B to A) (1400) (1405 ch A-4 to A-5)

A's friend, A-2, loses by theft a mysterious object, X, supposed to bring good fortune to its possessor, and A seeks to recover X for A-2 * A finds the thief, A-5, by looking for a man who suddenly becomes prosperous. A-5, stealing X, is inspired by superstition to put forth efforts which make him prosperous ** (724) (1425) (1427b)

(b) (1380) (1380; 114) (1075a; 1380)

B, in order to help backward and unenterprising A achieve success, gives him a mysterious little object, X, which, she solemnly assures him, will make him successful in all his undertakings (1075b) (1098) (1104) (1354b)

1378

(681b) (1327) (1329)

A has long been mysteriously missing * A's father, F-A, has a conviction born of simple faith that A, long mysteriously missing, will some day come back to ⁺im ** (698 ch A to F-A & CH to A) (1212b ch A to A-4 & A-8 to F-A)

(54) Becoming Involved in a Puzzling Complication that Has to do with an Object Possessing Mysterious Powers

1379

(259-3) (555b)

A is a man of adventurous nature who seeks to accomplish a dangerous enterprise * A, hearing of a mysterious and dangerous object, X, in a canyon of the lonely mountains, decides to investigate ** (691) (693)

1380

(7a) (1377ɔ)
A is told that a certain object, X, has power for evil (or good), and he decides to make a test (8a) (1134) (1330) (1343) (1352) (1354b) (1360)

1381

(562) (1211 ch A to A-5) (1387) (1389a, b)
A is puzzled to account for certain objects, X1, X2, X3, which come mysteriously into his possession * A, unable to explain events of a seemingly supernatural nature, has a feeling that a ghostly visitor is at work ** (1400) (1424a) (1435)

1382

(a) (789) (980-*) (985) (1343) (1369)
A comes innocently into possession of an object of mystery, X, highly prized by the person, or the people, who lost it or had it stolen * A suffers weird adventures and undergoes strange dangers when unknown persons seek by stealth to take from A a mysterious object, X, which has come innocently into his possession ** (867 tr A & A-2) (980*-**) (1367a)

(b) (1384 ch B to A) (1401) (1400)
A buys a little trick box, X, in an old curiosity shop and is unable to open it * A has a little trick box, X, which he is not able to open. One night it opens of its own accord, and A finds a jewel in the box ** (729) (1144 ch A to A-5) (803b)

1383

(1389b) (1427b)
A, proceeding about his business and caught in a crowd, is confronted suddenly by a strange woman, BX, who thrusts a mysterious object, X, into his hand and, without a word, disappears (541) (561) (1343) (1367a)

1384

(739 ch B to B-8) (1293c ch B to B-8 & A to A-8) (1440)
B buys an object, X, in a pawnshop * B wonders why the pawnbroker, A-9, tries to buy back from her an unredeemed pledge, X, which she bought in his pawnshop ** (1444) (586) (1044b ch A to B & A-2 to B-2)

(55) Becoming Involved in a Mysterious Complication and Seeking to Make the Utmost of a Bizarre Experience

1385

(603b, c, d; 168) (1160) (1334b, c)
A's friend, A-2, has just died suddenly, and the fact is not known to any one but A * A is believed to be his dead friend, A-2, and he leaves those who suppose him to be A-2 with the statement that he "goes to keep a tryst with death" ** (5) (1275)

1386

a) (1023) (1388 ch A-4 to A-8)
A, a young artist in needy circumstances, is conducted secretly by A-8 to a house in which B, a beautiful young woman, lies dead with a dagger in her heart * A, a young artist, is hired by A-8 to paint a mystery picture ** (771a) (802a)

(b) (903) (1143b)
A, a young artist in needy circumstances, has a picture rejected by a customer, B * A, a needy young artist with an ordered picture left on his hands, discovers in the picture a map locating buried treasure ** (1394) (1399) (1403)

1387

(233) (1389) (1400)
A, carrying out an occult enterprise, falls into a strange sort of trance during which he accomplishes remarkable things of which he has no remembrance when he awakes (1381) (1418a)

1388

(111) (656) (1085)
A, a young man in dire need of money, has a mysterious caller, A-4 * A is offered
a large sum of money by A-4 if he will take part in a secret enterprise, the nature
of which A-4 will not disclose ** (662 ch A-2 to A-4) (1387) (1386a ch A-8 to
A-4)

1389

(a) (179a, c) (233) (265a) (572) (786)
A has recurring spells by day or night when he becomes a somnambulist, doing
things of which he has no remembrance in his waking moments (1374) (1381)
(1117)

(b) (586) (1113) (1137a)
A is a dreamy, mysterious person who makes a study of occult phenomena * He
encounters a trying experience ** (541) (853) (1046)

1390

(548a) (681b) (734)
A receives a blow on the head which causes him to lose his original personality
and return to a fictitious personality which he had previously assumed (1036)
(1124) (1128a)

1391

(749) (1061) (1074) (1111a) A, a novelist, meets personally in real life a
fictitious character, AX, from one of his stories (1451d) (1455b) (1461b)

1392

(110-3) (1401) (1441a)
A will receive knowledge of an important secret if he has the ingenuity to solve
the mystery of a figure in an Oriental rug (1400) (1403) (1408)

1393

(1024) (1029)
A receives a call from a mysterious stranger, AX, who is peculiarly dressed and
seems to have hypnotic powers * A tries to solve the mystery of a stranger, AX **
(1388 ch A-4 to AX) (1404a ch A-4 to AX) (1405 ch A-4 to AX)

(56) Seeking to Test the Value of a Mysterious Communication and Becoming Involved in Weird Complexities

1394

(47a-*) (1384; 1444) (1386b) (874) (1046)
A, treasure trove, finds a mysterious old parchment document which describes
the place where the treasure is buried (47a*-**) (662) (691)

1395

(419) (460)
A receives a mysterious communication from B, sent from a distant place where
B is residing. It is evidently an important communication, but difficult to de-
cipher (501) (1394)

1396

(1093) (1111b)
A is a "cub" reporter. The "star" reporter, A-8, from a distant place sends a
cipher despatch which the best minds in the newspaper office are unable to translate. A attempts the task (1098) (1330)

1397

(513) (1111b)
A discovers that his cigar will not burn. On investigation, he discovers that
the cigar is merely a rolled paper, X, camouflaged with a tobacco wrapper—the
rolled paper, X, being an important message (541) (561) (1369) (1400)

1398

(1427b) (1444) (1459; 1444)
A, investigating a psychic problem, finds that he must begin by placing his faith
in so-called "automatic writing" (1411) (1437)

(57) Seeking to Unravel a Puzzling Complication

1399

(110-3) (117) (1286)
A seeks wealth, his by right, which has been concealed * A seeks wealth which his father, F-A, has left him, but concealed in a place whose location has been lost ** (1451b) (1452) (1461d tr A & B)

1400

(541) (1046) (1245) (1352-*) (1382a)
A seeks to solve a puzzling enigma that has to do with X, an object of mystery (1077) (1352*-**) (1392)

1401

(739) (1370b ch A to A-8)
A's curiosity and interest are aroused by a certain unredeemed pledge, X, in a pawnshop * A buys a mysterious object, X, in a pawnshop, and attempts to satisfy his curiosity regarding it ** (792a) (1384 ch B to A)

1402

(701 tr A & A-2) (705 ch A to A-2) (1021b)
A, his curiosity aroused by the mysterious actions of his friend, A-2, decides to investigate the cause (704) (807) (841) (1334c)

1403

(109) (1392)
A secures knowledge of an important secret, and his curiosity involves him in a queer enterprise (832 tr A & A-2) (1077)

1404

(a) (619 ch A to A-4) (1393 ch AX to A-4)
A's curiosity is aroused by the queer actions of A-4, a stranger * A, discovering that a stranger, A-4, is trying to commit suicide, investigates the cause ** (1391 ch AX to A-4) (1461b ch AX to A-4)

(b) (1111b) (1369) (1414a ch A to A-4) (1444)
A endeavors to find A-4, who has mysteriously disappeared * A's only clue in his search for A-4 is the picture of a beautiful woman, X, left at the place where A disappeared, and a legend connected with the picture ** (1400) (1143b ch A to A-4 & B to B-4)

405

(1175a ch A to A-4) (1194-* ch A to A-4)
A's curiosity is aroused by the strange actions of A-4, a stranger * A, his curiosity aroused, investigates a suspicious person, A-4. A robbery has just occurred and A-4 seems to have a guilty knowledge of it ** (774) (1283) (1413a ch A-5 to A-4) (1448 ch A-5 to A-4) (1194*-**)

1406

(1372a ch A to A-5) (1437)
A sees a stranger, A-5, stealthily remove papers, X, from the pocket of another stranger, A-8, who is asleep. A follows A-5 (1435) (1451b)

1407

(675; 1080) (1080)
A is a reporter assigned to "cover" a story which involves a closely-guarded secret (596) (828) (1019) (1076 ch A to A-8)

1408

(109) (147) (874)
A obtains knowledge of a closely guarded secret * A, obtaining knowledge of a closely guarded secret, goes on a hunt for buried treasure ** (47a) (1148b)

1409

(147) (600) (953)
A seeks to discover what is in a mysterious room behind a locked door (608) (623) (1414a)

1410

(1403) (1414a ch A to A-8) (1414b ch A to A-8)
A, endeavoring to solve a mystery, has for his only clue, X, the portrait of a beautiful woman, painted on ivory (1386b) (1404b)

1411

(1398) (1427b)
A, skeptically investigating a psychic communication, finds many things to corroborate the message, but he does not find the one important thing, X, whose location the message purports to reveal * A, when the death of a spiritualist medium, B, brings an occult investigation to an end, finds his skepticism at the blank wall of enigma ** (1242b) (1328) (1355)

1412

(a) (1383) (1444 ch B to BX)
A, in a city street, has a glimpse of BX, a strange woman who has caused him to become involved in a puzzling mystery * A, trying to overtake BX and secure information from her regarding a certain mystery, sees BX, under his very eyes, suddenly killed in a street accident ** (1375) (1411)

(b) (816b; 744) (1360) (1433b ch A to B)
A, friend of B, meets B in a foreign country, and invites her to dine with him at an appointed time and place * B meets A in a foreign country; and then, returning to her own country, B meets A and receives the astounding information that he has not been away from his native land for years ** (1387) (1389a)

1413

(a) (1302 ch A to A-5) (1305) (1334c)
A, by mind-reading, secures a confession from a transgressor, A-5 (1451d) (1461b ch AX to A-5)

(b) (1097b ch A-2 to A-5) (1261 ch A-3 to A-5)
A, a detective, unmasking A-5 as the leader of a criminal gang, finds that he cannot secure A-5's arrest as the police authorities refuse to act * A discovers that A-5 is a government secret service man, merely posing as a criminal in order that he may secure an advantage in prosecuting his work for law and order ** (1222a ch A-3 to A-5) (1228 ch A-3 to A-5)

(58) **Engaging in an Enterprise and then Mysteriously Disappearing**

1414

(a) (770a) (897) (953)
A, while carrying out an enterprise of small importance, vanishes completely and mysteriously, baffling every attempt of the police and of his friends to find him (917) (918a)

(b) (1347) (1367b-*)
A is carrying out an unusual enterprise * A vanishes mysteriously from a ship in mid-ocean ** (1367b*-**) (1357; 705)

1415

(837; 1446c) (1220b ch A to A-5; 806 ch B-4 to B)
A, an honest bank messenger, disappears mysteriously with a satchelful of money * A, with a large amount of money in his possession, disappears; he is later found in jail, his reason obscured, his money gone ** (1447 ch A to A-2) (1456 ch A-5 to B)

1416

(540 ch B to B-8 & B-3 to B)   (977a)   (1069)
B, waiting in the lobby of a crowded hotel until her father, F-B, can secure rooms, vanishes completely (643)   (743b)   (1105)   (1446c tr A & B)

1417

(470)   (1025)   B disappears, apparently a suicide when, in desperate danger, she implores aid and it is denied (802b)   (1207)   (1240)

(59)   Engaging in a Mysterious Enterprise and Becoming Involved with the Occult and the Fantastic

1418

(a)   (922b)   (925)
A, while engaged in an important enterprise, drinks of an enchanted water and falls asleep (918b)   (1418b)   ('419b)   (1433b)   (1438a)

(b)   (853)   (964a)   (1374)
A, an inefficient, futile sort of person, comes to believe that he is the reincarnation of AX, a powerful personage of antiquity * A, because of a strange delusion, proves himself a person to be reckoned with ** (1134)   (1387)

1419

(a)   (693)   (856)   (1379)
A, caught in a trap and held powerless under a huge burning glass, is saved by an eclipse of the sun (888)   (918b)   (1426a)

(b)   (1367b)   (1433b)
A, appearing suddenly among a tribe of savages, is encased in a diver's suit from which he cannot free himself unaided; nor, hailed as a god, can he ask his savage captors to free him (197)   (713)

1420

(1330)   (1342a)   (1418a)
A, while trying to discover perpetual motion, dreams that he has invented a machine, X, that defies the power of gravitation (1424b)   (1455b)   (1416b)

1421

(619)   (1027)
A, under the heel of adversity and almost at the starvation point, secures an object of mystery, X, which grants his every wish—but at the expense of years of his life for every wish granted (1330)   (1354a)

1422

(a)   (1421)   (1423)   (1427b)
A, while seeking to carry out an enterprise, is brought gradually under the power of a dreadful force, intangible, invisible and evil, until at last his body seems to become the abode of the accursed Thing (51a, b)   (1019)   (1424b)   (1433a)

(b)   (1113)   (1353)
A, seeking to express musically the odor of tube roses, is almost killed by a bolt of lightning * A, following a tragic experience, has a superstitious fear of a certain odor ** (1325)   (1333a)   (1359)

1423

(1389b)   (1422a)
A, late at night, enters a room of his house and sees another man, AX, sitting in a chair before the fireplace * A, thinking AX is a friend, steps toward him; whereupon, AX vanishes into thin air ** (1332)   (1424a)   (1455a, b)

1424

(a)   (1334a)   (1342a)   A, in a mysterious manner, receives a warning of danger * A, at a loss to account for a mysterious stranger, AX, who appears to him, warns him and then disappears, comes to believe that the messenger was sent by Divine Providence ** (1347)   (1348a)

(b) (540) (1414a)
A, friend of B, is reported to B, on unquestionable authority, to have been seen in two places, widely distant from each other, at the same identical moment (249) (1163a)

1425

(541) (586)
A is vastly puzzled in his attempts to solve the mystery of a strange object, X *
A, puzzled by an object of mystery, X, goes to sleep with X on a table in his bedroom. On arising in the morning, A finds X disintegrated into a fine powder, all hope of a solution of its mystery gone ** (1054) (1075a)

1426

(a) (74a, b) (953) (1409)
A seeks to unravel the mystery of a strange house * A, seeking to unravel the mystery of a strange house in the hills, is caught in an electrical storm. During the storm the house vanishes, and the site on which it stood becomes a lake ** (54a) (1414a)

(b) (691) (1082b) (1404b)
A, engaged in a hazardous searcn for A-4, finds himself in a strange lost community that has no direct communication with the outside world * A is made a prisoner in a strange lost community; and he finds A-4, for whom he is searching, also a prisoner ** (181c) (888)

1427

(a) (1061) (1082a. b)
A encounters a weird experience when he finds nimself in a mysterious place, surrounded by people who are the victims of a hypnotic delusion inspired by an idol (888) (1019)

(b) (898) (899)
A is a skeptic in all matters that have to do with the supernatural * A, a skeptic, encounters an experience which he finds disturbing ** (1342a) (1343)

1428

(852) (1433a) (1443a)
A dreams that he falls from a great height * A dies of psychic shock **

(60) Becoming Involved, Through Curiosity Aroused by Mystery, in a Strange Enterprise

1429

(730 ch A to A-8) (832 ch A to A-8; 705 ch A to A-8)
A, a thief, breaking into a building at night to commit a robbery, finds a man, A-8, dead on the floor, a revolver clutched in his tense fingers (819 ch A-5 to A-8) (906 ch A-2 to A-8)

1430

(a) (245) (697b)
A, who evidently is a person oī quality, cannot prove his station in life as he knows nothing of his birth and parentage (1051) (1054) (1055)

(b) (898) (926)
A sees a stranger, A-4, leave a baby, CH, on a doorstep * A appropriates CH **
(911) (914) (1229)

1431

(1180) (1199-*)
A is held up and robbed oy a masked woman road agent, BX * A struggles with a masked woman road agent, BX, and twists from her wrist a peculiar bracelet, X **
(801) (822) (828) (833)

1432

(1127 ch A to A-8 & CN to NW) (1270) A dies and leaves his fortune to a nephew, NW * A dies and leaves his fortune to a nephew, NW, who has been mysteriously missing for years ** (1001b ch U to A & A to NW) (1107a ch A to NW)

1433

(a) (51a) (852)
A, in a waking vision, sees a grave being dug for himself (1040) (1358)

(b) (991) (1366)
A has a dream so vivid that it seems a part of his waking experience * A has a dream which he conceives to be an actual experience ** (1348a, b) (1433a)

(c) (1389b) (1433b)
A, in a waking vision, becomes clairvoyantly aware of grave danger that is threatening B (1137a) (1333b) (1446b)

1434

(756) (791)
A, if he carries out a professional obligation to call at a certain house in a certain street, is daily warned by anonymous letters that it will be at the peril of his life (1019) (1447)

1435

(985) (1111b) (1046) (1381) (1406)
A investigates a mysterious package, X, that has fallen into his hands * A discovers that a mysterious package, X, contains stolen property. With X as a clue, he apprehends the thief, A-5 ** (596) (623) (1098)

1436

(1399) (1402)
A, investigating the mysterious actions of his friend, A-2, discovers that A-2 has a strange enterprise on hand * A discovers that his friend, A-2, is seeking the recovery of a buried chest containing long-lost gold ** (662) (1369)

1437

(455b) (1024) (1041 ch A to A-4)
A's fortune and happiness hang upon a technicality of the law: Both A-4 and his wife, B-4, are killed in an accident; if B-4 died first, A inherits, while if A-4 died first, others inherit (1052a) (1398) (1406)

(20) Becoming Involved with Conditions in Which Misfortune is Indicated

1438

(a) (677 ch B to A) (1117)
A, while in an abnormal mental condition, receipts for a valuable registered letter, X. Afterward, A has no recollection of receipting for X (1451b ch A to A-7 & A-8 to A) (1457 tr A & A-9)

(b) (63) (798) (985) (1267c)
[1] A, unknown to himself, has in his possession an object, X, which, at any moment, may bring disaster or death to him [2] A, unaware of his danger, is associating with people, or is ignorantly dealing with deadly circumstances, which may bring upon him a catastrophe at any time (153) (1333a) (1333b)

(c) (339) (1310) (1313a)
A is a member of a strange secret society in which all the members are bound by oath to avenge the wrongs, real or fancied, of each individual member * A is a member of a strange secret society in which all members have red hair. The watchword of the society: "One Bricktop for all, all Bricktops for one" ** (1154a*-**) (1319a)

1439

(a) (1402) (1436) (1437 ch A to A-2) A is informed regarding an important secret which, if revealed, will wreck all A-2's hope of acquiring gain (1325) (1290 ch A to A-2 & A-2 to A-8)

(b) (1147) (1260a)
A is evilly dealt with by A-8 and brought to the brink of ruin * A, evilly dealt
with by A-8, puts a curse on A-8 and all of his name ** (606 ch A to A-8) (619
ch A to A-8) (661 ch A to A-8)

(c) (1423) (1427b)
A always encounters a person of forbidding appearance with a demoniacal face,
AX, just before some great misfortune overtakes him (53) (552a, b) (606)
(681a) (1424a)

1440

(1283 ch A to A-8) (1293b ch B to A)
A, in great financial distress, pawns a valuable and mysterious object * [1] An
ivory box with a false bottom [2] A silver candelabrum with a cunningly concealed
opening in which something of value is hidden [3] A large brooch with a false
back in which smuggled gems are concealed [4] A jade box, a "trick" box which
can only be opened by one acquainted with the secret method ** A dies before
he can redeem the object, X, which he has pawned *** (1384) (1384 ch B to A-8;
1394 ch A to A-8) (1384 ch B to A-8; 1400 ch A to A-8)

1441

(a) (1354a) (1392)
A seeks to discover the secret of Life * A, seeking to discover a great secret, uncovers an unhappy complication ** (746 ch B to A) (888)

(b) (552b) (1311)
A has a wound, an invisible, psychic wound, which causes terrible pain in flesh
and tissue which, otherwise, are perfectly healthy and normal * A has an invisible
wound, caused by a tragic act of injustice he has committed, and no physician or
surgeon can heal him ** (1357) (1358)

1442

(1249) (1283) (1301) (1337) (1447)
A tears that A-2, who is plowing a field, will unearth evidence of a crime which,
A knows, has been buried there (1291a) (1461a)

1443

(a) (731) (1366)
A, a captured criminal, has a particularly vivid dream in which he is making a
successful escape (866) (875a tr A & A-2) (1428)

(b) (438) (1236) (1133) (1147 tr A & A-8) (1260a)
A is trapped in the woods by a falling tree * A, trapped by a falling tree in an isolated place, is unable to extricate himself, and dies **

(c) (438) (1236) (1133) (1147 tr A & A-8) (1260a)
A falls into an old well that has been covered with boards and earth * A, falling
into an old well, is unable to extricate himself and dies of his injuries **

1444

(586) (1062) (1091) (1093)
B induces A to attempt the solution of a mystery (802a, b ch B to B-8) (1045)

1445

(1244a, b)
B is strongly influenced by a supernatural vision in which her life is reviewed before her * B receives benefit when a psychic experience proves an obstacle to a
certain undertaking ** (1245) (1258)

1446

(a) (850b; 1243) (1297)
B loses her handbag, X, which contains the key to her jewel box * B finds her lost
handbag, X, and the key to her jewel box is in the bag—but the jewels in the jewel
box are missing ** (1254) (1284)

(b) (645) (647) (677) (1154a)
B seeks to escape from mysterious dangers * B falls asleep and, while she sleeps, terrible danger threatens her ** (179a, b) (1433c)

(c) (383) (1279a) (1325)
B is a hypnotist who, in carrying out an enterprise, hypnotizes A (471) (1206) (1258 ch A-6 to A) (1309b ch A-3 to A)

(61)   Becoming Aware of an Important Secret that Calls for Decisive Action

1447

(791)   (1019)   (1031)   (1130)   (1434)
A, a doctor, summoned to give attention to a sick man, A-8, finds that A-8 is dying *
A learns from A-8, dying, the details of a crime ** (456 ch A to A-8)   (1228)

1448

(1038 ch A-8 to A-5) (1042a ch A to A-5) (1280 ch A-3 to A-5) (1405 ch A-4 to A-5)
A secretly discoves A-5 counting money taken from a murdered man, A-8 (828
ch B-5 to A-5)   (836 ch A-2 to A-5)

1449

(1334c)   (833)   (1291b-*)
A investigates the murder of a friend, A-2 * A, investigating the murder of a friend,
A-2, is horrified to discover that all the circumstantial evidence points to him-
self as the murderer ** (642)   (732)   (750)   (787)   (879)   (951)   (1291b*-**)

1450

(1220a, b)   (1263)
A is compelled to alter certain plans very materially when he makes the astounding discovery that he is the father of B's son, SN (675)   (945)

1451

(a)   (1408)   (1430a)   (1437)
A for a long time seeks in vain to solve a puzzling mystery * A, trying to solve
a puzzling mystery, discovers a clue in a little box concealed in an old phonograph bought at auction ** (1392)   (1394)

(b)   (1305 ch A-5 to A-8)   (1399)
A, poor, secures from A-8 information that brings him a fortune (1052a)   (1408)

(c   (742)   (743a)   (870a)
A is happy in rescuing B from an unpleasant situation (869)   (876a)   (870b ch
A-6 to A)

(d)   (690 ch A to F-A)   (1414a, b ch A to F-A)   •
A, receiving information which he thinks trustworthy, embarks upon a hazardous
enterprise * A goes on a hazardous search for his father, F-A, long mysteriously
missing ** (1286)   (1404b ch A-4 to F-A)

1452

(1387)   (1395)   (1399)
A is puzzled by a mystery that seems too deep for solution * A slips and falls into
a chasm; and in the chasm he discovers a clue to a baffling mystery ** (1398)
(1403)   (1409)

1453

(1369)   (1389a)
A is at his wits' end in an attempt to solve a puzzling riddle * A, by chance, overhears a scrap of conversation in the street; and what he overhears proves a clue
to the whereabouts of stolen property, X ** (1045)   (1283)

1454

(61)   (87)   (1207)
A discovers that his pal, A-2, is a girl masquerading as a boy * A, discovering that
A-2 is a girl masquerading as a boy, keeps the knowledge to himself and does his
utmost to save the masquerader from annoying experiences ** (837)   (1100)
(1451c)

1455

(a)   (917)   (1379)
A, because of certain revelations he has received, firmly resolves that he will not carry out an enterprise that had formerly been dear to his heart (1432 ch A to U and NW to A)   (1433a)

(b)   (715a)   (1391)
A, in his overweening pride, is taught a lesson by AX * A, rescued from critical misfortune by AX, receives a revelation from AX which results in a beneficial character change ** (918b)   (922a)

1456

(516 ch A to A-5)   (624)   (783 ch A-7 to A-5)
A, by shrewd deduction and skilful reasoning, proves that A-5 is a criminal (802b) (803a)   (1222a ch A-3 to A-5)

1457

(1389a ch A to A-9)   (1394 ch A to A-9)   (1397 ch A to A-9)   (1438a ch A to A-9)
A is accused of having stolen a valuable document, X * A, accused by A-9 of having stolen a valuable document, X, has his innocence proved when X is found between the leaves of a book which A-9 had been reading ** (662 ch A-2 to A-9)   (1337 ch A-8 to A-9)

1458

(129)   (331)
B supposes herself to be a white woman and prides herself on her white heritage * B, a white woman, is told that there is a taint of alien and inferior blood in her veins ** (23a, b)   (873)   (1054 ch A to B)

1459

(1296)   (1304)   (1308)
B finds an old notebook, X, which contains the record of a dishonest transaction * B finds an old note book. X, which contains information that has an important bearing on some of her plans ** (1204)   (1244b)   (1279b)

(57)   Seeking to Unravel a Puzzling Complication

1460

(932)   (1074)
A, a writer, is in doubt as to whether a story he has in mind will interest the general public * A, seeking to discover whether a story he has in mind will interest the general public, tells the story to a group of strangers, A-4, A-4, A-4, *** (598) (1305 ch A-5 to A-4)

(21)   Becoming Involved with Conditions in Which Misfortune is Indicated

1461

(a)   (68)   (456)   (701)   (703)   (951)
A fights a hard battle with his conscience; he finds it a losing battle, and makes an important revelation in order that he may achieve peace of mind (51a, b) (952)

(b)   (783)   (1111a)
A receives an important communication from a mysterious person, AX, which enables him to correct a serious error (1064)   (1333b)

(c)   (797 ch D-A to B)   (1183 ch SR to B)   (1146; 29)
A reveals his identity to B * A, revealing his identity to B, shatters her ideals and plunges her into unhappiness ** (53)   (1187)   (1188)

(d)   (1461a, b)   A sends an important communication to B, a communication that vitally concerns his welfare (1278b)   (1461c)

(11) Confronting a Situation in Which Courage and Devotion Alone Can Save the Fortunes of One Beloved

1462

(85a; 340) (540; 589)
B's friend, B-2, makes an important revelation regarding A which causes B to correct a serious error (94a) (506a) (546b)

Index to Classification by Symbols

192

Index to   **PLOTTO**   *Classification*

PAGE No.

A & U,	A and uncle	241
A & CN,	A and cousin	241
A, A-8 & CN,	، A, male utility character and cousin	241
A, U & CN,	A, uncle and cousin	241
A, GCH & X,	A, grandchild and inanimate object or object of mystery..	241
B,	female protagonist	241
B & B-2,	B and female friend of B	246
B & B-3,	B and female rival or enemy of B	247
B & B-4,	B and female stranger	247
B & B-5,	B and female criminal	247
B & B-7,	B and female inferior	247
B & B-8,	B and female utility character	247
B & AUX,	B and mysterious aunt	248
B & X,	B and inanimate object or object of mystery	248
B, B-4 & X,	B, female stranger and inanimate object or object of mystery	248
B & M-B,	B and mother of B	248
B & F-B,	B and father of B	283
B & BR-B,	B and brother of B	284
B & SR-B,	B and sister of B	249
B & SN,	B and son	285
B and CH,	B and child	286
B & D-B,	B and daughter of B	2′9
B & AX,	B and man of mystery	285
B & A-2,	B and male friend of A	281
B & A-3,	B and male enemy or rival of A	282
B & A-4,	B and male stranger	282
B & A-5,	B and male criminal	282
B & A-6,	B and male law officer	283
B & A-8,	B and male utility character	283
B, A-2 & B-2,	B, male friend of A and female friend of B	300
B, A-4 & A-6,	B, male stranger and male law officer	300
B, A-5 & A-6,	B, male criminal and male law officer	299
B, A-9 & X,	B, male superior and inanimate object or object of mystery	300
B, M-B & F-B,	B, mother of B and father of B	300
B, F-B & A-3,	B, father of B and male rival or enemy of A	300
A & B,	male protagonist and female protagonist	250
A, B & A-2,	A, B and male friend of A	271
A, B & A-3,	A, B and male rival or enemy of A	272
A, B & A-4,	A, B and male stranger	276
A, B & A-5,	A, B and male criminal	276
A, B & A-6,	A, B and male law officer	277
A, B & A-7,	A, B and male inferior	277
A, B & A-8,	A, B and male utility character	278
A, B & A-9,	A, B and male superior	278
A, B & AX,	A, B and man of mystery	279
A, B & X,	A, B and inanimate object or object of mystery	279
A, B & BX,	A, B and woman of mystery	291
A, BX & X,	A, woman of mystery and inanimate object or object of mystery	291
A, B & F-A,	A, B and father of A	281
A, B & F-B,	A, B and father of B	280
A, B & SN,	A, B and son	281
A, B & BR-B,	A, B and brother of B	281
A, B & U,	A, B and uncle	281

NOTE

A mere reading of this list of characters in their various combinations is in itself highly suggestive to the trained imagination. Certain combinations will have their appeal and, by their reference numbers, may be immediately referred to in the various Conflict Groups.

The use for which this list is designed, however, primarily covers the selection of terminal Conflicts. The C Clauses of the Masterplots are numbered in parentheses; and, in the Classification by Character Symbols, the terminal suggestions are all grouped with their corresponding numbers at the end of each sub-group of Conflicts. If the number of the desired terminal Conflict is not found in the sub-group, other sub-groups should be scanned for a Conflict approximating the one desired, and the situation altered to correspond with the needs of the moment. Or, another terminal Clause may be almost synonomous with the one required, and its number substituted.

Very often, in writing a story a knotty point will be reached where the ingenuity of the writer wavers, or where he wishes to give the action a different trend. A study of the Classification by Symbols will be found rich in suggestions of means for meeting such an emergency. Such a study may be best approached in this manner: Resolve the leading characters of your story's situation into Plotto character symbols; if possible, not more than two or three symbols. Then look up the combination of symbols in the foregoing index and follow the references to the Classification by Symbols and, if necessary, on into the Conflicts.

If desired combinations of symbols cannot be found, a single symbol of the desired combination may be changed into the Plotto utility symbol, A-8 or B-8, or any other symbol which nearest approximates the one desired. Here, as elsewhere in Plotto, transposition, change and manipulation will bring the utmost in results.

A

Love's Beginnings

A, who knows nothing of the sciences, pretends to be engaged in scientific research 1f

A, a poor clerk, finances a "fling" in high society 2a

A, one of the "idle rich," gratifies his love for adventure by frequenting the slums in the character of a city "tough" 2c

A, seeking to uncover duplicity by crafty enterprise, encounters the unexpected 4a

A, traveling the high road, drops a purse of money unnoticed 6a

A, a judge, loses his brief case 6b

A is crude, unhandsome and repellant to the ladies although he desires to be a gallant 7a

A has a repellant personality and, knowing it, he is timid in love 8a

A has taken vows that proscribe the love of woman 16b

Love's Misadventures

A, a publisher, rejects a novel because of personal pique 44a

A seeks to escape annoying manifestations of love 71a

A pretends that he is married 71a

A pretends that he is engaged to be married 71a

A, young and romantic, sees a ruinous old house in a city street, a house said to be deserted 74a

A, his curiosity aroused, secretly watches an old house, said to be deserted; then, one day, he sees a beautifully rounded arm and a small, shapely hand emerge from behind the broken blind and place something on the window sill 74a

A, hearing a woman's voice calling for help in a house he happens to be passing, rushes up the steps, through the front door—and into a romantic complication 74b

A is so besieged by match-making mammas that their meddling seriously interferes with the practice of his profession. He resolves to escape the annoyance by a stratagem 101a

A is a sentimental person, fancy free but yearning for love 101b

A is a poet, fancy free, who keeps his lightning rods up in the hope of attracting a bolt of the divine passion 101b

A is a crabbed, disagreeable person whose misfortune it is to find no pleasure in life 106

A is timid in love but, armed with a love charm, X, he becomes bold and wins success 8a

Marriage Proposal

A is absent-minded 204-265b

Love's Rejection

A fears that he has inherited the evil traits of an ancestor 2b8

A hopes, by a surgical operation on his skull, to be made immune from the "master passion" 231

A, an aviator, is a person of masterful character 234b

A, in spite of the fact that there are reasons why he should not marry, nevertheless plans to do so 258

A becomes involved in a love affair at the same time that he becomes involved in a divorce proceeding as "the other man" 274

(1)   A, overwhelmed by misfortune in love, commits suicide 281b

(14) A, victim of an apparently hopeless love affair, seeks contentment in befriending all who are in need, especially those who are unjustly treated 246b

(14) A, by his enterprises in altruism, finds that his hard nature undergoes a beneficial change 246b

(14) A becomes a crook 263

Married Life

A embarks upon an ill-considered enterprise of gambling and loses money that is not his to lose 380

A, supposed to be dead, returns mysteriously as from the grave 402

A's marital discontent prompts him to reckless and questionable adventures 420

A—Married Life, Cont'd.

A indulges a taste for low companionship and questionable adventures 485

A is prevented by family and business obligations from embarking upon a cherished enterprise 512

A, innocent, is arrested on a murder charge 520

A secretly and mysteriously sequestrates himself and fosters the deception that he is dead 438

A flees to a distant part of the country and tries to bear his hard lot with fortitude 460

A faces failure in business, a failure which he knows will bring disaster to his married happiness 461

A, facing ruin, seeks to save himself by committing a transgression 484b

Misfortune

A exercises mistaken judgment in forwarding a certain undertaking 595

A loses his initiative, his enterprise and his ambition and becomes merely a cog in the wheels of his employer's business 595

A secures knowledge of a closely-guarded secret 596

A, an author, impersonates the crook hero of a story he is writing and becomes involved in an unpleasant complication 598

A, in a foreign seaport and seeking to return at night to his hotel, loses his way and finds himself in the lawless slums 600

A, a pugilist, loses a ring battle and all the money he has wagered on himself 602

A has invested all his money in a certain enterprise 606

A, investing all his money in a certain enterprise, sees the enterprise fail and himself plunged heavily into debt 606

A's youthful escapades, committed thoughtlessly and not with malice, constitute the wrong which has given him a bad name among the people of his native place 611a

A leaves his native place, squanders his substance in riotous living, comes to want and experiences remorse 611b

A, a coward and a braggart, is manoeuvered into a dangerous test of courage, and must either eat his words or acquit himself with credit 615

A, a coward who has been manoeuvered into a dangerous test of courage, is almost beside himself with fear as he sets forth to meet the test 615

A, annoyed by a **faux pas** he has committed, seeks to "save his face" 617

A is bored by certain duties he is obliged to perform 618

A, bored by certain duties he is obliged to perform, finds a way out—with unpleasant results 618

A loses all his life's savings 619

A plans to take his own life, but fate intervenes 619

A loses his job 620

A suffers misfortune when he departs from the strict line of duty to carry out a cherished ambition of his own 620

A, innocent, is supposed to be a transgressor 623

A is supposed to be a transgressor because he is found with contraband goods in his possession 623

A considers himself a transgressor until he finds that his supposed transgression was never committed 624

(4)   A, in need of money to finance an enterprise, holds up a stage 628

A mixes truth with delusion in an earnest investigation of a psychic problem 633

(1)   A, mixing truth with delusion in an earnest investigation of a psychic problem, finally loses his reason 633

(1)   A, imagining he sees a fast motor car almost upon him, leaps in front of a car that is not imaginary and is instantly killed 634

A suffers false suspicion as a transgressor 635

A is a professional burglar who throws caution to the winds in one of his burglaries 636

A, a burglar, breaks into a house that is quarantined 636

A contracts a contagious disease 636

A robs a heathen temple of jewels and proceeds about his work with reckless audacity 637

(1)   A, committing a robbery, is caught red-handed and turned over to the law for punishment 637

(4)   A, ruined financially, takes to drink and "dies in his cups" 638

A—Misfortune, Cont'd.

A is caught in an unpleasant complication and disaster threatens him unless he is crafty enough to devise plans for his own safety 652

A, facing misfortune, seeks desperately to evade disaster 654

A's ancestral estates have been heavily mortgaged and he is about to lose the property 656

A, by hook or crook, seeks to save his mortgaged paternal acres from foreclosure 656

A is a person of ability but of a race considered inferior 657

A takes part in a football game and falls innocently under a suspicion of treachery 657

A, innocent of transgression, seeks to prove his innocence by subtle enterprise 657

A, a man of high standing in his community, fears that through unusual conditions his character will be discredited 658

A seeks to safeguard his reputation which is threatened by unusual conditions 658

A, wealthy and powerful, goes alone to bathe in a mountain stream 661

A finds himself unexpectedly locked and barred in a room in a strange house 664

A, suddenly finding himself a helpless prisoner, tries to bear his fate with equanimity 664

A struggles against an overwhelming sorrow that proves an obstacle to enterprise and holds his abilities in subjection 674

A is a confirmed procrastinator, and the habit inhibits enterprise and circumscribes his abilities 675

A is taught a lesson which shows him how reprehensible a pet failing may become 675

A was in the World War 680a

A, before the war, was a successful business man; after the war, a physical wreck and a bankrupt 680a

A, happy and optimistic, undergoes a critical illness which makes of him a morbid, melancholy, superstitious pessimist 681a

A undergoes a critical illness 681b

A recovers from a critical illness but loses all remembrance of his personal identity 681b

A, a white man of brilliant intellectual attainments, battles for existence in an isolated, primitive, savage wilderness 682

A, battling for existence in a savage wilderness, suffers a deterioration of character until, after some years, he sinks to the level of his primitive surroundings 682

A is a telegraph operator at a lonely railroad way station 683

A is a sheep-herder, isolated with his flock of sheep 683

A is a lighthouse keeper on a lonely coast 683

A gradually, because of loneliness, becomes demented 683

A, traveling alone, is caught in a snowstorm 685

A is caught in a snowstorm in the mountains, becomes snowbound, and finds it impossible to reach a place of safety 685

A, of gentle birth and breeding, is isolated in a primitive, uninhabited wilderness and compelled to battle with Nature for his very existence 686

A finds himself the only white man in a half-savage tribe of natives 687

A, finding himself the only white man in a half-savage tribe of natives, is compelled to struggle against their primitive superstitions 687

A is traveling through a savage wilderness 689

A, traveling through a savage wilderness, is captured by natives and threatened with death 689

A takes a sea voyage in the hope of recovering his health 690

A, taking a sea voyage, is shipwrecked and cast away on a desert island 690

A, an explorer, loses his way in a trackless wilderness 691

A, without food or water, is adrift in a small boat at sea 692

A, wandering alone among the mountains, is trapped and held powerless 693

A, caught in a trap, faces death 693

A's neighbors persist in thinking him guilty of a crime for which he was tried and acquitted 695a

A, tried for a crime and acquitted, seeks happiness in freedom from suspicion 695a

A suffers imprisonment for a crime he did not commit 695b

A, finishing a term of imprisonment for a crime he did not commit, finds that his character as an ex-convict seriously hampers him in his honest enterprises 695b

A, a patriot but a wanderer and an outcast, is deprived of all news of his native land 696

A—Misfortune, Cont'd

A is a foundling and knows nothing of his birth and parentage 697b
A knows nothing of his birth and parentage, and he finds this a serious and humiliating handicap 697b
A is a fugitive from justice who dares not present himself to receive a rich estate that has been left to him, for he knows he will be arrested 699a
A, driven to bay by pursuers, takes refuge in an old house 699b
A is a man who believes that poverty is the true source of contentment 700
A is a minister of the gospel 703
A, a religious teacher of the people, errs secretly on his human side and becomes the prey of conscience 703
A's life-work, nearing completion, is threatened with destruction by a great storm 706a, b, c
A, after a mysterious absence of many years, returns to his old home town 708
A, returning as an Unknown to his native place, discovers that no one recognizes him 708
A is expected by a large crowd of people to appear and carry out an obligation of professional duty 710
A is forced to give up an enterprise when he is taken suddenly so ill he cannot leave his bed 710
A, engaged in an important enterprise, suddenly finds himself in quarantine because of an outbreak of a contagious disease 711a
A, engaged in an important enterprise, becomes involved in an automobile accident 711b
A is removed in an unconscious condition from the scene of an accident 711b
A, seeking to carry out an important enterprise, meets with obstacles that defeat his plans 711c
A, a doctor, is a fugitive from justice 712
A, deprived of food through misfortune, faces slow death by starvation 713
A, wealthy, finds that his pretentions to place and power are treated as a joke 715a
A, a poor man and crippled, finds his life in a sad tangle 715b
A is found guilty of a political conspiracy 715c
A knows something others do not know, something that proves the greatest obstacle to his enterprising and capable nature 718a
A is a youth who, sheltered from the world and pampered by doting parents, has no true conception of life and no ability to face its rugged issues 718b
A disappears mysteriously 719a
A's whole future is wrapped up in a mighty work which he has brought almost to successful completion 721
A's life work is threatened with destruction 721
A, a matador, is getting ready in his room to appear in the bullring 726a
A, making ready to undertake an enterprise, has his plans suddenly interfered with 726a
A, ill and worn by a long journey, is suddenly called upon to undertake an enterprise which would be difficult if he were physically at his best 726b
A, a judge presiding at a murder trial, finds himself unexpectedly confronted with a circumstance which makes his work a torture to his soul 727
A digs a pit for a tiger trap and baits it with a quarter of bullock meat 728
A is honest, but he is a stranger and regarded with suspicion 731
A is arrested as a criminal "suspect" because he happens to be in the vicinity when a crime is committed 731
A has a conviction that he is going insane and that, sooner or later, he will be confined in an asylum 732
A finds a banknote of large denomination 733
A, poor, comes into possession of a banknote of large denomination. There is no bank in the village in which he lives and he can find no one who can, or who would if he could, change the bill for him 733
A is mistakenly reported dead during the World War 734
A, victim of amnesia in a foreign land, wanders back to his native country 734
(1) A, dies of starvation 713
(1) A, convicted of being a traitor to his country, is expatriated and forced to live abroad 715c
(1) A undertakes an enterprise when he is prosperous; and then, suffering loss and becoming a bankrupt and a cripple, he has not the heart to go on with the enterprise 680b
(1) A constructs a deadly trap and, by accident, falls into it himself 728

A—Misfortune, Conc'd

(2)   A, a white man cast away among bloodthirsty savages, has his life spared because he is a ventriloquist and supposed to be a god 650

(5)   A, because he is a ventriloquist (a conjuror or a magician) saves his life among savages; then loses his voice 714

(5)   A, wealthy and influential, loses his clothes, personal belongings and all other means of identification 715a

(6)   A, unable to conquer his misfortunes, seeks to escape them by committing suicide 705

(8)   A, desperately in need of money, can recoup his finances at the expense of his integrity. He resists the temptation 729

(11)   A cannot convince others of his identity, and undergoes the hardships and evil treatment accorded an upstart and imposter 715a

(11)   A, believed by all to be a white man, knows there is negro blood in his veins 718a

(13)   A, in the World War, is shell-shocked and loses all knowledge of his identity 731

(14)   A, callow and inefficient, learns some real truths through hard experience 718b

Mistaken Judgment

A, poor, is happy in the belief that poverty is the source of contentment 748

A, a writer, is happy in producing a literary masterpiece 749

A flees to escape the consequences of a crime 750

A believes he is guilty of a crime, but no crime has been committed 750

A, informed that he has only a few months to live, undertakes an unusual enterprise 751

A resigns himself to fate and seeks to bear patiently a supposed bereavement; but the bereavement is imagined, not real 755

A, confronting a hard and dangerous duty, is suddenly taken very ill and compelled to go to bed 757

A is a hard-hearted man of the world, seeking gain by exploiting the misfortunes of others 758

A, a crook who has acquired wealth, in a quest for happiness returns to his native place to foregather with pals of his younger criminal days 763

A, with no social distinction whatever, entertains the grandiose delusion that he will be greatly missed if he drops out of society 768

A is mistakenly convinced of his great business ability 769

A is heavily in debt 770a

A thinks a crime has been committed, but he is mistaken 771a

A finds a paper containing the signals of his football team 771b

A is seriously injured by a motor car 776

A, although not really a criminal, has become convinced that he is one 777

A looks upon others as people to be exploited 781

A, week-end guest at a country house, prowls about the place at night on a perfectly honest enterprise 786

A, through circumstantial evidence, believes himself guilty of a crime which he cannot remember of having committed, and which he did not really commit 787

A, seeking information as to his proper course, is under the delusion that every one is giving him false directions 789

A, a doctor, comes of a proud old Southern family 791

A, a doctor, considers it his duty to give medical assistance to outcasts and the morally inferior 791

A, by trickery, is mistakenly convinced that he has achieved a cherished ambition 795

A is a transgressor, long mysteriously missing from his home 797

A commits a fault against propriety 799

(1)   A is discovered burglarizing a house 752

(1)   A, an intruder in a strange house, is discovered; he flees through the nearest door into a windowless closet and is trapped by a spring lock 752

(1)   A accomplishes his work so completely that his success results in failure 760

(1)   A meets with a fatal accident 762

(1)   A is mistaken for a burglar 786

(1)   A, a judge, proving false to his high duty, ever afterwards bears a "crooked" reputation 790b

(1)   A, a doctor, in following his ideals, loses caste with his friends and neighbors 791

(4)   A, believing poverty the source of contentment, refuses to develop resources in his possession that would give him wealth 748

A—Mistaken Judgment, Conc'd

(4)   A, a writer, unconsciously plagiarizes from the work of another author in producing a literary masterpiece 749

(4)   A, seeking to finance himself, gambles with money not his own—and loses it 753

(4)   A gambles with money he is holding in trust 754

(4)   A, in order to secure money to pay off his pressing obligations, leaves home to take a position at a distance; and he leaves suddenly and mysteriously without telling his creditors he is going 770a

(4)   A, heavily in debt, seeks to save himself by fraudulently using trust funds in his possession 770c

(4)   A, seriously injured by a motor car, ever afterward has a weird delusion while he is in the streets that motor cars are trying to run him down 776

(5)   A conceals his identity, avoids people, and leads a furtive, hermit-like existence 777

(7)   A, honest and high-minded, recommends a certain proposition, and then discovers that it is a swindle 747

(7)   A, told that he has only a few months to live, discovers that the doctor was in error and that he still has a long life ahead of him 751

(8)   A, by prayer, achieves success in an enterprise 796

(10)   A, a crook, discovers that his former pals are all married and "going straight" 763

(10)   A, supposing himself a criminal, discovers that no crime has been committed 783

(10)   A discovers that a coroner's verdict of "accidental death" should have been one of cold, premeditated murder 803a

(14)   A, grasping and relentless, and sparing no one in his greed for gain, encounters an experience which transforms his character 781

Helpfulness

A is old, believes he is slipping in his work, and considers himself a failure 810

A, undertaking charitable enterprises when he thought he was soon to die regrets the enterprises when he finds he still has a long life ahead of him 811

A is on his way to keep an important engagement 816a

A is an outlaw, hunted by the authorities and dodging about to escape capture 817

A, well-to-do and of good family, is impersonating a person who is "down and out" 818a

A sifts the circumstantial evidence of a crime in an attempt to discover the perpetrator 833

A, becoming secretly aware of the plans for a holdup, endeavors to prevent it 834

(1)   A is thrown into prison through false evidence in a political conspiracy 826

(7-12)   A overhears a chance conversation and secures information of the utmost value 835

(9)   A, by chance, overhears a conversation that gives him material for a literary masterpiece 835

(11)   A, a miser, is lured into a charitable enterprise by the prospect of death 811

(14)   A, a miser, would recover money given in charity until he discovers how popular his bounty has made him. Charmed by his popularity, he continues to be generous, and so consummates a most remarkable character change 811

Deliverance

A, a mediocre person, undergoes a weird experience 853

A, caught in a trap that holds his body powerless but leaves his mind alert, seeks to achieve physical freedom 856

A seeks to achieve emancipation from a fear which dogs his life, shows in his face and manner, and plunges him into misfortune 857

A is made miserably unhappy by the fear of death and would emancipate himself from it 858

A, falsely accused of crime, seeks to clear himself of the accusation 859

A fears that he will commit a transgression 862

A's popularity becomes so great that it annoys him 863a

A desires a place of seclusion where he can be absolutely alone, away from cables, wireless, mails and the public 863a

A seeks to enhance his social prestige 863b

A, keeper of a hotel at a summer resort, faces failure in business through lack of custom 863c

A is a man of wealth and high character whose conscience is troubled by a transgression committed in his earlier years 864

A—*Deliverance, Conc'd*

A seeks to escape financial disaster by undertaking an honest but secret enterprise that will bring him in enough money to discharge his pressing obligations 874
A's philanthropic enterprise is about to fail 882
A, an agnostic, is caught in a terrific storm 884b
A, a barbarian, is compelled to deal with a civilization which he once knew but now has forgotten 887b
A undergoes a strange experience among people hypnotically deluded 888
(1) A is heavily in debt and facing bankruptcy 874
(1) A, a ventriloquist, is captured by savages and threatened with death 878a
(2) A, a ventriloquist, captured by savages and threatened with death, makes an animal talk—and is given his freedom and loaded with honors 878a
(2) A, adrift at sea in a small boat and near death from exposure, lands on an unknown coast 878b
(2) A's philanthropic enterprise faces financial failure; and A, a reformed gambler, keeps the enterprise going with crooked card games 882
(4) A dreams of danger but discredits the dream and believes the danger real 852
(4) A, impoverished, seeks to recoup his fortunes by a wealthy marriage 860
(5) A, recovering his reason after it has long been obscured, relates a strange story of his experiences, a story which his friends find it difficult to believe 889
(12) A, fearing he will commit a transgression, seeks to emancipate himself from the fear, and from the possibility of doing evil 862
(12) A, under a fictitious name, returns to his native place, where he had committed a youthful transgression, and, as an Unknown, seeks to carry out an enterprise 864
(14) A, a mediocre person, undergoes an experience which inspires him with grandiose ideas of his power and ability 853

Idealism

A's popularity becomes so annoying that he seeks what he conceives to be ideal seclusion to escape from it 897
A is a selfish person, constantly looking out for "Number One" 898
A, selfish and miserly, finds that his methods are mistaken and that he is making no progress toward happiness 898
A is wealthy and avaricious and happy only when he is adding to his riches 899
A is a white man who seeks to make his white civilization a pattern for halfsavage peoples 901
A is a conscientious artist whose ideal is Truth 903
A's consuming desire is for friendship, for some one with whom he may associate and converse; but he is old and ugly, and no one pays him any attention 912a
A is a gambler pursuing his blackleg profession 914
A mysteriously disappears from his own community; and, when he reappears among strangers, he bears a fictitious name 917
A, in carrying out a worthy enterprise, changes his name and goes to a place where he is unknown 918a
A, a soldier, disappears from the ranks 919a
A, a soldier, is a deserter under fire but falsely reported "missing in action" 919b
A, after long years of wandering as an outcast, returns as an Unknown to his own home 919b
A searches everywhere for a Good Man, whom he envisions and personifies, but who evades him 922a
A becomes a "bum," an outcast and a wanderer 922b
A, a crook, is trying to "go straight" 923
A, wealthy, desires with all his heart to live as a poor man 924a
A, wealthy, seeks to live a life of idleness and luxurious leisure 924b
A is wealthy and his ideal life is a life of leisure—but he meets with an experience that challenges his ideal 924b
A is a "man of the world," relentlessly looking out for "Number One" and having little regard for others 925
A, trying to realize his ideal of being a benefactor of mankind, meets with a disturbing experience 926
A seeks to throw open his home to friends and strangers alike, and be generously hospitable, but certain unpleasant conditions make it difficult 927
A in a spirit of altruism, befriends all in need 928a
A is never too busy to give aid to others and, because of it, he has an unpleasant experience 928a

A—Idealism, Cont'd

A is a writer who plans to work up a pet idea into a story 932

A, a writer, before he begins work on a story, wishes to make sure that the tale he has in mind will be interesting to the general public. He plans to settle the question by secret enterprise 932

A, penniless, exchanges ten years of servitude for a college education 935

A's cherished ideal is the sea, and far-flung adventures 936

A is a morally superior person 937

A is a clever craftsman who struggles to earn a living while upholding his ideals 938

A, if he chooses, could win vast wealth by sacrificing his high principles 938

A seeks good in evil by culling lessons in good out of his association with transgressors—inspiration for contentment out of his misfortunes 939

A enlists as a private in the army when he might easily have secured an officer's commission 940

A seeks, through idealism, to be content with life in spite of a grinding poverty that makes life wretched 941

A is a police magistrate with lofty humanitarian ideals 949b

A, a police magistrate who wishes to know more of the private lives of those who are brought before him for judgment, disguises himself as a "bum" and plunges into the underworld 949b

A's half knowledge of the world constitutes his handicap 950

A believes he can be happier and more successful as a lawyer than as a doctor, as a general than as a private, as his own "boss" than by working for somebody else 950

A feels he can do more good outside the priesthood than as a priest 950

A's happiness lies in freeing himself of a torturing conscience 951

A will suffer ruin and disgrace if he carries out his plan to free himself of a torturing conscience 951

A's ambition, one that is necessary to his happiness, is to fall out of the world that knows him 952

A, for reasons of his own, craves peace and quiet 953

A, desiring peace and quiet, finds his ideal retreat in a vacant house, and there he secretly takes up his quarters 953

A, through erring imagination, becomes discontented with his life and surroundings 954

A, discontented, in a spirit of revolt seeks to achieve contentment 954

A, a highwayman, is robbing the mails 955

A becomes so wealthy and powerful that, in the overweening pride of his mistaken ideals, he voices the query: "Is there any god greater than I?" 957a

A is a general in the army 957b 960b

A is captain of a steamship, racing across the Atlantic in an attempt to cut down the time of the passage 957c

A takes issue with the accepted belief that poverty is the source of discontent, and conceives it to be the true source of happiness 958

A struggles against difficulties in seeking to avoid wealth 958

A is a soldier, eager to fight but who is commanded to retreat before a superior force of the enemy 960a

A receives orders from his superiors which he considers discreditable 960a

A's pride rebels against the loss of his ancestral acres through poverty 961

A's one desire is to achieve a high honor, an honor that is unmerited, and to enjoy that honor is a condition necessary to happiness 965

A has set his heart on accomplishing something beyond his powers, and his happiness depends upon his success 966

A has been mysteriously absent from his home for long years 967

A, for many years mysteriously absent from his home, seeks a happy renewal of old ties by returning suddenly and unheralded to his native place 967

A is a young man of lofty ideals 968

A, a young man of lofty ideals, craves all sorts of experiences in order that he may find the best and noblest in life 968

A, a city toiler, cherishes a dear desire for the open fields and the song of the lark 969

A befriends any strangers who may be in need of assistance, often neglecting his own family in carrying out his generous enterprises 970

A believes solitude the greatest of human blessings 971

(1) A, wealthy and avaricious, loses all by grasping for trifling gains 899

(1) A, a soldier, is reported "a deserter under fire" 919c

A—Idealism, Cont'd

(1-12)　A, a soldier facing a large force of the enemy, fights against overwhelming odds until he is killed 919c

(1)　A, a morally superior person, is cast away in a vicious, isolated, primitive environment, where moral inferiority assails his high idealism on every side 937

(1)　A has fallen upon evil days, and luck goes against him in every way 942

(1)　A, a general in the army, is engaged in an unimportant enterprise, and he is so absorbed in it that he gives no attention to the attacking enemy. A's troops are defeated 957b 960b

(2)　A flees to a foreign country to escape the consequences of a transgression 915

(4)　A, a fugitive in a foreign land, becomes so homesick for his own country that he has to return 915

(4)　A's capricious fancy, groping toward happiness, leads him to depart from the strict line of duty 949a

(4)　A, with negro blood in his veins, aspires to all the opportunities of the white race 959

(6)　A, unable to find a noble ideal for which he has long and vainly searched, dies 907

(6)　A, a soldier, disappears from the ranks and dies secretly and heroically for an ideal of duty; but he is reported "a deserter under fire" 919a

(7)　A, wealthy and desiring to live as a poor man, finds that his wealth makes it impossible 92?a

(7)　A, believing poverty the key to happiness, changes his ideals when he finds himself wealthy, and happy as he had never been in the days of poverty 929

(8)　A, given all he thought necessary for his happiness, finds there is still something lacking—something in himself 900

(8)　A, after searching in vain for a noble ideal, dies unaware of the fact that he himself, because of his earnest search, has come to exemplify the ideal 907

(8)　A seeks to rebuild his life, wasted in dissipation, along the lines of exemplary ideals 918a

(8)　A's lofty aim is to be a benefactor of mankind 926

(8)　A clings to his lofty ideals through all his vicissitudes of fortune 942

(8)　A starves to death in holding fast to a lofty conception of duty 943a

(8)　A starves to death rather than amass wealth by shattering his ideals 943a

(8)　A, a prisioner, dies holding fast to a lofty conception of duty rather than win freedom by shattering his ideals of loyalty 943b

(8)　A is a gentleman of the "old school," who comes through life enduring with patient fortitude every manner of misfortune; and then, at last, poverty stricken and pronounced a failure according to all the material standards of the world, he still clings to his high ideals and counts his vicissitudes, which could not overcome his ideals, as blessings in disguise 944

(8)　A, a highwayman, opening a letter that falls into his hands, secures information that sends him away on an altruistic undertaking—all by the way of proving that there is "good in the worst of us" 955

(8-12)　A discards low ideals for high ideals 963

(8)　A, a white man battling against the superstitious frenzy of a half-savage tribe stricken with the plague. upholds the highest ideals of the white man's civilization 973

(10)　A's imagination leads his mind astray, and in seeking emancipation from fancied misfortunes he is plunged into real misfortunes 900

(10)　A has a passion for a certain pastime; and he becomes so absorbed in his trifling pastime that big events demandin~ his immediate attention, are neglected with disastrous results 902

(10)　A, believing solitude to be the greatest of human blessings, encounters difficulties in his search for it 971

(11)　A's pride will not allow him to discontinue benefactions for which his family has long been noted, although his poverty forces him to many shifts of simulation, demands pinching sacrifices, and taxes his ingenuity 905

(11)　A cannot realize his cherished ideal because he is compelled to work at a desk job in order to support himself and his dependents 936

(12)　A, seeking to forward an enterprise which those who know him might consider absurd or unworthy. changes his name and goes secretly to a place where he is unknown 917

(12)　A has low ideals, but changes them abruptly for high ideals 922a

(12)　A is a man of wealth and influence who feels that the gold of his true worth is obscured by the dross of his riches 940

A—Idealism, Conc'd

(12) A leaves his coat on a cliff at the seaside, drops his hat in a stunted tree below the brink, and vanishes from the scenes that know him 952

(12) A, becoming aware of an old prophecy, unconsciously seeks to become like the exalted protagonist of the prophecy 964a

(14) A, seeking seclusion because his popularity annoys him, becomes hungry for the old applause and suffers remorse because of his flight from it 897

(14) A undergoes a tragic experience which results in a beneficial character change 918b

(14) A has high ideals but, on suffering misfortune, he changes his high ideals for low ideals 922b

(14) A, discarding low ideals for high ideals, struggles in vain to realize his high ideals; but, although baffled in realizing his cherished ambition, he effects a beneficial character change 963

Obligation

A has innocently caused a number of people to invest money in a worthless enterprise 979

A, by undertaking an obligation, finds himself threatened by misfortune 980

A's family all worked in order that he might be helped to a technical education 990

A conceives it to be his duty to work at a calling he dislikes so that he may repay his family for their sacrifices 990

A seeks theoretical adventure, "arm-chair" adventure—the thrill of high emprise caught second-hand from travel-books 991

A, with a half million, must be "broke" within a year, and he must not give away any money nor spend a cent foolishly 997b

A is the scion of a proud old line whose greatest pride has been to keep its estates intact 1000

A, in desperate need, ignores a family obligation 1000

A finds it necessary to carry out a certain distasteful enterprise if he would attain wealth 1001a

A is a woman-hater 1002

A is under an obligation to commit a crime 1003

A is a United States consul 1015

A is the recipient of anonymous threats of violence if he tries to carry out an obligation 1019

(1) A, in order to carry out an obligation, gives up his chosen profession and enters another line of work 1006b

(8) A, unable to realize his ambition because of family obligations, comes as near realizing the ambition as he can 991

(12) A, having innocently caused a number of people to lose money in an enterprise, feels that he cannot rest content until, by his own efforts, he recovers the money for the losers and restores it 979

(12) A, under an obligation to commit a crime, is not a criminal at heart and cannot fulfill the obligation 1003

(12) A, threatened anonymously with violence if he carries out an obligation, proceeds boldly with what he believes to be his duty 1019

(6) A cuts a Gordian Knot by taking poison 1016a

Necessity

A is desperately in need of money 1023

For A, beating back to "Easy Street" has its difficulties 1024

A is an outcast son, sorely in need of money 1026

A, a man of ability who has fallen upon evil days and is almost bankrupt, meets with unpleasant complications in seeking to recoup his fortunes 1029

A, innocent, is in the hands of the police on a groundless charge 1030

A, in the hands of the police, must be free at once in order to carry out a certain enterprise, and cannot wait to prove his innocence 1030

A, a doctor, while taking an evening stroll, is summoned hurriedly to attend a sick person. He meets with evil experiences 1031

(1) A is young, and had considerable money, but, by a wild life, he impoverishes himself and comes to want 1024

(4) A, desperately in need of money, undertakes a rash enterprise and becomes involved in an unpleasant complication 1023

(4) A, hard-pressed for money, is beguiled by the devil into an unwise proceeding 1027

A

Chance

A, an inventor, is secretly testing out an invention 1034
A is a plain man of mediocre abilities 1036
A is on his way to keep an important engagement 1040
A is injured in an accident and taken unconscious to a hospital 1040
A, in a half doze, overhears a chance conversation that concerns a transgression; but he is in doubt as to whether he overheard a real conversation, or was deceived by a dreaming mind 1045
A is strolling through the streets of a large city at dead of night 1046
A, a blind man, is groping his way along a city street 1047
(1) A, an inventor secretly testing out an invention, so delays in mid-ocean a ship carrying a fabulous cargo of bullion that fears are entertained for the ship's safety 1034
(1) A, on his way to execute a new will disposing of his estate, meets death in an accident 1041
(1) A, engaged in a secret enterprise, suffers a chance intrusion and discovery owing to his own carelessness 1042a
(4) A carelessly leaves a door unlocked while engaged in a secret enterprise 1042a
(4) A, when in doubt regarding his course of action in any enterprise, flips a coin to let luck decide. This has always been his custom, and it has invariably been successful; but there comes a time when the coin proves unreliable 1049
(9) A's gold mine, seemingly of little value, is turned into a "bonanza" by a lucky strike 1043
(9) A hears by chance a familiar name, and the name solves a riddle of the past 1053
(9) A solves a mystery involving his happiness 1054
(9) A solves an important mystery when falling plaster reveals the place where some old love letters are concealed 1054

Personal Limitations

A, although simple minded and genuine, is awkward in speech and forward and uncouth in manner 1059
A attempts audacious enterprises, but his confidence has a way of leaving him "flat" before the enterprises are carried through to completion 1060
A is told by a clairvoyant that he has inherited the trait of cowardice 1061
A's belief in the statement that he has inherited the trait of cowardice, makes a coward out of him 1061
A is so content with what he has that any impulse toward enterprise is throttled 1062
A's mistaken ideals are an obstacle to his advancement 1063
A, on trial for murder, could establish an alibi and prove his innocence—but only by a dishonorable act 1070
A finds that the duties of his position are so numerous it is physically impossible for him to carry them out 1071
A's high official position makes it impossible for him, in his own person, to acquire information which he thinks of first importance 1072
A, a successful business man, has an overwhelming desire to break away from commercial affairs and go adventuring in quest of Romance 1073
A is obsessed with fear of a pursuing peril 1078
A, obsessed with fear of a pursuing peril, seeks to gain contentment of mind 1078
A finds it beyond his power, in any ordinary manner, to secure a man of courage for a dangerous piece of work 1081
A proceeds by secret enterprise to find a man of courage 1081
A is a man who finds cowardice an obstacle to enterprise 1082a
A lives in a strange lost community which is ruled by an idol of Fear 1082b
A seeks escape from a community ruled by Fear, but finds it difficult to develop sufficient courage to accomplish his purpose 1082b
A lacks initiative, and the ability unaided to advance his material fortunes 1083
A seeks to forward an honest enterprise but lacks the means to finance it 1084
A would like to achieve a lofty enterprise, but he is so poor he cannot finance the undertaking 1086
A, a crook, would like to restore some of his ill-gotten gain, but finds it difficult without revealing his culpability 1087
A's happiness is wrapped up in his ambition 1088

A—Personal Limitations, Cont'd

A is hampered in his work, and his success imperiled, by a lack of new ideas 1090

A's knowledge of the profession he seeks to follow has been obtained solely by reading stories about it; he has had no practical experience 1091

A reaches a point in his chosen work where his ingenuity and enterprise grow stale and will not help him onward 1092

A is considered a very inferior person intellectually 1093

A, considered an inferior person intellectually, seeks to solve a mystery that has puzzled the most sagacious 1093

A is a celebrity; and the written requests for his autograph become so numerous that they interfere seriously with his work 1094

A seeks to free himself from certain meddlesome influences that interfere seriously with the practice of his profession 1095

A, a playwright, having no new ideas for a play, goes forth in quest of them 1096

A has a cherished ambition which he cannot realize because he is hampered by certain obligations 1097a

A is a subordinate, and considered mentally inferior 1098

A's ignoble weakness is lack of courage in investigating events that have great news value; for A is a newspaper reporter, and news is his stock in trade 1104

A, on one side of the Atlantic, must arrive on the other side at a certain time or he will lose a rich inheritance 1107a

A, pursuing an important enterprise, catches a swift steamer for a hurried trip across the Atlantic 1107a

A has committed a crime but has never fallen under suspicion 1110

A, an author, becomes suddenly aware of deterioration in his creative work 1111a

A finds that his obligations as a "quack" doctor are too difficult for his powers 1112

A has a theory that the perfume of flowers may be blended into musical conceptions 1113

A is hastening across the ocean on a fast steamer in order to carry out an important enterprise 1116

A manufactures a hand-made product in a worthy manner no machinery can duplicate 1122

A, by manufacturing a hand-made product by machinery, on a large scale, and so keeping up with the demand, will amass wealth; but the standard of quality will be lowered 1122

A is a bibulous person, and his ultimatum from his doctor is this: "Either quit drinking or resign yourself to die within a very few months" 1126

A, apparently dead, is really in a cataleptic state and sees and hears everything that takes place around him although powerless to move a muscle 1128a

A is in a mine when a charge of giant powder explodes prematurely 1128b

A's character weakness is superstition 1132

A seeks a courageous person who will recover property that has been stolen from him 1129b

A, publicly, is honest and prosperous, but privately he is a transgressor 1140

(1) A has assumed the furtive manner of a criminal for so long that it has become habitual with him and he cannot act like an honest man 1064

(1) A, a writer, discovers that he is losing his grip on his reading public and is becoming unable to write salable material 1074

(1) A's character weakness is betting; and he seems unable to conquer the failing, although he invariably suffers loss 1079

(1) A lacks ingenuity, and the power to force circumstances to contribute their utmost in forwarding his undertakings 1088

(1) A's obligations, which prevented him from realizing a cherished ambition, pass, but the habit of excusing himself from enterprise on account of the obligations remains and his cherished enterprise is never undertaken 1097a

(1) A's guilty conscience handicaps him in the field of enterprise 1110

(1) A, engaged in an important enterprise, is delayed in mid-ocean by an accident to his steamer; the vessel's wireless is out of commission and A faces failure in a pet undertaking 1116

(1) A, in his absent-minded moments, mechanically draws odd designs on a piece of paper, unaware of what he is doing, or that it may have an adverse effect upon some of his secret enterprises 1124

(1) A, suffering a terrible mental shock, seemingly falls dead 1128

(1) A loses his eyesight in a powder explosion 1128b

(1) A is so superstitious that it prevents him from winning success in his enterprises 1132

A—Personal Limitations, Conc'd

(4) A, a young man of mediocre abilities, is happy in considering himself a very superior person 1060
(4) A's ideal of labor is to do just enough to "get by" and hold his job 1063
(4) A, a reporter, assigned to "cover" a certain story and finding it impossible, decides to write up an imaginary interview, pretending it is bona fide 1080
(4) A, in order to secure means to finance an honest enterprise, becomes a bootlegger for a time 1084
(4) A, for worthy purposes, poses as a criminal 1097b
(4) A seeks to overcome personal limitations in an honest enterprise by a resort to dishonest methods 1101
(4) A, reading de ective stories, is fired with the desire to become a detective 1111b
(4) A, highly confident of his own ability, takes up a line of work with which he has had no practical experience 1111b
(4) A's obstacle to enterprise is laziness; and he submits to it cheerfully 1131
(4) A is an agnostic who, in his arrogance and presumption, defies a Higher Power 1133
(9) A, a craven at heart, deliberately forces himself into danger as a method of developing his courage 1082a
(9) A, a subordinate, attacks a problem that defies solution by his superiors, and solves it, thereby winning just recognition and preferment 1098
(9-14) A, a coward, by deliberately forcing himself into risky situations in order to acquire first-hand information, transforms his character and becomes a star reporter 1104
(12) A makes the mistake of thinking himself a criminal; then he discovers that he is not a criminal 1064
(13) A, a somnambulist, deceives himself in a certain enterprise by opposing, in an unconscious state, all the efforts of his waking moments 1117
(14) A, supposed to be a hoodlum, is transformed into a gentleman in an astonishingly short period of time 1076
(14) A, a very ordinary young man, suddenly becomes afflicted with megalomania, and his character is completely changed 1134
(14) A, who was timid and shirked enterprise, undergoes a character change which impels him to rush audaciously into the most difficult undertakings 1134

Simulation

A has a violent distaste for ghost stories and stories of the supernatural 1141
A pretends to be ill in order to avoid listening to ghost stories 1141
A, in his coffin and just before burial, revives from a cataleptic trance 1142a
A is mistakenly supposed to have met his death in a storm 1142b
A is a connoisseur of precious stones and has a valuable collection 1143a
A, a crook, seeks by substituting a worthless counterfeit for the valuable original to secure an object carefully safeguarded 1144
A, a crook, in order to carry out a crafty enterprise, disguises himself as a person of wealth and social standing 1146
A desires to get away frequently to the city and have his "fling" with boon companions but fears the gossip of the rural community in which he lives 1148
A, in order to protect his collection of valuable stones against robbery, displays replicas of them, comparatively worthless, to would-be customers 1143a
A, an innocent transgressor under ban of the law, owes a large sum of money which he must pay 1148b
A is a lad away from home, very unhappy because he does not receive letters from home as all his other young friends do 1149
A, lonely and never receiving any letters from his home folks, writes letters to himself and shows them to his friends 1149
A is an art collector 1165
A seeks to demonstrate his ability to enact a certain role in a forthcoming play 1169
A, in order to prove his ability to enact a certain role in a forthcoming play, assumes the role off the stage 1169
A, wealthy and of high social standing, desires adventures in the underworld 1170
A is a fugitive from justice who has assumed an alias and is posing as an innocent and worthy member of society 1175a
A, a banker, has juggled with the bank's funds 1177

A—*Simulation, Conc'd*

A, a transgressor, covers up his criminal acts by a painstaking simulation of honor and excellence 1177

A, highly respected in his community, has committed a murder 1178

A is a criminal who is posing as an officer of the law hunting for another criminal 1179

A is a transgressor who poses as an honest man for the purpose of carrying out another transgression 1181

A, in order to achieve happiness, seeks to be free of suspicion 1183

A's high place in society is at odds with an enterprise he wishes to undertake 1181

A, in order to proceed with certain plans, finds it necessary to hide his identity 1184

A, to the public, is highly placed, honest and successful. This reputation is necessary as a "cover" for his private transgressions 1185

A, pursuing a worthy enterprise, changes his name and goes to a place where he is unknown 1186

A, a tramp, in order to have more success in his "panhandling", pretends to be a missionary 1190

A is a thief, who has an honest profession which he uses as a "cover" for his dishonest practices 1194

A is a wanderer, "under a cloud," who returns as an Unknown to his home town, scene of his youthful transgressions 1199

(2) A, a fugitive from justice, supposed to be dead, assumes an alias and escapes to a distant place 1142b

(3) A, just before burial, revives from a cataleptic trance, puts weights in the coffin, closes it, and secretly escapes from the house 1142a

(4) A is a coward who seeks, by arrogant boasting, to convince everybody that he is a hero 1150

(4) A, desiring adventures in the underworld and unable to realize his desire in his own character, assumes a fictitious character 1170

(4) A is a poor clerk who, with a limited capital, dons a dress suit and takes a brief "fling" in high society 1187

(4) A, to secure relief from desperate misfortunes, pretends to be a victim of lost identity 1188

(4) A, pretending to be a victim of lost identity, appeals to the police and is given food and shelter while the authorities try to discover who he is and where he comes from 1188

(4) A is a murderer who, for his own protection and gain, impersonates the man he has murdered 1195

(5-10) A plays the role of a "rube" so successfully that he defeats the purpose for which he undertook the impersonation 1202a

(8) A seeks to rebuild his life, wasted in dissipation, along the line of exemplary ideals 1186

(9) A, a fugitive from the law, assumes a fictitious character and an alias and wins a large sum of money in a certain enterprise 1148b

(9) A, returning to his home town as an Unknown, prevents a bank holdup 1199

(11) A, discovered masquerading under a false name and in disguise, is compelled to flee for his life 1193

(11) A, for the purpose of discovering what obstacles a certain person will meet and how he will react to them, assumes the role of a fictitious character and falls into very real misfortunes 1198

Craftiness

A, a fugitive from justice, disguises himself and, as an unknown, risks discovery and arrest to carry out a romantic enterprise 1209a

A is told by a doctor that he has only three months to live 1210

A, having committed a transgression, seeks to make restitution without betraying his guilt 1211

A is a bold thief who wishes to hide his identity and appear free of ulterior motives while carrying out an audacious robbery 1217a

A, secretly searching for a man of courage, stages a crafty enterprise in order to find a man of sufficient courage to face a dangerous test 1219

A tries to discover what obstacles a certain person will meet and how he will react to them 1223a

A has taken up his quarters in a vacant house 1225

A—Craftiness, Conc'd

A is obsessed with a fear of burglars 1230
A, obsessed with a fear of burglars, places a wax figure in his bed and sleeps in a locked closet 1230
A wagers all his money on a boxing bout 1231
A pretends to lead a dissipated life 1237a
A, a crook, launches a benevolent enterprise as a means of making secret restitution of his ill-gotten gains 1239
A seeks craftily to keep the good opinion of the public 1247
A closely guards an evil secret which, if known, would reflect upon his character and make impossible a cherished enterprise 1247
A is a doctor who follows his honest profession by day, and makes it a "cover" for his activities as a burglar by night 1248
A attempts craftily to clear himself of a suspicion of robbery 1249
A, rich and unscrupulous, has set his heart on acquiring a certain piece of ground 1260a
A represents guilt-masquerading-as-innocence 1262
A decides to use secret information for blackmailing purposes 1263
A is selling luck charms among a superstitious people 1273
A, supposed to be dead, assumes a fictitious name 1275
A, a crook, commits a robbery and escapes in woman's clothes 1282
A plans by crafty enterprise to secure a rich inheritance 1285
A is threatened with violence if he carries out an enterprise connected with his profession 1287
A, a white man among savages, seeks to avert a calamity by prayer 1289b
(1) A, a writer, slipping in his work as the years advance, draws on material of his early days to keep himself going. The material exhausted, A dies 1238
(1) A is influenced to engage in an enterprise that will bring about his punishment for transgression 1262
(1) A, influenced to carry out an enterprise, falls into a trap—a trap of mysterious dangers unknown to him 1267a
(1) A is so worried about a certain secret enterprise that, in his absent-minded moments he pencils, on anything that happens to be convenient, diagrams that offer a clue to his enterprise 1289d
(4) A, a Beau Brummel, wealthy and aristocratic, disappears inside a public washroom at a railway station with a suit case. When he reappears, he has transformed himself into a typical hoodlum A checks his suit case and plunges into the underworld in quest of adventure 1209b
(4) A, a wealthy miser, told by his doctor that he has only three months to live, decides to spend all his money before he dies so none will be left for his heirs 1210
(4) A, taking refuge in a vacant house and desiring to stay on secretly in the place, moves into the attic when the house is rented 1225
(4) A's plan to commit a robbery becomes known, and a trap is laid for him at the scene of the intended crime 1268
(4) A, by a stratagem, fosters the delusion of his own death in an attempt to realize money on his life insurance 1277b
(6) A kills himself, but contrives to make his death appear accidental 1237b
(6) A kills himself in order that money, to be secured as life insurance, may take care of his pressing obligations 1237b
(9) A renounces an inheritance because of a distasteful obligation attached to it; and then, after giving up the inheritance, a codicil to the will restores it to him, stating that the supposed obligation was merely a "test of merit" 1242b
(9) A, in the face of threats, carries out an enterprise and discovers that the threats were merely a stratagem to prove his courage 1287
(12) A craftily fosters the delusion of his own death 1277b

Transgression

A's estate has been in his family for hundreds of years, and it is an unwritten law of the family that it is to be held intact 1291c
A, a poor man going about his honest duties, is suddenly afforded the opportunity to commit a secret transgression whereby he will acquire great gain without incurring suspicion 1297
A fights against the temptation to acquire gain through transgression 1297
A is a notorious outlaw, at large and craftily avoiding apprehension 1298
A has committed a crime and fled to escape the consequences 1300

A—Transgression, Conc'd

A seeks to evade the legal consequences of a crime he has committed 1301
A, a minister of the gospel, errs secretly on his human side and commits a moral transgression 1306
(4)   A commits a transgression when he sells a piece of woodland, part of an inherited estate 1291c
(8)   A, committing a transgression and escaping unsuspected, is so tortured by conscience that he has to give himself up and confess 1291a
(8)   A, suffering remorse because he has committed a transgression, seeks to make restitution 1295
(9)   A, a prospector, discovers gold 1296
(12)   A commits a transgression and escapes unsuspected 1291a
(12)   A, highly placed and universally respected, protects his reputation by keeping a moral lapse a close secret 1306
(13)   A finds it important that he show himself where he is known; but it is also important that he remain in hiding 1300

Revenge

A is a malefactor of small pretentions, a down-and-outer of striking appearance masked by rags and squalor 1320
(1)   A, high born, falls under the ban of death as a political conspirator in his native country 1327
(2)   A evades a conspiracy aimed at his life and escapes to a distant land 1327
(3)   A, supposed dead, plays the role of a ghost 1313b
(4)   A seeks revenge against his native country for a grievous wrong 1312
(8)   A, in a spiritual victory, decides to forego a cherished enterprise and spare an innocent woman her happy but mistaken ideals 1323a

Mystery

A, dabbling in things he does not understand, seeks to accomplish wonderful results 1330
A, with a fearful oath declares: "I will see home to-night in spite of the storm, or I will never see home!" 1331
A flees from a pursuer who is wholly imaginary 1332
A, a chemist, with the aid of subtle poisons, develops a flower of unusual color and beauty 1333a
A, a needy person, picks up two pairs of cast-off shoes, one pair discarded by a clergyman and the other by a man of reckless nature and "shady" reputation 1336
A is a transgressor posing as an honest man 1339
A, a man of wealth and influence, holds his place in society by closely guarding a tragic secret 1346
A represents guilt-masquerading-as-innocence 1349
A thinks himself obsessed with a fear of speeding automobiles, and that the cars that are trying to run him down are phantom cars 1350
A decides that what he has come to consider a danger is merely a fancied danger inspired by fear 1351
A is caught in a snare of superstitious delusion 1355
A's will is waging a psychic battle against fear 1356
A is investigating psychic phenomena 1357
A has a prophetic vision which forecasts his death 1358
A has a delusion in which a certain odor, manifesting itself during a tragic experience, fills him with superstitious dread 1359
A has an evil dream which haunts his waking moments, works on his mind and has its effect on his behavior 1361a
A is sure that an occult experience he has had portends success in a certain enterprise 1361b
A believes that he hears strange voices talking to him 1365
A counters the belief that he hears strange voices talking to him with the auto suggestion that he is merely the victim of superstitious delusion 1365
A is influenced unduly by his dreams 1366
A, influenced unduly by his dreams, strives to master the ignoble weakness and control his dreams by sheer force of will 1366
A has invented a life-preserver for the use of shipwrecked persons 1367b
A undergoes a memory lapse and forgets everything about himself 1368

A—*Mystery, Cont'd*

A, a Fortyniner, returning with a wagon train from California, has with him a fortune in gold dust 1370b

A has a character weakness that prevents him from achieving success in enterprise 1374

A has long been mysteriously missing 1378

A is a man of adventurous nature who seeks to accomplish a dangerous enterprise 1379

A, a needy young artist with an ordered picture left on his hands, discovers that the picture is a map locating buried treasure 1386b

A is a dreamy, mysterious person who makes a study of occult phenomena 1389b

A encounters a trying experience 1389b

A will receive knowledge of an important secret if he has the ingenuity to solve the mystery of a figure in an Orental rug 1392

A, investigating a psychic problem, finds that he must begin by placing his faith in so-called "automatic writing" 1398

A seeks wealth, his by right, which has been concealed 1399

A secures knowledge of an important secret, and his curiosity involves him in a queer enterprise 1403

A is a reporter assigned to "cover" a story which involves a closely-guarded secret 1407

A obtains knowledge of a closely-guarded secret 1408

A, obtaining knowledge of a closely-guarded secret, goes on a hunt for buried treasure 1408

A is carrying out an enterprise 1414b

A vanishes mysteriously from a ship in mid-ocean 1414b

A, an honest bank messenger, disappears mysteriously with a satchel full of money 1415

A, while engaged in an important enterprise, drinks of an enchanted water and falls asleep 1418a

A, following a tragic experience, has a superstitious fear of a certain odor 1422b

A seeks to unravel the mystery of a strange house 1426a

A encounters a weird experience when he finds himself in a mysterious place, surrounded by people who are the victims of a hypnotic delusion 1427a

A is a skeptic in matters that have to do with the supernatural 1427b

A, a skeptic, meets with an experience which he finds disturbing 1427b

A dreams that he falls from a great height 1428

A, who evidently is a person of quality, cannot prove his station in life as he knows nothing of his birth and parentage 1430a

A, in a waking vision, sees a grave being dug for himself 1433a

A, if he carries out a professional obligation to call at a certain house in a certain street, is daily warned by anonymous letters that it will be at the peril of his life 1434

A is a member of a strange secret society in which all the members are bound by oath to avenge the wrongs, real or fancied, of each individual member 1438c

A is a member of a strange secret society in which all members have red hair. The watchword of the society: "One Bricktop for all; all Bricktops for one" 1438c

A, in great financial distress, pawns a valuable and mysterious object 1440

A seeks to discover the secret of life 1441a

A, a captured criminal, has a particularly vivid dream in which he is making a successful escape 1443a

A is trapped in the woods by a falling tree 1443b

A falls into an old well that has been covered with boards and earth 1443c

(1) A, involving himself recklessly in matters he does not understand, succeeds only in making himself ridiculous 1330

(1) A is haunted by a superstitious delusion that arouses fear and causes him to give up an enterprise 1334a

(1) A, seeking to carry out a certain enterprise, climbs into a building and suddenly discovers that the room he has entered is a trap; all windows bar themselves, and the stout door locks against him 1335

(1) A, during a storm, has a narrow escape when lightning strikes a tree under which he is standing, throwing A to the ground and injuring him severely 1353

(1) A, discovering a magic method for **wishing** and **having** makes a last wish that he shall live forever; but his magic fails him, and he dies 1354a

(1) A meets with disaster when illusion becomes reality through the overthrow of his reason 1357

A—Mystery, Cont'd

(1) A, taken ill, is haunted by a vision that forecasts his death, and he dies 1358

(1) A, unreasoningly fearful regarding a certain odor, succumbs and dies, a victim of his own delusion 1359

(1) A has supernatural experiences which prove an obstacle to enterprise 1360

(1) A is so sure of success in an enterprise that he puts forth no effort to win; and the enterprise fails 1361b

(1) A and his companions are attacked by Indians, A's companions are killed and A is mortally wounded 1370b

(1) A, discovering a "pocket" of gold in the desert, dies before he can take the gold out 1370c

(1) A, a detective, is falsely suspected of being a professional crook by those unaware of his secret motives 1376

(1) A, appearing suddenly among a tribe of savages, is encased in a diver's suit from which he cannot free himself unaided; nor, hailed as a god, can he ask his savage captors to free him 1419b

(1) A, while seeking to carry out an enterprise, is brought gradually under the power of a dreadful force, intangible, invisible and evil, until at last his body seems to become the abode of the accursed Thing 1422a

(1) A, seeking to express musically the odor of tube roses, is almost killed by a bolt of lightning 1422b

(1) A, seeking to discover a great secret, uncovers an unhappy complication 1441a

(1) A has an invisible wound, caused by a tragic act of injustice he has committed, and no physician or surgeon can heal him 1441b

(1) A, trapped by a falling tree in an isolated place, is unable to extricate himself, and dies 1443b

(1) A, falling into an old well, is unable to extricate himself and dies of his injuries 1443c

(4) A is under the delusion that he lives in a chaotic world, such a world as is pictured by pessimists 1345

(4) A, seeking sincerely to investigate psychic phenomena, begins unconsciously to mix truth with delusion 1347

(4) A, in order to disprove a fancied hallucination, deliberately throws himself in front of a speeding automobile which he supposes to be a phantom 1350

(4) A, in order to shatter his fear complex, plunges into a supposed danger that proves to be real 1351

(4) A, during a storm, defies the Supreme Power 1353

(4) A discovers a magic method for realizing all his wishes but at the expense of years of his life for every wish granted 1351a

(4) A is a performer whose specialty is a daredevil act of great danger; but in A there is growing the feeling that he will fail, although he knows that death is sure if he even contemplates failure 1356

(4-12) A, in order to prove the value of a life-preserver he has invented, dons the rubber suit, inflates it, and secretly by night drops overboard from a steamer on the high seas 1367b

(4) A, as a method of reprisal against his country, seeks to sell important government information to a foreign country 1372a

(4) A, as a method of reprisal against his native land, turns traitor in time of war and joins the forces of the enemy 1372b

(4) A sells his shadow for an inexhaustible purse 1373

(4) A seeks to discover what is in a mysterious room behind a locked door 1409

(5-10) A, slowly recovering from injuries in a hospital, changes his views on certain important questions 1353

(6) A, near death, draws a cryptic map on the page of a note book, locating the spot where a store of gold may be found 1370c

(6) A dies of psychic shock 1428

(9-14) A has a dream, or an unusual experience, psychic or otherwise, which enables him to conquer a serious character weakness and become successful in his undertakings 1374

(9) A, in a desperate mental conflict with a superstitious obsession, succeeds in scoring a victory for sense and reason—all by his own unaided powers 1375

(9) A, treasure trove, finds a mysterious old parchment document which describes the place where the treasure is buried 1394

(9) A, caught in a trap and held powerless under a huge burning glass, is saved by an eclipse of the sun 1419a

(10) A has a dream so vivid that it seems a part of his waking experience 1433b

A—Mystery, Conc'd

(11) A, in one pair of shoes, is meek and circumspect in his behavior · when wearing another pair, he is wild and profligate 1336
(12) A, in a mysterious manner, receives a warning of danger 1424a
(13) A, homeward bound, drives and drives; and he is still driving, no nearer his home than he was when he first started 1331
(13) A, unable to explain events of a seemingly supernatural nature, has a feeling that a ghostly visitor is at work 1381
(13) A, carrying out an occult enterprise, falls into a strange sort of trance during which he accomplishes remarkable things of which he has no remembrance when he awakes 1387
(13) A has recurring spells by day or night when he becomes a somnambulist, doing things of which he has no remembrance in his waking moments 1389a
(13) A, while carrying out an enterprise of small importance vanishes completely and mysteriously, baffling every attempt of the police and of his friends to find him 1414a
(13) A, seeking to unravel the mystery of a strange house in the hills, is caught in an electrical storm. During the storm the house vanishes and the site on which it stood becomes a lake 1426a
(13) A has a dream which he conceives to be an actual experience 1433b
(13) A has a wound, an invisible, psychic wound, which causes terrible pain in flesh and tissue which, otherwise, are perfectly healthy and normal 1441b
(14) A, victim of lost identity, assumes a fictitious name and character 1368
(14) A receives a blow on the head which causes him to lose his original personality and return to a fictitious personality which he had previously assumed 1390
(14) A, with a large amount of money in his possession, disappears; he is later found in jail, his reason obscured, his money gone 1415

Revelation

A for a long time seeks in vain to solve a puzzling mystery 1451a
A, receiving information which he thinks trustworthy, embarks upon a hazardous enterprise 1451d
A is puzzled by a mystery that seems too deep for solution 1452
A is at his wits' end in an attempt so solve a puzzling riddle 1453
A, a writer, is in doubt as to whether a story he has in mind will interest the general public 1460
(8) A fights a hard battle with his conscience; he finds it a losing battle, and makes an important revelation in order that he may achieve peace of mind 1461a
(9-12) A, trying to solve a puzzling mystery, discovers a clue in a little box concealed in an old phonograph bought at auction 1451a
(9-12) A slips and falls into a chasm; and in the chasm he discovers a clue to a baffling mystery 1452
(11) A, because of certain revelations he has received, firmly resolves that he will not carry out an enterprise that had formerly been dear to his heart 1455a

A and A-2

Love's Misadventures

(4-5) A and A-2 meet with a tragic adventure, and A-2 is killed 169

Married Life

A calls on his friend, A-2 446b
(12) A-2, falsely suspected of transgression, finds himself in a most unhappy position until A, by a statement of the facts, clears A-2 of suspicion 390

Misfortune

A, seeking to help his friend, A-2, lends him all his money 601
A and his friend, A-2, are attacked by robbers in a lonely wood 603b
A's friend, A-2, receives a wound from which he dies 603b
A, and his friend, A-2, on horseback, are swimming a flooded river. A-2 is struck by a piece of floating drift, but A rescues him and gets him to the river bank 603c
A's friend, A-2, is so badly injured that he dies 603c

A and A-2—Misfortune, Conc'd

A and his friend, A-2, are wandering afoot in the desert. A-2 is injured, and their water supply fails 603d

A's friend, A-2, dies from injuries and hardships 603d

A and his friend, A-2, explorers, are alone in the jungle 607

A's friend, A-2, goes insane from eating the berries of a strange plant, and makes a murderous attack upon A 607

A helps A-2 secure treasure in a secret place 662

A's friend, A-2, commits suicide before A can help him overcome his misfortunes 671

A plans a secret enterprise in an effort to help A-2 672

A seeks wealth by craftily defrauding his friend, A-2 701

A, because of a disturbing experience, is compelled to turn against his friend, A-2 704

A and A-2, before the war, were fast friends 716

A is captain in the army, and his men capture and bring before him A-2, a bosom friend of A's, who is one of the enemy and a spy 716

(1) A s friend, A-2, fails to repay money borrowed from A, and A is left penniless 601

(1) A suffers defeat because his friend, A-2, does not efficiently carry out his part in a certain enterprise 603a

(1) A finds himself ruined, and his reputation gone, when his "double," A-2, bungles an important enterprise while posing as A 629

(1) A, through his confederate in an enterprise, A-2, suffers loss 630

(1) A is ruined when his appeal to his supposed friend, A-2, for financial aid, is denied 631

(1) A, helping A-2 secure treasure in a secret place, is abandoned to die in a deep pit by A-2, who makes off alone with the treasure 662

(1) A, seeking wealth by craftily defrauding A-2, is tortured by conscience 701

(1) A loses his small fortune in trying to help a friend, A-2 715b

(4) A, in order to oblige his friend, A-2, acts contrary to his own principles and experiences unpleasant results 599

(4) A dons A-2's mask and costume and assumes A-2's role at a carnival, A-2 being called away suddenly on pressing business and promising to return shortly. A is against masquerades on principal; and, when A-2 fails to return, he is in a dilemma 599

(4) A has his "double", A-2, take his place in an important enterprise 629

Mistaken Judgment

A, believing that a certain proposition has merit, buys stock in it himself and sells stock to his friends, A-2, A-2 747

A seeks to manage A-2's languishing business and place it on a paying basis 769

A's bibulous friend, A-2, influences A to take to drink, scoffing at the doctor who has forbidden A to indulge in spirituous liquors 779

A, before the war, had a friend, A-2, who had rendered him a very great service 790a

A-2, during the war, is captured as an enemy spy and brought before Captain A 790a

A, a judge, has a friend, A-2, brought before him for trial and sentence 790b

A is persuaded by his friend, A-2, to engage in an enterprise 793a

A is influenced by his friend, A-2, to take charge of some important papers 793b

A supposes his friend, A-2, is dead 794

(1) A, through the influence of a reckless friend, A-2, comes to his death 761a

(1-5) Captain A allows an enemy spy, A-2, to escape, and ever afterward is regarded as a traitor to his country 790a

(1-5) A, a judge, presiding at the trial of his friend, A-2, so manipulates proceedings in favor of A-2 that A-2 is acquitted 790b

(1) A, obliging his friend, A-2, by taking charge of some secret documents, is arrested, and accused, on the strength of the documents, of having a part in a criminal conspiracy 793b

(4) A, heavily in debt, seeks to save himself from ruin by forging the name of a friend, A-2, to a note 770b

(4) A is persuaded by his friend, A-2, to undertake an enterprise which A knows to be extremely difficult and which his judgment warns him to let alone 793a

(7) A is astounded when his friend, A-2, whom he supposed to be dead, suddenly appears before him 794

A and A-2

Helpfulness

A learns that his friend, A-2, is accused of a crime 820
A, learning that his friend, A-2, is accused of a crime, seeks to prove his innocence 820
A is a ne'er-do-well who has a friend, A-2, of worth in the world 823
A, a sprinter, is on the point of losing a footrace because he believes he hears the voice of a dead friend, A-2, calling to him 827
A, ill and starving, receives food and money from his friend, A-2 831
A-2 tells his friend, A, in confidence, that he is a bootlegger 831
A meets with unhappy experiences when he tries to help his friend, A-2, who has fallen into misfortune 836
A, in order to help his friend, A-2, puts aside his principles and engages in distasteful enterprise 838
A seeks to correct a character weakness in his friend, A-2 839
A seeks to prevent his friend, A-2, from committing a reckless act that would have fateful consequences 840
A discovers that his friend, A-2, has committed suicide 841
A seeks to save the family of A-2 from shame and disgrace because of a reckless act committed by A-2 841
A, poor and humble, at great self-sacrifice helps A-2, an old man poorer than A himself 845
A's friend, A-2, falls from exhaustion while engaged in an enterprise 846
A completes a task for his friend, A-2, which A-2 is unable to finish 846
(1) A, trying to be of service to his friend, A-2, is suspected of treachery by A-2 807
(6) A's friend, A-2, is unjustly condemned to death; and A, by subtility, takes A-2's place in the prison cell and dies in his stead 823
(9-12) A plies his friend, A-2, with drink until he is intoxicated and helpless in order to prevent him from committing a reckless act that would have fateful consequences 840
(9) A, through his enterprise, restores A-2 to friends and fortune 845
(10) A seeks to correct a character weakness in his friend, A-2, by telling him a story which subtly suggests a method of self-correction 839

Deliverance

A, a sheriff, believes A-2, the man he is about to hang, innocent of the crime for which he was sentenced 877
A, a sheriff, delays hanging a condemned man, A-2, in the hope that a Higher Power will intervene to save A-2 877
(2) A, by a stratagem of his friend, A-2, is saved from an act of folly 880a
(2) A, rescued by a stratagem of his friend, A-2, from an act of folly, comes to realize his intended folly, forgive the stratagem, and thank A-2 880a
(5) A, about to commit an act of folly, is abducted by his friend, A-2, and held a prisoner as the only means of restraining him 865
(8-12) A, destroying a letter in which his friend, A-2, declares he is about to commit suicide, makes it appear that A-2 died of a contagious disease 868
(9-12) A, suspected of treachery by his friend, A-2, in a daring rescue saves the property and perhaps the life of A-2, and proves his faithfulness by a revelation of the danger to which A-2, unknown to himself, was exposed 867
(9) A, an old man, a homeless outcast and a "bum", is restored to relatives and to fortune by a friend, A-2 880b
(9) A, once a cultured gentleman but now a barbarian, was rescued from an unfortunate situation by his old friend, A-2 887b
(9) A, visiting A-2 in his prison cell, exchanges clothes with him and A-2 leaves the prison as A 875a
(14) A, a sheriff, is by duty compelled to hang a condemned man, his friend, A-2 877

Idealism

A discovers that his friend, A-2, is a defaulter 906
A suffering misfortune, seeks happiness in the companionship of A-2 and in playing golf 913
A is a worthless ne'er-do-well, while his friend, A-2, is a man of worth in the world 972

A and A-2—Idealism, Conc'd

A resolves, at any cost to himself, to save his friend, A-2, from threatening misfortune 972

(1-4-12) A-2 has important responsibilities, which A has not, and A flees, thus making it appear that he is the defaulter, and not A-2 906

(14) A grievously wrongs his friend, A-2, and is taught a beneficial lesson when A-2 freely forgives him 925

Obligation

A, in return for a service A-2 has rendered him, agrees to grant any favor within his power that A-2 may ask 981

A is indirectly the cause of danger to his friend, A-2—danger of which A-2 is ignorant and of which A cannot tell him 987

A, on his sacred honor, has promised his friend, A-2, that he will do whatever A-2 shall require of him 997

A-2 begs relief at A's hands as an act of mercy 1007

A, as a favor to his friend, A-2, promises to undertake a certain enterprise 1021a

A promises his friend, A-2, to undertake a certain enterprise, and then forgets his promise 1021a

A and A-2 are as Damon and Pythias, David and Jonathan 1021b

(1) A carries out honorably the heart-breaking obligation of killing his friend, A-2, hopelessly ill and tortured with suffering 1007

(1) A, an army officer, has a friend, A-2, one of the enemy and a spy, brought before him for punishment by court-martial 1016b

(1) A and A-2 have their ideal of friendship challenged by an unusual experience 1021b

(6-12) A's friend, A-2, rescues A from a heart-breaking situation by killing himself 1016b

(12) A, influenced by a compelling idea of responsibility, finds it necessary to protect his friend, A-2, from a secret danger 987

Chance

(1) A, thinking he has a robber to deal with, by mistake shoots his friend, A-2 1035

Personal Limitations

A lightly assumes a task to oblige his friend, A-2 1058

A would like to save his friend, A-2, from disaster, but money is necessary—and A has no money 1085

A, wealthy and too old to have his "fling," gives A-2, a spendthrift, a large sum of money to squander as he sees fit 1102

A hopes to enjoy A-2's spendthrift experiences second hand 1102

A seeks to be loyal to his friend, A-2, but certain conditions render it difficult 1115

(1) A, posing as a criminal, finds that he is arrayed against some of his friends of the elite, A-2, A-2, A-2, who are engaged in a swindling enterprise and are fortified with police protection 1097b

(4) A, an elderly writer who runs out of ideas, copies material which his friend, A-2, long dead, wrote in his younger days 1103

(10) A, assuming an enterprise to oblige his friend, A-2, finds it completely beyond his powers 1058

Simulation

A, inspired by altruistic motives, assumes the name and character of A-2, using A-2's clothes and other belongings, and seeking to carry out an enterprise begun by A-2 1168

A and A-2 are crooks, seeking escape through the closing net of the law 1174

A drops his own name and assumes the name of a deceased friend, A-2 1183

A, wealthy, entertains his friends lavishly; consequently, he counts his friends by scores 1202b

(1) A, posing as A-2, does not know that A-2 is a transgressor 1168

A and A-2—Simulation, Conc'd

(10) A, wealthy, as a test of his friends' loyalty, pretends to lose his wealth; then he tries to borrow, but not one of his former friends will lend him so much as a plugged nickel, or even notice him in the street as he passes   1202b

(13) A and A-2 are friends, but one of them is a criminal and a fugitive from justice. Which of the two is the criminal?   1175b

Craftiness

A, for his own selfish reasons, gives aid to his friend, A-2, who is suffering misfortune   1212a

A, friend of A-2, learns that A-2 is to be made the victim of a transgression. A discovers this too late to warn A-2, and determines to help him by secret enterprise   1214

A recovers property stolen from his friend, A-2   1234

A explains that he invested money belonging to himself and A-2 in an enterprise that failed   1249

A persuades his friend, A-2, to undertake a hazardous piece of work—and does not tell him it is hazardous   1264

A discovers his friend, A-2's, secret transgression   1269

A challenges his friend (really his enemy) A-2, to a mock duel, the pistols to be loaded with blank cartridges—a performance ostensibly for the entertainment of their friends   1288

(3) A's friend, A-2, is waylaid and robbed by three men; and one of the men is A   1227a

(4) A informs the authorities of his friend, A-2's, secret transgression and receives the reward for A-2's capture   1269

(6) A, in what is supposed to be a mock duel with A-2, falls at the first exchange of shots, craftily killing himself in such a way that it appears the killing was done by A-2   1288

(8) A's friend, A-2, reaps a rich reward from a discovery he has made, and offers to share with A; but A, knowing he is unworthy of such generosity, refuses it   1235

(9) A, a fugitive from justice, succeeds by a stratagem in rescuing his pal, A-2, from the toils of the law   1209c

(9) A, recovering property stolen from his friend, A-2, seeks to restore it by stealth so A-2 will not know it has been out of his possession   1234

(11) A attempts to deceive his friend, A-2, thinking to profit by the deception, but fails   1235

Transgression

A, in a drunken brawl, quarrels with A-2   1291b

A and A-2 are placer mining in partnership   1304

(1) A, recovering sense and reason after a drunken brawl, discovers A-2 dead at his feet and thinks he has killed him   1291b

(4) A, a prospector, makes a rich "strike." Of right, he should share his discovery with his partner, A-2, but decides to exploit the discovery for himself alone   1296

(4) A, under cover of the night, takes all the wealth belonging to himself and A-2 and decamps with it   1304

Revenge

A seeks revenge upon his friend, A-2   1313a

A and his friend, A-2, are of high and honored station; and A, seeking revenge against A-2, must conceal his purpose and proceed by indirection   1313a

Mystery

A's friend, A-2, is killed in an accident at A's side   1334b

A's friend, A-2, is mysteriously murdered   1334c

A seeks to discover the murderer of his friend, A-2   1334c

A has a delusion that he is haunted by A-2   1344

A's friend, A-2, has just died suddenly, and the fact is not known to any one but A   1385

A, his curiosity aroused by the mysterious actions of his friend, A-2, decides to investigate the cause   1402

A and A-2—Mystery, Conc'd

A, investigating the mysterious actions of his friend, A-2, discovers that A-2 has a strange enterprise on hand   1436

A discovers that his friend, A-2, is seeking the recovery of a buried chest containing long-lost gold   1436

A is informed regarding an important secret which, if revealed, will wreck all A-2's hope of acquiring gain   1439a

A fears that A-2, who is plowing a field, will unearth evidence of a crime which, A knows, has been buried there   1442

(1) A believes that the blood of A-2 is on his hands   1344

(1) A is haunted all his days by an act which he committed in an effort to help a friend, A-2   1355

(5) A, transformed into an ass by witchcraft when he was seeking to transform himself into a bird, is given a garland of flowers to eat and becomes his normal self—plus sorely garnered wisdom   1363

(5) A, plunged into misfortune through mistaken judgment and folly, is rescued by a devoted friend, A-5   1363

(12) A is believed to be his dead friend, A-2; and he leaves those who suppose him to be A-2 with the statement that he "goes to keep a tryst with death"   1385

(13) A, superstitious, believes he is haunted by the ghost of his friend, A-2   133.b

(13) A, a pugilist, believes that A-2, a friend whom he killed by a chance blow in a practice bout, is present in the ring every time he has a battle   1338

Revelation

A investigates the murder of a friend, A-2   1449

A discovers that his pal, A-2, is a girl masquerading as a boy   1454

A, discovering that A-2 is a girl masquerading as a boy, keeps the knowledge to himself and does his utmost to save the masquerader from annoying experiences   1454

(1) A, investigating the murder of a friend, A-2, is horrified to discover that all the circumstantial evidence points to himself as the murderer   1449

A and A-3

Love's Misadventures

A's rival in love, A-3, pretends to be A's friend in order to lure him into an undertaking in which he will lose his reputation or his life   79

Love's Rejection

A is accused by A-3, his rival in love, of having been born under a "bar-sinister" 245

Married Life

A's enemy, A-3, who wronged A grievously, is dead   433

(1) A is manoeuvered by A-3 into gambling with money not his own, and losing it 434a

(1) A is craftily manoeuvered into misfortune by A-3   434b

Misfortune

A, the idol of his people, is about to lose a wrestling match to A-3, his rival   652b

(1) A's deadly enemy, A-3, has A at his mercy, and there seems nothing for A to do but to make the best of his hard lot   663

(1-12) A-3, having slain A, places a revolver in A's stiffening fingers in order to make it appear that A is a defaulter and a suicide   730

(6) A, wrestling in the open with A-3, a rival wrestler, prevents A-3 from winning a victory by falling from a cliff, apparently by accident, and losing his life   652b

Mistaken Judgment

1) A's success is mistakenly credited to his enemy, A-3   796

A and A-3

Helpfulness

(1) A is arrested for transgression on charges trumped up by a jealous rival, A-3
829

Deliverance

A, a hunted outlaw in disguise, takes refuge with an enemy, A-3   883

Idealism

(2) A becomes reconciled with an enemy, A-3, when A-3 renders him a service   912b

Obligation

A's life is saved by his enemy, A-3   1022
(1) A's life, saved by his enemy, A-3, is mutually agreed to be forfeit to A-3 whenever A-3 so desires   1022

Chance

A is seeking the life of A-3, an enemy   1039

Personal Limitations

A, a simple mountaineer, comes to a large city in pursuit of an enemy, A-3   1109
(3) A, from the mountains, seeking his enemy, A-3, in the city, is so overawed and impressed by his unfamiliar environment that his enmity fades away   1109

Simulation

(4) A, assuming a disguise and an alias, secures employment from A-3 for the purpose of obtaining certain information   1193

Craftiness

A believes A-3 guilty of a crime   1222a
A, as a means of forcing a confession of guilt from A-3, throws both himself and A-3 into a situation where death for both of them seems imminent   1222a
A possesses knowledge inimical to A-3   1228
A discovers that A-3 has knowledge of a secret that will bring disaster to A if revealed   1232
A finds it necessary to abduct A-3 and hold him incommunicado   1232
A pretends that he is "going to the dogs" in order to deceive his mortal enemy, A-3, and lead A-3 to believe he is not to be feared   1237a
A is helpless against an armed enemy, A-3   1250
A pretends to be hors du combat for the purpose of luring A-3, his enemy, within arm's reach   1250
A is inveigled into a gambling game by A-3   1255a
A's rival, A-3, when A fails to join him in an enterprise as agreed, carries out the enterprise alone   1265b
A's enemy, A-3, is a connoisseur of wines   1266
A's enemy, A-3, seeks to avert a calamity by an incantation   1289b
A, by prayer, and A-3, by an incantation, seek to avert a calamity. The calamity is averted   1289b
(1) A is manoeuvered into jail by the politically powerful A-3 in order to prevent A's information from causing A-3 any damage   1228
(1) A is lured into a trap by A-3   1253
(1) A's enemy, A-3, lures A into a gambling game and arranges for a fake police raid   1255a
(1) A, seeking to obtain unfair advantage of A-3, induces him to take charge of some contraband goods, knowing he will be apprehended   1265a
(3-9) A, lured into a trap by A-3, has set a counter trap for A-3   1253
(3) A's enemy, A-3, arranges for a fake police raid on a gambling game; but A, secretly informed, has the police make a real raid   1255a
(3) A catches his enemy red-handed in a transgression   1280

A and A-3—Craftiness, Conc'd

(4-12)   A, to escape suspicion, places the body of A-3, the man he has murdered, on a railroad track in an attempt to make it appear that A-3 was killed by a train   1277a

(5)   A, seeking to convert a savage people to Christianity, has all his efforts set at naught by A-3, a witch doctor   1274

(9)   A, by subtle enterprise, forces a confession of guilt from A-3, and thus wins success in a difficult undertaking   1222b

(9)   A, when his mortal enemy, A-3, is lulled by a false sense of security, strikes and kills   1237a

(9)   A, by working on A-3's pride as a connoisseur of wines, lures him into a wine vault where he is faced with death   1266

(9)   A who "has the goods on" A-3, keeps his information from the authorities and holds A-3 in his power and subject, through fear of the law, to his will   1280

Revenge

A revenges himself upon an enemy, A-3   1311

A seeks revenge against A-3 for a disrespectful remark against A's family   1315

A seeks revenge against A-3 for a persecution that results in the death of A's parents and sisters   1316

A seeks revenge against A-3 for a terrible wrong   1318

A constructs a deadly trap in a place where, he thinks, his enemy, A-3, will fall into it   1319b

A seeks to be revenged on A-3; but A-3 is powerful and constantly on his guard   1322

A, prosperous and successful, is hated by a rival, A-3   1323b

A's enemy, A-3, seeks craftily to encompass the death of A   1321a

(1-7)   A revenges himself upon an enemy, A-3, unaware of the fact that A-3 is his brother   1311

(1)   A has no personal enmity against A-3, but he is caught in the toils of a family feud and his obligation requires that he kill A-3   1314

(1)   A is brought under suspicion as a political conspirator through the craftiness of a rival, A-3   1323b

(1)   A, an aristocrat, is trailed and spied upon by enemies, A-3, A-3, A-3, seeking his life   1329

(2)   A secretly examines a letter in the possession of A-3, his traveling companion, and discovers that the letter is his own death warrant. A carefully erases his own name and fills in the name of A-3   1324b

(2)   A disguises himself as a hoodlum and lives in the underworld as a means of escaping enemies, A-3, A-3, A-3, who are seeking his life   1329

(3)   A, by subtle enterprise, brings upon A-3 the fate A-3 was seeking to bring upon him   1324a

(3)   A, supposed to be dead, plays the role of ghost and, as a method of reprisal, haunts his enemy, A-3   1313b

(10)   A, seeking revenge against A-3, discovers after   long search that A-3 is dead   1318

Mystery

A, in a dream, sees a person he hates, A-3, in his room   1361a

(5)   A, in early life, killed A-3 in the heat of passion by striking him with the weighted handle of a riding crop. A, unsuspected, escapes from the scene of the tragedy   1346

(10)   A supposes he has murdered A-3; then, suddenly, A-3 appears before him   1342b

A and A-4

Misfortune

A, in desperate danger, appeals for rescue, to A-4   632

A's appeal to a selfish power, A-4, for rescue, is denied because commercial interests would be imperiled by the delay necessary to save A's life   632

A, a professional man, is captured in his office at night by mysterious strangers, A-4, A-4, A-4, blindfolded and taken to a secret place   660a

A, spirited away by A-4, A-4, A-4, is compelled to perform a professional service   660a

A and A-4—*Misfortune, Conc'd*

A invites a number of guests to meet a celebrity, A-4 702
A has invited a number of hero-worshipers to meet A-4, a celebrity. The hero-worshipers arrive, but A-4 does not 702
(1) A is abandoned and left to die by A-4 632
(4) A asks A-4, a stranger, to remove a pair of handcuffs from his wrists 707

Mistaken Judgment

A befriends a needy stranger, A-4 772
(1-7) A befriends a needy stranger, A-4, who proves to be a criminal 772

Helpfulness

A seeks to help A-4, an old man in misfortune 805
A finds a stranger, A-4, ill, exhausted and unconscious, lying in the road 816a
(1) A, seeking to help a stranger, A-4, meets with an unpleasant experience 805
(4) A's sympathy goes out to A-4, a fugitive from the law, and he attempts to rescue him 815a
(8) A subordinates his own affairs to those of a stranger, A-4, who is ill, and helps him to a place where he can receive medical attention 816a

Deliverance

A invites a celebrity, A-4, to be guest of honor at a reception in his home, and A-4 accepts 863b
A, a hotel keeper at a summer resort, facing failure, invites A-4, a celebrity, to be a guest at his hotel, and A-4 accepts 863c
A refuses to delay his important enterprise long enough to rescue A-4, a person in distress and facing death 957c
(7-10) A, attempting to commit suicide, is prevented from doing so by A-4, who comes to the same place to make an attempt on his own life 879

Obligation

A is threatened with misfortune because of a mysterious parcel which he has obligingly taken from A-4 and promised to deliver 985
A secretly discovers a delinquency A-4 wishes to conceal 998
(3) A, secretly informed regarding a transgression A-4 wishes to conceal, threatens to inform the authorities unless A-4 does something A wants him to do 998

Chance

A, of an humble station in life, is mistaken for A-4, a celebrity 1036
A unwittingly takes a suit case belonging to a stranger, A-4, when leaving a train, leaving his own suit case in place of A-4's 1044a
A, hiding in a place where there is no food, steals from the larder of his nearest neighbor, A-4 1056
(2) A's suit case is in the hands of a stranger, A-4. The train is wrecked and A-4 is killed. A, on the evidence of his own suit case, is reported a casualty 1044a

Personal Limitations

(10) A, in spite of certain character defects, seeks the friendship of A-4, but only succeeds in annoying A-4 and so fails of his purpose 1059

Simulation

A, in order to help A-4 poses as A-4 1161
A, a crook, in order to overcome the difficulties of a certain enterprise impersonates a celebrated novelist, A-4 1180
A, a crooked gambler, seeks to fleece a stranger, A-4, out of his money 1191
A, a crooked gambler, pretends to be a friend of A-4, a stranger, in order to lure him into a card game 1191
(1) A's "double," carries out an enterprise as A which A finds disastrous to his own fortunes 1163c

A and A-4—Simulation, Conc'd

(2)   A unloads upon A-4 certain romantic affairs which he (A) finds distasteful 1163b

(4)   A, falling in with A-4, a stranger who has been injured in an accident, agrees to take over an enterprise which the accident prevents A-4 from finishing   1161

(4)   A finds his "double" in A-4, and he hires A-4 to attend to certain duties which devolve upon himself (A)   1163a

(9)   A, a crook, impersonating a celebrated novelist, A-4, proceeds to a small town and becomes the lion of a ladies' literary society   1180

Craftiness

A hires A-4 as a catspaw and sends him uninformed into various misadventures 1223a

A pretends to be a novelist, A-4, writing a burglar story   1271

A, a "dummy-chucker," pretends to have a fit on the walk in front of the mansion of A-4, a wealthy man   1285c

Mystery

A, a reporter, writing up an imaginary interview as fact, quotes A-4 as being in town on a certain day   1310

A, a young man in dire need of money, has a mysterious caller, A-4   1388

A is offered a large sum of money by A-4 if he will take part in a secret enterprise, the nature of which A-4 will not disclose   1388

A's curiosity is aroused by the queer actions of A-4, a stranger   1404a

A, discovering that a stranger, A-4, is trying to commit suicide, investigates the cause   1404a

A endeavors to find A-4, who has mysteriously disappeared   1404b

A, his curiosity aroused, investigates a suspicious person, A-4. A robbery has just occurred and A-4 seems to have a guilty knowledge of it   1405

A, engaged in a hazardous search for A-4, finds himself in a strange lost community that has no direct communication with the outside world   1426b

A is made a prisoner in a strange lost community; and he finds A-4, for whom he is searching, also a prisoner   1426b

(2)   A-4, accused of a crime, establishes an alibi through an interview innocently faked by a reporter, A   1340

(2)   A is hired by A-4 to recover stolen property which, unknown to A-4, was stolen by A himself   1339

(4)   A murders a stranger, A-4, in a lonely wood where the soil is of a peculiar color, unlike any other soil for miles around. A sulks back home with the mud on his shoes   1341

Revelation

(7)   A, seeking to discover whether a story he has in mind will interest the general public, tells the story to a group of strangers, A-4, A-4, A-4   1460

A and A-5

Misfortune

A seeks to defeat a grafter, A-5 at the grafter's own game   630

A, abducted by A-5 and held for ransom, is a meddlesome, disagreeable person, and his family and friends are glad to be rid of him and will not pay the ransom 639

A, faced by a robber, A-5, with a gun, tries craftily to delay yielding up his valuables   655

A, captured by mutineers, A-5, A-5, A-5, is placed in a small boat and cast adrift on the high seas   719b

A is an officer of the law hot on the trail of a fleeing criminal, A-5   722

A, a police officer, owes a debt to A-5, a criminal, but has no money and cannot pay   723

A seeks to reveal to the authorities the identity of a criminal, A-5 who, so far, has been unsuspected   725

(1)   A, securing knowledge of a closely-guarded secret, is hounded by a guilty persecutor, A-5, until his life is made miserable   596

A and A-5—Misfortune, Conc'd

(1) A, standing sponsor for A-5, discovers that A-5 is a crooked gambler who uses A's sponsorship for the purpose of mulcting A's friends   612

(1) A befriends a tramp, A-5; and A-5, taking advantage of A's hospitality, steals valuable property from him   613

(1) A is swindled out of his life's savings by A-5   621

(1) A is abducted by A-5 and held for ransom   639

(1) A is a captive, held by his captor, A-5, in a physical environment which constitutes a trap, and from which there seems absolutely no means to escape   653

(1) A is shot and seriously wounded by a robber, A-5   655

(1) A, passenger on a vessel on the high seas, is made a prisoner when the vessel is captured by mutineers, A-5, A-5, A-5   719b

(1) A, an officer of the law, while pursuing a criminal, A-5, meets with misfortune   722

(1) A, in trying to lodge information with the police against a criminal, A-5, meets with misfortune   725

(2-12) A, mistakenly supposed to be a transgressor, is finally cleared of suspicion by a confession of the real transgressor, A-5   635

(2) A, abducted by A-5 and held for ransom, makes A-5's life so miserable that he pays a round sum to have A taken off his hands   639

(4) A, given to altruistic enterprises, befriends a tramp, A-5   613

Helpfulness

A seeks to help A-5 in a certain enterprise   809

(4) A, seeking to help A-5, does not know that A-5 is a crook   809

Deliverance

(1) A is bitterly persecuted by a relentless enemy, A-5   884a

(2) A, bitterly persecuted by a relentless enemy, A-5, sees no possible escape from the coil; then, suddenly, A-5 is killed in an accident   884a

Idealism

(1) A, a crook trying to "go straight," is compelled by A-5, the leader of his old gang, to take part in a criminal enterprise   923

Obligation

A, a lawyer, honorably discharges the distasteful duty of defending a crim nal, A-5   1006a

A, an officer of the law, is under a personal obligation to a criminal, A-5   1011

(1) A, an officer of the law, is compelled by duty to arrest a criminal, A-5, to whom he is under an obligation   1011

A, a police officer, has captured a criminal, A-5   1016a

A, a police officer, is under an obligation of professional duty to arrest A-5, and he is under a counter-obligation of a personal nature to help A-5   1016a

A, an officer of the law, is old; and A-5, his prisoner, is young, and there are extenuating circumstances in his case   1017

(1) A, a cashier responsible for the funds of the firm employing him, is ordered by A-5, junior partner of the firm, to give him secretly a large sum of the firm's money   1014

(1) A, an officer of the law, and A-5, his prisoner, are lost in the desert, afoot, without food and with only a small supply of water—not enough for the two of them   1017

(6) A and A-5, officer of the law and prisoner, are lost in the desert with only a small supply of water between them. They draw lots to see which shall take the water and make his escape. A cheats in the drawing so that A-5 can win. A-5 picks up the water canteen and abandons A to die   1017

Chance

(1) A, a blind man, answering a wild call for help, stumbles into a nest of crooks, A-5, A-5, A-5, who are engaged in a criminal enterprise   1047

A and A-5

Personal Limitations

A's cattle have been stolen by A-5, a notorious "rustler" whose very name inspires fear in the law-abiding 1129b

Simulation

A, for worthy purposes, plays the role of a fictitious criminal, A-5 1167
(4) A, for worthy purposes playing the role of a fictitious criminal, A-5, is sought by the police for a crime committed by the real A-5 1167
(4) A, a criminal, poses as an officer of the law looking for A-5, another criminal Authorities pick up A-5, turn him over to A, and A starts with his prisoner for the scene of A-5's crime—and his own 1179

Craftiness

A is secretly drugged by enemies, A-5, A-5, A-5 1221
A learns that he has been cast by A-5 for the role of victim in a confidence game 1226
A, a detective, captures A-5, who was once an old friend of his 1284
A, a detective, owes A-5, a criminal he has captured, a sum of money which he has not been able to repay; and A-5 hopes to make use of the debt in securing his release from custody 1284
(1) A is captured by a brigand, A-5, and held for ransom 1218
(1) A, a miser who is deaf and dumb, is made a prisoner in his home by A-5, who seeks to force him to reveal the whereabouts of hidden wealth 1237b
(1) A, captured by A-5 and taken to a secret place, is being held for ransom 1281
(3) A, secretly drugged by enemies, A-5 A-5 A-5, is a drug addict and the potion has no effect; but A, realizing the attempt has been made, simulates unconsciousness to discover why it was made 1221
(3) A simulates guilelessness in an attempt to lure designing A-5 to his own undoing 1226
(3) A detects A-5 cheating at cards and denounces him; in the fight that follows, A-5 is killed 1276
(3) A, supposed dead, discovers an imposter, A-5, using his name and pretending that he is A 1275
(12) A, a detective, gives A-5, a criminal he has captured, a written order for the reward offered for A-5's apprehension; thus A, having paid the debt, takes A-5 to jail 1284

Transgression

A, in his safe, has a fortune in valuables. During his absence, crooks, A-5, A-5, A-5, attempt to open the safe and loot it of its contents 1307
(2) A captures a buglar, A-5, who is looting his house 1305

Mystery

A finds that A-5, in absent-minded moments, beguiles his leisure with a trifling proceeding that has become habitual with him 1362
A suspects A-5, seemingly an honest man, of a crime, and tries to prove him guilty 1371
A, seeking evidence against a gang of crooks, A-5, A-5, A-5, assumes the character of a burglar in order the more successfully to achieve his aims 1376
(5) A, a detective, unmasking A-5 as the leader of a criminal gang, finds that he cannot secure A-5's arrest as the police authorities refuse to act 1413b
(9) A, investigating a crime, discovers the criminal, A-5, through a most unusual clue 1362
(9) A, by mind-reading, secures a confession from a transgressor, A-5 1413
(10) A discovers that A-5 is a government secret service man, merely posing as a criminal in order that he may secure an advantage in prosecuting his work for law and order 1413b

Revelation

(9) A, by shrewd deduction and skillful reasoning, proves that A-5 is a criminal 1456

A and A-6

Misfortune

A is a fugitive from justice, hunted by A-6, an officer of the law   610

A, a fugitive driven to bay by officers of the law, takes refuge in a house which is a place of mystery   651

(1)   A, in a strange part of the country, is arrested by the police as a criminal "suspect"   608

(1)   A is in a trap in the town of X. He can escape only by passing through the towns of Y or Z, and detectives, A-6 and A-6, are watching for him in both places   610

(1)   A, a fugitive from justice seeking to avoid capture, finds himself in a tight corner with sheriffs, A-6, A-6, A-6, apparently approaching him from every direction   651

(2)   A is rescued from pursuers, A-6, A-6, when the old house in which he has taken refuge is blown away by a tornado   699b

(4)   A is impersonating an officer, A-6   717

(8)   A, a doctor, who is fleeing from A-6, an officer of the law, by his skill restores sight to A-6 who had become temporarily blind   712

Mistaken Judgment

A thinks a certain crime has been committed and lodges information with the police, A-6   771a

Deliverance

(1)   A is arrested and is being taken to prison by A-6   866

(2)   A's captor, A-6, an officer of the law, is killed in an accident, and is supposed to be A; consequently, A secures his freedom   866

Obligation

A, a fugitive from justice, will be arrested if he rescues A-6, the officer who is pursuing him, from misfortune; and if A abandons A-6, A-6 will die   1013

(9)   A, a fugitive in the desert, discovers that the officer who is pursuing him, A-6, is sunblind and dying from thirst   1013

Simulation

(1)   A, a crook, is trapped and surrounded by officers of the law, A-6, A-6, A-6   1176

(2)   A, a crook, trapped and surrounded by officers of the law, A-6, A-6, A-6, escapes by pretending to be another A-6 who is hunting for himself   1176

(2)   A is a captured criminal who, when the detective who has him in charge, A-6, suddenly dies, appropriates the clothes and belongings of A-6 and seeks to escape by impersonating him   1189

Craftiness

(1)   A had local fame as a female impersonator; and A-6, a detective, makes use of this fact as a clue in apprehending A for transgression   1282

(1)   A's secret is discovered by A-6, who craftily makes use of clues furnished unwittingly by A himself   1289d

A and A-7

Misfortune

A shows his ignorance of the usages of high society by unpacking his satchel when a servant, A-7, is expected to do it for him   617

Mistaken Judgment

(1)   A allows himself to be blackmailed by A-7, because he is convinced that he unintentionally committed a crime   783

(4)   A trusts his servant, A-7, and makes a confidant of him   775

(10)   A discovers that his trusted servant, A-7, is a thief   775

A and A-7

Deliverance

(2) A, held on a murder charge, wins freedom by an unusual plea of his attorney, A-7 887a

Craftiness

A invents a fictitious servant, A-7 1213
(9) A invents a fictitious servant, A-7, on whom he pretends to depend, and whose unreliability, while seeming to occasion A much embarrassment is really a convenience to A 1213

Mystery

(1) A, representing guilt-masquerading-as-innocence, is influenced by his valet, A-7, through a curiosity-arousing suggestion, to visit a certain place where, unknown to A, a deadly trap has been laid for him 1349

A and A-8

Married Life

(4) A's evident purpose is to shift the resopnsibility of a crime to the shoulders of innocent A-8 467

Misfortune

A is in the employ of A-8, a man in whom he has implicit confidence 604
A, against his wish and inclination, has been left a fortune by a deceased relative, A-8 700
A is annoyed by a person, A-8, who constantly crosses his path with the most untimely intrusions 735
(1) A's fear that he has inherited the evil traits of an ancestor, A-8, paralyzes his will in enterprise 720
(5) A's employer, A-8, has been "using the mails to defraud" 604
(7) A rids himself of a meddlesome person, A-8, and later regrets his harshness 735
(13) A is a fugitive from justice, who discovers that a relative, A-8, has died and left him a rich estate 699a

Mistaken Judgment

A, a tenderfoot in the west, takes offense at the slurs of a cowboy, A-8 759
A and A-8 proceed to settle their differences with their fists 759
A struggles in vain for the friendship of A-8 762
A, arisocrat, endeavors to pound a comprehension of class distinction into the thick skull of A-8, a plebian 782
A discovers, as he supposes, plain circumstantial evidence of a crime, and informs the police where A-8, the criminal, can be found 780
(1) A, after his death, receives the friendship of A-8—for which he had vainly struggled in life 762
(5) A-8, arrested as a criminal on information furnished by A, easily proves that no crime has been committed 780
(10) A, an aristocrat, and A-8, a plebian, fight a drawn battle. Equal prowess spells equality, and A and A-8 become fast friends 782

Deliverance

(9) A, undergoing a strange experience among a people weirdly deluded, discovers the secret of the delusion written in a notebook belonging to A-8, one of the victims who had died. By means of information obtained from the note book, A succeeds in rescuing the other victims of the delusion 888

Obligation

A, in order to get A-8 into his power, craftily manoeuvers him heavily into debt 983
A hopes to secure A-8's help in an undertaking by offering to free him from debt 983

A and A-8—Obligation, Conc'd

A, a doctor who is also a crook, is returning at night from a successful burglary job, when he is hastily summoned to attend a very sick person, A-8   1004

(2)   A, by concealment and stratagem, transfers a dangerous obligation to A-8, a stranger   980

Chance

A sells a gold mine of little value tentatively to A-8 at a bargain price. A-8 delays turning over the money and getting the deed   1043

(1)   A is impersonating A-8, when he is confronted by A-8 in person   1037

(1)   A, highly placed, wealthy and influential, has exactly the same name as a characterless individual, A-8, who lives in the same community   1038

(3-7-9)   A, by chance, meets A-8 who, under the influence of l.quor, reveals an important secret   1052a

(9)   A learns from A-8 whether a man or his wife died first in an accident—a secret of tremendous importance   1052a

Personal Limitations

(10)   A desires a piece of ground on which to build a mansion. The ground is owned by A-8, a poor man, in whose family it has been for generations. Influenced by family sentiment, A-8 refuses to sell   1140

Simulation

A seeks to appropriate a large sum of money which a dying man, A-8, has in his possession   1194

A bears a striking resemblance to A-8   1197

A, a crook, assumes the role of an honest, cultured gentleman, A-8   1200

(4)   A buries the body of his murdered victim, A-8, in a swamp and, by his usual exemplary conduct, seeks to escape suspicion   1178

(4)   A impersonates A-8 for the purpose of acquiring gain   1197

(4)   A, a crook, assuming the role of an honest, cultured gentleman, A-8, undergoes an experience which breaks down his nerve and exhausts his resourcefulness   1200

Craftiness

A, a crook, pretends to be a lover of precious stones while calling on a collector of gems, A-8   1217a

A is aware that A-8 knows too much for his (A's) good   1251

A gives A-8 money with which to take himself out of the country   1251

A is in a wild race with A-8 for a fortune   1255b

A's fortune depends on winning a race with A-8, and in reaching town and securing a certain document before A-8 can get his hands on it   1255b

A, rich and unscrupulous, craftily manoeuvers A-8 into debt   1260b

(1)   A, a confidence man selling "luck charms," finds his business languishing because miserly and influential A-8 has warned the people that his wares are a delusion   1278e

(4)   A, for his own selfish reasons, pretends to be the long-lost son of wealthy A-8   1212b

(4)   A to rid himself of the body of his murdered victim, A-8, and escape suspicion, hides the body in an old tomb   1252

(9)   A desires property which A-8 refuses to sell; so A ruins A-8 financially and forces him to sell   1260a

(9)   A, by using confidential information, convinces A-8 of his supposed ability and secures a position at a good salary   1278c

(9)   A agrees to go "fifty-fifty" with respectable and influential but miserly A-8; and A-8 recommends the luck-charms A is selling, and A's business flourishes   1278e

(12)   A, manoeuvering A-8 into debt, offers to cancel the debt if A-8 will agree to a certain proposition   1260b

Transgression

(4)   A seeks to acquire a rich estate in spite of A-8's legal rights   1299

A and A-8

Revenge

A's relative, A-8, has been grievously wronged by the authorities of their common country   1312

A, down and out, is hired by A-8, a revengeful rich man, to wear evening clothes, appear at a social gathering and act as a catspaw in carrying out a vicious scheme of reprisal   1320

(4)   A, a poor young man, inspired by anger and a desire for revenge, seeks to ruin wealthy A-8, a powerful captain of industry   1317

A commits an act of reprisal against A-8 with more serious results than he had intended   1323c

Mystery

A stumbles over the body of a murdered man, A-8   1337

A, a young artist, is hired by A-8 to paint a mystery picture   1386a

(1)   A, evilly dealt with by A-8, puts a curse on A-8 and all of his name   1439b

(5)   A is evilly dealt with by A-8 and brought to the brink of ruin   1439b

(13)   A is a cub reporter. The star reporter, A-8, from a distant place sends a cipher dispatch which the best minds in the newspaper office are unable to translate. A attempts the task   1396

(13)   A, a thief, breaking into a building to commit a robbery, finds a man, A-8, dead on the floor, a revolver clutched in his tense fingers   1429

Revelation

A, a doctor, summoned to give attention to a sick man, A-8, finds that A-8 is dying   1447

A learns from A-8, dying, the details of a crime   1447

(9)   A, poor, secures from A-8 information that brings him a fortune   1451b

A and A-9

Deliverance

(1)   A, because he has knowledge of A-9's guilty secret, is persecuted, spied upon and thrown into prison on a trumped-up charge   854

(3)   A discovers a fateful secret of his rich and powerful employer, A-9   854

Obligation

A, trusted butler in the household of A-9, is really a crook   1008

Necessity

A, for services rendered, receives the cast-off clothes of a young millionaire, A-9   1028

(2)   A, in needy circumstances, acts as a tailor's dummy for a young millionaire, A-9, who dislikes the annoyance of trying on his new clothes   1028

Chance

(1)   A is abandoned to die in mid-ocean by A-9, captain of a steamship, who refuses to delay his vessel to make the rescue   1052b

(2)   A is rescued from a boat adrift in mid-ocean when an accident delays the steamer of which A-9 is captain   1052b

Personal Limitations

A applies for the position of butler in the home of wealthy A-9   1107b

A, private secretary to A-9, knows that A-9 is jealously guarding some weighty secret   1114

(4)   A's curiosity gets the better of him and he meddles with the personal affairs of A-9   1114

A and A-9

Craftiness

(1)   A, at the instigation of A-9, unknowingly commits a crime   1272
(1)   A, innocent, is arrested for a crime; and his employer, A-9, testifies against him 1272
(1)   A, selling luck charms in a town, is denounced by the mayor of the town, A-9, as an imposter because A has not crossed A-9's palm with silver   1273

Transgression

(3)   A discovers secretly that his employer, A-9, is a murderer and a fugitive from justice   1303

A, A-2 and A-3

Misfortune

A decides to undertake a secret enterprise for the purpose of protecting helpless A-2 from a powerful enemy, A-3   671
(1)   A's friend, A-2, is helpless against the persecutions of a powerful enemy, A-3   671
(1)   A's friend, A-2, is the owner of a flock of sheep. A-3 is a cattle baron, rich and influential. A-3's men kill nearly all A-2's sheep, and A-3 is scheming to take A-2's land away from him. A-2, deep in debt, scarcely knows which way to turn 672

Mistaken Judgment

(4)   A, in order to save his friend, A-2, picks a quarrel with A-2's enemy, A-3, and slays him   764
(7)   A, in order to protect A-2 slays A-3, quondam enemy of A-2's, unaware that A-2 and A-3 have composed their differences, and that A-3 has become A-2's friend and financial backer   764

Revenge

(1)   A sets a trap for A-3 but A-2 is caught in it   1319b

A, A-2 and A-5

Misfortune

(1)   A, seeking to defeat the schemes of a grafter, A-5, is betrayed by a confederate, A-2, whom A asks to help him   630
(4)   A receives A-5 on a forged letter of recommendation from a friend, A-2, and introduces A-5 into his own social circle   612

Helpfulness

(3)   A, friend of A-2, exposes A-5, a spiritualist charlatan who is mulcting A-2 of large sums of money   830
(3)   A, threatening A-5 with arrest, forces him to return money out of which he has swindled A's friend, A-2   830

Obligation

A lives on an island, and on the same island are two other white men, A-2 and A-5, both friends of A's   1015

Simulation

(4)   A induces a friend, A-2, to play the role of A-5 in order to carry out an enterprise in which the presence of A-5 is necessary   1162

A, A-2 and A-5

Craftiness

A's friend, A-2, plans to rescue A from a brigand, A-5, who is holding A for ransom, and he plans to make the rescue without paying the ransom   1218

(3)   A's friend, A-2, is robbed by A and A-5· then A, in turn, robs A-5   1227a

(3)   A robs A-5 of valuablès stolen from A-2, and returns the property to A-2   1227a

Mystery

A is positive, in his own mind, that his friend, A-2, has been murdered by A-5   1371

A, A-2 and A-6

Simulation

(2)   A and A-2, crooks trying for a "get-away" after a successful "job," slip through the police net, A-6, A-6, A-6, when A disguises himself as a woman   1174

A, A-2 and A-8

Helpfulness

(2)   A, superstitious, is on the point of suffering defeat in an enterprise because he thinks he hears the voice of a deceased friend, A-2, calling to him; but he is saved when A-8, one of the spectators, turns the tragic call into a mere incident by a counter-call which allays A's superstitious fears   827

Craftiness

A tries to make two pugilists, A-2 and A-8, who are fast friends, stage a spirited ring battle   1215

A, for certain reasons, seeks to make enemies of two friends, A-2 and A-8   1215

(7)   A, wagering all his money on a boxing bout between A-2 and A-8, learns that the pugilists are fast friends, and that neither will fight to win   1231

Mystery

(13)   A, stealthily entering the house of his friend, A-2, finds the body of a murdered man, A-8   1337

A, A-2 and A-9

Helpfulness

(4)   A steals money from his employer, A-9, to help his friend, A-2, over a financial crisis, intending to make good the shortage when A-2 gets back on his feet and repays the loan   832

A tells his friend, A-2, that he has stolen money from A-9 in order to help A-2   832

A, A-3 and A-4

Chance

(4)   A, seeking the life of A-3, follows A-4 with murder in his heart; for A-4, by chance, is wearing the hat and coat of A-3   1039

A, A-3 and A-5

Revenge

(4)   A is sent abroad with a companion, A-3. A-3 bears a letter to a clique of conspirators, A-5, A-5, A-5, ordering the death of A   1324b

A, A-3 and A-6

Deliverance

(2)   A, a hunted outlaw, takes refuge with an enemy, A-3; and A-3, considering himself bound by the laws of hospitality, conceals A and saves him from his pursuers, A-6, A-6   883

A, A-3 and A-7

Love's Rejection

A-7 is a mercenary of A-3, A's rival in love   213

Deliverance

(2)   A, held on a murder charge, is released from custody when his lawyer, A-7, proves that A, "drunk with sleep," had believed his victim, A-3, was trying to kill him 887a

A, A-4 and A-6

Helpfulness

A is overtaken by a fugitive, A-4, who is being pursued by A-6, an officer of the law   815a

Personal Limitations

(1)   A, an escaped prisoner, finds it impossible to free himself from his handcuffs; and when, in desperation, he appeals for help to a stranger, A-4, A-4 notifies a police officer, A-6, and A is recaptured   1066

A, A-4 and A-8

Simulation

(4)   A, having invited friends to meet a celebrity, A-4, who does not arrive, persuades A-8 to impersonate A-4 in order that the guests may not be disappointed   1164

Craftiness

A, in order to forward a certain enterprise, contrives a test of merit for two men, A-4 and A-8   1223b
A, by chance, receives confidential information sent by A-4 to A-8   1278c
A-8, a doctor, is called in by A-4, and A-8 informs A privately that he is an imposter   1278d
A, a crook, pretends to have a fit, and is befriended by A-4, who calls in a doctor, A-8, to attend him   1285c
(9)   A, a crook, pretends to be a novelist, A-4, writing a burglar story; and a banker, A-8, obligingly gives A information about his own bank vaults   1271
(9)   A is discovered by A-8, a doctor, to be shamming illness. By collusion they foster A's pretentions, whereby A secures bed and board from wealthy A-4, and A-8 secures a fat fee   1278d
(14)   A pretends to disappear and to be in great danger, and so lures A-4 and A-8 into real danger in a quest for him   1223b

A, A-4 and A-9

Personal Limitations

A, applying to A-9 for a job, is asked for references as to character and ability, and is referred to A-4 by A   1107b

Craftiness

A, seeking a job from A-9, refers A-9 to A-4 for a recommendation as to character and ability, telling him A-4 can be reached at a prominent hotel at a certain hour by phone   1212c

A, A-4 and A-9—Craftiness, Conc'd

(9)   A, when A-4 is paged in a prominent hotel, answers the call, assumes the character of A-4 and gives himself such a flowery recommendation over the phone that he secures a job from A-9   1212c

A, A-5 and A-6

Deliverance

(8)   A, robbed by A-5 and wishing to save him from the law, declares to A-6, the officer who has arrested A-5, that he gave A-5 the stolen property in his possession   894

Obligation

A-6, an officer of the law calls on A to help him arrest A-5   1015

A, A-5 and A-8

Revelation

(3)   A secretly discovers A-5 counting money taken from a murdered man, A-8   1448

A, A-6 and A-8

Misfortune

(1)   A, employed by A-8, comes to work one morning and finds the office in the hands of federal agents, A-6, A-6   604

A, A-7 and A-8

Misfortune

(1)   A's chauffeur, A-7, driving A's car by A's orders at a high rate of speed, apparently injures a pedestrian, A-8   597

(5)   A, when his car apparently injures a pedestrian, A-8, seeks to evade consequences by having his chauffeur A-7, drive on at high speed   597

A and AX

Misfortune

(1)   A is robbed by AX, who secretly puts on A's clothes, takes his horse and flees 661

(1)   A, set upon by mysterious persons, AX, AX, AX, in the cellar of his house, is spirited away through a concealed passage   719a

Deliverance

A struggles against an hallucinary enemy, AX, who fights with superstition as a weapon   855

Personal Limitations

(1)   A, a doctor, is about to leave his office on a night emergency call when he is made a prisoner by mysterious strangers, AX, AX, AX, and spirited away   1130

Simulation

(4)   A, wishing to carry out an enterprise that would cause gossip, puts gossip to sleep by inventing a fictitious relative, AX, who is always in trouble and always calling on A to help him out   1148a

A and AX

Mystery

A receives a call from a mysterious stranger, AX, who is peculiarly dressed and seems to have hypnotic powers   1393

A tries to solve the mystery of a stranger, AX   1393

A, late at night, enters a room of his house and sees another man, AX, sitting in a chair before the fireplace   1423

A, thinking AX is a friend, steps toward him; whereupon, AX vanishes into thin air   1423

(1) A's property and high place in the world are appropriated by AX, and when A would claim his earthly possessions he is treated as an imposter   1348a

(1) A, inventing a mechanical giant, AX, and endowing it with life, is pursued by AX and brought to his death   1348b

(2) A, at a loss to account for a mysterious stranger, AX, who appears to him, warns him and then disappears, comes to believe that the messenger was sent by Divine Providence   1424a

(4) A's mortal pride would transgress the Divine Power; so fate, seeking to discipline A, materializes a spirit, AX, in A's image   1348a

(4) A invents a mechanical giant, AX, and endows it with life   1348b

(9) A because of a strange delusion, proves himself a person to be reckoned with   1418b

(10) A, a novelist, meets personally in real life a fictitious character, AX, from one of his stories   1391

(10-11) A always encounters a person of forbidding appearance with a demoniacal face, AX, just before some great misfortune overtakes him   1439c

(14) A, an inefficient, futile sort of person, comes to believe that he is the reincarnation of AX, a powerful personage of antiquity   1418b

Revelation

A, in his overweening pride, is taught a lesson by AX   1455b

(10) A receives an important communication from a mysterious person, AX, which enables him to correct a serious error   1461b

(14) A, rescued from critical misfortune by AX, receives a revelation from AX which results in a beneficial character change   1455b

A, A-2 and AX

Craftiness

(4) A, for personal reasons, impersonates the fictitious character, AX, invented by his friend, A-2   1216

A's friend, A-2, has invented a fictitious character, AX, for personal reasons 1216

A, A-5 and AX

Misfortune

(2) AX, a mysterious "righter of wrongs," at the point of a gun takes from A-5 money out of which A-5 has swindled A, and restores the money to A   621

(2) A, swindled out of his life's savings by A-5, is about to take his own life when his lost money is returned to him by a mysterious person, AX   621

A and X

Love's Misadventures

(4) A pretends that a wax figure, X, is his invalid wife   71a

(7) A discovers that a certain charm, X, with which he has won success in love, is no charm at all. The person who gave X to him tells him that faith in the charm is all that counts. Let a man be sure of himself, with or without a charm, and he is sure to conquer love   161

A and X

Married Life

(13) A, whenever he attempts to have X, a certain object of mystery, explained to him, meets with misfortune   541

Misfortune

A loses a valuable diamond, X, in a place where there is a flock of chickens, and he insists that the chickens must be killed, one by one, until X is found. The chickens are all killed   614

A, desperately in need, is offered a large sum of money for a diamond, X, which he knows is an imitation   729

(1) A loses a valuable diamond, X   614

(1) A loses a valuable diamond, X, and has his suspicions as to where it can be found, but discovers that his suspicions are unfounded   614

(1) A, custodian of a valuable object, X, misses X and believes it has been stolen   709

(1) A loses an important object, X, on the scene of an accident   711b

(1) A, on his way to return to the owner a stolen object, X, which he has recovered, loses the object and again seeks to recover it   724

(2-12) A finds a valuable paper, X, between the leaves of the family Bible   733

A has recovered a stolen object, X, and is on his way to return it to its owner   724

Mistaken Judgment

A finds an object of mystery, X, seemingly of great value   798

(4) A finds and keeps an incriminating document, X, with the intention of discovering the author of it at a later time   771b

(4) A is a thief who plans to steal what he believes is a very valuable gem, X   778

(4) A, believing that a counterfeit gem, X, is genuine, plans to steal it   778

(4) A highly prizes an object of mystery, X, carries it about with him and is unaware of the fact that his possession of X is fraught with terrible danger   798

(9) A, in desperate need, discovers that a gem, X, which he supposed to be worthless, is in reality genuine and immensely valuable   803b

Helpfulness

(1) A finds a satchel, X, which, unknown to him, contains evidence of an incriminating nature   804

(4) A, tramping along a country road, sees a satchel, X, drop from a passing automobile, and takes possession of it   804

Idealism

(8) A, humble and supporting himself by menial tasks, loses a work of art about which there are no marks of identification. The work of art, X, is found and pronounced by connoisseurs to be the production of a master. In the public prints the unknown artist is invited to come forward and receive the honor and wealth to which his genius entitles him. But A's ideal is "art for art's sake," and he will not be tempted   920

Chance

A is suddenly arrested by an object, X, that drops in front of him from the upper window of a house   1046

Personal Limitations

(1) A has lost the ticket of a pawned object, X, and the pawnbroker will not give up the pledge without the ticket   1077

A and X

Simulation

    A is a thief who has a real gem, X-1, which he supposes is a counterfeit   1166a

(5-7)   A, a thief, has a real gem, X-1, which he supposes is a counterfeit; and, adroitly, he substitutes X-1 for X-2, a counterfeit which A thinks is a genuine stone   1166a

(9)   A, making a replica, X-1, of a valuable original, X-2, secures X-2 by leaving X-1 in its place   1166b

Craftiness

    A discovers where a certain object, X, small but immensely valuable, has been concealed   1283

    A, to secure a certain object, X, must proceed warily and without arousing suspicion   1283

(1)   A finds himself in danger because he has innocently undertaken the custodianship of a mysterious package, X   1233

(2)   A, in danger because he is the custodian of a mysterious package, X, contrives a dummy package exactly counterfeiting X in appearance   1233

Transgression

(1)   A, a transgressor, seeks to forget a transgression, but a certain object, X, or circumstance, continually reminds him of it   1302

Mystery

    A carries in his pocket an object of mystery, X   1343

    A, annoyed by a certain object, X, destroys it   1367a

    A is told that a certain mysterious object, X, has power for evil (or good) and he decides to make a test   1380

    A comes innocently into possession of an object of mystery, X, highly prized by a person or a people, who lost it or had it stolen   1382a

    A buys a little trick box, X, in an old curiosity shop, and is unable to open it 1382b

    A seeks to solve an enigma that has to do with X, an object of mystery   1400

    A's curiosity and interest are aroused by a certain unredeemed pledge, X, in a pawnshop   1401

    A, endeavoring to solve a mystery, has for his only clue, X, the portrait of a beautiful woman, painted on ivory   1410

    A, while trying to discover perpetual motion, dreams that he has invented a machine, X, that defies the power of gravitation   1420

    A is vastly puzzled in his attempts to solve the mystery of a strange object, X 1425

(1)   A, apparently as the result of carrying in his pocket a queer object of mystery, X, experiences all sorts of misfortunes   1343

(1)   A, carrying in his pocket a small object of mystery, X, is harried by ill-luck and comes to believe in the malefic powers of X   1352

(1)   A suffers weird adventures and undergoes strange dangers when unknown persons seek by stealth to take from him a mysterious object, X, which has come innocently into his possession   1382a

(3-4)   A investigates a mysterious package, X, that has fallen into his hands   1435

(4)   A, staring at a certain object, X, falls under a spell which leads him to believe certain events are transpiring—events which are partly true but mostly grotesquely false   1342a

(4)   A, hearing of a mysterious and dangerous object, X, in a canyon of the lonely mountains, decides to investigate   1379

(4)   A buys a mysterious object, X, in a pawnshop, and attempts to satisfy his curiosity regarding it   1401

(4)   A, unknown to himself, has in his possession an object, X, which at any moment, may bring disaster or death to him   1438b

(6)   A, alone and near death, buries his store of gold dust and draws a map of the cache on a water canteen, X   1370b

(6)   A dies before he can redeem an object, X, which he has pawned   1440

(9)   A, under the heel of adversity and almost at the starvation point, secures an object of mystery, X, which grants his every wish—but at the expense of years of his life for every wish granted   1421

A and X—Mystery, Conc'd

(10) A discovers that his cigar will not burn. On investigation, he discovers that the cigar is merely a rolled paper, X, camouflaged with a tobacco wrapper—the rolled paper, X, being an important message   1397

(13) A encounters seemingly supernatural experiences which have to do with a small idol, X   1360

(13) A destroys a certain object, X, but mysteriously it reappears; again and again A destroys X, but always it reappears   1367a

(13) A is puzzled to account for certain objects, X-1, X-2, X-3, which come mysteriously into his possession   1381

(13) A has a little trick box, X, which he is not able to open. One night it opens of its own accord, and A finds a jewel in the box   1382b

(13) A, skeptically investigating a psychic communication, finds many things to corroborate the message, but he does not find the one important thing, X, whose location the message purports to reveal   1411

(13) A, puzzled by an object of mystery, X, goes to sleep with X on a table in his bedroom. On arising in the morning, A finds X disintegrated into a fine powder, all hope of a solution of its mystery gone   1425

(13) A, while in an abnormal mental condition, receipts for a valuable registered letter, X. Afterward, A has no recollection of receipting for X   1438a

Revelation

(1) A is accused of having stolen a valuable document, X   1457

(9) A, by chance, overhears a scrap of conversation in the street; and what he hears proves a clue to the whereabouts of stolen property, X   1453

A, A-2 and X

Misfortune

(4) A assumes charge of a valuable object, X, for a friend, A-2   709

Chance

(4) A unwittingly takes an object, X-1, belonging to his friend, A-2, leaving for A-2 a similar object, X-2, in place of X-1. Close inspection is necessary to discover the difference between X-2 and X-1   1044b

Personal Limitations

A calls at a pawnshop to redeem an object, X, pawned by his friend, A-2, who died leaving the pledge unredeemed   1077

Mystery

A's friend, A-2, is in the dark regarding an important secret that surrounds X, an object of mystery that has been stolen from him   1370a

A knows the secret of X, an object of mystery that has been stolen from A-2, and seeks to use his knowledge in recovering X   1370a

A's friend, A-2, loses by theft a mysterious object, X, supposed to bring good fortune to its possessor, and A seeks to recover X for A-2   1377a

A, A-3 and X

Misfortune

A fights with A-3 to safeguard valuables, X, of which A is custodian   730

(1-6) A is slain by A-3, who takes valuables, X, of which A is custodian   730

(1) A is accused of transgression by his rival, A-3, and an incriminating paper, X, is found in A's possession   771b

Craftiness

(2) A smashes an idol, X, supposed by a savage people to be a god, and immediately good fortune comes to the tribe. A-3 is discredited   1274

A, A-3 and X

Revenge

(4) A, in order to be revenged upon his enemy, A-3, manufactures an infernal machine, X 1319a

A, A-4 and X

Mistaken Judgment

A pursues a stranger, A-4, to recover from him an object, X, which has been stolen 774

(1-4) A, pursuing a stranger, A-4, and taking from him a valuable object, X, which, A thinks, was stolen from him, later discovers that X, which he supposed was stolen, has all the time been in his own possession 774

Helpfulness

A, finding a satchel, X, in the road, picks it up and carries it on with him, in the hope of returning it to the stranger, A-4, who lost it 804

Personal Limitations

A desires a certain object, X; but X is in the hands of A-4, who guards it carefully 1129a

Mystery

A is given an object of mystery, X, by a stranger, A-4, and assured that its possession will bring misfortune 1352

A receives half of an important message, X, and is looking for a stranger, A-4, who has the other half. The message cannot be read until both halves are joined 1369

A's only clue in his search for A-4 is the picture of a beautiful woman, X, left at the place where A-4 disappeared, and a legend connected with the picture 1404b

(10) A, meeting A-4, a stranger who has given him a small object of mystery, X, which has brought A ill-luck, is informed by A-1 that only A's belief in the misfortunes inspired them, and that he was merely the victim of suggestion 1352

A, A-5 and X

Personal Limitations

A has been robbed of valuable property, X, by A-5, a notorious criminal; and A tries to secure a courageous man who will recover X for him 1129c

Simulation

(1-5) A owns an objet d'art, X-1; and he buys X-2, as he supposes, which is an exact duplicate of X-1, from A-5, only to discover that he has repurchased X-1 which the scheming A-5 had stolen from his collection 1165

Mystery

(3) A finds a thief, A-5, by looking for a man who suddenly becomes prosperous. A-5, stealing X, is inspired by superstition to put forth efforts which make him prosperous 1377a

(3) A discovers that a mysterious package, X, contains stolen property. With X as a clue, he apprehends the thief, A-5 1435

A, A-6 and X

Misfortune

(1) A, arrested by the police as a criminal "suspect," has in his possession a satchel, innocently come by. The satchel, X, is found to contain burglar's tools 608

A, A-7 and X

Love's Beginnings

A receives from A-7 a small object of mystery, X, which, A-7 declares, will make A redoubtable in love. A takes X and fares forth to try it   7a

A, A-8 and X

Simulation

A, a crook, seeks unlawful gain by selling A-8 an object, X, which A-8 already owns   1145

(1) A calls on A-8 for a valuable object, X, which A has left with A-8 in the hope of making a sale; but A-8 declares A never left X with him, and has A ejected from the premises   1147

(4) A, poor, at the request of a rich man, A-8, leaves with A-8 a valuable object, X, which he has in his possession and wishes to sell   1147

A, A-9 and X

Simulation

(9) A, adroitly, secures an object greatly desired, X, from A-9, who will not dispose of it   1166b

Revelation

(2) A, accused by A-9 of having stolen a valuable document, X, has his innocence proved when X is found between the leaves of a book which A-9 had been reading   1457

A, A-5, A-8 and X

Mystery

(3) A sees a stranger, A-5, stealthily remove papers, X, from the pocket of another stranger, A-8, who is asleep. A follows A-5   1406

A, A-2, A-3 and X

Revenge

(1) A sends an infernal machine, X, to his enemy, A-3, and it falls into the hands of A's friend, A-2   1319a

A and F-A

Misfortune

A induces his father, F-A, to advance him his patrimony   611b

Helpfulness

(2) A, a dissolute son, is freely forgiven by his father, F-A   815b

(8) A, a dissolute son, in want, returns to his home and his father, F-A, a better and a wiser man than when he went away   815b

Obligation

(12) A, the son of F-A, feels it to be his duty to sell all his property in order to help pay the debts of the deceased F-A   1018

Craftiness

A finds the fly-leaf of the Bible owned by his father, F-A   1286

(10) A finds evidence to prove that his father, F-A, is dead   1286

A and F-A

Transgression

(1)   A, posing as F-A, is unmasked when discovered removing F-A's clothes   1290b
(4)   A, profligate son of wealthy F-A, cast off and disowned, murders F-A and then poses as F-A in an attempt to secure F-A's property   1290b

Mystery

A's father, F-A, has a conviction born of simple faith that A, long mysteriously missing, will some day come back to him   1378
A seeks wealth which his father, F-A, has left him, but concealed in a place whose location has been lost   1399

Revelation

A goes on a hazardous search for his father, F-A, long mysteriously missing   1451d

A, A-8 and F-A

Craftiness

A, the outcast son of F-A, seeks to borrow money of A-8 with the approval of F-A   1217b
A, seeking to borrow money of A-8 on the supposed approval of F-A, asks A-8 to call on F-A and secure authority to make the loan   1217b

Necessity

A seeks to borrow a large sum of money from A-8, a money lender, on his prospects of inheriting the estate of his wealthy father, F-A   1026

Personal Limitations

A is a profligate son who seeks to borrow money of A-8 on the prospect of inheriting the estate of his wealthy father, F-A. A-8 is skeptical regarding A's inheriting the estate   1139

A and BR-A

Obligation

A and BR-A are twin brothers with the same likes and dislikes   1005
(8)   A and BR-A, brothers, carry out honorably the distasteful obligation of living apart   1005

A and SN

Married Life

(4)   A craftily keeps from his son, SN-A, a family secret   425 .

Misfortune

A mistakenly supposes his son, SN, to have perished in a tragic accident   622
(14)   A loses his son, SN, in whom all his ambitions were centered   674

Helpfulness

A seeks to protect his son, SN, from what he conceives to be disgrace and dishonor on his own part   813
A's son, SN, is arrested for committing a crime   821
A seeks to save his son, SN, from misfortune and becomes involved in an unpleasant complication   821

A and SN—Helpfulness, Conc'd

(2)   A is inspired to carry on successfully because of the faith his son, SN, has in him 810

(10)   A's son, SN, wins for his college in a gruelling contest; and SN tells A, who is gloomy and despairing and considers himself a failure, that his success was inspired by the thought that his father had never been beaten 810

Deliverance

A has turned his back upon happiness because of an obligation he fancies himself under to his son, SN 881

(9)   A's son SN discovers a fateful secret of A's, and persuades him to correct an error and regain lost happiness 881

Idealism

A is proud of his son, SN 928b

(5-10)   A's son, SN, dies a shameful, inglorious death, bringing dishonor and sorrow to A 928b

(8)   A, father of SN, renounces happiness in order to uphold a lofty conception of duty and save SN from disgrace 934

Chance

(2)   A, hearing by chance a familiar name, finds his long-lost son, SN 1053

Personal Limitations

A is so preoccupied with business affairs that, while he intends writing to his son, SN, he somehow never gets around to it 1108

A, A-4 and SN

Chance

(2)   A, a supposed "ghost," is caught in a trap set by A-4; and A-4 proves to be A's missing son, SN 1056

A, A-5 and SN

Craftiness

A is a wealthy man whom sharpers, A-5, A-5, are seeking to influence to disinherit a son, SN 1289a

A and NW

Obligation

(1)   A's nephew and ward, NW, is wild and reckless and A is unable to manage him 999

Mystery

A dies and leaves his fortune to a nephew, NW 1432

A dies and leaves his fortune to a nephew, NW, who has been mysteriously missing for years 1432

A, A-2 and NW

Obligation

(4)   A agrees to take in hand and control an incorrigible youth, NW, who has proved too hard a problem for his uncle and guardian, A's friend, A-2 982a

(5)   A passes his unmanageable nephew and ward, NW along to a friend in the West, A-2, who declares that he will either kill NW or tame him 999

A, A-8 and NW

Craftiness

A disapproves of his nephew, NW; and A, sick unto death, sends for a lawyer, A-8, to draw his will   1270

(1) A's nephew, NW, tricks A into thinking that he is A-8, the lawyer who has come to draw A's will   1270

A and U

Obligation

A has $500,000. A rich relative, U, bequeaths a million dollars to A, provided he shall spend his half million within a year   997b

A is to inherit a fortune from his uncle, U, on condition that he shall never leave his native land   1101b

Personal Limitations

(1) A, giving ten years of his life to a miserly uncle, U, in exchange for a college education, loses his ambition and enterprise   1065

(1) A's uncle, U, has promised A all that he has when he dies, but U dies a banrupt; and A is thrown out on the world with abilities obscured and enterprise strangled 1065

Craftiness

(4) A, seeking by strategy, to secure a rich inheritance, fails in his plan when his uncle, U, discovers A's "son and heir" to be a girl   1289c

A and CN

Simulation

A's cousin, CN, has long been mysteriously missing   1201

A, U and CN

Simulation

(4) A's uncle, U, dies and leaves A's cousin, CN, a large estate. A impersonates CN 1201

A, A-8 and CN

Personal Limitations

A is a cousin of CN, and CN is to inherit the wealth of a deceased relative, A-8. If CN were out of the way, A would be the legal heir   1127

A, GCH and X

Obligation

A's impecunious grandchild, GCH, buys A a birthday present, X, on credit 1012

(5) A pays for X, a birthday present, which his impecunious grandchild, GCH, is giving him   1012

B

Love's Beginnings

B, wealthy, devotes much time to settlement work; and, in carrying out her philanthropic enterprises, she pretends to be a shop girl   2e

B is discouraged regarding her romantic affairs   13a

B, unmarried, cherishes motherhood as her ideal   39

(1) B's cattle ranch has been left to her by her father; and every man B hires as foreman, makes love to her sooner or later   9c

B—Love's Beginnings, Conc'd

(1)   B finds herself in a great city, penniless and the victim of evil intrigue   14b

(1)   B, desiring love, has never had a lover and feels the misfortune keenly   32

(1)   B is attractive, but no man pays her any attention   36

(4)   B, poor and humble but romantic, acquires unexpectedly a small sum of money; thus financed, she pretends for a time to be wealthy and aristocratic   2f

(4)   B, a maid, uses the wardrobe of her wealthy mistress and pretends to be a distinguished personage   2g

(4)   B, a criminal, assumes an alias and makes use of stolen funds in evading the law   2h

(4)   B, attrative, and humiliated because of her lack of admirers, resorts to simulation to gain contentment   36

(4)   B considers love and marriage the great adventure, and eagerly proceeds with them   38

(10)   B, discouraged regarding her love affairs, meets with a "sign" which prophesies her marriage within a year   13a

Love's Misadventures

B is convinced that several eligible men are in love with her   56

B is unaware of the fact that she is the victim of egotistical self-deception   56

B, in a fit of discouragement over an unhappy love affair, meditates suicide and writes a note to her friends telling of her motives   57

B is harrassed by gossip concerning men falsely rumored to be in love with her, and by relatives of the supposed lovers calling on her and making complaint   62

B is in doubt as to which of her many lovers is in love with her rather than with her money, and she resolves to settle the doubt by secret enterprise   103

B, unmarried, seeks motherhood because of a lofty ideal that does not shrink from public censure   121

B has so many lovers that she has no time to give to any one or anything else   143

B, an attractive girl, is so absorbed in serious pursuits that she subordinates everything else, even love, to her high ambition   145

B, a poor unfortunate, meditates suicide as the only way out of her misfortunes   162b

B, a rich widow, has so many suitors she finds it difficult to make a choice   164

(1)   B, contemplating suicide, writes a note explaining her motives; then she changes her mind—and loses the note   57

(1)   B is falsely suspected of being in love with various men. She decides to free herself of the suspicion by a stratagem   102

(1)   B has been betrayed, and her child is to be born out of wedlock   162b

(2)   B, wealthy, pretends to lose all her money in an unfortunate investment, by way of discovering which of her lovers loves her for herself alone   93a

(4)   B, single, pretends that she is a married woman and assumes the name of "Mrs. Blank"   58c

(4)   B is so fully aware of the fact that she is beautiful and attractive that she thinks every man is in love with her   65

(4)   B, in order to escape annoying manifestations of love, resorts to simulation   71b

(4)   B pretends that she is engaged to be married in order to be free of certain annoying experiences   83

(4)   B, in order to carry out an enterprise considered necessary, offers to sell herself in marriage to the highest bidder   88

Marriage Proposal

(1)   B, out in a storm on a pitch-dark night, receives a proposal of marriage. Unable to see her lover, and scarcely able to hear him, she nevertheless accepts—and meets with a disagreeable surprise   195

Love's Rejection

B, disapproving of the men she meets in her own social and business world, envisions her ideal, the man she would like to meet, and fares forth secretly in search of him   242

B is a white woman who knows nothing of her birth and parentage   305

B—Love's Rejection, Conc'd

(7)   B disapproves of the men she meets in her own social and business world   242
(8)   B, denied love, seeks happiness in a mental personification of love   251
(8)   B, suffering disappointment in love, resigns herself philosophically to her fate 325

Marriage

B must be married when she reaches a certain age if she would receive a rich inheritance   354b
(1)   B, a white woman, contemplates suicide when a mystery of her birth and parentage apparently yields an evil secret   364a
(2)   B, unworthy, achieves a reward of married happiness   359
(4)   B pretends to be wealthy and merely masquerading as a shop girl   358

Married Life

(4)   B seeks to save herself from the consequences of transgression by taking to flight 453
(6)   B dies in childbirth   515
B's great desire is to become an actress   413

Misfortune

B is accused of transgression, but the accusation is unjust   648
B is leading an exemplary life and trying honestly to live down an unfortunate past   665
B, unless she conceals a personal delinquency, will seriously compromise herself 667
B is intellectual and of an artistic temperament   676
B is engaged in forwarding an important undertaking   677
B fights against insomnia brought on by overwork   677
B is riding alone through a wilderness country   694
B inherits the trait of disguising her affections, a trait which proves an obstacle to her success and happiness   736
B is greatly discontented because of an unfortunate state of affairs   737a
B discontented, seeks to gain contentment, but the obstacles seem insuperable 737a
B finds that the knob and lock on the door of a hotel bedroom are in disrepair; the lock apparently locks itself, and the knob will not turn   737b
B, near-sighted, unsophisticated, on leaving her room in a big city hotel, ties a black ribbon to the doorknob so she can easily find the door on her return   737c
B writes a note, and the note contains a very important secret   742
(1)   B, tired, and unable to get a room in a hotel in a large city, wanders about the lobby and neighboring rooms. It is very late; and B, unfamiliar with her surroundings finds a dark, deserted room with comfortable chairs and large mirrors, and falls asleep in one of the chairs. She does not awaken until morning; then, to her horror, she discovers that she has spent the night as no respectable woman ought to have done   643
(1)   B finds herself, innocently and through error, a prisoner at night in a bedroom not her own   645
(1)   B, innocently caught in a compromising situation, discovers a state of affairs that renders her dilemma tragic   645
(1)   B is accused of being a transgressor because she is found in an environment, or because she has property in her possession, which indicates transgression   648
(1)   B, riding alone through a wilderness country, is thrown from her horse and sprains her ankle. The horse runs away, and B is left helpless in an uninhabited region 694
(1)   B, in a large city hotel, returns at night from her bath and, through error, enters through an unlocked door into a room which proves to be not her own   737b
(1)   B is shunned and ostracised because of a misfortune for which she is not responsible   740
(1)   B writes a note; and it is picked up by a gust of wind, carried across a narrow court, through an open window, and deposited in a neighboring apartment   742
(1)   B writes a very important note, then loses it. If the note is found and read by other persons, B will be greatly humiliated   742

B—*Misfortune, Conc'd*

(1)   B, who was thought by the people of her community to have supernatural powers, is discovered to have been insane—a condition caused by a great sorrow 746
(4)   B commits a secret transgression 669
(4)   B commits a transgression   B in order to escape the consequences of a transgression, flees secretly to a distant place and assumes a fictitious name 743b
(6)   B, a victim of unpleasant conditions, seeks to escape them by self-destruction 738
(6)   B becomes the victim of such desperate misfortunes that she plans to take her own life 743a

Mistaken Judgment

B has a character weakness which proves a bar to many of her enterprises 766
(2-10)   B, thinking herself a criminal, seeks to evade the law by various makeshifts 784
(4)   B, a school teacher, unknowingly violates the rules set up by the school board by going to dances and taking long walks at night 765
(4)   B, a plain woman, believes herself surpassingly beautiful 766
(7)   B discovers that she is innocent of a crime she supposed she had committed 784

Helpfulness

(1)   B, attacked by a huge snake, suffers a psychic shock 848b

Deliverance

B, harrassed by gossip that reflects on her integrity, seeks deliverance from false suspicion 870a
B, fearing she is going insane, seeks emancipation from the demoralizing fear 872
B discovers an evil secret of her past 873
B is a prisoner in one of the upper floors of a tall building 885b
(1)   B fears she is going insane 872
(1)   B, discovering an evil secret of her past, meditates suicide 873
(2)   B, prisoner in a room on one of the upper floors of a tall building, saves herself by making use of the fire-escape 885b

Idealism

B, her lot cast in a lonely place, craves excitement as a condition necessary to happiness 916
B is happy in her mistaken ideals 931
B, as the world regarded her, was a moral transgressor; but, in her own estimation, she was seeking the best and noblest in life 945
B, who finds her happiness in a beautiful garden, learns that the garden is about to be destroyed 962
B, reared in the slums of a large city and seeking her ideal of happiness in the woods and open fields, comes finally to live in a drab, cheerless countryside 974
B is in failing health and her days numbered 975
B, in failing health and her days numbered, feels that she cannot die happy until she sees again her native place, and re-visits the well-remembered haunts of her childhood 975
B is determined to protect the honor of her family, but she can do so only by following the path of relentless duty 977a
(1)   B dies a broken-hearted victim of her own high ideals 909
(4)   B is a selfish, hard-hearted, worldly-minded woman who seeks to live for herself alone. She wonders why she is not happy and contented 908
(7)   B decides that there is more to be gained by suffering defeat in an enterprise than by being successful 933
(8)   B realises that her happiness and her duty lie in rehabilitating her character; in establishing, under an assumed name, an exemplary character and thus to make amends for a grievous wrong committed under her real name 921
(8)   B, considered a moral transgressor, through her magnetic personality and the sincerity of her convictions, disarmed criticism in life and was praised by all after she died 945
(8)   B, a transgressor, tries to live down her unfortunate past by exemplary conduct 946

B—Idealism, Conc'd

(8) B seeks to remain a good woman in spite of a vicious, morally inferior environment 947
(8) B believes that the practice of the religious virtues is the crying need of the world,
and seeks by her own life to exemplify her convictions 976

Obligation

B, a widow, finds her happiness in being independent 994
B labors for years at a lonely task 995
B, a widow, wishes to be independent and to have a home of her own; but there
are certain obligations at war with her desire 1009a

Necessity

B seeks employment, but her sex is against her 1032
B, in order to carry out an enterprise, resorts to a stratagem 1032
(1) B is carrying out a secret enterprise and falls into danger 1025
(4) B, sorely in need of money, undertakes a rash enterprise 1033

Personal Limitations

B fails to understand how her fretful disposition makes herself and all around
her unhappy 1067
B is too young, too attractive, too modern for the scholarly position she occupies;
and her success, which means happiness to her, is endangered 1099
B, young and attractive, in order to win success in her chosen work, dresses the
part of a spinster, and makes herself appear prim and old-fashioned 1099
B's happiness and success hang upon her successful impersonation of a boy 1100
B is ambitious to "get ahead," to advance herself in her chosen line of work;
but she has difficulties that are disheartening 1121
B, in poor health, is ordered by her doctor to leave the city and live in the country
1137b
B, city bred, undergoes unpleasant experiences when she goes to the country
to live 1137b
(1) B, a banker's wife, trying to subscribe to the social conventions of a farming
community, finds her efforts embarrassing and distasteful 1118
(1) B, in a small boat, has lost her oars and is drifting out to sea in a fog 1137a
(1) B, ocean bathing, is caught by the undertow and is being swept out to sea 1137a
(4) B, impersonating a boy, is subjected to the rough pranks of her male companions,
who do not suspect her true sex 1100
(4) B is young and pretty, and believes that Youth, seeking self-expression, is warranted in overriding any and all conventions 1105
(4) B, of an humble station in life, yearns for efforts social prestige 1106
(4) B, who lacks every qualification of a successful writer, nevertheless believes herself highly gifted as a novelist 1119
(14) B, overhearing a conversation which brings home to her a bitter truth regarding
her unpleasant disposition, alters her mental attitude and undergoes a beneficial character change 1067

Simulation

B is the owner of a gem so valuable that she fears to wear it in public; so she
keeps it in a strong box and wears a replica of it which is of comparatively little
value. The fact that she owns the real stone is well know, and the counterfeit
is supposed to be the original 1152
B innocently commits a transgression 1156
B, innocenly committing a transgression, for fear of the law keeps the transgression a close secret 1156
B's happiness requires a complete escape from her life and enviroment 1204
'1) B fails in an undertaking dear to her heart 1153
.1) B, mistaken for another woman who is under ban of death by a strange secret
society, seeks to escape from her pursuers 1154a
(4) B simulates ignorance regarding a certain compromising event in her life 1151
(4) B, failing in an undertaking dear to her heart, seeks to make others think she
has succeeded 1153

B—*Simulation, Conc'd*

(4) B seeks to convince the home folks that she is a celebrity when she is really a failure 1203

(4) B's sex prevents her from securing employment among men, so she disguises herself as a boy 1207

Craftiness

B undertakes for extravagant pay to carry out a secret investigation in which it is necessary for her to pretend to be deaf and dumb, and in which she must have a knowledge of "sign" language 1211a

B, engaged in an enterprise that might cause gossip or censure, defers to public opinion by a stratagem 1242a

B plans to forward an enterprise, but cannot do so openly and must resort to stratagem 1244a

(2) B, engaged in an enterprise that might cause gossip or censure, escapes from a room by picking the lock of a door with a bent hairpin 1211c

(4) B, middle-aged, is so adept in the arts of the toilette, that she keeps her beauty youthful and blooming. Apparently in her early twenties, she is really in her late forties 1279

(12) B fires a revolver and pretends that she is shooting at a thief who got away in the night 1279b

Transgression

(1) B, seeking happiness as a reformed transgressor, has her old transgression discovered 1292

(1) B, committing one transgression to hide another, is apprehended for her crime, brought to trial and sentenced 1294

(4) B secretly borrows money on property she is holding in trust in order to forward a certain enterprise 1293b

(4) B commits a transgression in order to conceal a less serious transgression 1294

(8) B seeks happiness as a reformed transgressor 1292

Revenge

(6) B seeks revenge as a lofty conception of duty—and comes to her death while seeking it 1328

Mystery

B disappears, apparently a suicide when, in desperate danger, she implores aid and it is denied 1417

B seeks to escape from mysterious dangers 1446b

(1) B receives a photograph; and on the back of it is written "You are in great danger! Beware!" 1364a

(1) B falls asleep and, while she sleeps, terrible dangers threaten her 1446b

(10) B receives benefit when a psychic experience proves an obstacle to a certain enterprise 1445

(13) B receives in a mysterious manner a photograph, not of herself but of some one greatly resembling her 1364a

(14) B is strongly influenced by a supernatural vision in which her life is reviewed before her 1445

Revelation

B supposes herself to be a white woman and prides herself on her white heritage 1458

(1) B, a white woman, is told that there is a taint of alien and inferior blood in her veins 1458

B and B-2

Misfortune

(1-11) B loses a valuable ornament she has borrowed from her friend, B-2 642

(4) B, as a sop to her vanity, borrows a valuable ornament from her wealthy friend, B-2 642

B and B-2

Helpfulness

B is convinced that her friend, B-2, is making a mistake 843

(4)   B, convinced that her friend, B-2, is making a mistake, resolves to correct the mistake in secret, since B-2 will not do it 843

Simulation

( )   B is impersonating B-2. In the midst of the impersonation, B-2, at a distance, is injured in an accident and expected to die. Great newspaper publicity is given the incident 1208

B and B-3

Deliverance

(6)   B dies of pneumonia brought on by exposure while rescuing B-3 from an accident 892

Craftiness

B-3, lurking in the doorway of B, pretends to be B and receipts for a package delivered by messenger 1278b

B and B-4

Simulation

(4)   B sends newspaper clippings regarding a celebrity, B-4, to the home folks, and pretends that she is B-4 under a stage (or pen) name 1203

B and B-5

Simulation

(12) B's striking physical resemblance to B-5 a criminal, causes her to be suspected of a crime 1172

B and B-7

Personal Limitations

B sends a telegram to her maid, B-7, to "come at once" 1136

B and B-8

Married Life

B bears a close physical resemblance to B-8 456

Mistaken Judgment

(2-3)   B places an identifying mark on the door of her hotel room. The mark is changed in an unusual manner to another door; and B-8, occupant of the other room, is found to have been murdered 792b

Simulation

(4)   B hires B-8, a woman who has not long to live, to take her name 1204
(9)   B-8 dies and is buried as B 1201

B and AUX

Simulation

(4)   B, traveling alone, invents a fictitious aunt, AUX, as a chaperone   1158

B and X

Love's Misadventures

B, thinking a symbol of lost love, X, has a magic power of its own, seeks to regain love by wearing the symbol   89

(4)   B, in order to be free of unwelcome lovers, invents a mechanical figure, X, which she pretends is her husband   84a

Misfortune

(1)   B, owing to financial difficulties, has been compelled to pawn an object, X, dearly prized   739

(1)   B is unable to redeem an object, X, necessary to her happiness, which she has pawned   739

Mistaken Judgment

(1)   B, poor, borrows a supposedly valuable object, X, and loses it   767

(5)   B, borrowing a supposedly valuable object, X, and losing it, labors for years to earn the money with which to replace X; only to discover that X was a counterfeit and of little worth   767

Mystery

B buys an object, X, in a pawnshop   1384

(1)   B loses her handbag, X, which contains the key to her jewel box   1446a

(13)   B finds her lost handbag, X, and the key to her jewel box is in the bag—but the jewels in the jewel box are missing   1446a

Revelation

B finds an old notebook, X, which contains the record of a dishonest transaction 1459

(2-3-7)   B finds an old notebook, X, which contains information that has an important bearing on some of her plans   1459

B, B-4 and X

Helpfulness

B, in charge of a booth at a charity bazaar, seeks to prevent B-4 from buying a certain object, X, on which she seems to have set her heart   849

Craftiness

(9)   B prevents a stranger, B-4, from buying an article, X, which B is convinced would bring her only misfortune, by tying to X a ticket labeled "sold"   1245

B and M-B

Love's Beginnings

B, daughter of M-B, a widow, desperately opposes, and for very good reasons, M-B's intention to marry again   33

Love's Rejection

(1)   B's mother, M-B, is determined that B shall marry wealth; so, rejecting the man she loves, who is poor, to marry the man she does not love, who is rich, B is plunged into unhappiness   341

B and M-B

Misfortune

B's mother, M-B, is a widow in poor health   659

M-B's life hangs on a change of climate, but she and her daughter, B, are penniless   659

B is desperately determined to do something, anything, to help her mother M-B   659

B's mother, M-B, is a drug addict   668

B's mother, M-B, is subject to recurring periods of temporary insanity   670

(1)   B makes a heavy personal sacrifise in order to help her mother, M-B, hide from the world a terrible secret   668

(1)   B is a strange, wild creature, marked at birth by an unfortunate experience of her mother, M-B's   740

(4)   B helps her mother, M-B, hide from the world a fateful secret   670

Mistaken Judgment

B's mother, M-B, is a widow in desperate misfortune   785

B's mother, M-B, is planning a move which B knows will have unhappy consequences, but B cannot persuade M-B against it   785

Deliverance

B's mother, M-B, is in straitened circumstances and estranged from B   886

(10)   B's mother, M-B, inherits a large sum of money unexpectedly, and becomes reconciled with B, from whom she was estranged   886

Idealism

B's mother, M-B, cherishes the fixed desire to give B a good education   978

B and her mother, M-B, are penniless, and B has to work to support the two of them   978

(7)   B is compelled to challenge the value of her ideals when she sees her mother, M-B, pursuing them   931

Obligation

B's mother, M-B, denies herself the necessities of life in fulfilling her duty to educate B   996

Craftiness

B, daughter of M-B, falling into error, conducts herself unwisely and scorns admonition   1246

(12)   B's mother, M-B, copies B's foolish conduct, thus giving B a visible demonstration of its absurdity   1246

B and SR-B

Misfortune

B is compelled to live with a sister, SR-B   678

(9)   B rebels against the tyranny and selfishness of her sister, SR-B, which makes B's life miserable   678

B and D-B

Personal Limitations

(14)   B, over the dead body of her daughter, D-B, experiences a psychic revelation that transforms her whole character   1069

Simulation

(4)   B, in order to avoid slander and evil gossip and protect a daughter, D-B, who is about to marry a man of wealth and social position, seeks to hush up a possible scandal in her own life   1151

A and B

Love's Beginnings

A, poor, is in love with wealthy and aristocratic B   1a
A, of humble birth, falls in love with aristocratic B   1b
A, elderly, is in love with youthful B   1d
A is in love with B; and B is devoted to scientific pursuits   1f
A falls in love with romantic B   1g
A quarrels with his sweetheart, B, and fears he is losing her love   1h
A, a poor clerk financing a "fling" in high society meets "wealthy" and "aristocratic" B   2a
A, a fugitive from the law and using a fictitious name, falls in love with B   2b
A, craftily engaged in a secret enterprise, falls in love with B, who has also embarked upon a crafty enterprise   2b
A, disguised as a city "tough," meets B, and they fall in love   2c
A is mistaken by B for A-8   2d
B has corresponded with A-8 but has never seen him   2d
B, while posing as a shop girl, meets A, and they fall in love   2e
B, poor and humble but pretending to be wealthy and aristocratic, meets "rich" and "influential" A, and they fall in love   2f
B, poor, but pretending to be a wealthy aristocrat, meets A, apparently rich and influential, and they fall in love   2g
B, a criminal in disguise, meets A, and they fall in love   2h
A is a judge, and B is a fugitive from justice, posing as a woman of wealth and fashion   3a
A, seeking to uncover duplicity, falls in love with B, supposed to be guilty of the duplicity   4a
A, in a spirit of altruism, restores property to a stranger, B,—and falls in love with her   4b
B, who has long desired to know A, picks up a purse he has dropped and restores it.   A and B fall in love   6a
B finds a lost brief case belonging to A, a judge, and restores it to him; and the acquaintance, thus begun, ripens into love   6b
A is in love with B, and fears his affair is hopeless   7b
A, in order to prosper his love affair with B, secures a love philtre from a Seventh Son of a Seventh Son—a philtre that is guaranteed to bring him the love of B   7b
A and B, young and single, enter into a business partnership   9b
B is a criminal, and A is the detective who has arrested her   10a
B, a criminal arrested by A, a detective, brings her charms to bear upon A in the hope of effecting her escape   10a
B, poor and in great misfortune, is befriended by wealthy A   10b
B, poor, seeks to win the love of wealthy A   10b
B makes love to A in an attempt to escape misfortune   10c
B, who is unworthy, finds that she has won the love of wrothy A   11c
A and B, each secretly, suppose themselves transgressors of the law   12a
B, an "inferior" person, falls in love with A, a "superior" person; and A's apparent love for B gives her the power to bear patiently the misfortunes of her humble estate   13b
B, almost overwhelmed by misfortune, meets A, and they fall in love   14a
B, helpless and in misfortune, meets a stranger, A, and they fall in love   14b
B, an attractive young widow, meets A, an equally attractive young widower   14c
B, plain and humble working girl, falls in love with A   15a
A does not dream that humble B is in love with him   15b
A, a detective, has arrested B, a criminal, and is returning her to the scene of her crime for trail and punishment   16a
A and B, while engaged in a commercial transaction, fall in love   20a
A and B are mutually involved in a snare of indirection; nevertheless, they are drawn to each other and fall in love   20b
A and B, during their meetings as lawyer and client, fall in love   20c
A meets B and thinks she is a transgressor; and B, on her part, thinks A is a transgressor   21
A and B, each thinking the other is a transgressor, nevertheless fall in love   21
A, a woman hater, falls in love with B   22a
A, wealthy, and of high social position, falls in love with humble B   23d
A, attracted by the loveliness of B, loses his heart to her   24b

A and B—Love's Beginnings, Cont'd

A sees a photograph of B, a woman he does not know   2⁴c

A, hearing of the character and charms of B, a woman he does not know, falls in love with her and resolves to win her in marriage   2'd

A, of an inordinately romantic temperament, sees the hand of B; and, because of the hand's shapeliness and beauty, falls in love with the owner, B   2 e

A, falling in love with B, whom he does not know, seeks an introduction   25

A and B have never seen each other; but they correspond, and through their correspondence become betrothed   26b

B, unworthy, wins the love of worthy A, and tense complications result   27

B, a stenographer, is in love with A, junior partner of the firm employing her   30

B, humble and self-effacing, worships A, her love alone seeming a sufficient reward of happiness   34

(1) A and B, supposing themselves fugitives from the law, meet in a foreign country and fall in love   12a

(1) A, unmarried, and B, married, are shipwrecked and cast away on a desert island   12b

(1) A, under threat of being disinherited, is ordered to commit an act that will prove a grievous injury to a near relative of B's, the woman he loves. A refuses   19b

(1) A meets B while engaged in an enterprise of indirection, and clever B finds a flaw in his explanations; B, also, is entangled in a snare of indirection, and A's suspicions are aroused   20b

(1) A has an experience with B which causes him to become a woman hater   22b

(4) A, poor, in love with wealthy B, pretends to be a man of wealth   1a

(4) A, of humble birth, in love with aristocratic B, pretends to be a man of high social standing   1b

(4) A, elderly, in love with youthful B, seeks to forward his love affair by simulating youth   1d

(4) A, a crook, outlaw, gambler, pretends to be an honest man in order to forward his love affair with B   1e

(4) A, in love with romantic B, pretends to be a hero   1g

(4) A, fearing he is losing the love of B, pretends to take poison with suicidal intent   1h

(4) A, falling in love with B, pretends that he is A-8   2d

(4) A, a judge, falls in love with B, a criminal   3a

(4) A, a detective, falls in love with B, a criminal he has arrested and is returning to the scene of her crime for trial and punishment   3b

(4) A and B, both single, craftily agree to ban love in their associations   9a

(4) A and B, entering into a business partnership, ban love with every legal device   9b

(4) B, middle-aged, and A, a youth, are in love with each other   11b   37

(4) B, plain and humble "slavey", secretly adores A   15b

(4) A, a detective, falls in love with B, a criminal, whom he has arrested   16a

(4) A, unmarried, and B, married, thrown together in a solitary and lonely environment, fall in love   17a

(4) B, an "inferior" person, falls in love with A, a "superior" person, and seeks to win him in marriage   23a

(4) B, of an inferior race, falls in love with A, of a superior race   23b

(4) A, of an inferior race, falls in love with B, of a superior race   23c

(4) A loses his heart to B, a woman he does not know, and wishes to marry her   24a

(4) A, studying a photograph of unknown B, falls in love with her   24c

(4) B, very ill and under the doctor's care, fancies herself in love with the doctor, A   28a

(4) B, undergoing misfortune with A, fancies herself in love with him   28b

(4) B knows nothing of A, having fallen in love with him at "first sight"   29

(4) B, rescued from an accident by A, whom she does not know, falls in love with him   31

(7) A, unmarried, and B, married, fall in love when B supposes A to be her ideal. And then B makes a discovery   12b

(7) B, a widow, and A, a widower, meet in a cemetery where each comes with flowers for his and her lost spouse—and they fall in love   14c

(7) A, although he has taken vows that proscribe the love of woman, nevertheless falls in love with B   16b

(8) B, winning the love of A, finds the courage to bear patiently with her hardships   14a

(9) B considers A too perfect for married happiness; so A assumes a "hard-boiled" character in order to prove that he is not so perfect as he seems   1c

(9) A recovers property belonging to an unknown woman, B   4b

A and B—Love's Beginnings, Conc'd

(10) A, in love with B, finds that B considers him too perfect for married happiness 1c

(10) A and B, engaging in an enterprise, mutually covenant and agree to ban love; but love enters into their little scheme in spite of their platonic notions 9a

(14) B hires A as foreman on her ranoh, and he promises to keep his place and not make love to her; but B falls in love with him, and is presently glad to learn that A's sole purpose in taking the job of foreman was to win her love 9c

(14) A is a woman hater, but he is rendered a service by B which causes him to revise his opinions of the opposite sex 22a

Love's Misadventures

A encounters disappointment in love when B fails to answer a note he sent her 40b

A has promised B, the woman he loves, that he will give up a practice which B considers discreditable 41b

A meets B, his love of other days, and is surprised to find that his success in distant lands has no charm for her that is not discounted by the meager opportunities of the home country 46

A asks that B allow herself to be hypnotized in order that he may learn where buried treasure has been concealed 47a

A and B, lovers, meet with tragic misfortune but escape death 49

A thinks B has merely gone away for a time, and spends years in a vain search for her 53

A, investigating a psychic mystery, falls in love with B 54b

A, his love rejected by B, revenges himself by cutting off B's long hair 66a

A, elderly, wealthy, is in love with youthful B 67

A seeks by a stratagem to discover the sincerity of B's professed love for him 67

A's family is at war with B's family; and A, in love with B, disguises his identity when calling on B 70

B disguises herself and meets A, the man she loves, as an Unknown 82a

B seeks to d scover whether A really loves her 82a

B resorts to simulation in order to discover whether A, the man she loves really loves her 82b

B seeks to prove A's love for her by a stratagem 85b

B deliberately manoeuvers herself and A into a compromising situation, and places the responsibility squarely upon A 85b

B, in love with A, seeks to save A from disaster by shrewd enterprise 91

B, seeking to prove whether or not A really loves her, has recourse to a stratagem 93b

A betrays B and does not marry her as he promised 96

A, in love with B, seeks to save B, by secret enterprise and at any cost, from misfortune 97

A believes that his sweetheart, B, is dead; and B, at a distance, learns of this mistaken belief on A's part 105

A's little world seems to crumble about his ears when he fancies that his sweetheart, B, is false to him 107

A, sweetheart of B, is condemned to die for a transgression he did not commit 108

A, in love with B, is promised her hand in marriage if he will successfully carry out a certain enterprise 110

A, in love with B, struggles to accumulate enough money to be able to marry 113

B informs A, the man she loves, that he will lose her love unless he overcomes his lack of enterprise and makes the determination to win his dominant trait 114

B is in love with A; but, before she will promise to marry him, she stipulates that he must do big work, wonderfully big work 115

B, in love with A, who is unfortunate and unenterprising, sees an opportunity for A to make great gain and influences him to take advantage of it 125a

B, in love with A, who is forgetful and absent-minded, is asked by A to marry him. B tells A to call for his answer on a certain day at a certain hour. If he can remember to come, B is resolved to accept him 125b

A believes that B will not marry him until he becomes wealthy 127a

A believes that B will not marry him until he overcomes his personal limitations 127b

A and B are in love; but certain unhappy conditions prevent the cherished culmination of their romance 129

A, if he carries out a certain obligation, will be unfaithful to B and will lose her love 132

A and B—Love's Misadventures, Cont'd

A loves B, and is compelled to stand helplessly by while B undertakes a dangerous enterprise   133

A, and the woman he loves, B, are lost in the woods; and it is evident that they will have to remain in the woods all night   13ᴀa

B, in love with A, has worn A's engagement ring for years   141

B, in the hands of enemies of A, is being forced to do their bidding by threats of violence against A, the man she loves   144

B shares with her sweetheart, A, an important secret which, if revealed, would bring misfortune to B   147

A, in love with B, has a valuable gift sent to B by a jeweler   153

B, in love with A, is uncertain of A's affections   162a

B learns that her lover, A, has fallen into desperate misfortune   163

B loses her watch (or a locket) and has her lovers search for it. The picture of A, the lover B favors, is in the watch   165

B wore a certain ornament when her false lover, A, proposed to her. She has an odd conviction that the same misfortune will befall any other woman who wears the ornament   173

B promises A that she will marry him if he will successfully carry out a difficult enterprise   176c

A, by mental telepathy, becomes aware of a terrible danger threatening B, the woman he loves   179a

A, at a long distance from B, and in a lonely country, hears an agonized call from his sweetheart over the phone   179b

A has a clairvoyant vision apprising him of danger that threatens his sweetheart, B   179c

(1)   A presents his sweetheart, B, with a gift which brings about an unpleasant complication   40a

(1)   A is so absorbed in his love affair with B that it has a disastrous effect on his business enterprises   44b

(1)   A hypnotizes B, and B dies of psychic shock   47a

(1)   A and B, lovers, escaping death in a tragic misfortune, each believes the other has perished   49

(1)   A's pretentions accepted, it develops that the person he is impersonating has a wife, who immediately claims A as her husband   50

(1)   A loves B; and, when A confesses to B that he once committed a murder, B's health declines and she worries herself into her grave   5ᴀa

(1)   A confesses to B that he once committed a transgression, and the result of the confession proves disastrous   51b

(1)   A, a fugitive from justice, hiding in the bush, through error shoots and kills B, his sweetheart, when he hears some one approaching his hiding place   52a

(1)   A really loves B, although he has taken vows that prohibit love for woman. A lives to regret his vows   55

(1)   B is abandoned by A, the man with whom she eloped   60

(1)   A, in love with B and thinking B has committed a crime, declares to the police that he committed the crime himself   69

(1)   B suffers remorse after rejecting A's love   124

(1)   A is on his way to marry B, and has only a few hours before the ceremony. He meets with misfortune   130

(1)   A, and B with whom A is in love, find themselves trapped in a ruinous old house from which escape seems impossible. Night is coming on, and B accuses A of seeking to compromise her so he may win her in marriage   134b

(1)   B, in love with A, discovers that A no longer loves her, although he is willing to marry her as he has promised   142

(1)   A sends a gift to B; through error, or by evil intent, packages are transposed; and the gift received by B as from A very nearly proves disastrous to A's love affair   153

(1)   A, planning to meet B at a country church where they are to be secretly married, becomes lost in a storm and does not reach the church until B, and all the others, have left   154a

(1-7)   A, a pretender, in love with B, secretly discovers B making fun of his pretensions; he retires from the scene in disgust, hurt and indignant, and gives B up   156

(2)   B will lose her lover, A, if she allows A to proceed with an enterprise instigated by herself. To avoid losing A, B defeats the enterprise by making a confession   95

(2)   A proposes marriage to B and is accepted   181a

A and B— Love's Misadventures, Cont'd

(4) A, in love with B, refuses the wise counsel of B in business affairs and an estrangement results   41a

(4) A, yielding to temptation, proves false to a promise he made his sweetheart, B, and an estrangement follows   41b

(4) A persists in taking measures against one of the family of B, A's sweetheart, in spite of the protests of B. An estrangement results   41c

(4) A discovers that B, unhappily married, is—innocenly on his own part—in love with him   45a

(4) A persuades his sweetheart, B, to assume a fictitious character for the purpose of acquiring gain by transgression—with unhappy results for both of them   47b

(4) A, in love with B, impersonates another person at B's instigation   50

(4) A, seeking to benefit B, undertakes an enterprise which results disastrously   52b

(4) A loves B; B dies, and A becomes demented through grief   53

(4) B, aristocratic, wealthy, romantic, falls in love with A, a designing rogue masquerading as a person of "quality"   59

(4) B, in love with A, makes A a gift which, she mistakenly thinks, will forward their mutual happiness   63

(4) B is persuaded into a secret marriage with A, the man she loves   64

(4) A, his love rejected by B seeks revenge on the sex by becoming a heartbreaker and a betrayer   66b

(4) A, his love rejected by B, seeks revenge by making love to eligible, wealthy women and getting money from them   66c

(4) B, in love with A, treats A harshly in an attempt to arouse his anger and spur him into proving his abilities   85a

(4) B disguises herself as a boy in order to be near A, whom she secretly adores   87

(4) B elopes with A, who promised her a theatrical engagement   90a

(4) A and B, both unmarried, enter into a business association. They covenant and agree that love between them shall be taboo   99

(4) A, in love with B, is determined to see B, although the determination will surely involve him in misfortune unless he resorts to crafty enterprise   100

(4) B, sweetheart of A, persuades A to seek wealth by transgression   126

(4) A is so much in love with B that his business languishes and he devotes all his time to courtship   131

(4) A, because of his romantic surroundings, imagines himself in love with B   148

(4) A, a widower, elderly, wealthy, temporarily bewitched by the vernal season, imagines himself in love with B, a servant of his own household   149

(4) B, seeking to make a test of her lover's devotion, capriciously plunges into danger to see if he will follow her   176b

(4) B, seeking to make a test of her lover's devotion, capriciously sends him into desperate danger   176a

(5) A is in love with B. One evening, as usual, A calls to see B; but where her beautiful home has stood, no later than the evening before, there is now only an ancient, time-stained tomb—the tomb of B, who had died a hundred years before A was born   54a

(5) A, fancying himself in love with B, corrects the error when his fancy is discredited   151

(7) A, whom B favors but who does not love her, seeks B out and bluntly tells her of her egotistical self-deception   65

(8) A loses wealth by marrying B against the wishes of a rich relative, who disinherits him   116

(8) B is older than A and feels that it will be unjust to permit A to marry her, although she dearly loves him   124

(9) A loses his sweetheart, B, loses his liberty on a false charge, escapes prison and survives shipwreck, at last to reach the island where great treasure is buried. And he recovers the tresure   109

(9) B, estranged from her lover, A, whom she dearly loves, sends a telegram to another person and unconsciously puts A's name and address at the top of it   172

(9) A rescues B from an accident   181a

(10) A, kind to humble B and considering her merely as a friend, is amazed to learn that she is in love with him   45b

(10) B, apparently in her early twenties, is dazzlingly beautiful; but she is really very old, and in her case the ravages of time were stayed in early youth by a psychic shock. A's love dissolves the spell; and, under A's eyes, B ages and her beauty fades   54b

(10) B, in male attire, is suddenly revealed to A, the man she loves, in her true sex   61

A and B—Love's Misadventures, Conc'd

(10) A and B, associating in platonic friendship, find that love will not be denied   140
(12) A wronged B, the woman he loved, but secretly; and A craftily retains his own high place in society while leaving B to bear the heartache and shame alone   68
(12) A is one of the "idle rich," who craftily retains his own high place in society in spite of the fact that he has secretly betrayed a young woman, B   98
(13)   B, in love with A, discovers that A, Narcissus like, is in love with A   42b
(14)   A, a crabbed, disagreeable person, falls in love with B and, under the inspiration of love, his character undergoes a transformation   106
(14)   A, discovering that B is still true to him, undergoes a character transformation; pep, persistency, and eloquence return and lead him to success and happiness   107
(14)   A is a youth who is "wild" and hard to manage; he falls in love with B, and his character is transformed   152a

Marriage Proposal

A is in love with B and is determined to ask her to marry him, but B is so closely guarded that A is in despair because of his lack of opportunity   185
A seeks by subtlity to make an opportunity to ask B to marry him   185
A, in love with B and wishing to propose marriage, finds it impossible because B is so busy he can never find her alone. He seeks to make an opportunity by stratagem   187
B, impelled by an unusual motive, agrees to marry A if she loses to him in a certain contest of skill 188a
B has the ability to defeat A in a certain contest if she so desires   188a
B, about to commit suicide, is restrained by a stranger, A. A is informed by B that life is too bitter, since there is no name for her unborn child   188b
B, asked by A to marry him, wants a little more light on A's character before making up her mind   189
B challenges A to a contest of skill, her acceptance or rejection to be determined by the result   189
A, because of timidity, is unable to ask B's hand in marriage   196
A, fearing that B will refuse him, finds it impossible to propose marriage   201
A, in love with B, has reasons for not proposing marriage   202
A and B, in love, are each too diffident to make the overture to the other   203
A asks B to marry him and forgets that he has done so   204
(1) A, of a proud old Southern family, impoverished in fortune, feels that he cannot ask wealthy B, with whom he is in love, to marry him   198
(1) A is poor and crippled, and his pride will not suffer him to ask B, the woman he loves, to marry him   199
(4) B, not in love with A, for certain reasons proposes to A, not in love with B   190
(4) A, lacking courage to propose to B face to face, proposes over the telephone   192a
(4) A, in love with B and eager to win her in marriage, procrastinates as a matter of habit in making the marriage proposal   200
(5) A, threatened with death by savages, is offered his life by B, the ruler of the tribe, if he will marry her   197
(8) A, in order to rescue B, who is ill and without funds, pretends to be in love with her and proposes marriage   186
(8) A, a stranger, offers to marry B and so save her from a crowning disgrace   188b
(9) A, seeking desperately his chance to propose marriage to B, rescues her from drowning and proposes while they are clinging to an overturned boat   191
(9) B, thinking A loves her and lacks the courage to make an avowal, proposes marriage to him after he has rescued her from a tragic accident   194a
(10) B takes the opposite meaning of an ambiguous sentence and accepts A's statement as a proposal of marriage   184

Love's Rejection

A, winning the love of B in his youth, and casting it aside, goes searching for it in later years   205
A, although he loves B, is a conceited person   218a
A, in love with B, becomes estranged from B through mistaken judgment   222a
B, the woman A loves, proves false to him; and A fears B will reveal a secret which will cause him trouble if it becomes known   224
B wears a rose in her hair to reveal her love for A, as A requested   228

A and B—Love's Rejection, Cont'd

A, impelled by an unusual motive, pretends to fall in love with B   230

A is an aristocrat; and B, the woman he loves, is a "daughter of the people" and hates the aristocracy   232

A loves B and would like to marry her, but B considers A a weakling and keeps him dangling   234a

B meets A clandestinely   2'0

A fights against the blandishments of B, a morally inferior woman who is in love with him   244

A, in love with B, of an inferior race, seeks to abandon B secretly in order to uphold a lofty conception of duty   246a

B is in love with A, but A avoids women, believing them all to be tempters of Satan   250

B refuses A's offer of marriage because she feels that he is too model a man for her to be happy with   252a

B refuses A's offer of marriage because she feels that he is so absent-minded he might forget he had married her   252b

A, falls in love with B; but love, in A's case, is a transgression   257a

A, absent-minded, forgets that B has rejected his love and continues to pay court to her   265b

A, poor, in love with B, suddenly puts forth a great effort and secures a large sum of money   281c

B loves, and is beloved by, A, a man who is poor but of admirable character; but B, accustomed to luxury, shrinks from the idea of poverty, even with love   291

A considers B the acme of womanly perfection   292

A considers B the acme of womanly perfection; yet B, on the contrary, is a woman of doubtful character   292

A is an aristocrat; and B, the woman he loves, is a "daughter of the people" and hates the aristocracy   293

A, if he marries B, the woman he loves, will be disinherited   302

A's love for B encounters an obstacle   303

A is resolved to marry B, but relentless duty stands in the way   304

B's rejected lover, A, spreads the report that there is negro blood in B's veins 305

A, in love with B and about to marry her, is detained and does not reach B's house in time for the wedding   314

A, when B fails to keep a tryst with him, considers the failure a rejection of his love   316

A, in love with B, thinks B is a confirmed coquette, and is merely playing with him   320

A, in love with B, finds her unresponsive, reserved and distant   322a

B advises A to go away somewhere and try to develop the generous side of his character   322b

B loves A, but A, apparently, does not return her love   327a

B believed that her lover, A, was what he seemed to be, poor and humble; but he reveals himself as a man of wealth and station, incognito   336b

(1)   A suffers remorse for telling B that he was married when he was not   207

(1)   A did not think that he loved B, but later finds that he does   207

(1)   B awakens her lover A from his apathy by arousing his ambition to get ahead in the world—which results in disaster to her love   225

(1)   B wears a rose in her hair to reveal her love for A; but the rose, unnoticed by B, falls from its place; and when A sees her, he turns without a word and goes away   228

(1-7)   B, of an inferior race, in seeking to win the love of A, of a superior race, learns how hopeless is the task of challenging racial conventions   229

(1)   A pretends to fall in love with B, and ends his make-believe by really falling in love   230

(1)   A is in love with B, and they are to be married; but A leaves town mysteriously, no one knows what has become of him, and he does not return until after the time set for the wedding   233

(1)   B, in love with A, rejects his love because she thinks him a man of evil mystery   249

(1)   A, with a taint of negro blood in his veins—known only to himself—loves, and is beloved by B, a white girl   255

(1)   A loves B, but is estranged from her because he is so absent-minded and forgetful; he writes B a letter, assuring her that he has cured himself of his great failing—and forgets to post the letter   260b

A and B—Love's Rejection, Cont'd

(1) B, in desperation and out of her great love, proposes marriage to A and is rejected   264

(1) A and B are in love; but A realizes that if he, of an inferior race, should marry B, of a superior race, the result would be disastrous to both of them   271

(1) B suffers persecution and sorrow by falling in love with A, who is married but unable to tell her that he is married   278

(1) A finds that he cannot do justice to his chosen career if he marries B, the woman he loves   287

(1) A is the presiding magistrate at the trial for murder of B, the woman he loves   297

(1) B and A are in love; but B, unknown to A, is already married   309

(1) A's love is rejected by B; and A, in an effort to forget, buries himself in an isolated part of the country   315

(1) A tries philosophically to make the best of fate when B, the woman he loves, refuses him   321a

(1) A's love is rejected by B because, as she frankly tells him, he is hard-hearted and has made money his god   322b

(1) B, of alien blood and inferior race, is abandoned by A, the white man with whom she is in love   323

(1) B loves A; and A, who is kind to B but not in love with her, does not even suspect that he is the object of her affections   327b

(1) A's profession is a hazardous one, and B considers this fact an obstacle to their marriage   334a

(1) A, in love with B, discovers that B's desire for a "career" is an obstacle to their marriage   335

(1) B, who considered A poor and humble, discovers that he is a man of wealth and station; and, oddly enough, in B's mind A's deception outbalances the wealth and rank, and she makes his high estate an obstacle to their love   336b

(4) A is pledged by B, the woman he loves, to undertake an enterprise that will bring him serious misfortune   212a

(4) B pledges A to an enterprise which, unknown to B, will bring him serious misfortune   212a

(4) A, an aristocrat, in love with a working girl, B, pretends to be a toiler   232

(4) A, in order to prove his "courage" to B, stages a mock rescue   234a

(4) B, poor, would like to marry wealthy A, whom she does not love, for the freedom from care his money would give her   239

(4) A betrays B, thinking mistakenly that there is no one to take her part and avenge the wrong   247

(4) B is loved by wealthy A. B does not love A, but, for certain reasons, she yields to his importunities and marries him   253

(4) A falls in love with B, after taking vows that forbid marriage, or love for woman   272

(4) A and B, their families at enmity, fall in love with each other   275

(4) B, unmarried, falls in love with A, married   279

(4) B, a Polynesian woman, challenges racial conventions by falling in love with A, a white man   331

(4) B, of alien blood and inferior race, seeks to marry A, the Caucasian with whom she is in love   332

(5) A, when B, the woman he loves, refuses to marry him, becomes blase and cynical, a misogynist; reckless, "goes to the dogs" or loses his mental balance in other ways; or seeks to forget his unhappiness by indulging in a love for adventure   259

(5) B, influenced by an anonymous communication, breaks her engagement to marry A   262a

(7) B, finding her supposed ideal lover, discovers that he has "feet of clay" like all the others   226

(7) A, discovering that he is not a fugitive from justice as he had supposed, returns to his native country, secretly abandoning B, for whom he had declared his love while thinking himself a transgressor   237

(8) A, having carried out successfully an enterprise instigated by capricious B, renounces her love   212b

(8) A, recognizing a relentless obligation, renounces B, with whom he is deeply in love   248

(8) B, although she loves A, realizes that she is not the intellectual equal of A, and that their marriage would prove a hindrance to him   254

(8) B refuses marriage with A, the man she loves, because of an obligation   268

A and B—Love's Rejection, Conc'd

(8) B sacrifices happiness when, faithful to an obligation, she refuses marriage with A, the man she loves. Her sacrifice, in time, brings the consolation of spiritual joy for a hard duty nobly done   268

(8) A, because he fears he has inherited the evil traits of an ancestor, dares not ask B, the woman he loves, to marry him   288

(8) A, in love with B and engaged to marry her, has almost wrecked his life with dissipation and feels that he should give B up   289

(10) A, in love with B, discovers that B is a confirmed coquette and is merely playing with him   208

(10) A, under abnormal conditions, falls in love with B; on returning to normal conditions, he sees B as she really is, and his love fades   210

(10) A, who has long cherished B in his heart as the loveliest and most perfect of her sex, returns home after a long absence and discovers that B has become an immoral character   211

(10) B, in love with A, receives an unsigned letter in which the writer states that she is the wife of A by a secret marriage, and asks B to use her influence in persuading A to return to her   262c

(10) B, in love with A, receives an unsigned letter in which the writer states that she is the mistress of A and begs B not to take A away from her   262b

(10) B, compelled by circumstances to be a companion of A in an isolated place, alters her rosy views of love and marriage when she discovers, through A, the selfishness of men   307

(10) B breaks her engagement to marry A because she feels unequal to the responsibilities of married life   310

(10) A, prevented by circumstances from marrying B as planned, discovers the unworthiness of B and decides not to marry her at all   314

(12) B loves A with all her heart, but refuses his proposal of marriage   326

Marriage

A's gift to his sweetheart, B, is returned by B to A on account of a lover's quarrel   349

A, enacting the role of a servant, rescues B from accident by heroic bravery not at all in the manner of a menial   352a

B, a working girl, discovers that her lover, A, is wealthy and only pretending to be a toiler   358

A loves B, but is uncertain of her affections and is too timid to propose marriage   360b

A proves false to B, the love of his youth   361b

A, middle-aged, goes searching for B, the sweetheart of his earlier years   361b

A and B are lovers, their families at enmity. A and B elope and are pursued by their rival kindred   362

B, in love with A and estranged from him, after various misadventures discovers that A still loves her   364b

A, with the help of B, overcomes an ignoble weakness   364d

A refuses an inheritance because of a restriction that he must not marry; then he marries B   366

B, a foundling, has a secret of her birth and parentage revealed to her by A. A rich estate awaits B's claim and proof of parentage   368b

(1) B, capriciously sending her lover into desperate danger, drains the bitter cup of remorse   342

(1) A is estranged from B, the woman he loves, because of a difference of opinion over a trivial matter   343

(1) A is estranged from his sweetheart, B, and B refuses to return money A has given her to save for him   344

(1) A and B, lovers, are innocently thrown into a compromising situation   351b

(2) A discovers B was right, acknowledges his error, achieves a reconciliation, and presently they are married   343

(2) A falls into misfortune; and his sweetheart, B, from whom he is estranged, returns money she has been saving for him, effects a reconciliation, and their marriage follows   344

(2) A, in order to win B, is compelled to confess his true rank and station   358

(2) A and B, eloping and hotly pursued by their rival kindred, are suddenly plunged into terrible danger. A makes a heroic rescue of B under the very eyes of their anguished relatives   362

A and B—Marriage, Conc'd

(2) A, with a taint of negroid blood in his veins, is in love with B, supposedly a white girl. He is about to give B up, when he discovers that B has also a taint of inferior blood 364c

(4) A is sent into desperate danger by capricious B, on the very eve of their marriage 342

(4) B has no lovers, but a "marriage of convenience" is arranged with A, on the understanding that it is to be secret, and that A is never to see B after the marriage 354b

(4) A and B, not in love with each other, nevertheless marry because it seems the logical outcome of their long, friendly association 365a

(4) A and B, unknown to each other, in a spirit of fun at a masquerade ball, go through with a supposedly mock marriage ceremony. It later appears that the marriage was legal 365b

(4) B offers to marry A and, as his wife, help him to rebuild his wasted life 367a

(4) B marries wealthy A, a man she does not love, in order that she may have money with which to help a parent who is in desperate need 368b

(8) A, seeking to uphold a lofty conception of duty, secretly abandons B, a woman he loves dearly 347a

(8) B, unworthy, wins the love of worthy A; and B, by pretending to be worthy, presently achieves worthiness 359

(9) B, capable of winning a contest against her lover, A, deliberately suffers defeat—because it has been agreed that she shall marry A if he wins 355

(9) B could easily win a contest, but she deliberately allows herself to be defeated, thereby losing wealth, but winning in marriage poor A, the man she loves 356

(9) B, knowing that her sweetheart, A, believes her to have perished in a tragic accident, discovers by secret enterprise that A has remained true to her, reveals her identity, and they marry 357

(9) B, having given A a Roland for his Oliver, reveals to A her own rank and station 358

(9) A joyfully proposes to B and is accepted 360b

(9) A finds B patiently waiting for him, and they marry 361b

(9) Out of A's heroic rescue of B is born a reconciliation of opposing houses and married happiness for A and B 362

(9) A revolts against opposing restrictions and achieves happiness in marriage with B 363

(9) B, still loyal, returns to A and there is reconciliation and marriage 361a

(9) A, B's loyal lover, working in secret, secures proof of B's unsullied lineage, and they marry 364a

(9) A and B, estranged, become reconciled and marry 364b

(9) A marries B 364c

(9) A's gratitude to B blossoms into love; and when A is sure he has rehabilitated his character, he proposes marriage to B and is accepted 364d

(9) B doubts A when he tells her he loves her; then, having convinced herself of A's love, B accepts him and they are married 367b

(9) A, in love with B, is poor, and feels that he may not aspire to the hand of wealthy B; but B proposes marriage to A, and happiness is the result 368d

Married Life

A and B, married and devotedly in love with each other, are hasty and intolerant 369

B mourns over the mistaken belief that she has lost A's love 370

A is suspected of having murdered his wife, B 371

A and B, devotedly in love with each other, through failure to understand each other's ideals, develop an incompatability which results in frequent quarrels 372

A believed B was of an artistic nature 374

A, after marriage, is sorely disappointed on discovering that B is indolent in the pursuit of a career 374

A, husband of B, holds B in subjection 376

A is a religious fanatic who makes B miserable with his petty domination 376

B is devoted to A, and he owes much of his prosperity to her loyalty and shrewd advice 377a

B, just divorced from A, falls heir to a large estate 377b

A is jealous of his wife, B 380

A's wife, B, has a birthmark which mars her beauty 383

A and B—Married Life, Cont'd

A, influenced by a birthmark which mars the beautiful features of his wife, grows discontented and his love begins to wane 383

A, and his wife, B, have frequent and violent quarrels 385a

A presents his wife, B, with a gift as a testimonial of his love 387

A divorces B, then seeks a second marriage with her 388

B's health was declining, and beauty fading, when A secured his divorce from her 388

A believes he sees the apparition of his dead wife, B 392

A, because of his memories, finds that his married happiness is not what it should be 393

A, married to B, escapes from B on plausible pretexts and lives in a furnished room for a few days each month 394

B discovers A's deceit, trails him, and learns how A is merely seeking home comforts denied him by B 394

A's wife, B, proves herself a termagant, and quarrels are frequent 395

B fancies herself neglected by her husband, A 398a, b

B is the sensible, devoted wife of A 399

A, advised wisely by B, thinks B is jealous of his great abilities 399

A and B are estranged from each other 399

B's husband, A, has failed to return home, and B is worried about him 401

B's husband, A, is brutal and tyrannical 403

B, giving her husband, A, poison, flees before the poison has time to take effect 403

B is the second wife of A, a widower 405

B is flogged by her husband, A, for a transgression she did not commit 407

B, happily married to A, commits an indiscretion 411a

B, wife of A, is annoyed by the little mannerisms of A—trifling banalities that so work on B's nerves that bitter quarrels result 412

B marries A, a man much older than herself 413

A must have his abilities recognized by his wife, B, in order to be happy 419

A leaves B to run their joint business enterprise alone, and goes to a distant place, knowing that his absence will cause B to discover his business worth 419

A's wife, B, is a mystery woman 432b

A, having secured B's money, grows tired of her 422b

A tells B he is a criminal and will shortly be arrested by the police 422b

A induces B to enter into a suicide pact with him 422b

A and B, man and wife, each secretly leaves home on the same day 423a

A believes he has deserted B, and B believes she has deserted A 423a

A and B, man and wife, are wealthy and socially popular 423b

A and B are so occupied with social engagements that they have no time for the enjoyment of each other's society 423b

A and B seek solitude where they can be alone together 423b

A and B find the solitude they crave in a lonely environment 423b

A, an artist, works secretly as a day laborer in order to help his wife, B, who is also an artist 424

A tells B he is "realizing money on his art" 424

A, married to B, is impelled by an unusual motive to furnish a suite of bachelor lodgings in another town. He does this unknown to B 427

A and his wife, B, are artists. Their art does not prosper 428

A, husband of B, is heavily in debt 430

A, wealthy and desiring to be poor, has married B in order that she may spend his money 431

A, married to B, seeks by secret enterprise to effect a change in unpleasant matrimonial conditions 432a

A does not know B, and has not seen her since the day of their romantic marriage 432b

A fears that he will be killed by some admirer of his wife, B's, so that the admirer may marry B 436

B, wife of A, is a drug addict 441

B is forbidden by her husband, A, to do a certain thing 442

B, ordered by her husband, A, not to do a certain thing, does it anyway, during A's absence from home 442

B, wife of A, seeks desperately to escape disaster 445b

B, wife of A, is guilty of an indiscretion 446a

A and B—Married Life, Cont'd

B seeks by secret enterprise to emancipate herself from fear of her husband, A 452

B believes she has killed her husband, A 453

B's husband, A, married her under false pretenses 454

B seeks by secret enterprise to be revenged upon her husband, A 454

B marries A. B has property in her own name which, by a marriage settlement, is to descend to A if he outlives B 456

A and B, just married, start by train on their honeymoon 458a

A, finding the beauty of his wife, B, a source of danger to himself, seeks to avoid the danger by a stratagem 458b

A, husband of B, is cruel and tyrannical 459

A is deeply in love with his wife, B 461

A revolts against the injustice he is compelled to suffer at the hands of his beloved wife, B 463

A is ill and about to die; B, his wife, could save him, but she will not 466b

B, attempting to poison her husband, A, mistakes a bottle of harmless white powder for the poison and gives A some of its contents 468

B, seeking to aid her husband, A, by secret enterprise, finds poverty a bar 469

B seeks to escape from her tyrannical husband, A, by running away 470

B falsely accuses her husband, A, of transgression 478

B, wife of A, desperately ill, sends A for a doctor 480

A, sent for a doctor by B, who is seriously ill, does not return—and he does not send the doctor 480

A and B, man and wife, struggle to realize a cherished ideal 484a

A, husband of B, is wealthy, cultured, and of high social standing 485

A is estranged from his wife, B 487

A marries B because he thinks she is poor 488a

A begins divorce proceedings against his wife, B 489

B is the wife of A and loves him devotedly 491a

B, through foolish extravagance, brings A close to ruin 491b

B's husband, A, loves her devotedly 492a

B's husband, A, is a poor man 492b

B loves jewels and fine clothes which her husband, A, is unable to give her 492b

B, wife of A, is shallow, foolish and faithless 494

A has recently lost his wife, B 497

A seeks to find his deceased wife, B 498

A and B, husband and wife, are estranged from each other 499a

A is seeking a divorce from B 500a

A, failing in business and almost a bankrupt, nevertheless marries B, a shrewd and thrifty woman 500b

A receives a letter from B, calling him home 501

B·supposes that her husband, A, is dead 502

B's husband, A, is brutal and tyrannical 503a

B seeks to win her husband, A, to a certain enterprise 504a

B is the second wife of A 504b

B thinks her husband, A, has committed a moral transgression 506a

B, through false suspicion, is estranged from her husband, A 506a

A, married to B, finds the necessity of supporting his wife and family a bar to cherished ambitions 511

A, married to B, is compelled to lead a prosy, middle-class life, drab and monotonous 513

A, married to prosy B, treasures in his heart of hearts dreams of knightly exploits and chivalrous adventures, himself the star of each performance 513

A, husband of B, is discovered by honest and high-minded B to be planning a transgression that will work untold hardship to the public 517

A learns that his wife, B, is in terrible danger 519a

A, if he leaves his post of duty to save his wife, B, who is in terrible danger, will sacrifice lives and property he is in duty bound to safeguard 519a

A, over the phone, receives an agonized call from his wife, B, for help. B is in terrible danger 519b

A, and his wife, B, find themselves face to face with starvation 522

A, because of extreme poverty, finds it impossible to remember his wife, B, with a Christmas present 523

A, husband of B, has a dangerously reckless passion for gambling in stocks 524

A and B—Married Life, Cont'd

A, husband of B, is a lawyer with trust funds in his possession; and B fears he will be tempted to use the trust funds for gambling purposes   524a

A, elderly husband of youthful B, will die if a limb is not amputated   524b

A struggles to carry out an obligation to his deceased wife, B, which he considers sacred   526

A seeks to be loyal to his wife, B   527

B, wife of A, is of alien blood and inferior race   527

A is the husband of worthy B whom he does not love   528

A dominates his wife, B, a nagger and a scold, by petty tyrannies, that are more masterful than any B has at her command   529b

B, wife of A, refuses to live with A in a house beside which there is a mysterious grave   530

B must have money in order to save her husband, A   532a

A, husband of B, is desperately ill, and will die unless he can have a change of climate   532a

B's long, beautiful tresses are greatly admired by her husband, A   532b

B, A's tyrannical wife, goes out for the evening and orders A not to leave the house while she is away   533

B is forbidden by her husband, A, to engage in a certain enterprise   534

B engages in a certain enterprise which her husband, A condemns and forbids her to take part in   534

A's wife, B, is murdered at a certain hour of the night   537

A, husband of B, enroute to his home in the country, is caught in a storm and is out all night   538

A, absent from home all night, finds, on reaching home in the morning, that his wife, B, is missing   538

A, husband of B, is the victim of egotistical self-deception and thinks himself a great man   539a

A believes that he is prevented from becoming famous by the jealously of his wife, B   539a

B divorces A on the grounds of desertion   539b

A labors under the mistaken belief that the altruism of his wife, B, is prompted by selfish motives   542

B labors under the mistaken belief that her husband, A, receives all the praise for her own kindly acts   544

B's husband, A, fails to return home. A blizzard is raging, and B fears that A has suffered misfortune in the storm   545

B, wife of A, during A's absence, sees destruction threatening A's life work   546a

B, homely, marries a blind man, A, who thinks her surpassingly beautiful   546b

A dearly loves his wife, B; and her love, which he does not possess, is necessary to his happiness   547

A is married to B, and his ideal is faithfulness   549

B's husband, A, is a tyrannical, churlish person whose dislike for his attractive wife inspires in his small mind a desire to persecute her   559

A finds that a delusion regarding the apparition of his deceased wife, B, is entangled with truth   560

A, husband of B, receives each morning a mysterious communication regarding B   562

A, estranged from his wife, B, whom he dearly loves, seeks a reconciliation   563a

A marries B, a beautiful woman notorious for her vicious temper and scorpion tongue   563b

A is deeply in love with his wife, B, a virago, and plans to transform her nature by a method of his own   563b

A and B, man and wife, deplore the insincerity and the mercenary spirit of modern city life   563c

A and B, man and wife, leave the city and search in the country for their ideal of what life should be   563c

B, young and attractive, has lost her husband, A   564c

B, a young and attractive widow, resolves to remain faithful to the memory of her deceased husband, A, and never marry again   564a

B cherishes the dear desire that her husband, A, shall become religiously inclined   565

B seeks to aid her husband, A, who is morose and discontented   566a

B pretends to be a shoplifter, but has honestly purchased the goods which her horrified husband, A, finds in her possession   566b

A and B—Married Life, Cont'd

A, married to B, discovers the unfaithfulness of B   568a   568c
B's husband, A, mysteriously disappears, and B mourns for him as dead   572
A, a toiler, tries to support his wife, B, and family by honest enterprise; but he is out of work, his wife ill and family in need   574a
A, husband of B, is in dire financial straits   574b
A becomes aware of the impending death of his wife, B   575
A suffers overwhelming sorrow because of the death of his wife, B   576a
B is convinced that all the misfortunes of herself and her husband, A, are due to A's irreligious nature   579a
A's wife, B, is racially, morally and mentally A's inferior   579b
B desires the love and consideration of her husband, A, which she delieves she has lost   581
B, if discovered doing something she has in mind, will find herself at odds with her husband A   583a
B, wife of A, is desperately in need of money for a certain purpose   583b, c
B, wife of A, discovers in a secret place her obituary notice (written by A?), the date of demise alone left blank   584a
B, wife of A, leaves home suddenly on important business while A is absent   585a
B, wife of A, is a "butterfly of fashion"   585b
B, wife of A, must have rich clothes and luxurious surroundings in order to be happy   585b
B, fourth wife of A, discovers shortly after her marriage that A's other wives have all died suddenly and mysteriously   590
B revolts against certain unpleasant conditions involving her husband, A   592
B, undemonstrative in her affections, surprises her husband, A, and arouses his suspicion by bringing his breakfast to him in bed   59 a
B, wife of A, innocently commits a transgression   59 d
(1) A and B quarrel, and an estrangement results   369
(1) A is so much older than B that, after their marriage, the discrepancy in their ages becomes the cause of quarrels and, finally, of estrangement   373
(1) A marries B, thinking she is wealthy; after marriage, he discovers that B is not wealthy   377b
(1) A, marrying a widow, B, discovers that he has "caught a tartar" and has wedded a domestic tyrant   378
(1) A suffers the loss of happiness in carrying out honorably a distasteful obligation to divorce his wife, B   379
(1) A finds a note, somewhat ambiguously worded, which leads him to a wrong conclusion regarding the conduct of his wife, B   381
(1) B is mysteriously murdered and A, innocent, is suspected of the crime   385a
(1) A finds B dead, slain by the gift he had presented to her   387
(1) A, through mistaken judgment, becomes estranged from his loving wife, B   391
(1) A, struggling to overtake the fleeing apparition of his dead wife, B, falls from a cliff and meets his death   392
(1) B learns that her supposed legal marriage to A was a farce   415
(1) B is abandoned by A and left penniless and alone   415
(1) B, wife of A, dies as the result of an enterprise undertaken for her supposed benefit   416
(1) B, while too severely reprimanding her husband, A, bursts a blood vessel and expires   417
(1) A lives unhappily with his wife, B   420
(1) B, carrying out a suicide pact with A, kills herself. A does not kill himself, but craftily explains that B committed suicide   422b
(1) A and B encounter dire misfortune. Each seeks some secret method of recouping their joint finances   428
(1) A, married to B, loses his identity   437
(1) B is happily married to A   449
(1) B, and her husband, A, have fallen upon evil days   455b
(1) A and B, married, finding they cannot live happily together, agree on the secret and honorable expedient of living apart undivorced   457
(1) B, the bride, seeks to escape annoying experiences when A, the groom, leaving the train to send a telegram, is left behind   458a
(1) A and B, married, find themselves cast away among a strange, half-barbarian people   458b
(1) A is estranged from his wife, B, whom he dearly loves   460
(1) A is unhappy with his wife, B   462

A and B—Married Life, Cont'd

(1) A's wife, B, dies   474

(1) A finds himself under a weird psychic spell because of a birthmark on the face of his wife, B   475

(1) B is accidentally killed by a series of manoeuvers set in motion by her husband, A   479

(1) B is abandoned by A, her husband by a secret marriage   481

(1) B is unable to prove her secret marriage to A; the marriage records disappear and the priest who performed the ceremony dies   481

(1) B, wife of A, sees happiness and beauty in everything and evil in nothing until A accuses her of causing his downfall   482

(1) B's bright outlook on life changes to one of darkness and despair when she is falsely accused of evil by her husband, A   482

(1) B, wife of A, falls into misfortune   483a

(1) A tries in vain to pay the debts incurred by his extravagant wife, B, whom he idolizes   484b

(1) A, estranged from his wife, B, seeks a reconciliation, and then quarrels with B as to which of them caused the estrangement—and the estrangement continues   487

(1) A's wife, B, deserts him and obtains a divorce   496b

(1) A dearly loves his wife, B, but B does not love him   499b

(1) A and B are estranged and living apart, their married happiness in a sad tangle   501

(1) A finds his marriage to B a bar to his contentment   508

(1) A is unhappy in his married life with B   510

(1) A is unable to find a job and support his wife, B   522

(1) A, deeply in love with his wife, B, is made defendant in divorce proceedings started by B   529a

(1) A, husband of B, discovers that B is unfaithful   552a

(1) A, husband of B, mysteriously disappears   572

(1) A's sorrow over the death of his wife, B, culminiates in hallucination   576a

(1) A, mistakenly supposing his beloved wife, B, is dead, kills himself   576b

(1) B, discovering that her husband, A, is dead, commits suicide   576b

(1) A suffers remorse and overwhelming sorrow—remorse for broken vows, and sorrow because of the death of his beloved wife, B   577

(1) A, goaded by sorrow for the death of his beloved wife, B, goes into seclusion   577

(1) B, wife of A, proves a hindrance to him socially and in a business way   579b

(1) B, alone, helpless and in terrible danger, sends to her husband, A, a despairing call for aid   591

(2) A, enlightened and transformed by the revelation of his error, returns humbly to his wife, B   391

(2) A seeks to escape difficulties, restore property and be free of an unloved wife, B, all by secret enterprise   465

(2) A's wife, B, from whom he is seeking a divorce, nurses him back to health   496a

(2) A becomes reconciled with B when she nurses him through a serious illness   500a

(2) B so reorganizes and manages A's affairs that he becomes prosperous   500b

(2) B loyally helps her huband, A, recoup his financial losses   505

(2) B becomes reconciled with her husband, A, when a suspicion is proved to be false   506b

(2) A rescues B   519b

(2) B, when properly subdued by her husband, A's, pretended tyrannies, finds A gentle, kindly and considerate   529b

(2) B, engaging in a certain enterprise forbidden by her husband, A, discovers that A has a part in it; and, because of this discovery, B comes to an agreement with A which enables them to go forward happily in life with a better understanding of each other's rights and privileges   534

(3) A, after his marriage to B, discovers that B was a married woman and neither divorced nor widowed   471

(3) A, B's husband, pretends to be innocent of a transgression, but B knows he is guilty   521

(3) B, fearing her husband, A, will commit a transgression, pretends herself to commit a transgression   566b

(3) A, discovering that his wife, B, is unfaithful, kills her and himself   568a

(4) A, husband of B, loves B devotedly, but he is so constituted that he never shows his true feelings but often masks them with something that suggests their exact opposite   370

A and B—Married Life, Cont'd

(4) A is more capable than his wife, B, although B thoughtlessly treats him as mentally inferior 375

(4) A, in order to restore to B, without a confession of culpability, wealth of which he has secretly defrauded her, marries her 382

(4) B, thinking her husband, A, is in danger, plunges into danger herself on the chance of finding him and helping him 401

(4) B, goaded beyond her powers of endurance, puts poison in a glass and gives it to A 403

(4) B, wife of A, keeps their house so well-ordered, and is so tyrannical and unreasonable about it, that A's home life becomes a hell 408

(4) B has committed a secret transgression in order to help her husband, A 410

(4) B does not love A but thought, when she married him, that he would help her realize her consuming ambition 413

(4) B, married, quarrels with her husband, A, and runs away from home in an attempt to find peace and contentment 418

(4) A secretly defrauds B of a large sum of money 422a

(4) A marries B in order to make a crafty restitution of property which, before marriage, he had stolen from her 422a

(4) A has married B for her money 422b

(4) A, married to B and desiring his freedom, resorts to craftiness 426

(4) A, married to B, is impelled by an unusual motive to drop out of sight, lose his personality and go adventuring in the underworld 429a

(4) A and B, married and devotedly in love with each other, are impelled by an unusual motive to drop out of sight, leave the world they know and search for an environment more to their liking 429b

(4) A, husband of B, a very beautiful woman, persuades B to pretend that she is his sister 436

(4) A seeks to achieve the refinement of cruelty in persecuting his wife, B 438

(4) A is impelled by an unusual motive to marry B, a woman he does not love 440

(4) B keeps her husband, A, in ignorance of the fact that she is a drug addict 441

(4) B drinks a potion which throws her into a condition resembling death, having been assured that A will appear and rescue her when she revives 445b

(4) B kills her husband, A, in order to prevent A from revealing an evil secret 448

(4) B marries A, a man of wealth and high social standing, and keeps her black past a close secret 447

(4) B married to A and neither widowed nor divorced pretends to be single 451

(4) A, married to B, is impelled by an unusual motive to lead a double life 464

(4) B attempts to poison her husband, A 468

(4) B craftily gives a birthmark a peculiar significance, and holds A under its power 475

(4) A marries B, a woman he does not love 488b

(4) A seeks to divorce B, thinking to find happiness in a new love 489

(4) A and B, man and wife, keep themselves in poverty by spending all their money for rich furnishings to put in the mansion they are going to build when they become wealthy 490a

(4) B insists on dominating A in business affairs 491a

(4) B, wife of A, insists on living beyond her husband's means 491b

(4) A is of a parsimonious nature and gives B little money 492a

(4) B's husband, A, is affectionate and kindly and puts on his "Sunday manners" in company; but, when he and B are alone together, he is cross-grained, petty and tyrannical 493

(4) A, rich and powerful, is determined to use all his wealth and influence in carrying out an iniquitous project. His wife, B, seeks in vain to persuade him against it 517

(4) A refuses to have a limb amputated, preferring "to die in one piece." B, his wife, upholds him in his determination 524b

(4) A, married to B, attempts to carry out an infamous project in spite of family obligations 525

(4) B, wishing to be free of her husband, A, writes anonymous "poison pen" letters regarding herself, and sends them to A 564b

(4) B writes anonymous "poison pen" letters regarding her husband, A, and sends them to herself 564b

(4) A and B, for certain reasons, keep their marriage a close secret 573a

(4) B secretly takes money from her husband, A, for her own use 593

(4) B, a termagant, supposes herself a widow, and marries A 594b

A and B—Married Life, Cont'd

(5)   A divorces his wife, B   377a

(5)   B suffers betrayal at the hands of A, her husband by a secret marriage   479

(5)   A and B keep themselves poor by buying rich furnishings for the mansion they are some day going to build; but the furnishings, inadequately housed, fall into ruin before A and B are able to build their air castle   490a

(5)   B, wife of A, loses her love for him when she discovers his cowardly nature   584b

(5)   B, dying, reveals to her husband, A, a closely guarded secret which he finds greatly perturbing   588

(6)   B meets her death while searching vainly in a storm for her husband, A   545

(6)   B, at the cost of her own life, heroically saves from destruction the life work of her husband, A   546a

(6)   B hires a noted eye-specialist to perform an operation on the eyes of her blind husband, A, whereby A's sight is restored   546b

(7)   B, just married to A, tells A she does not love him   406

(7)   A, husband of B, proves a brutal tyrant and gives B nothing but harsh and inconsiderate treatment   413

(7)   A discovers, after his marriage to B, that she is wealthy in her own right   488a

(7)   B, opening a letter addressed to her husband, A, discovers that A has lied to her   582

(8)   B secretly disposes of a dearly-prized possession in order to buy her husband, A, a Christmas present   455a

(8)   A finds his memories of his deceased wife, B, an inspiration and a sustaining power   497

(8)   A wins the love of his wife, B, by patience, forbearance, kindliness and devotion   499b

(8)   A, unhappily married to B, proves true to his obligation to run a charted course as a family man, even through he must sacrifice cherished ambitions   510

(8)   B, in order to finance a certain enterprise involving her husband, A, sells her long hair   532b

(8)   A, because of his great love for his wife, B, forgives her delinquency and glories in her moral courage in making a confession of it   535

(8)   A, in order to save his wife, B, declares that he is guilty of a transgression committed by B   594d

(9)   B, with the help of the elements during a devastating storm, succeeds in winning her husband, A, to an enterprise long cherished by B   501a

(9)   A, by being cruel in order to be kind, insures the married happiness of himself and B   529b

(10)   B, her health restored, considers herself well rid of A   388

(10)   A learns that his wife, B, has been true to him   396

(10)   A, desperately ill, fired by tales of his wife, B's, unfaithfulness, makes up his mind to live and takes treatment that cures him   435b

(10)   A and B discover that their cherished ideal is a mistaken one   484a

(10)   B reads in a newspaper that her husband, A, whom she had supposed dead, is alive   502

(10)   A finds a bundle of love letters in a locked drawer of his wife, B's, desk—letters written after B's marriage to him, but not by him   552b

(10)   A and B, man and wife, discover that they are searching for an ideal that does not exist   563c

(12)   B, in order to "keep the wolf from the door," finds work in a laundry, but tells A she is working as an "art director"   455b

(12)   A has committed a transgression; B knows of the transgression, and A marries her in order to safeguard his evil secret   488b

(12)   A, discovering that his wife, B, is unfaithful, strangles her while she sleeps   552b

(12)   B, the deceased wife of A, appears to a relative of A's and describes her mortal reactions to A's lack of affection for her   587

(13)   Tricky so-called spiritualists pretend to materialize the spirit of deceased B in order to influence A to give them money by advice of the supposed B   474

(13)   A believes that his deceased wife, B, has returned to earth to comfort him   498

(13)   A, husband of B, vanishes mysteriously   540

(13)   A hears the voice of his deceased wife, B, and there seems absolutely no doubt that it is her voice   560

(13)   A finds an anonymous communication regarding his wife, B, on a sheet of paper in his typewriter   562

(13)   A receives mysterious "poison pen" letters regarding his wife, B   562

A and B—Married Life, Conc'd

(13) A, mysteriously missing, returns to his home and his wife, B, in a dazed condition, unable to give any explanations   571

(13) B, leaving home suddenly during the absence of her husband, A, writes a line to A explaining her departure, but the wind whisks the note out of an open window, and away. B's absence is accounted a "mysterious disappearance"   585a

(14) A reads in a newspaper that his wife, B, has divorced him   539b

(14) A, because of the death of his wife, B, suffers great sorrow and undergoes a character transformation   578a

(14) B, realizing suddenly the injustice her exacting nature has been causing A, promises to be different—and there is a reconciliation   394

Misfortune

A, striken with fever in a wilderness country, is attended by an old woman, B   605

A is tricked by B in a certain enterprise   640

B knows the combination of A's safe; and she knows, also, that there is a small fortune in jewels in the safe   666

B, unless she reveals a personal delinquency, will cause an innocent man, A, to suffer for transgression   667

A, a fugitive from justice, seeks to resue B from her misfortunes   673

B rebels against A's method of appropriating as his own the brilliant achievements which B accomplishes at his command   679

A and B, strangers to each other, are together thrown into misfortune   688

B goes to a restaurant to keep a dinner engagement with A. A does not appear   744

(1) A falling ill in a wilderness country, is attended by an old woman, B, to whom, years before, he had taught a fake method of healing   605

(1) A awakens in B a consuming desire to leave the city and return to her home in the country to live. All of which was farthest from A's plans, since he seeks a business engagement from B which can only be carried out in the city and with B's help   625

(1) A unintentionally causes the death of B   627

(1) A, seeking to save B by giving her an antidote for a certain poison, causes her death   627

(1) A, robbing a stage, discovers that B, who knows him and recognizes him, is one of the passengers   628

(1) A, tricked by B in a certain enterprise, dies when the trickery is discovered   640

(1) B is overshadowed and dominated by her mentally inferior employer, A   679

(1) A and B find themselves cast away in a desolate, primitive environment where they must fight for their very existence   688

Mistaken Judgment

A finds a mysterious note. It contains a woman's fateful secret—the secret of B in desperate misfortune   758

A removes a birthmark from the beautiful face of his wife, B, with chemicals   761b

A, in a spirit of altruism, befriends B   773

A forces his way into the room of an unmarried woman, B   799

B wins the protection of A   801

(1) A befriends B, who proves to be a transgressor and has lied to A regarding her identity   773

(4) A, seeking to help B, falls into tragic error   761b

(5) B reveals herself to A in the character of a transgressor   801

(8) A, attempting to exploit B's troubles for his own gain, ends by yielding his sympathy and befriending B   758

(10) A discovers that B, supposed to have been murdered, really committed suicide   802a

(10) A discovers that B, supposed to have committed suicide, was really murdered   802b

Helpfulness

A is older and more experienced than B and seeks to advise her wisely and help her avoid making mistakes   808b

B resents the superior attitude assumed by A   808b

A and B—Helpfulness, Conc'd

A's friend, B, is in a foreign country, alone, homesick and discouraged   816a
B, in a foreign country, unexpectedly meets A, a friend from "home"   816b
A, a hoodlum, rescues B from an attack by footpads   818b
B befriends A, picks him out of the gutter and makes a man of him   818b
A supposes that B is a transgressor   822
B, an attractive married woman, clever and influential, seeks diversion by help-
ing her friend, A   844a
A rescues B, who has been attacked by a huge snake   848b
B discovers in backward A a promise of great things, and attempts to guide him
to a high goal   850a
B seeks to rescue A from a life of dissipation and make a man of him   850b
B picks A out of the gutter and gives him employment   850b
(1) A, taking possession of B's property in order to save it for her, is falsely suspected by B of trying to steal it   808a
(') A, seeking to help B, who is in distress, meets with unpleasant complications   848a
(4) A takes possession of B's property in order to save it for her   808a
(8) A, under ban of the law, runs the risk of capture in order to aid B, a stranger who
is in critical misfortune   817
(8) A, a burglar, seeks to aid B, who was his friend before he "went to the bad"   819
(8) A, honest, poses as a transgressor in order to help B   822
(9) A succeeds in an enterprise secretly devised by B as a test for his abilities   814
(9) B, working secretly, rescues A from prison by proving his innocence   826
(9) A working "under cover," contrives to prove B's innocence of a certain crime   828
(9) B, working in secret, proves A's innocence of a certain transgression   829

Deliverance

A, of an inferior race, rescues B, of a superior race, from accident   861
B makes use of A's hound dog in tracking A   875b
A and B find themselves prisoners in a deserted house   876b
B knows that A is innocent of the crime for which he was convicted   895
(1) A rescues B from imminent danger, but only by bringing the danger upon himself   851
(1) A is unable to extricate himself from the peril from which he rescues B   851
(1) A, when he rescues B, becomes involved in an unpleasant complication, due to
mistaken judgment   861
(2) A is rescued by B   875b
(2) A and B, trapped in a deserted house, seek some method of escape. A hurls
himself from an upper window and, his arm broken, secures aid and rescues B
876b
(2) A, a prisoner, bound, helpless and facing death, is rescued by resourceful B   878c
(2) B, while carrying out an enterprise, is rescued from imminent danger by A   885a
(2) A, unable to rescue himself from danger incurred in saving B, is in turn rescued
by B   885a
(8) A, an agnostic, is persuaded into a belief in God by B when, together, they escape
a terrible danger through prayer   884b
(9) A, a fugitive from justice with a price on his head, prevents B from committing
suicide   869

Idealism

(1) A, hired by B to paint her portrait, puts so much character and so little beauty
into his work that B is deeply offended   903
(4) A "goes native" and marries a native woman, B   901
(4) A, a morally superior person thrown into a savage environment, is conquered
by moral inferiority in the person of B, a native girl   904

Obligation

A, after B dies, carries out honorably the distasteful obligation to travel   984
A, a detective, returns B, a criminal, to the scene of her crime for trial and punishment   986
(1) A, pledged to die if B dies, learns that B has committed suicide   1020
(4) A is disloyal to B, his ward   988

A and B—Obligation, Conc'd

(4)   A, against his wish and inclination becomes the guardian of a beautiful woman, B   1002
(14) B, a criminal who has undergone a character change and become an honest woman, is given her liberty by the jury before whom she is tried   986

Chance

(5)   A is disagreeably surprised when, by chance, he finds stolen jewels in the possession of B   1050
(9)   A and B achieve happiness when a questionable story is proved to be false   1055

Personal Limitations

A could save his life by revealing a secret that would compromise the good name of B   1070
A, struggling hopelessly against a character weakness, forms a platonic friendship for B   1075a
A, transformed almost over night from a hoodlum into a cultured gentleman, imparts to B, his friend, the secret of his surprising rehabilitation   1076
A secures the help of B, a woman friend, in a difficult enterprise   1083
B, unhappy because of A's sins, appeals to God to save him   1120
B, in great danger, seeks to apprise A, at a distance, of her danger by occult methods—methods with which they have often experimented   1137a
(2)   A rejects unfeelingly the friendship of B because he finds her too capricious   1125a
(4)   A and B, impelled by an unusual motive, enter into a suicide pact   1125b
(4)   A and B pledge each other that he or she will die whenever the other dies   1125b
(8)   A's admiration for his friend, B, and his desire to please her, inspires him to bring out the best in his nature   1075b

Simulation

B masquerades as an Unknown in order to prove or disprove an evil story about A   1154b
B, the friend of A, learns that A is heavily involved in debt   1155
B is forced to weep at an appointed time; and A strikes her in order to make her grief more realistic   1157
A and B are pretenders, yet neither knows that the other is not what he or she seems to be   1173
A, a pretender, encounters B, who is also a pretender   1173
(2)   B, unknown to A, settles with A's creditors and frees A from debt   1155
(12) A, B's best friend, in order to save B, who is suspected of a certain crime, declares that he alone is guilty   1171
(13) A, an artist, is hired by B to paint a miniature; and into the miniature he is to weave an intricate series of lines which constitute a concealed map of great importance   1143b

Craftiness

A is a grafter who forces B to help him in his grafting enterprises   1220b
A compels B to wander about the streets in rags, forlorn and weeping, with the idea of securing money from guileless strangers   1220b
A appears during a fake holdup and "rescues" B   1227b
A "rescues" B during a mock abduction   1227c
A, painting a house, finds the purse of B lying on a bench in the garden   1254
A finds a purse which contains the key to B's strong box   1254
A, a sculptor, models a bust of B at B's order   1257
A discovers an evil secret of B's past   1263
A sends a package to B by messenger   1278b
B seeks to recover, by stratagem, wealth which was stolen from her by A   1279b
A, unknown to B, holds a large sum of money in trust for her   1285b
(1)   A rifles the safe of B, his employer, and returns the key of the strong box to the place where he found it. **But there is a smear of yellow paint on the key** 1254
(1)   A has a valuable work of art destroyed by a lady, B, in a tantrum   1256
(1)   B, displeased with the work of a sculptor, A, destroys a bust in an angry outburst   1257

A and B—Craftiness, Conc'd

(3) B steals into the room of A, who is spending the night at her house, and appropriates a bag of jewels that is under A's pillow   1279b

(4) A, craftily seeking gain, overcomes the opposition of B with the use of strong drink   1200a

(4) B, in order to forward a certain enterprise, assumes a fictitious name and secures the position of private secretary to A   1244b

(4) A, desperately in need, secretly appropriates to his own use money belonging to B   1285b

(8) B subtly places obstacles in the path of A, obstacles which, when overcome, will profit A and develop his moral courage   1243

(9) B, a very great personage, snatches A's cane and belabors A with it. A auctions off the cane as a priceless piece for a collection   1256

Transgression

(1) B, engaged in carrying out an enterprise, finds that she must give it up for lack of funds when her guardian, A, misappropriates her resources   1308

(3) B, seeking to protect herself from A, shoots and kills him   1309a

(4) B's guardian, A, appropriates to his own use the property of B   1308

Revenge

A seeks by craftiness to be revenged on B   1310

(4) B, suffering a grievous injury at the hands of A, seeks to kill him by making use of a certain odor which A regards with superstitious fear   1325

B, wronged, is helpless in reprisal; her friend, A, champions her cause   1326

(4) A, seeking revenge against B, overreaches himself   1310

Mystery

A, with a hobby for collecting curios, presents B with an old, hand-painted miniature   1333b

B finds a note, ostensibly written by A, which causes her great perturbation 1364b

A, friend of B, meets B in a foreign country, and invites her to dine with him at an appointed time and place   1412b

A, in a waking vision, becomes clairvoyantly aware of a grave danger that is threatening B   1433c

B induces A to attempt the solution of a mystery   1444

B is a hypnotist who, in carrying out an enterprise, hypnotizes A   1446c

(1) A gives B, who loves flowers, some of his rare blooms—with unhappy results 1333a

(1) A, a young artist in needy circumstances, has a picture rejected by a customer, B   1386b

(9) A, spurred into putting forth an unusual effort by B, succeeds in winning a fortune   1354b

(13) A receives a mysterious communication from B, sent from a distant place where B is residing. It is evidently an important communication but difficult to decipher   1395

(13) B meets A in a foreign country; and then, returning to her own country, B meets A and receives the astounding information that he has not been away from his native land for years   1412b

(13) A, when the death of a spiritualist medium, B, brings an occult investigation to an end, finds his skepticism at the blank wall of enigma   1411

(13) A, friend of B, is reported to B, on unquestionable authority, to have been seen in two places, widely distant from each other, at the same identical moment 1424b

Revelation

A reveals his identity to B   1461c

A sends an important communication to B, a communication that vitally concerns his welfare   1461d

(1) A, revealing his identity to B, shatters her ideals and plunges her into unhappiness   1461c

(9) A is happy in rescuing B from an unpleasant situation   1451c

A, B and A-2

Love's Beginnings

A, carrying the news of the death of his friend, A-2, to B, the girl to whom A-2 was betrothed, is mistaken by B and her parents for A-2. B and her parents have never seen A-2   5

A, posing as his dead friend, A-2, falls in love with B and withholds the news of A-2's death   5

Love's Misadventures

A, and his friend, A-2, traveling together, meet with a tragic accident in which A-2 is killed. Before he dies, A-2 requests A to carry the news of his death to his sweetheart, B. A proceeds with his mission   168

A falls in with his friend, A-2, who is on his way to meet B, a girl he has never seen but to whom he is betrothed   169

(1) A discovers that his best friend, A-2, is in love with B, the girl A is seeking to marry   139

(4) A, unmarried, elopes with B, the wife of his dearest friend, A-2   119

(13) A, in love with B, pretends to be his deceased friend, A-2, who was betrothed to B. B and her family, hearing of the death of A-2 at last, believe A to be the specter of A-2   72

Marriage Proposal

A sends his friend, A-2, to B with a proposal of marriage   192b

(1) A-2 proposes to B for A; and B, thinking A-2 is speaking for himself, accepts him   192b

Love's Rejection

A's friends, A-2, A-2, believe that B, whom A is about to marry, is a woman of immoral character and that A should be restrained   220

A discovers that his friend, A-2, is cruelly fickle in his love affair with B   294a

A, discovering that his friend, A-2, is cruelly fickle in his love affair with B, takes him to task for it   294a

A falls in love with B in spite of the fact that his friend, A-2, has warned him against her   329

A, wealthy, is in love with B. A's friends, A-2, A-2, think that B is a designing fortune hunter   330a

(1) A, in love with B, secretly discovers that B is about to marry his friend, A-2   319

(4) A falls in love with B, who is betrothed to his friend, A-2   273

(4) A, in order to arouse the jealousy of his friend, A-2, and cure him of fickleness in love, pretends to be in love with B, A-2's sweetheart   294b

(10) A, in love with B, renounces his love when told by his friend, A-2, that it is unwise   221a

Marriage

A's gift, returned by B on account of a lover's quarrel, is sent back to B, unknown to A, by A-2, a friend of both B and A; and attached to the gift is a note requesting B to keep it until A calls for it in person   349

(10) A, estranged from B, is influenced by A-2 to call on B; and the result of the call is a reconciliation and marriage   349

Married Life

A persuades his friend, A-2, to elope with B   426

A's wife, B, is untrue to him, a fact of which A is in ignorance. A-2 discovers B's unfaithfulness, and informs A, who is on his deathbed obstinately refusing treatment that would heal him   435b

B's husband, A, leaves for town, as he declares, to meet a friend, A-2   443

A's friend, A-2, sends a letter to A; it arrives during A's absence, and B opens it   443

B, wife of A, calls on her lover, A-2   446b

A-2 conceals B so A will not see her   446b

A and B, man and wife, are to inherit money from a rich relative, A-2, when a child shall bless their union   490b

B is the wife of A, a friend of A-2's   580

A's friend, A-2, discovers that A's wife, B, is a "vamp"   580

A, B and A-2—*Married Life, Conc'd*

(1)   A-2, friend of A, is in a foreign country; and B conceals the letter from A-2 and, the next time A leaves home "to meet A-2", B trails him   443

(1)   A discovers his wife, F., concealed in the apartment of A-2   446b

(4)   B, wife of A, persuades A-2 to elope with her   477

(4)   A's wife, B, elopes with A's friend, A-2, a man more successful in business than A   549

(4)   B, wife of A, elopes with A's friend, A-2   557b

(6)   B, wife of A, and A-2, with whom B is eloping, meet death in an automobile accident   557b

Obligation

A's friend, A-2, was the father of B; and, when A-2 died, A promised him he would care for B as though she were his own child   988

A-2 is the brother of B, who is very dear to A   1007

Chance

A, years after he has stolen money from A-2, by merest chance and unwittingly happens to stop for the night with A-2 and his wife, B   1048

B, and her husband, A-2, meeting A, by chance discover that A has with him a bag of unset diamonds   1048

Craftiness

(4)   A, in order to convince B that he is a man of "courage," arranges with A-2 to stage a fake holdup with B the supposed victim   1227b

(4)   A hires a confederate, A-2, to abduct B   1227c

(4)   A hires A-2 to abduct B under pretense that she is to be held for ransom   1227c

A, B and A-3

Love's Misadventures

A and A-3 are in love with B. A seeks by craftiness to eliminate A   75a

A and A-3 are rivals for the hand of B. A-3 plans to forward his own aims at A's expense   76

B, if she wins a certain contest, also wins A-3, a lover of wealth and distinction whom she does not love, although she does love riches and social prominence; and if she loses the contest, she wins A, a poor lover whom she does love   104

A and A-3 are in love with B   136

A and A-3, twin brothers, are both in love with B   137a

A's rival for the hand of B, A-3, is more energetic and enterprising than A and seems more favored   158

A is in love with B and does not know he has a more favored rival, A-3   159

A has a rival in love, A-3, whose assurance is the key to his extraordinary resourcefulness   160

A, a humble lover, has a rival for the love of B—A-3, who is cultured, polished and a man of the world   171

A and A-3, rivals in love, agree to meet at a certain hour, call on B, and ask her to choose between them   174

B puts the love of two suitors, A and A-3, to the test   175

(1)   A, obliged to carry out the orders of his rival for the hand of B, A-3, is commanded to commit suicide, or to leave the field clear for A-3   136

(1)   B loves A; but A's rival, A-3, makes a captive of B and intends compelling her to marry him   146

(1)   A and A-3, once bosom friends, become enemies through their rivalry for the love of B   157

(4)   A and A-3, in love with B, are persuaded by capricious B to undertake a dangerous enterprise to prove their love   78

(6)   A and A-3 are rivals for the love of B, and A learns that B prefers A-3. A, in order to insure the happiness of B and A-3 slays himself and leaves his estate to B and A-3   80b

A, B and A-3—Love's Misadventures, Conc'd

(8)   A, in order to insure the happiness of B, whom he loves, and who, he thinks, loves his rival, A-3, flees secretly so it may appear that he, and not A-3, committed a certain transgression   80a

(8)   A and A-3 are both in love with B.   A seeks to protect A-3 from arrest   122

(9)   A kidnaps his sweetheart, B, from an automobile while she is on her way to marry A-3, A's rival in love   81

Marriage Proposal

(1)   B, thinking she has received a proposal of marriage from A, accepts. Later, she discovers it was A-3 who proposed   182a

(2)   B, accepting A-3's proposal of marriage by telegram, through error sends the telegram to A, the lover from whom she is estranged   194b

Love's Rejection

A, in love with B, discovers that his rival, A-3, is unworthy.   B seems to favor A-3   206

A's rival for the love of B, A-3, basely deceives B with false suspicions of A   217

A and A-3 are rivals for the hand of B.   B secretly favors A, but because A is self-effacing and less enterprising than A-3, B pretends to favor A-3 in order to spur A into proving his worth and ability   235

A and A-3 are in love with B.   B is about to marry A-3, whom A knows to be a crook   236

A loves B, but is rejected for a rival, A-3, who, known to A but unknown to B, is a transgressor   230a

A would save B, the woman he loves, from marriage with a rival, A-3, when he discovers A-3 to be a scoundrel   266

A tells B, with whom he is in love, that he has killed A-3   296

A is in love with B; and B is plighted to A-3—a fact which A suddenly discovers   300

(1)   A's rival in love, A-3, abducts A and holds him a prisoner as a means of preventing him from marrying B   221b

(1)   A loves B; but, after A meets with misfortune, B gives her favor to A-3, A's rival in love   257b

(1)   B is in love with A, but the sentiment of her family is against A and ranged on the side of A-3, A's rival in love   290

(1)   A and B are in love and betrothed; A, supposed dead by B, returns and finds B arrayed for marriage with A-3, and accuses her of faithlessness   328

(3)   B, discovering the perfidious nature of A-3, the man she has promised to marry, turns from him to accept A, by whose shrewdness A-3 was unmasked   267

(4)   B rejects A, an honorable lover, and accepts A-3, who is a knave   263

(5)   A sees in a newspaper the announcement of the engagement of B, the woman he loves, to A-3   318

(6)   A discovers that A-3, his rival for the love of B, is a transgressor.   A-3, to prevent the truth from becoming known, kills A   280b

(8)   A tells B, the woman he loves, that he has killed A-3, and asks her to call the police   296

(8)   B loves A and is about to marry A-3.   Accused of faithlessness by A, B shows A a dagger, and declares that she intends to kill herself at the altar steps before A-3 can claim her for a bride   336a

(10)   A, while in a psychic state, has a prophetic vision of his rival in love, A-3, discredited, and of himself achieving happiness in love   265a

(10)   A discovers that A-3, his rival for the love of B, is a defaulter   280a

Marriage

A's enemy, A-3, is captain of a ship on which A has taken passage, and on which B is a stowaway   348

(1)   A's enemy, A-3, as a means of persecution, by subtlity compels A to marry B   347a

(1)   A-3, knowing a secret of A's, compels A to marry B, A-3 performing the ceremony   318

(1)   B accepts her lover, A, and A secures a marriage license; then, before B and A can marry, B suddenly marries A-3, A's rival in love   368c

A, B and A-3—Marriage, Conc'd

(3-9)   A rescues B, the woman he loves, from a villainous rival in love, A-3   352b
(9)   A and A-3 are lured into a secret ordeal to prove their merit; A-3 flunks completely, but A succeeds almost at the cost of his life   350
(9)   A kidnaps his sweetheart B while she is on her way to marry A-3, A's rival in love, and marries her himself   351a

Married Life

A gambles with A-3, the man with whom A believes his wife has an "affair"   380
B, married to A, supposes A dead and marries A-3   402
A seeks to force B to give up A-3, whom she has married   402
B, after a loveless marriage with A-3, obtains a divorce and begins searching for A, the man she loves and from whom she became estranged   404
A seeks to revenge himself upon B, the wife of A-3, for a grievous wrong committed by A-3   433a
A's wife, B, is loved by A-3   433b
A-3 seeks craftily to win B, the wife of A   433b
A's wife, B, seems to have an affair with another man, A-3   434a
B's friend, A-3, seeks to save her from persecution at the hands of her brutal husband, A   439
B, wife of A, is mistakenly supposed by A to have an "affair" with A-3   445a
B, wife of A, detests A-3, but calls on him at his apartment at night   445a
A seeks craftily to kill A-3, an unmarried man with whom B is in love   459
A discovers that B has married another man, A-3   472
A becomes the second husband of B, whose first husband, A-3, had mysteriously disappeared and was supposed to be dead   473
A-3 threatens to reveal to B's husband, A, a fateful secret unless B will agree to a certain proposition he makes to her   476b
B, wife of A, falls in love with young and reckless A-3   495
A, hen-pecked husband of B, discovers that B has an undivorced husband, A-3, living   496c
B discovers that her husband, A, is seeking the life of her lover, A-3   503b
B seeks desperately to save her lover, A-3, from the vengeance of her husband, A   503b
B is eloping with A-3, the man who destroyed her faith in her husband, A   507a
B, married to A, elopes with A-3   507b
A mistakenly supposes that his wife, B, has eloped with A-3   538
A believes that his wife, B, is in love with A-3   553
A unhappily married to B, falls in love with B-3, a girl much younger than himself   555b
B, wife of brutal and tyrannical A, has a loyal friend in A-3.   A-3 seeks to help B escape from A   558
A, the brutal and tyrannical husband of B, is a huge man and as powerful as he is brutal; and A-3, who would save B from A, is a coward   558
A, husband of B, receives anonymous communications regarding B and A-3   561
A's wife, B, is dishonored (and slain?) by A-3   567
A tries to find A-3 and be revenged upon him for a grievous wrong committed against A's wife, B   567
A seeks craftily to be revenged upon his wife, B, for falling in love with A-3, the man who has befriended her   568b
A, husband of B's lover, attempts to kill B's lover, A-3   568d
A-3, B's undivorced husband, appears secretly to A, B's present husband, and tries craftily to get A to pay him money for not claiming B as his wife   594b
(?)   Married B is away with unmarried A-3 when A-3 suddenly dies   397
(1-10)   B wife of A, informs A that she is in love with A-3   409
(1)   A, in the power of A-3, is compelled to divorce his wife, B   434b
(1-7)   After A and B are married, B's first husband, A-3, appears secretly to A   473
(1)   B, wife of A, finds herself in the power of an old lover, A-3   476b
(1)   A-3, a man of evil character, seeks by violence and while intoxicated, to dishonor B, wife of A   483a
(1)   B, wife of A, is by subtlity made a prisoner by A-3, a rejected lover, in his apartment   483b
(1)   A, married to B, after a long, mysterious absence returns to find B married to A-3   550
(1)   A secretly discovers that his wife, B, has an "affair" with A-3   554

A, B and A-3—Married Life, Conc'd

(1) A, husband of B, is killed in an accident while on the way to elope with B-3   **556**

(1) A dies as the result of a conspiracy between B and A-3, and B suffers remorse **557a**

(1) B, wife of brutal and tyrannical A, is loved by A-3. B, although she loves A-3, is too high-minded to consider an elopement, or to be a party to any sort of intrigue   **559**

(1) A's wife, B, is dishonored and slain, during the war, by an enemy officer, A-3 **567**

(1) A, missing and supposed to be dead, returns secretly and finds his wife, B, married to A-3   **573b**

(2) A secretly abandons B and leaves her to A-3, B's undivorced former husband **496c**

(3) A kills A-3, the lover of his wife, B   **568c**

(3) A-3, murderously assaulted by A, husband of B, slays him in self-defense   **568d**

(4) B, married to A, has a flirtation with A-3, unmarried   **307**

(4) A-3, the "other man," appears and, by flattering married B, and sympathising with her, causes her to imagine she in in love with him   **398a**

(4) B, in order to win back her husband, A's, love by arousing his jealousy, flirts with A-3   **398b**

(4) B deserts her husband, A, for another man, A-3   **400**

(4) B, wife of A, secretly borrows money from her old lover, A-3, for a certain purpose   **411b**

(4) A marries B who, unknown to A, is already married to A-3, a husband who is living and undivorced   **435a**

(4) B elopes with A-3, who has artfully inspired doubts of her husband, A's, loyalty **444**

(4) B, wife of A, impelled by an innocent motive, clandestinely meets an old lover, A-3   **449**

(4) B seeks by secret enterprise to be free of A, her husband who is poor, in order that she may marry wealthy A-3   **450**

(4) B, wife of A, is craftily persuaded by A-3, the "other man" in a "love triangle," to elope with him   **476a**

(4) B is persuaded to accept a valuable piece of jewelry from an old admirer, A-3 **492b**

(4) B tells A, her husband, that a valuable piece of jewelry given her by A-3, is set with imitation stones and that she bought it herself   **492b**

(4) B, married to A, flirts with an unmarried man, A-3   **494**

(4) B, married to brutal and tyrannical A, loves and is beloved by A-3   **503a**

(4) A abandons his loving, devoted wife, B, to elope with B-3, a younger and prettier woman   **555a**

(4) A, abandoning his wife, B, to elope with B-3, pays a penalty of remorse and unhappiness   **555a**

(4) A, married to B, pretends to be single in making love to B-3   **556**

(4) B's husband, A, has a weak heart, and is lured into over-exertion by A-3. B permitting   **557a**

(4) A-3, a rejected lover of B's, promises to help B, wife of A, if she will come to his apartment for an interview   **583b**

(4) B, wife of A, happens to meet an old lover, A-3, and is compelled to borrow a sum of money from him   **583c**

(6) B's friend, A-3, forces a quarrel on B's brutal husband, A, hoping A will kill him, thus entangling himself with the law and freeing B of his brutal tyranny. A-3 accomplishes his heroic sacrifice   **439**

(7) A-3, the man with whom A thought B had eloped, A discovers, was married several days before the date of the supposed elopement   **396**

(8) B, wife of A, saves A-3, a supposed transgressor, from the law by a public confession of her own delinquency   **535**

(8) A, married to B and in love with B-3, takes a long journey in an attempt to forget B-3   **555b**

(8) A, discovering that his wife, B, dearly loves A-3, whom she has married thinking A to be dead, secretly goes away and takes himself out of her life   **573b**

(9) B forces A-3, at the revolver point, to return to her money which he has taken craftily from A   **445a**

(10) B has an experience with A-3 which proves to her that running away from her husband, A, was a mistake   **418**

A, B and A-3

Deliverance

B's escort to a dance, A-3, gets into a fight with another man, A   891
(2)   B saves A from a knife in the hands of his enemy, A-3   891

Craftiness

(11)   A's confederate, B, with a woman's wiles, lures A-3 into a trap that has been set for him   1261

A, B and A-4

Love's Misadventures

A, a publisher, in love with B, receives a manuscript novel from A-4, in which a woman character, approximating B physically and temperamentally, is made the rogue of the story   44a
(2)   A is in love with B; and B, rescuing A and A-4 from their captives, flees with them when they effect their escape   181c
(9)   A and A-4, held prisoners in a strange lost city, escape with the help of B, a supposed goddess   181c

Love's Rejection

(1)   A, in love with B, secretly discovers B in the arms of A-4   222b

Misfortune

A finds a motor stage wrecked and the U. S. mail it was carrying scattered from the torn pouches. The stage-driver, A-4, has gone for help. A picks up a torn letter, reads it, and discovers that B is in misfortune   673

Helpfulness

A has been hired by A-4 to circulate an infamous slander against B   818b
(8)   A, hired by A-4 to injure B, meets B, his sympathy goes out to her, and he revolts against A-4's scheme and warns B   818a

Simulation

A, a confederate of B's, seeks damages from A-4, the owner of an automobile that apparently injures B   1192

A, B and A-5

Love's Misadventures

A's secretary, B, is a criminal, "planted" in A's home by A-5, a crook   152b
(1)   B, a criminal, confederate of A-5, a crook, falls in love with her employer, A   152b

Married Life

A-5, A-5, tricky so-called spiritualists, pretend to materialize the spirit of deceased B in order to influence A to give them money by advice of the supposed B   474
B's husband, A, is killed by A-5   569
B's husband, A, is killed by A-5; and A-5, through the law's delay and technicalities, escapes with only a light sentence   569
(9)   B invokes the Mosaic law in seeking revenge upon A-5 for the murder of her husband, A   569
(9)   B, wife of A, takes the law in her own hands and shoots A-5, who has murdered A   594e

A, B and A-5

Misfortune

A, captured by enemies of B, is threatened with death by A-5 in an attempt to extort from him a secret of B's 660b
A, threatened with death by A-5 in an attempt to force him to reveal a secret of B's, defies A-5 to do his worst 660b

Helpfulness

A, friend of B, breaks into a building for the purpose of committing a robbery, and finds a trusted employee, A-5, B's husband, dead at his desk, a defaulter and a suicide. A-5 has left a note explaining his guilt 819
(8-9)   A, in order to save his friend, B, from disgrace, destroys a letter that would have proved B's husband, A-5, a defaulter and a suicide, "blows" a safe, and pretends to have committed a robbery 819

Obligation

B, ordered by thieves, A-5, A-5, A-5, to open a safe belonging to A, refuses in spite of threats against her life 1010

Personal Limitations

(1)   B, in the hands of crooks, A-5, A-5, A-5, and being forced to do their will, is tortured by having A, the man she loves, threatened with death by one of the crooks who is "drawing a bead" on A from behind a window curtain 1135a

Transgression

B, A's secretary, is made a prisoner, by crooks, A-5, A-5, A-5, when they fail to open A's safe 1307

A, B and A-6

Love's Misadventures

(1)   B is in love with A, who has been arrested on a criminal charge by A-6 92
(4)   B, in order to help her lover, A, escape from A-6, who has arrested him, makes love to A-6 92

Misfortune

(1)   A, impersonating A-6, meets A-6's sweetheart, B, and she recognizes him as an imposter 717

Mistaken Judgment

B, in order to protect herself from A, calls a policeman, A-6 799

Helpfulness

A is a prisoner of A-6, and A-6 seeks to secure from A information inimical to B 824

Deliverance

A sees a policeman. A-6, watching B, who is about to pick a pocket 876a
A warns B of danger from A-6 876a

A, B and A-7

Love's Misadventures

(1)   B promises to meet A, her lover, at her home and introduce him to her parents. A, arriving in advance of B, is mistaken for A-7, a man who is expected to call and apply for the position of butler 178

A, B and A-7

Love's Rejection

(10) A and B are in love; but one of A's employees, A-7, tells B of a (seeming) transgression that A has committed. B credits the story   213

Married Life

(4) B, young wife of elderly A, has an intrigue with a servant of A's, A-7   466b

A, B and A-8

Love's Beginnings

(4) A, unmarried, out of sympathy for B, who is unhappily married to brutal and tyrannical A-8, falls in love with B   17b

Love's Misadventures

(1) A, unmarried, falls in love with married B; B's husband, A-8, will not divorce B, nor will B divorce him   120

(1) A, in love with B, discovers that B is married to A-8   128

Marriage

(2) A in order to safeguard B's good name, has a marriage ceremony performed by a wandering circuit rider, A-8   351b

Married Life

A has seen her husband, A, secretly as he thought, exchange a pair of muddy shoes for the clean shoes of A-8   467

Mistaken Judgment

A believes B is an adventuress, seeking unlawful gain by pretending to be the daughter of A-8   788

(12) B proves to A that she is the daughter of A-8   788

Craftiness

A, deaf and dumb, is dying and desires to make a will. The lawyer who has been summoned, A-8, thinks chicanery is afoot, and hires B to go with him to read A's "sign language"   1267c

(9) A, counseled by artful B, makes use of important papers belonging to A-8 in forwarding a certain enterprise   1278a

Mystery

(13) A, a young artist in needy circumstances, is conducted secretly by A-8 to a house in which B, a beautiful young woman, lies dead with a dagger in her heart   1386a

A, B and A-9

Love's Misadventures

A, unjustly imprisoned, is pardoned and restored to liberty when B appeals to high authority, A-9   108

Deliverance

B implores A-9, the governor of the state, for a pardon for A, a condemned prisoner   895

Obligation

(9) A, using his position in the household of A-9 as a "cover" for his black designs, loots the jewel box of A-9's wife, B, and departs secretly between two days   1008

A, B and AX

Love's Misadventures

(1)   B, running away from home to marry A, by a mistake marries AX. Immediately after the ceremony, AX disappears   166

Love's Rejection

(1)   A, in love with B, is persuaded by Old Dry-as-Dust, the sage, AX, to turn from love as from something evil   214

A, B and X

Love's Beginnings

A seeks to buy an object, X, from B, an object he greatly desires. B will not sell X   20a

Love's Misadventures

A and B, lovers, have a violent quarrel, and B returns a gift, X, she has received from A   170

Love's Rejection

(1)   A makes a gift, X, to B, the woman he wishes to marry; and X is a gift of value which it is proved has been stolen   333

Marriage

(2)   A finds an object, X, which B has lost, an object that proves her love for him   360b

Married Life

B believes that her husband, A, loves her less than he does a certain small statue, X, that stands on his desk   586
(13)   A, showing X, a mysterious object, to his wife, B, is astounded when B, without explanation, begins divorce proceedings   541

Misfortune

A has confided to B the combination of his safe, X   616
A, confiding to B the combination of his safe, X, brings danger to B   616

Mistaken Judgment

B mistakenly supposes A to be a thief when he restores to her an object, X, which she has lost   792a
A, restoring to B an object, X, which she has lost, mistakenly supposes her a thief because X seems too valuable to be honestly owned by one in B's straitened circumstances   792a

Personal Limitations

A seeks professionally to secure a desired object, X, from B   1138
A, seeking to secure a desired object, X, from B, finds the object so dearly prized because of family associations that B will not part with it at any price   1138

Transgression

(4)   B, in order to carry out a certain enterprise, sells a valuable heirloom, X, confided to her for safe-keeping by A   1293c

Mystery

(13)   B, in order to help backward and unenterprising A achieve success, gives him a mysterious little object, X, which, she solemnly assures him, will make him successful in all his undertakings   1377b

A, B and F-B

Love's Beginnings

A is a young lawyer, retained by B to help her settle the involved estate of her deceased father, F-B   20c

Love's Misadventures

A, in love with B, is required by F-B, father of B, to secure a certain amount of money before he will be seriously considered as a son-in-law   111

A loves B; and B's father, F-B, promises him B's hand in marriage if he will carry out successfully an enterprise of great difficulty and danger   112

B is in love with A, who is engaged in settling the estate of B's deceased father, F-B   125c

A mistakenly believes that F-B, father of B, the girl he loves, is his enemy   177

(1)   B's father, F-B, is mysteriously slain, and innocent A is arrested for the crime 43

(4)   A, in love with B, quarrels with F-B, father of B   43

(9)   B's father, F-B, deceased, was heavily in debt; and A, wealthy, pays the debts unknown to B   125c

Love's Rejection

A carries out successfully a very difficult enterprise when promised the hand of B in marriage by F-B, father of B   209

A is in love with B; and he sues F-B, father of B, for damages sustained in a certain proceeding   295a

A, in love with B, and disapproved of by F-B, father of B, is forcibly ejected from the home of B and F-B. A brings suit for damages against F-B   295b

(1)   B's father, F-B, a religious fanatic, sends B away from home because she falls in love with A, who is not of their religious belief   223

(1)   B is unable to marry A because her father, F-B, in using B for his subject in a scientific experiment, has instilled a poison into her blood   227

(1)   B, revealing the fact that she is in love with A, of a family at war with her own, is denied further intercourse with A by her father, F-B   240

(1)   B cannot marry A, the man she loves, because of her promise to live with her widowed father, F-B, and make a home for him   285

(1)   A is in love with B; but F-B, father of B, orders A to keep away from the house and away from B   299

(1)   B, in love with A, is detained by her father, F-B, when she seeks to keep an appointment with A   306

(1)   B is locked in her room by her father, F-B, in order to prevent her from meeting her lover, A, and telling him of her love   308a

(1)   B sends a letter to her sweetheart, A, but it is intercepted by B's father, F-B, who does not approve of A   308b

Marriage

F-B believes he is fully warranted in compelling A, at the point of a gun, to marry B   347b

A masquerades as a servant in the household of F-B, father of B, the girl he loves 352a

(1)   B, having rejected A, the man she loves, because of an obligation she feels herself under to her father, F-B, is informed by F-B that he is going to be married— and B finds herself turned out on the world   368

(2-9)   F-B approves of A, and he marries B   350

(5)   A is compelled by F-B, father of B, to marry B   347b

(9)   F-B approves of A, and A and B are married   352a

(9)   A renounces an enterprise against F-B, father of B, the girl he loves, when F-B withdraws his objections to A as a son-in-law and allows him to marry B   363b

(9)   A, thinking his love rejected by B, receives a letter from B telling him how much she loves him, and that her father, F-B, has consented to their marriage   360a

Helpfulness

B's father, F-B, fails in his attempt to control and subdue A, a "wild" and unmanageable youth left in his charge   812b

A, B and F-A

Love's Misadventures

A, and his father, F-A, are both in love with B and wish to marry her   135

Love's Rejection

B, in love with A, and disapproved of by F-A, the father of A, seeks as an Unknown to impress F-A with her character and charm   241

A's father, F-A, disapproves of B, A's sweetheart   330b

(1) A's sense of filial obligation is so strong that, when ordered by his father, F-A, not to marry B, the girl he loves, he gives her up   282a

(1) A, an Indian, in love with B, a white girl, is commanded by his father, F-A, and by the head men of the tribe, to renounce B   282b

(9) B, by secret enterprise, proves her charm and worth to A's father, F-A, and he withdraws his objections to her marriage with A   330b

A, B and SN

Love's Misadventures   •

A's son, SN, is determined to marry B, whom A thinks is unworthy   181b

(4) A, seeking to prevent his son, SN, from marrying B, makes love to B and plans to marry her himself   181b

Simulation

A is mistaken by B for her son   1196

A, mistaken by a dying woman, B, for her son, SN, altruistically fosters the delusion in order to give B a few last moments of earthly comfort   1196

Revelation

(10) A is compelled to alter certain plans very materially when he makes the astounding discovery that he is the father of B's son, SN   1450

A, B and BR-B.

Simulation

B does not know that her brother, BR-B, is dead. She corresponds with a man, A, who pretends to be BR-B   1205

(1) B, after corresponding with A, whom she supposes to be BR-B, calls on A unannounced and discovers A's deception   1205

A, B and U

Obligation

(1) B, an enemy of U who has left a fortune to A on condition that he shall never travel abroad, wins a promise from A that he will travel abroad after she dies 1001b

Craftiness

A's rich uncle, U, promises to leave his wealth to A when A and his wife, B, shall be blessed with a son and heir   1289c

B and A-2

Married Life

(4) B, in order to escape consequences of personal culpability, falsely accuses innocent A-2   446a

B and A-3

Marriage Proposal

(5)   B, while in an irresponsible state of mind, promises to marry A-3; and later, realizing what she has done, regrets the promise   183
B sends a telegram to A-3, accepting his proposal of marriage   194b

Love's Rejection

(4)   B, her life's romance apparently wrecked, decides to marry the man, A-3, she does not love   261

Married Life

A-3 seeks to use his power over B to advance his own selfish aims   411b
(4)   B, married, assumes another name and marries A-3   451

Misfortune

(1)   B, a reformed transgressor, going about doing good, has her transgression revealed by A-3, who knew her in the old days   665

Craftiness

B goes innocently with a friend, A-3, to pass a few days at a summer resort   1240
(12)   B's friend, A-3, dies suddenly in his room at a summer resort hotel; and B, first to discover A-3's death, flees secretly in order that her name may not be compromised   1240

Transgression

B's friend, A-3, mysteriously disappears while in B's company   1309b
(1)   B is arrested on suspicion of having murdered A-3   1309b

B and A-4

Helpfulness

B, sympathetic, befriends a needy stranger, A-4   812a
(1)   B, through befriending a needy stranger, A-4, becomes involved in an unpleasant complication   812a

Deliverance

B, engaged in carrying out a secret enterprise, finds herself in danger and calls upon a stranger, A-4, for aid   890

Necessity

(1)   B, carrying out a secret enterprise, and falling into danger, appeals for aid to a stranger, A-4; but A-4 is wary and refuses assistance   1025

Simulation

(4)   B pretends she has been injured in an automobile accident in order to collect damages from the owner of the car, A-4   1159

B and A-5

Married Life

(1)   B finds herself in the toils of A-5   410
B, in her extreme youth, was lured into marriage with a criminal, A-5   447
A-5, a criminal, is killed, and B, his widow, leaves home and goes to a distant country   447

B and A-5

Misfortune

B, committing a secret transgression, has her secret discovered by A-5   669

B is threatened by crooks, A-5, A-5, A-5, in an attempt to force her to open a strong box   666

(1)   B, a respectable working girl seeking employment, follows the advice of a supposed friend, A-5 and finds herself in an immoral dance hall where she is compelled to dance with patrons and serve drinks   647

(1)   B's secret transgression is discovered by A-5, who seeks to use his knowledge for purposes of blackmail   669

Personal Limitations

B is forced, to battle for her honor with A-5 when finding herself trapped in a room   1135b

Craftiness

(2)   B traps A-5, a thief, by telling him her valuables are in a clothes closet—and then locking the closet   1259

B and A-6

Deliverance

B, her integrity seriously compromised, finds a friend in A-6, a detective   870b

Simulation

B, seeking to carry out an enterprise in a large department store, finds the enterprise endangered by A-6, a detective   1206

(2)   B, faultlessly dressed, in order to escape A-6, a detective, steps into the show window of a large department store and poses as a life-size wax figure, one of several figures displaying the latest suits and cloaks   1206

Craftiness

B, a woman criminal arrested by A-6, a detective, seeks to effect her escape by artful strategy   1258

B and A-8

Idealism

B volunteers to nurse a sick person, A-8, when no one else will undertake the work   956

(6)   B, nursing A-8, contracts a contagious disease and dies   956

B and F-B

Misfortune

B, elder daughter of F-B, is the sole support of the family when F-B dies   745

B rebels against the authority of her father, F-B, who compels her to do all sorts of rough farm work   676

B's father, F-B, is an unworthy character long mysteriously missing   684

(1)   B, trying to make a home for her widowed father, F-B, is neglected and cruelly treated by F-B   641

(1)   B is forced by her father, F-B, to leave home and become a domestic drudge in a distant town   741

(1)   B's father, F-B, pursuing rustlers who have stolen his cattle, is shot down and killed   745

B and F-B—Misfortune, Conc'd

(8)   F-B renounces his intention to disclose his identity to his daughter, B, and shambles away as an Unknown, leaving B happy with her mistaken ideals   684

(11)   B's father, F-B, long mysteriously missing, returns to his old home as an Unknown and discovers that his daughter, B, thinks him dead, believes his character to have been noble and holds him in hallowed remembrance   684

Helpfulness

B, when her father, F-B, fails in an enterprise, takes the enterprise off his hands 812b

Deliverance

B's father, F-B, is compelling B to take a step which she believes will be fatal to her happiness   871

(2)   B, compelled by her father, F-B, to take a step which she believes will be fatal to her happiness, escapes the catastrophe by a stratagem   871

Idealism

B builds a monument to her father, F-B, whom she mistakenly thinks is dead, and whose memory is to her a source of pride and honor   930

Obligation

B's father, F-B, dies heavily involved in debt   993

(1)   B makes a great personal sacrifice in order to carry out a filial obligation to live with her father, F-B, and make a home for him   992

(4)   B, the only child of her father, F-B, considers herself in honor bound to pay the debts of the deceased F-B, and undertakes a strange enterprise in order to carry out the obligation   993

(9)   B labors for years at a lonely task in order to clear the name of her father, F-B, from dishonor   995

Simulation

B's father, F-B, is suspected of a certain crime   1171

(1)   B, in order to save her father, F-B, who is suspected of a certain crime, confesses that she is the culprit   1171

Craftiness

(12)   B, compelled by her father, F-B, to engage in a distasteful enterprise, evades the enterprise by pretending suddenly to have been stricken deaf and dumb 1241b

Transgression

(4)   B forges the name of her father, F-B, to a note in order to secure money for a certain purpose   1293a

(5)   B forges the name of her father, F-B, to a note. Unknown to B, F-B dies suddenly before the date of the note   1293a

Mystery

(13)   B, waiting in the lobby of a crowded hotel until her father, F-B, can secure rooms, vanishes completely   1416

B and BR-B

Misfortune

(1)   B, sister of BR-B, in order to prevent BR-B from bringing dishonor upon their family, unintentionally causes his death   649

B and BR-B

Idealism

B indirectly causes the death of her brother, BR-B, by opposing a discreditable enterprise he was trying to carry out   909
B's brother, BR-B, has committed a crime   977
(12) B, apprised of a crime committed by her brother, BR-B, informs the police and has BR-B arrested   977b

B and SN

Mistaken Judgment

B has a weird delusion regarding her son, SN   800
B considers her son, SN, brilliant and highly talented, whereas he is less than mediocre in mentality   800

Deliverance

B learns that her son, SN, is suspected of having committed a crime   896
B knows that her son, SN, is innocent of the crime of which he is accused, and she knows who is guilty, but this knowledge makes the task of protecting SN dangerous and difficult   896

Obligation

B, a widow, is compelled by family obligations to live with a married son, SN   994
B, a widow, has given all her money to her son, SN   1009b
(1) B, penniless, is compelled to live with her son, SN   1009b

B and AX

Love's Misadventures

(1) AX, a gay young blade traveling through the country, takes refuge from a storm in a rural church. To his astonishment, he is hailed at once as a bridegroom, and is hurried to the altar where a pretty girl, B, in an exhausted condition, seems to be waiting for him. In a spirit of recklessness, he allows himself to be married to her; and when she, after the ceremony, seems to realize that he is not the man she thought he was, he hurriedly makes his escape   155
(4) B pretends that she is engaged to be married to an imaginary person, AX, buys herself an engagement ring and has the betrothal announcement published in a newspaper   86
(11) B invents a wholly imaginary lover, AX; and, most unexpectedly, a man of AX's name and general characteristics presents himself to her   58a

Marriage

B, impelled by an unusual motive, invents a fictitious character, AX   354a
(9) AX, a fictitious character invented by B, "comes to life," falls in love with B, and they marry   354a

Misfortune

B befriends an Unknown, AX, in a spirit of altruism   646
(1) B discovers that AX, an Unknown whom she has befriended, is a notorious criminal and is being hunted by the authorities   646
(4) B pretends that she is engaged to be married to an imaginary lover, AX, buys herself an engagement ring and has the betrothal announcement published in a newspaper   58b

Personal Limitations

B pretends that she is entertaining a duke, AX   1106
(1) B, alone and in a strange bedroom, discovers a man, AX, dead in the bed   1135b

B and CH

Married Life

(10) B lives for her children, CH, CH, gives all to them and loses her moody despondency 505

Deliverance

(6) B performs an act of great heroism in rescuing a child, CH, from death, but sacrifices her own life in making the rescue 893

Personal Limitations

(5) B comes to understand the evil of her selfish outlook upon life when one of her children, CH, dies 1068

A and B-2

Married Life

A has no admiration at all for B-2 and her ways 414

A and B-3

Love's Rejection

(4) B-3 flatters A's vanity and so manoeuvers him into an engagement to marry her 218a

Marriage

(1) B-3 abandons A after he loses his money and is injured and sent to a hospital 361a

Married Life

A, married to B, is haunted by memories of a former sweetheart, B-3 393
B-3 is a heartless coquette whom A loves 421
A, while traveling abroad, marries B-3, a woman of inferior race, abandons her and returns to his own country 425
A could prove an alibi and win freedom of a murder charge, but only by involving B-3, another man's wife 520
(1) B-3 whom A, divorced, seeks to marry marries another man 377b
(1) B-3 is wealthy, but shallow; and A, in following her advice, fails miserably in all his undertakings 386
(2) A finds B-3, his love of other days, and discovers that her beauty and charm have faded 393
(4) A falls in love with B-3 382
(4) A assumes a fictitious identity and marries B-3 437
(4) A, married to B, falls in love with B-3 486
(8) A's obligation to save himself, is opposed by an obligation to protect B-3, another man's wife 52͡

A and B-4

Helpfulness

A walking in the street, sees B-4, a stranger, weeping 806
(5) A, giving aid to a stranger, B-4, later regrets his impulsiveness 806

A and B-7

Chance

(12) A, finding by chance an aged nurse, B-7, learns from her a secret of birth and parentage which means happiness for him 1051

A and BX

Love's Misadventures

(4)   A, annoyed by unwelcome love affairs, pretends that he has an invalid wife, BX 84b

Love's Rejection

A is left a fortune by a deceased relative provided he will marry BX, a woman he does not know   298b

A is appealed to for aid by BX, a woman he does not know   298c

(10)   A, appealed to for aid by a stranger, BX, refuses aid, and regrets the refusal when BX mysteriously disappears. A considers himself under an obligation to find BX   298c

A, an eligible young man, is mystified by discovering in a newspaper the announcement of his betrothal to BX, a woman he does not know   298a

Marriage

A and BX, husband and wife, go their different ways immediately after the marriage ceremony   365d

(4)   A marries BX, a woman he does not know   365d

Mystery

A, in a city street, has a glimpse of BX, a strange woman who has caused him to become involved in a puzzling mystery   1412a

A is held up and robbed by a masked woman road agent, BX   1431

(13)   A, trying to overtake BX and secure information from her regarding a certain mystery, sees BX, under his very eyes, killed in a street accident   1412a

A, B and B-2

Misfortune

(1)   B and her husband, A, poor, are compelled to labor hard and deny themselves every comfort for years in order to replace a valuable ornament B borrowed from B-2, and lost   642

Mystery

B's friend, B-2, perpetrates a hoax by forging a note which has to do with B and A   1364b

Revelation

(10)   B's friend, B-2, makes an important revelation regarding A which causes B to correct a serious error   1462

Love's Beginnings

(4)   B, a plain girl who has no lover, is persuaded by her friend, B-2, to accept an escort to a dance—A, a man she does not know   35

Love's Misadventures

(13)   A, in love with B, discovers that B is in love with B-2   42a

Love's Rejection

B falls in love with A, who jilts a friend of B's, B-2, in order to pay suit to B   277

B-2 grieves so terribly over losing her false lover, A, that B's heart is wrung   277

(1)   B, in love with A, rejects his love when she learns that he jilted B-2, B's dearest friend, to pay attention to her   243

A, B and B-2

Married Life

A is asked by B-2, a friend of his deceased wife, B, for a bundle of love-letters, which B-2 had given to B for safe-keeping   385b

B, wife of A, admires the personal independence of B-2, and would pattern after her   414

(5)   A, husband of B, suspects B of receiving love-letters—and discovers that the letters were merely being held by B for B-2, for safekeeping   385b

(7)   B discovers through a friend, B-2, that the moral transgression of which she has accused her husband, A, was never committed   506a

A, B and B-3

Love's Beginnings

B, unworthy, seeks to have her lover, A, transfer his affections to B-3, who is worthy   11c

(4)   A falls in love with B; but A already has a wife, B-3, whom he has never loved, a wife whom he considers it his duty to care for   18

(8)   B, elderly, in love with youthful A, seeks to have A transfer his affections to B-3, who is nearer his own age   11b

Love's Misadventures

B and SR-B, twin sisters, are both in love with A   137b

(1)   B and A are in love. B-3, by craftiness, steals A away from B   94a

(3-9)   B, matching her own craftiness against B-3's, steals B-3's thunder and wins A back from B-3   94a

(4)   B's ambition is to do B-3 an injury; so she elopes with A, who is engaged to marry B-3   90b

(4)   A, engaged to marry B, receives a request from B-3, his former sweetheart, that he come and see her   138

Marriage Proposal

(1)   A is in love with B. Intending to propose marriage to B, he discovers that he has proposed to B-3   182b

(1)   A, thinking he is proposing marriage to B, finds that he has proposed to B-3, who accepts him   182b

Love's Rejection

A is in love with B and B-3   215b

A is about to marry B-3, who has deceived him into thinking B, the woman he loves, is unfaithful   216

A wishes to marry B, but is already united to B-3 by a secret marriage   281a

A renounces his love for B and seeks to win wealthy B-3   281c

B, a white woman, is in love with A, also white. B-3, a woman of alien race, seeks to win A away from B   336c

B-3 sues A for breach of promise   337b

(1)   While A debates within himself whether he shall marry B or B-3, B and B-3 engage themselves to marry other lovers   215b

(1)   B loses the love of A when B-3 comes into his life   324

(1)   A, in love with B, meets with misfortune when he leaves B for B-3, a woman who flatters his vanity   337a

(1)   B, who loves A and is beloved by him, loses him to B-3 through the wily strategy of B-3   340

(4)   A, because of the wiles of B-3, a coquette, breaks his engagement to marry B, the woman he loves   215a

(4)   A sends a gift to B, the woman he loves; B-3 intercepts the gift and craftily replaces it with a photo of herself, lovingly inscribed to A   218b

(4)   A, in love with B, leaves B for B-3, a woman who flatters his vanity and whose bold beauty has an appeal for him   256

(8)   B adores A in secret; and when A disappears and reappears with a bride, B still finds her happiness in the great unselfish love she has for him   270

A, B and B-3—Love's Rejection, Conc'd

(3)   B, unmarried falling in love with A, husband of B-3, is overcome with remorse. B flees from A, and from the world, to a solitary spot where she seeks to do penance and obtain a spiritual victory over her evil nature   279

(4)   A, engaged to marry B-3, abandons her and marries B   337b

Marriage

B, of an inferior race, rescues A, of a superior race, and falls in love with him. A is engaged to marry B-3, a girl of his own people   346

A, unhappily married to B and in love with B-3, is too high-minded to seek a divorce   368e

(1)   B-3, filled with remorse because she has rejected A's love, goes searching for him, finds him, and is informed by him that he is presently to marry B   345

(1)   A, telling B of an inferior race who is in love with him, that he is going away and will soon return. never returns, but marries B-3, a girl of his own people   346

(2)   A's unworthy wife, B, is killed in an accident, and A is free to marry B-3, whom he has long loved   368e

(4)   A proves false to B, the woman he loves, and has a disastrous affair with B-3   361a

(10)   A, his love rejected by B-3, goes to a distant part of the country and meets B. A falls in love with B   345

Married Life

A, bankrupt. divorces B and plans to marry wealthy B-3   377b

A leaves his loving, devoted wife, B, to take up with B-3, a woman who flatters his vanity   386

A, thinking he has been disloyal to his first wife, B-3, makes B unhappy by his brooding   405

A falls ill. B-3, who loved A before he married B, nurses A back to health   496b

A's sorrow for his deceased wife, B-3, causes B, his second wife, much unhappiness   504b

A finds his marriage to B a hindrance in his love affair with B-3   509

A, married to B, whom he does not love, is haunted by memories of a former sweetheart, B-3, whom he still loves   528

A, husband of B, and B-3, both vanish mysteriously at the same time   540

Gossip has it that A, husband of B, has eloped with B-3   510

A's wife, B, dies. B, A's wife, on her death bed, has A promise that he will marry B-3, B's best friend   578b

B-3 loved A before he married B   578b

B is convinced that her husband, A, has eloped with B-3   589

(1)   A is suspected of having murdered his wife, B; but, at the hour the murder was committed, A was with B-3   537

(1)   A is a bigamist; and his two wives, B and B-3, meet by chance and compare notes   548b

(4)   A has two wives, B and B-3, two homes several miles apart, two names by which he is known in two different communities, two circles of acquaintances, and and practices two professions   486b

(4)   A, married to B, suffers a memory lapse and marries B-3   548a

(4)   A marries B in order to emancipate himself from the evil influence of B-3   421

(9)   A realizes that his emancipation from the evil influence of B-3 is complete, and he returns to B a better and a wiser man   393

(9)   A succeeds by a stratagem in leaving his unloved wife, B, and, under a fictitious name, marries B-3, the woman he loves   440

(9)   B, second wife of A, discovers that B-3, A's first wife, was unfaithful   504b

(10)   B, wife of A, dons the mask and costume of B-3, A's paramour, and meets A as B-3 at a masquerade ball   594f

(13)   A, husband of B, suffers an attack of amnesia and marries B-3; his memory returns, and he forgets B-3 and goes back to B   548a

Simulation

(10)   B discovers that B-3 has told an untruth about A   1154b

A, B and B-5

Helpfulness

(12) A, proving B innocent of a certain crime, proves also the guilt of B-5, a criminal whom B physically resembles   828

A, B and B-7

Love's Rejection

(1) A is told by B-7, a maid in the home of B, A's sweetheart, that B has informed the police of A's criminal operations, and that he is an ex-convict   338

Personal Limitations

B, intending to send a telegram to her maid, B-7, through error addresses the message to A   1136

A, B and B-8

Married Life

(4) B-8 dies, and A contrives to make it appear that it was B who died   456
(9) B, as B-8, is immured in an insane asylum, and A inherits the money belonging to B   456

A, B and CH

Marriage Proposal

(9) A, in love with B, but too backward and diffident to propose, is horrified to hear a child, CH, who knows of his passion, propose to B on his behalf   193

Married Life

A has a son, CH, by his white wife, B; B dies   425
B is married to A and they have one child, CH   466a
B loves her child, CH, but she does not love her husband, A   466a
B, wife of A, forsakes cherished ambitions in order to carry out the desire of A that she bear him a son, CH   515
B divorces her husband, A, and is awarded the custody of their child, CH   594c
A steals his child, CH, from his divorced wife, B   594c
(1) B, married to A, her second husband, finds her domestic happiness imperiled by the obligation to care for CH, a child by her first husband   514
(5) B's love for her child, CH, left with her husband, A, when she deserted him, draws her back to CH and A   507b
(5) A learns that a child, CH, has been born during his absence. Result: Reconciliation with B, and happiness   501
(6) B deliberately sacrifices herself at the hands of her husband, A, in order to save their son, CH, who is falsely accused of transgression by A, the real transgressor   516
(14) A and B, estranged, undergo a character transformation through love for their child, CH   499a
(14) B, wife of A, suffers a critical illness at childbirth and her character is transformed   505

Misfortune

CH, a child, playing in the corridor of a large city hotel, transfers a black ribbon from the knob of B's door to that of A   737c

Craftiness

(2) A, with a strange baby, CH, on his hands, secretly leaves CH in the care of B, who has other children   1229
A finds himself with a strange baby, CH, on his hands   1229

A, B and SM-B

Married Life

B is the daughter of A and the step-daughter of A's wife, SM-B   570

(4) B seeks revenge upon her step-mother, SM-B, because she thinks SM-B has stolen the affections of her father, A, away from her   570

A, B and M-A

Married Life

A and B, married, live with A's mother, M-A   384

B quarrels with M-A, and with A on account of M-A   384

A and B are married, and A's mother, M-A, lives with them   518

B, wife of A, is jealous of the attentions A gives his mother, M-A   543

B has a mistaken idea that her husband's mother, M-A, is trying to interfere between her and A   543

A, and his wife, B, are compelled to live with A's mother, M-A, and avail themselves of her slender resources   574b

(1) A and B quarrel regarding M-A, and A is forced to choose between M-A and B   518

A, B and M-B

Love's Beginnings

B's mother, M-B, a middle-aged widow, introduces A, her youthful lover, to B   11a

(8) B's mother, M-B, plans that her youthful lover, A, shall transfer his affections to B. M-B's plans are successful   11a

A, B and BX

Love's Beginnings

(2) A falls inl ove with B, and renounces wealth which he was to inherit by marrying BX   19a

A, BX and X

Mystery

A strugles with a masked woman road agent, BX, and twists from her wrist a peculiar bracelet, X   1431

(13) A, proceeding about his business and caught in a crowd, is confronted suddenly by a strange woman, BX, who thrusts a mysterious object, X, into his hand, and, without a word, disappears   1383

A, B and SR

Love's Misadventures

B and SR-B, twin sisters, are both in love with A   137b

Love's Rejection

(1) A, influenced by his maiden sisters, SR-A, SR-A, renounces his affair with B, the woman he loves   219

A and D-A

Misfortune

(1)   A, in making a scientific experiment, has unintentionally caused his daughter, D-A, a grievous injury   626

Mistaken Judgment

(1)   A, a transgressor, returning as an Unknown to his home, finds his daughter, D-A, reverencing his memory as of a great and noble person   797

Helpfulness

A, aware that his end is approaching, seeks to protect his adopted daughter, D-A, by making a will   825

Idealism

A seeks happiness in being the pal of his daughter, D-A, and in making her happy 910

A is ultra-old-fashioned, and his daughter, D-A, is ultra-modern   910

A, a transgressor, returns to his home as an Unknown after a long absence, and meets his daughter, D-A   964b

(8)   A, a transgressor, learning that his daughter, D-A, thinks he is dead, and that his character was high and noble, does not reveal his identity but leaves D-A happy in her mistaken ideals   964b

A and M-A

Obligation

(1)   A's promise to his mother, M-A, prevents him from undertaking a cherished enterprise   989

A and CH

Misfortune

A, temporarily in charge of two mischievous children, CH-1 and CH-2, finds himself in more dilemmas than he can successfully manage   609

(1)   A seeks to live down his bitter grief over the loss of his only child, CH, but finds it impossible   698

(1)   A constructs a concealed trap, and a person dear to him, CH, falls into the trap and cannot escape   728

(14)   A cripples himself in rescuing a child, CH, from death   715b

Helpfulness

A finds a small child, CH, on the beach after a shipwreck   818c

A takes CH, a foundling, into his heart and his home and rears her as his own child   818c

A rescues a baby, CH, from death in a shipwreck   818d

A, unable to learn anything about a foundling, CH, adopts the child as his own 818d

A, a rough frontiersman in a rough frontier camp, undertakes to care for an orphan baby, CH   847

(6)   A tries to rescue a child, CH makes a heroic attempt, and both die   842a

(9)   A rescues a child, CH   842b

Idealism

A handicaps himself by taking charge of an abandoned child, CH   914

(5)   A seeks happiness in his love for a child, CH, but for certain reasons finds it difficult to realize his desire   911

A and CH

Personal Limitations

A seeks to find the relatives of CH, a foundling of whom he has taken charge 1089
(13) A writes to government authorities sending a copy of a coat of arms found on a foundling, CH's, coat, but receives no information regarding CH 1089

Craftiness

A finds himself with a strange baby, CH, on his hands 1229

Mystery

A appropriates CH 1430b

A and SR-A

Personal Limitations

A, brother of SR-A and her only living relative, is poor, while SR-A is wealthy and unmarried 1123
(1) A, poor, will not inherit the money of his wealthy sister, SR-A, if she marries, as she seems likely to do 1123

Craftiness

(4) A, through deception involving his sister, SR-A, wins a large estate 1236

Revenge

A seeks revenge for a wrong committed against his sister, SR-A 1321
(13) A, seeking revenge for a wrong committed against his sister, SR-A, has difficulty in discovering the name of the wrong-doer 1321

A, A-2 and CH

Personal Limitations

(4) A borrows an infant, CH, from a married friend, A-2, in order to carry out an unusual enterprise 1057b

A, A-2 and SR

Simulation

A-2, deceased, has a sister, SR; and SR, not knowing of A-2's death, corresponds with A, thinking him her brother 1183

Transgression

(4) A kills A-2, who is about to marry his sister, SR-A 1290a
(4) A kills A-2, who is about to marry his sister, SR-A, in order that he may inherit wealth possessed by SR-A 1290a

A, A-2, F-A and M-A

Simulation

A's friend, A-2, is the sole support of his parents, F-A-2 and M-A-2 1160
(8) A's friend, A-2, the sole support of his parents, dies, and A withholds the knowledge from the needy parents, writes them in A-2's name and continues sending money for their support 1160

A, A-2, B-5 and X

Married Life

(1) X, an object belonging to A-2, is lost by A in a questionable place; and, found, is sent by a mischief maker to A-2's wife with a note stating just where it was found   390

(4) A, through accident, loses an object, X, belonging to his friend, A-2, at the door of a woman whose character is not of the best   390

A, A-3 and B-3

Revenge

A, seeking revenge against B-3 for a wrong committed by her husband, A-3, who is dead, finds that B-3 treasures A-3's memory most sacredly, unaware of his evil character   1323a

A could destroy the beautiful love and devotion of B-3 for her dead husband, A-3, by telling her the sort of man A-3 was   1323a

A, A-3 and B-5

Love's Misadventures

(1) A, through the wily manoeuvers of A-3, his rival in love, is innocently lured into a compromising situation by B-5, woman confederate of A-3   75b

A, A-4 and B-4

Mystery

(13) A's fortune and happiness hang upon a technicality of the law: Both A-4 and his wife, B-4, are killed in an accident.   If B-4 died first, A inherits, while if A-4 died first, others inherit   1437

A, A-4 and CH

Mystery

A sees a stranger, A-4, leave a baby, CH, on a doorstep   **1430b**

A, A-8 and SR

Craftiness

(4) A, by trickery, prevents his sister, SR-A, from marrying A-8   **1236**

A, A-8 and CH

Craftiness

(4) A seeks for his own gain to impersonate a widower, A-8, who has a child, CH. A has no child, but overcomes the handicap by a stratagem   1224

A, A-8 and D-A

Love's Misadventures

(1-5) A knew very well that he would suffer adversity all his life when, in order to cancel an obligation he gave his daughter, D-A, in marriage to A-8, a man she did not love   48

A, B, A-2 and A-5

Craftiness

(9) A's friend, A-2, captures B, daughter of A-5, and makes overtures to exchange B for A, whom A-5 is holding for ransom   1281

A, B, A-3 and A-5

Love's Misadventures

(4) A's rival in love, A-3, learning of the plans of A and B for a secret marriage, sends an automobile to the church with a confederate, A-5, who lures B away by telling her A has sent for her   154b

A, F-A and M-A

Misfortune

(1) A's parents, F-A and M-A, insist that he study to be a doctor, while all his soul is yearning to make another profession his life work   697a

Mistaken Judgment

(1) A, desiring a musical career, defers to the wishes of his parents, F-A and M-A, and becomes a doctor; but, all his life long, he feels that he has made a mistake   756

Simulation

(1) A, through no fault of his own, is estranged from his parents, F-A and M-A   1182
(9) A, estranged from his parents, F-A and M-A, effects a reconciliation with them by proving his true worth in an assumed character as an Unknown   1182

A, SR-A and CH

Obligation

(4) A, a bachelor, undertakes to care for CH, the child of his married sister, SR-A, while SR-A is away on a vacation   982b

A, B, A-2 and A-9

Chance

(1) A's presents to A-2 and B are in packages, and the packages are transposed by A-9 with unfortunate results   1042b
(4) A has a jeweler, A-9, send to his friend, A-2, a silver whisky flask, and to B an expensive "slave" bracelet   1042b

A, B, B-2 and B-3

Love's Misadventures

(3) B's friend, B-2, an attractive married woman, seeks to save A, B's fiance, from the wiles of a designing woman, B-3, and restore him to B. B-2 does this by winning A away from B-3   94b

Love's Rejection

(3) A is engaged to marry B. B-3, a designing woman, seeks to compromise A so B will give him up. B-2 is a generous woman who seeks by secret enterprise to rescue A from the wiles of B-3 and restore him to B   238

A, B, B-2 and B-3

Helpfulness

B's friend, B-2, seeks to save A, B's fiance, from the wiles of a designing woman, B-3, and restore him to B   844b

B's friend, B-2, seeks to save B's lover, A, from a designing woman, B-3, by winning A away from B-3   844b

A, B, F-B and A-3

Love's Misadventures

A, a man of great strength and skill, is in love with B. F-B, father of B, sure of A's prowess and proud of it, in order to lure the champion of a rival clan, A-3, into a wrestling match with A, offers the hand of B to the victor of the bout   180

Love's Rejection

A's rival in love, A-3, is favored by F-B, father of B   301a

(1) A has been promised B in marriage by F-B, father of B; but F-B, false to his promise, compels B to marry A-3, a wealthier man than A   313

(8) A, discovering secretly that B loves a rival, A-3, refuses to hold B to a promise of marriage made by F-B   209

B's father, F-B, seeks to discover by secret enterprise whether A or A-3 is the more worthy of B   77

Marriage

A and A-3, rivals for the love of B, are put to a secret, gruelling test of worthiness by F-B, father of B   350

Married Life

(1) B's father, F-B, insists that B, already united to A by a secret marriage, shall marry A's rival in love, A-3   573a

A, B, A-2 and CH

Married Life

A and B, man and wife, are to inherit money from a rich relative, A-2, when a child, CH, shall bless their union   490b

A-2 writes A and B that he is coming to see their child, CH; and A and B find it necessary to resort to further simulation   490b

(4) A and B, childless, write a rich relative, A-2, that a son, CH, has been born to them   490b

(12) A discovers that his wife, B, is the mother of A-2's son, CH   551

A, B, A-2, A-3 and AX

Married Life

(3-9) B, wife of A, is eloping with A-3 when they meet a stranger, A-2; and A-2 in the presence of both B and A-3, tells about a man, AX, who broke up a home by eloping with a friend's wife and then abandoning her. A-2 has recognized A-3 and, in order to save B, tells this story about him, hiding A-3's identity under a fictitious name. But it is enough. A-3 sneaks away and B nevers sees him again   536

A, B, A-2 and A-3

Love's Misadventures

(1) A, unmarried, elopes with B, the wife of his best friend, A-2; then B leaves A to elope with A-3   150

A, B, A-2 and A-3

Married Life

(3) A-2, a friend of A's, sends A-3, B's undivorced first husband, to A, B's second husband, and exposure of deceitful B follows 435a

(9) B, wife of A, eloping with A-3, meets A-2, A's friend, and is rescued by A-2 from an act of folly 507a

A, B, CH and A-3

Married Life

(4) B loves A-3, and elopes with him, leaving her child, CH, with her husband, A 466a

A, B, A-3 and B-3

Married Life

(1-10) B, deserting her husband, A, for A-3, discovers that A-3 is in love with another married woman 400

(1-5) B informs her husband, A, that she married him from pique, and because A-3, the man she loves, married B-3 406

A, B, B-3 and CH

Married Life

A, thinking his first wife is dead, marries again and has children by his second wife 389

A learns that his first wife was living at the time of his second marriage, but that she has died since his second marriage 389

(1) A's second marriage unwittingly invalidated 389

(1) A seeks to make a new will and go through a second marriage ceremony with his wife, but is killed in an accident on the way to his lawyer's 389

(1) A's children by his second marriage are illegitimate, and A's property descends to the relatives of his deceased first wife 389

A, B, F-B, M-B and A-2

Marriage

(4) A is supposed by B's parents, F-B and M-B, to be A-2, to whom B is betrothed 353

(9) A elopes with B and marries her; A then returns B to F-B and M-B, tells them that A-2, to whom B was betrothed, is dead, and asks and receives the parental blessing 353

A, B, F-B, M-B and A-3

Love's Rejection

(4) B, in love with A, is compelled by her parents, F-B and M-B, to marry A-3 284

(4) B, supposing A, the man she loves, to be dead, yields to the wishes of her parents, F-B and M-B, and consents to a marriage with A-3 339

A, B, F-B and M-B

Love's Misadventures

A and B are in love, but B's parents, F-B and M-B, do not favor A; and A and B plan to elope, marry, and then seek forgiveness of B's people 73

A, B, F-B and M-B

Love's Rejection

B is ordered by her parents to have nothing to do with A   286

B's parents, F-B and M-B, disapprove of A, B's lover, because of his lack of enterprise   311

B's love for A encounters obstacles through her parents, F-B and M-B   312

(1) B allows herself to be governed by filial duty when her parents, F-B and M-B, order her to have nothing to do with A, the man she loves   286

(1) A, in love with B, was divorced from his first wife.   B's parents, F-B and M-B, have religious scruples against B's marrying a divorced man   334b

(9) A, an aviator, in love with B and in disfavor with B's parents, F-B and M-B, induces B to take a ride in his airplane; and then A elopes with B along the sky lanes   234b

A, B, F-A and M-A

Love's Rejection

(10) A falls in love with B and intends to marry her.   A's parents, F-A and M-A, do not approve of B, and A is shipped off to South Africa to get him out of danger and give him a chance to do some serious thinking   321b

A, B and AU-B

Love's Beginnings

(1) A's love affair with B is not prospering.   A secures a love philtre and mixes it secretly in a cup of tea; but B's maiden aunt, AU-B, drinks the tea   8b

Love's Rejection

(1) B sends a gift to A, the man she loves.   Unknown to B, AU-B, an aunt of B's who does not approve of A, secretly alters or marks the gift in such a way as to make it offensive to A, or exchanges the gift for some other object which will offend A   308c

A, B, A-3 and X

Love's Rejection

A's rival in love, A-3, finds a certain object B has lost, an object, X, that proves B's love for A.   A-3 appropriates X and says nothing about it   301b

(3) A induces his rival in love, A-3, to send B a certain gift, X; then, after X is sent, A proves that it was stolen by A-3   236

A, B, F-A and F-B

Love's Beginnings

(4) A and B have never seen each other; but, through their fathers, F-A and F-B who are old friends, it is arranged that A and B shall meet and marry   26a

Love's Misadventures

(1) A, to protect a parent, F-A, is compelled to take measures against F-B, father of B, the girl he loves   123

Love's Rejection

(1) A and B fall in love; but their fathers, F-A and F-B, are bitter political enemies   276

(5) B loves A, but rejects his love because of petty differences, and because her father, F-B, is an enemy of A's father, F-A   283

A, B, A-4 and BR-B

Love's Rejection

(1) A, secretly discovering his sweetheart, B, in the arms of A-4, leaves in anger, unaware that A-4 is B's brother, just returned after a long, mysterious absence 222b

A, B, AX and BX

Love's Misadventures

(2) A, married to BX, a woman he does not know, and B, married to AX, a man she does not know, meet, fall in love, and A presently discovers that BX is B, while B discovers that AX is A   167a

A, B, GF-A and F-B

Love's Misadventures

A will be disinherited by his wealthy grandfather, GF-A, if he does not perform an act which will prove a grievous injury to F-B, father of B, the woman A loves 118

A, B, A-5 and X

Craftiness

A wishes to buy an object, X, in the possession of B.   B will not sell X.   A-5, a crook, steals X from B and tries to sell it to A   1217c

A, B-4 and CH

Personal Limitations

(1) A volunteers to care for an infant, CH, for a woman stranger, B-4, but A finds himself with CH on his hands when B-4 fails to return   1057a
(4) A, young and unmarried, assumes temporary charge of an infant, CH, for a woman stranger, B-4   1057a

A, F-A and BX

Love's Misadventures

A, a wanderer, is left a fortune by F-A, his father, in case he can be found and will marry BX, a woman he has never seen   117

A, BX and A-8

Marriage

(1) A is married to an unknown woman, BX, by an insane clergyman, A-8, at the point of a gun   365c

B, A-5 and A-6

Deliverance

(3-12) A-6 proves that B's enemy, A-5, is a crook, and has him sent to prison   870b

B, A-4 and A-6

Misfortune

(1) B innocently befriends a stranger, A-4; and it later develops that A-4 is a political offender whom government officials, headed by A-6, are straining every nerve to capture 644

(5) If A-6 knew that B had befriended A-4, B would be considered a confederate of A-4's and suffer accordingly 644

B, A-2 and B-2

Married Life

B uses her weird powers of mental telepathy in reshaping the destiny of an unhappily married couple, A-2 and B-2 594g

(1-5) B, having succeeded in reconciling A-2 and B-2, married and estranged from each other, discovers herself to be in love with A-2 594g

B, A-9 and X

Mystery

(13) B wonders why the pawnbroker, A-9, tries to buy back from her an unredeemed pledge, X, which she bought in his pawnshop 1384

B, M-B and F-B

Idealism

B's parents, M-B and F-B, are "just poor white trash," but lowly B struggles for an education that will lift her out of her squalid environment 948

B, F-B and A-3

Love's Rejection

(2) B's father, F-B, bankrupt, refuses to give B in marriage to wealthy A-3, a man she does not love, in discharge of his debts 269

(THE END)

CPSIA information can be obtained at www.ICGtesting.com
Printed in the USA
LVOW100354120712

289764LV00001B/37/P